By Flesh and Toil

By Flesh and Toil

How Sex, Race, and Labor Shaped the Early French Empire

MÉLANIE LAMOTTE

HARVARD UNIVERSITY PRESS

Cambridge, Massachusetts
London, England
2026

Printed in the United States of America
First printing

EU GPSR Authorised Representative
LOGOS EUROPE, 9 rue Nicolas Poussin, 17000, LA ROCHELLE, France
E-mail: Contact@logoseurope.eu

Library of Congress Cataloging-in-Publication Data

Names: Lamotte, Mélanie, author.
Title: By flesh and toil : how sex, race, and labor shaped the early French empire / Mélanie Lamotte.
Description: Cambridge, Massachusetts ; London, England : Harvard University Press, 2025. | Includes bibliographical references and index.
Identifiers: LCCN 2025008662 (print) | LCCN 2025008663 (ebook) | ISBN 9780674272835 (cloth) | ISBN 9780674302211 (pdf) | ISBN 9780674302204 (epub)
Subjects: LCSH: Slavery—France—Colonies—History | Enslaved persons—Atlantic Ocean Region—Social conditions. | Enslaved persons—Indian Ocean Region—Social conditions. | Enslaved women—Violence against—Atlantic Ocean Region—History. | Enslaved women—Violence against—Indian Ocean Region—History. | Interracial marriage—Atlantic Ocean Region—History. | Interracial marriage—Indian Ocean Region—History. | Multiracial people—Legal status, laws, etc.—Atlantic Ocean Region—History. | Multiracial people—Legal status, laws, etc.—Indian Ocean Region—History. | Human reproduction—Economic aspects—France—Colonies—History. | France—Colonies—Race relations—History.
Classification: LCC HT1180 .L36 2025 (print) | LCC HT1180 (ebook) | DDC 909/.097124407—dc23/eng/20250604
LC record available at https://lccn.loc.gov/2025008662
LC ebook record available at https://lccn.loc.gov/2025008663

For Daniel

Contents

Maps

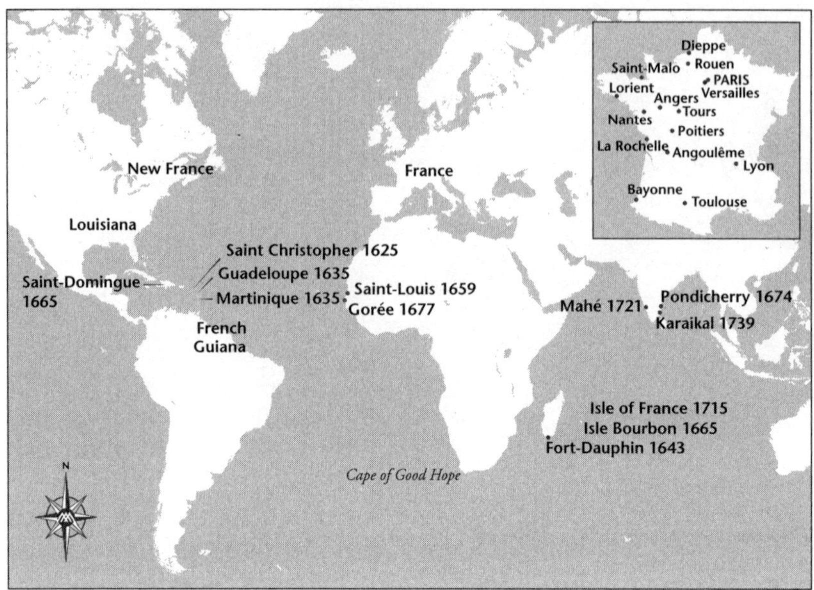

The Early French Empire

Bold characters designate the main colonies and outposts that were colonized by the French from the early seventeenth century to the Seven Years' War. These include New France, Louisiana, and French Guiana in America; Saint-Domingue (1665), Saint Christopher (1625), Guadeloupe (1635), and Martinique (1635) in the Caribbean; and Saint-Louis (1659) and Gorée (1677) in Senegambia. In the Indian Ocean, these include Isle of France (1715), Isle Bourbon (1665), and Fort-Dauphin (1643) in the Southwest, as well as Mahé (1721), Pondicherry (1674), and Karaikal (1739) in India.

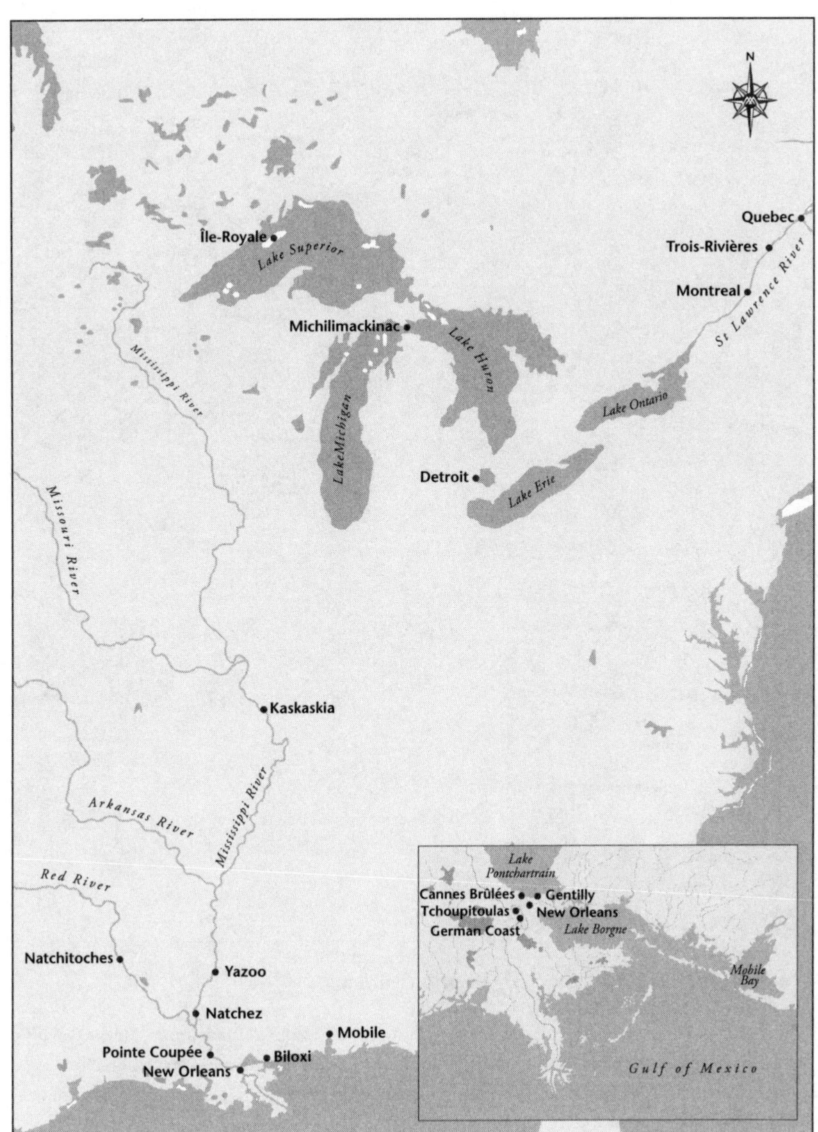

New France and French Colonial Louisiana in the Eighteenth Century

Featured locations are the French cities, settlements, and outposts in New France and French colonial Louisiana that appear throughout this book.

The Caribbean Islands in the Eighteenth Century

Bold characters designate French positions, including Martinique, Guadeloupe, Marie-Galante, Saint Christopher, and Saint-Barthélemy in the Lesser Antilles (southeast) and Saint-Domingue in the Greater Antilles (northwest). Inset maps show the parishes of Martinique (bottom left) and Guadeloupe (top right).

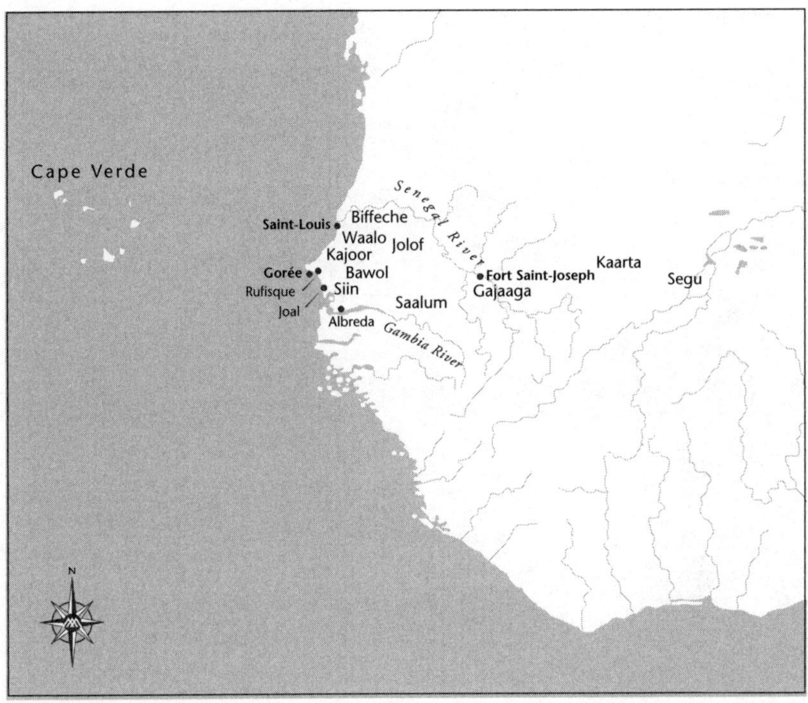

Senegambia in the Eighteenth Century

Bold characters designate the French outposts of Gorée and Saint-Louis on the coast and Fort St. Joseph in Gajaaga (Galam) on the Senegal River. Also featured are several African kingdoms, including Waalo, Bawol, Kajoor, and Jolof.

Southern Madagascar in the Seventeenth Century

Featured locations include the regions, towns, and valleys that appear in this book. Bold characters designate the French outpost of Fort-Dauphin.

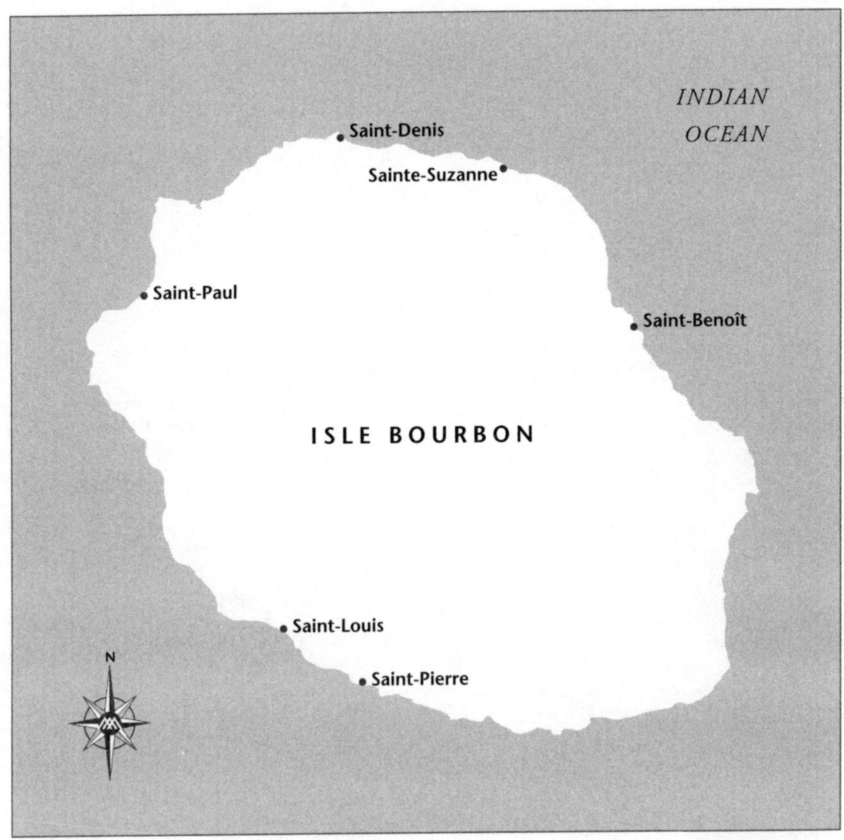

Isle Bourbon in the Eighteenth Century

Featured locations are the various parishes that appear in this book: Saint-Pierre and Saint-Louis (south), Saint-Paul, Saint-Denis, and Sainte-Suzanne (north), and Saint-Benoît (east).

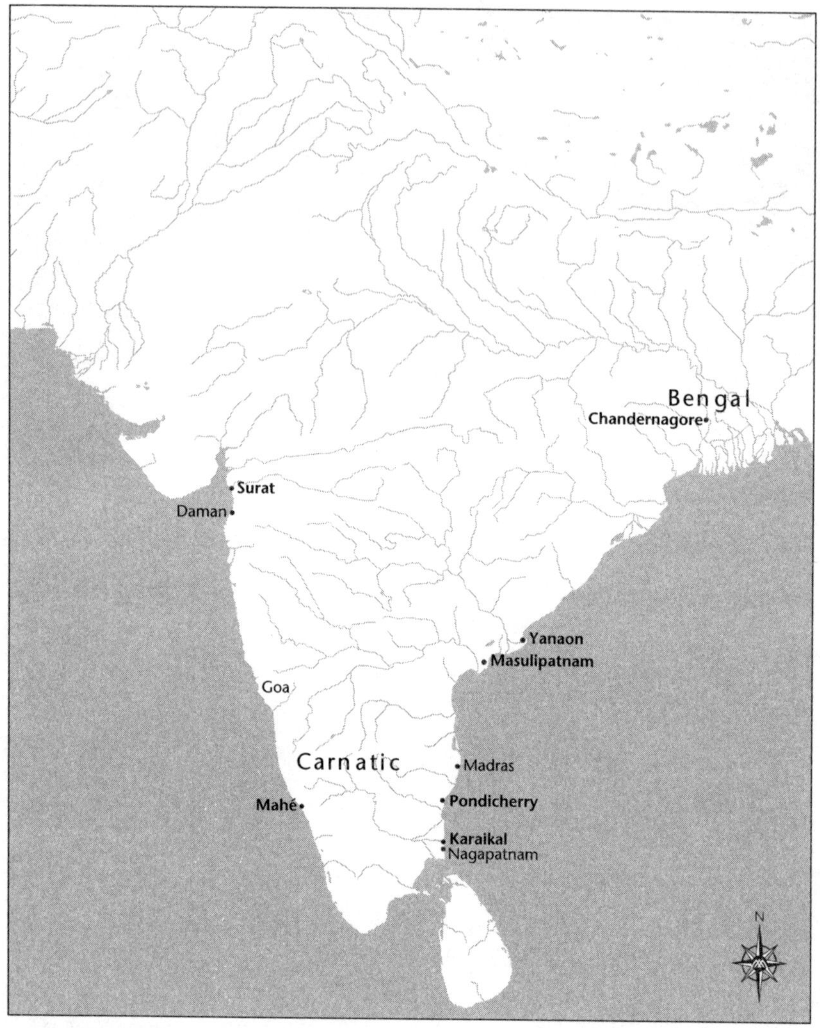

India in the Eighteenth Century

Bold characters designate French outposts, including Surat and Mahé on the west coast; Karaikal, Pondicherry, Masulipatam, and Yanaon on the east coast; and Chandernagore, Bengal, northwest of India.

By Flesh and Toil

Introduction

A Tale of Two Mariannes

In the 1720s, on Isle Bourbon, a small French island in the southwest Indian Ocean now called La Réunion, lived a woman named Marianne Payet. Marianne was born free on the island in 1710, and she was of Malagasy ancestry. Her paternal grandparents, a freeborn widow from the southeastern Madagascan province of Anosy named Louise Siaram and a French carpenter named Antoine Payet, had married in the Catholic Church of Isle Bourbon in 1677.[1] Like many other free creoles (people born in the colony) of Malagasy ancestry, Marianne was legally treated as a "white" woman on Isle Bourbon because she was Christian, Europeanized, and comfortable financially. When, in 1728, she married a Frenchman from Limousin named Joseph Choppy Desgranges, this meant that their marriage was unaffected by the series of laws prohibiting marriage and sex between whites and Blacks on Isle Bourbon, first enacted in 1673 and reiterated in letters patent issued by the French crown in 1723.[2] Joseph's reputation was not tarnished by his relationship with Marianne either, as evidenced by his later rise to political prominence.[3] Like many settlers on Isle Bourbon in the first half of the eighteenth century, Marianne and Joseph made their fortune as coffee planters. By 1732, they owned several heads of cattle, as well as four coffee bean plantations, where much of the manual labor was performed by their sixteen enslaved laborers. The origins of these enslaved people spoke to the demographics of the French Indian Ocean slave trade: while one came from India, and a few others were born on Isle Bourbon, the majority came from Madagascar.[4] By the eighteenth century, when Europeans in the Americas mostly relied on enslaved Africans and Native Americans, the French on Isle Bourbon imported enslaved captives not only from West and East Africa but also from Madagascar and India—all were categorized as "Blacks" (*Noirs* or *nègres*) in historical documents. After fourteen years of marriage and the births of their three children, Joseph died some time before December 1742.[5] Seven years later, Marianne married another Frenchman, named Bidot-Duclos, a humble captain in the French army.[6] The wealth that she had accumulated through her first marriage and her work in Isle Bourbon's coffee economy would have made her a very attractive bride.

At the same time, thousands of miles away, on the shores of Lake Pontchartrain, a few miles north of New Orleans, Louisiana, lived another woman, also named Marianne. Marianne of Lake Pontchartrain was Black, and she was enslaved. By the 1740s, she shared a home with her French owner, Claude Vignon, nicknamed La Combe.[7] La Combe and his business partner, Chavannes, ran a factory by the lake near a bayou that now bears La Combe's name. The factory produced pitch and tar, a substance used to caulk the ships that sailed across the Mississippi River and out into the Atlantic Ocean.[8] Marianne was the mother of two boys, Joseph and Pierre, who were also enslaved and described as *mulâtres* (mixed Black and white children) in historical documents.[9] Marianne and her children would have spent a lot of time assisting La Combe in the manufacture of pitch and tar. Joseph and Pierre lived next door to Marianne, in the home of another Frenchman, Pierre Boyer, who worked as a cooper.[10] It was common for white settlers in Louisiana to live under the same roof with enslaved people. But a number of facts make this particular story intriguing: the gifts of cattle and money given by La Combe to Marianne and her sons; the fact that La Combe freed Marianne some time before his death in 1747; the fact that Joseph and Pierre were also manumitted some time before 1745; and finally, the fact that Boyer, on his deathbed in 1745, gave everything he owned to those boys.[11] Although we will never know for sure, these gestures can prompt us to wonder: were these two white men Marianne's lovers, or was she pressured into living in concubinage with them? Might one of Marianne's sons have been fathered by La Combe and the other by Boyer? (We do know that Joseph went by the name "Joseph La Combe.")[12] In practice, Marianne's probable concubinage with La Combe was outlawed by the *Code Noir* of Louisiana, a 1724 metropolitan edict that reiterated word for word the content of the letters patent issued by the French crown for Isle Bourbon one year earlier, which banned intermarriage and sexual intercourse between whites and Blacks.[13]

The stories of the two Mariannes—one a prominent slaveowner on Isle Bourbon (also called Mascarin), the other an enslaved person freed in Louisiana—bridge the two oceans that were colonized by the French beginning in the seventeenth century. They illustrate this book's two core arguments about the formation of the French empire in the early modern period. First, as a result of transoceanic exchanges and legal standardization, French colonies and outposts across the Atlantic and Indian Oceans grew increasingly united through a coherent set of imperial policies that targeted peoples of non-European ancestries: this is exemplified in the letters patent of 1723 and the *Code Noir* of 1724, which both prohibited relationships between whites (*Blancs*) and Blacks (*Noirs*) on Isle Bourbon and in Louisiana. Second, in addition to racial policies, interracial sex and labor played a critical role in the making of the early French empire. By producing mixed children, Catholic marriages between freeborn or manumitted women of non-European descent and European men helped offset shortages of European colonists in the first decades of French colonization. Marianne Payet's Malagasy grandmother, Louise Siaram, had a total of ten mixed children with Antoine between 1678 and 1695, all of whom were integrated into the free creole population of Isle Bourbon. Like Marianne, many of the descendants of these Christian mixed children were assimilated into the "white" population of the colonies and outposts, being treated and categorized as such by colonial officials. European observers noted with fascination and satisfaction that some of these children almost completely blended into the "white" master class in the end, because their skin had been literally "whitened" by generations of intermixing with white men.[14] On the other hand, when they were born to enslaved women of non-European descent and white men, mixed children were typically incorporated into enslaved labor forces: Marianne of Lake Pontchartrain's two boys initially joined the enslaved labor force and then the free population of French colonial Louisiana. The labor of both enslaved and free people of non-European descent was critical to the development and commercial exploitation of the colonies and outposts: Marianne of Lake Pontchartrain and her children presumably helped La Combe make pitch and tar, for example, to patch sailing vessels, and Marianne of Isle Bourbon cultivated coffee beans with the support of her sixteen captives.[15]

This book explores the making of France's transoceanic empire, an early imperial formation that was largely built in a bottom-up manner, through the actions of people on the ground. Specifically, it examines what historians Jane Burbank and Frederick Cooper have called the "repertoires of imperial power," defined as the "different strategies empir[e] chose as

[it] incorporated diverse peoples."[16] I refer to the early French imperial formation as an empire of "flesh and toil," for several reasons. First, because sexual relations between women of non-European descent and white men played an important role in populating the French colonies and outposts in the seventeenth century, and in the formation of diplomatic and commercial alliances that were key to the protection and exploitation of several French overseas positions. Second, because the French empire was rooted in extreme physical violence, and in particular sexual violence, which helped subjugate overseas populations.[17] Third, because, by the eighteenth century, French policymakers tried to create hierarchies based on race by controlling interracial sex and marriages and by trying to prevent the socioeconomic ascendency of people of non-European ancestries, in order to consolidate the French empire and maintain ferocious slave-labor regimes. Finally, because the French empire was largely built on the labor of enslaved and free people of non-European ancestries. By studying their labor, I intend to counterbalance a growing historiography by France-based economic historians that risks overshadowing enslaved people's important contribution to French economic and cultural history.[18]

Spanning the Atlantic and the Indian Oceans, this book is the first pan-imperial study of the early French empire in the English language. After several failed French colonization attempts, most notably in Brazil (France Antarctique between 1555 and 1560, and Equinoctial France from 1612 to 1615), beginning in the seventeenth century, the French imperial formation grew to encompass islands in the Caribbean (starting in 1625), along with settlements and outposts in New France (starting in 1608), Guiana (1643), Senegambia (including Saint-Louis, Gorée and Fort Saint-Joseph de Galam, starting in 1659), and Louisiana (1699)—a territory that, as claimed by France, encompassed the vast Mississippi river basin from the Great Lakes to the Gulf of Mexico.[19] During this period, the French also began to make regular use of Vasco de Gama's sea route from the South Atlantic to Asia via the Cape of Good Hope. In 1643, a short-lived French garrison called Fort-Dauphin was established in the north of the peninsula of Tolagñare, in the kingdom of Anosy, Madagascar, followed by colonies on Isle Bourbon (as of 1665) and Isle of France (1715), as well as by several French trading outposts on the Indian subcontinent, beginning with Surat in 1668. While much of the early French colonial historiography remains fragmented into local and regional studies, the pan-imperial approach in this book is necessary to unveil converging and diverging repertoires of empire, illuminate oft-shared responses to imperialism among people of non-European descent, and reveal unsuspected transoceanic exchanges of ideas.

This book also departs from another historiographical tradition to show that free and unfree people of African, Malagasy, and South Asian descent played a critical role in the story of both the making and unmaking of France's overseas empire. Many studies of early French empire-building embrace top-down perspectives centering on the aspirations and actions of French administrators—with some exceptions, including a rich New France, Illinois, and Louisiana historiography considering empire-building through the lens of French-Indigenous contacts, which has had an enormous influence on this book.[20] While these studies have made an essential contribution to the field of French colonial history, reconstructing the story of the formation of the early French empire also requires that we engage with "history from below"—or "way below,"—to use the expression coined by Black studies scholar Marlene Daut. It is true that the legal actions and aspirations of French administrators are an important part of the story, and indeed, this book aims to show that France's early modern Atlantic and Indian Ocean legal regimes were far more connected than previously acknowledged. Yet to truly understand how the French empire was built, colony by colony, we must also consider how ordinary people on the ground—especially those of non-European descent—contributed demographically, socially, economically, legally, and politically to the formation of empire. This book is a response to Vincent Brown's call, in his groundbreaking work on Jamaica, to recast African-descended populations in this period as "an integral part of the development of European empires."[21] I also explore attempts by people of non-European ancestries to limit the expansion of French influence, as well as the specific factors that led many of them to contribute to the construction of empire (whether or not they were aware of it), by forming alliances with the French.

Because the sexuality, cultural identities, and social and political aspirations of free and unfree *women* of African, Malagasy, and other non-European ancestries played an especially important role in the story of French empire building, this book pays particular attention to their experiences. Despite their central role, women of non-European descent have received relatively little notice in early French colonial histories, partly as the result of a double "racialized and gendered forgetting."[22] This is especially true of those who lived in the Indian Ocean world.[23] For example, although the lineage of most free colonists on Isle Bourbon could—by the early eighteenth century—be traced back to a Luso-Indian or Malagasy woman like Marianne Payet's grandmother Louise Siaram, the experiences of these "black first mothers" have received very little attention in the English-speaking scholarship.[24] The important place of all these women of non-European descent in the story of the French empire was not restricted to their role as progenitors. The following pages are filled with stories of women of African, Malagasy, and South Asian descent who played very important roles in local and global economies as well as in areas like religion and culture, trade, diplomacy, and even political intelligence.

Reconstituting the lives of many of these women and men of African, Malagasy, and South Asian descent—especially those who lived in slavery—is a challenging task because of the many archival silences surrounding their lived experiences.[25] Those silences are entangled with the structures of knowledge production that contributed to their exploitation in the seventeenth and eighteenth centuries.[26] As Marisa Fuentes puts it in her study of the history of enslaved women in eighteenth-century British Barbados, because they left us few firsthand accounts, enslaved people (here, in particular, Black women) "appear as historical subjects through the content of archival documents in the manner in which they lived: spectacularly violated, objectified, disposable, hypersexualized, and silenced. The violence is transferred from the enslaved bodies to the documents that count, condemn, assess, and evoke them, and we receive them in this condition."[27] I use three methods to circumvent these difficulties. First, I acknowledge how patterns of knowledge production shaped the content of early modern sources on slavery.[28] Second, I read archival evidence "along the bias grain" of white colonizers, to borrow Fuentes's phrase.[29] Third, I stitch together a vast patchwork of historical fragments from a broad range of archival and printed sources, including not only censuses, marriage and baptism records, official correspondence, legislation, and travel narratives but also court testimonies by enslaved people and notarial documents—such as manumission acts, wills, acts of property sales and donations, and estate inventories.

By shifting the perspective from French officials to people on the ground across the Atlantic and Indian Oceans, this book sheds new light on the social, economic, and cultural histories of women and men of African,

Malagasy, and South Asian descent—in particular, their attempts to integrate the political sphere to advance their interests, to seek justice and protection for themselves and their kin, to improve their social condition, and to find economic opportunities, often in the face of tremendous adversity and violence. It is plausible, for example, that free and unfree women like Marianne Payet and Marianne of Lake Pontchartrain strategically used their relationships with French men to secure opportunities for themselves, their children, and their communities. This pattern has been theorized by many Black feminist scholars, including Hilary Beckles, and—more recently—historian Jessica Johnson, who coined the notion of *Black femme freedom*: the idea that enslaved and free Black women's freedom resided in their capacity to belong to themselves and to each other as white colonists tried to use their bodies to commodify, exploit, and violate them. Black women, Johnson argues, challenged these people with their own understandings of how their bodies should be used.[30] As Doris Garraway puts it, "Desire as a concept allows, in certain cases, for the careful redistribution of agency across the power dichotomy, such that enslaved women and free women of color may be viewed as agents and negotiators of desire, as well as victims of sexual violence."[31] Although the agency of women like Marianne of Lake Pontchartrain was drastically confined by their enslavement, by engaging in such practices, they could still position themselves as willful agents who in a few cases obtained freedom for themselves and for their loved ones.[32]

A Pan-Imperial History of the Early French Empire

By adopting a pan-imperial perspective, this book offers an innovative contribution to the field of French colonial history. Although Atlantic history—an area of study focused on imperial, transnational, and multicultural connections within the Atlantic basin—has since the early 2000s generated multiple interconnected studies of the French Atlantic colonies, the field of early French colonial history is still dominated by local and regional studies which typically examine one colony or outpost, or one cluster of colonies or outposts, within one oceanic basin—the Atlantic or the Indian Ocean.[33] A few scholars have recently begun to move away from these established approaches, by seeking to reconnect one or two

French Atlantic position(s) to one or two others in the Indian Ocean.[34] This book is deeply indebted to this groundbreaking trend in US and European historiographies. In order to remedy the fragmentation in the scholarship, I also take this approach one step further by reconnecting an unprecedented number of Atlantic and Indian Ocean colonies and outposts.

The lingering fragmentation of French colonial history into local and regional studies has to do with the heavy compartmentalization of historical research.[35] Regional scholars in the United States and Britain often evolve through separated subject groups, historical associations, journals, and area studies.[36] Researchers in France are dispersed across research institutions that are likewise separated by geographical and cultural divisions.[37] Atlantic history's belated arrival on the scene of French academia has further contributed to this fragmentation. While the field of Atlantic history in the United States and Britain began to flourish as early as the postwar era, French historians were, until the early aughts, reluctant to address it.[38] As Cécile Vidal explained at the time, one of the reasons for this was the exclusion of French colonial history from the national narrative, which was itself partly a consequence of the challenges that colonialism posed to the French ideal of universalism.[39] All of this only began to change around the early 2000s, when more French scholars began to contribute to a renewal of French interest in the era of colonization and several, like Vidal herself, began to work within the Atlantic history framework.[40] As a result of the continued rise of the field of Atlantic history in the United States, some US-based scholars have also contributed to the growth of the field.[41]

While all this was happening, however, multiple scholars—including many world historians—began to voice apprehensions regarding certain aspects of the Atlantic history framework, noting in particular its risk of obscuring important transoceanic connections.[42] It is true that one of the most significant limitations of Atlantic history is its failure to capture the transoceanic dimension of early European empires. There are already many inspiring pan-imperial and transoceanic studies of the early modern Spanish, Portuguese, and British empires.[43] In fact, as historian François-Joseph Ruggiu puts it, "empire is [currently] imposing itself as a historical object [. . .] and as an indispensable category of analysis across the world."[44]

Comparatively little work has been produced that embraces a pan-imperial approach to the French empire, especially when it comes to its formation in the early modern period.[45] In fact, Ruggiu is right to point out that early modern French history continues to demonstrate "a lack of interest in the colonial dimension of this period compared to the empire at the end of the 19th and the 20th century."[46] Similarly, British historian Trevor Burnard recently lamented "the absence of a single treatment of the French colonial empire in the eighteenth century in English and the comparatively limited attention by French historians writing in French to 18th-century colonialism."[47] France's territorial losses in the aftermath of the Seven Years' War (1756–1763) and the Haitian Revolution (1791–1804) have probably been central to this neglect, "blind[ing]" scholars to this history, to use the words of Christopher Hodson and Brett Rushforth.[48]

Yet the seventeenth and early eighteenth centuries are important because it was during that period that people laid the foundations of the French overseas empire. The French empire then continued evolving until the twentieth century, losing and acquiring new territories but also eventually retaining several of its older colonies and outposts in the Indian Ocean, Senegambia, and the Americas (including several Caribbean islands and Guiana). France also kept some of the "repertoires of imperial power" that had emerged in the early modern period, as illustrated by the continuities Saliha Belmessous has identified between the well-known policy of assimilation formulated for New France in the seventeenth century and the "civilizing mission" promoted by French authorities, especially from the late nineteenth century.[49]

Contours of This Book

This book focuses on France's forming Atlantic and Indian Ocean empire in the seventeenth and eighteenth centuries. It begins with the establishment of France's first permanent settlement in Quebec in 1608 and ends with the conclusion of the Seven Years' War (1756–1763), because this conflict wrought major transformations across the French empire. The British occupied numerous French colonies and outposts during the war, and once the conflict ended, France was forced to relinquish Louisiana and New France, along with several other positions, under the terms of the Treaty of Paris.[50]

The geographical scope of this book is also wide. I do not pretend to systematically give the same level of attention to every French overseas colony or trading post during this period. Instead, this book offers a bird's-eye view of the early French imperial formation, prioritizing a carefully selected range of overseas locations at the center and on the peripheries of empire. Those places include islands that eventually grew to become slave plantation societies, as well as settler colonies and small military and trading outposts in continental settings, along with the vast borderlands that lay beyond them.[51] Specifically, in the Atlantic world, this book pays particular attention to Lower Louisiana and Guadeloupe. It also offers insights into the histories of Saint-Louis and Gorée and, to a lesser extent, New France, Guiana, and other French Caribbean islands.[52] In the Indian Ocean, it focuses especially on Isle Bourbon and Anosy in southeastern Madagascar (especially Fort-Dauphin and its surroundings), while also providing some insight into the histories of India and, to a lesser extent, Isle of France.

My decision to prioritize certain colonies and outposts over others is intentional, partly meant to start remedying the unevenness in local and regional historiographies of the French empire. By contextualizing New France through a pan-imperial approach, I aim to clarify which New France imperial practices were unique and which were part of a wider imperial tradition.[53] I also seek to offer a better sense of how New France, the first permanent overseas colony established by the French, influenced wider pan-imperial strategies. I treat the history of the Lower Mississippi valley more extensively because much work is yet to be done to further our understanding of French imperialism in this region and much is to be gained from situating Louisiana within a wider Atlantic and Indian Ocean perspective.[54] Along with the Illinois Country, this region has already been the focus of a rich scholarly tradition.[55] US and French historians have produced excellent studies of slavery, intercultural exchanges, and race in Lower French Louisiana.[56] Yet a pan-imperial approach to French Louisiana is long overdue because the Indian Ocean had an almost completely overlooked impact on its legal framework and racial regime.[57] This book pays particular attention to *African-descended people's role* in the making of France's empire in *Lower* Louisiana because important research has already been produced on the ways Native American peoples—especially the Illinois in the Illinois Country but also the Small Nations of the Gulf Coast—have shaped European empires.[58] This book also devotes particular attention to Guadeloupe in the seventeenth and early eighteenth centuries, since the early period of its colonization has received relatively little attention, particularly in the English-speaking world.[59] Unlike Saint-Domingue, and just like the isle of Guadeloupe, most French-ruled islands in the Caribbean were part of the Lesser Antilles—an arc of much smaller islands, some of which became relatively easier for French authorities to control.[60] Importantly, the history of Saint-Domingue is less representative of wider French Caribbean processes because it shared a border with a Spanish colony and was by far the largest and most productive of the French Caribbean sugar islands—and home to the most successful slave revolt in history.[61]

By putting the Atlantic world in dialogue with the Indian Ocean, I illuminate common transoceanic patterns and show how developments that took place in the Indian Ocean came to shape French imperial stances in the Atlantic world—and vice versa. I pay special attention to Isle Bourbon in the early era of colonization because this island came to have an outsized influence on France's wider imperial policies in the early eighteenth century. There have been some excellent Francophone studies of this island in the seventeenth and eighteenth centuries—notably by Reunionese scholars. However, very little work has been produced on this important colony in the Anglo-American sphere.[62] Isle of France, by comparison, has enjoyed more attention.[63]

I also consider the period of French presence in Fort-Dauphin and the surrounding Anosy country in the seventeenth century since it remains understudied despite the huge impact it had on people's experiences on Isle Bourbon and in the wider French world.[64] Scholars in the United States, Germany, Madagascar, and South Africa have produced very important research on slavery, imperialism, and missionary work in Madagascar.[65] However, with the exception of a few trailblazing publications, relatively little work has been produced on the crucial early era of French presence in Anosy and Fort-Dauphin, perhaps because this French outpost was short-lived and left behind few primary sources. Focusing on this period is important, partly because there were critical continuities as French settlers, their Malagasy wives, and their bonded servants began to move from Madagascar to settle Isle Bourbon starting in the 1660s. The tradition of intermarriage initiated in Anosy, in particular, along with the agricultural background of mixed couples in that region, had a critical impact on the peopling and exploitation of Isle Bourbon.

This book also follows the trail of the people of Indian (South Asian) and Luso-Indian descent who lived on Isle Bourbon by offering some insights into the history of the French commercial outposts in India, especially Pondicherry. The presence of Luso-Indian people in India and across the Indian Ocean dated back to the Portuguese occupation, beginning in the fifteenth century. The Portuguese were pioneers in establishing a direct link between Europe and India via the Cape of Good Hope. Luso-Indian women and Indian *engagés* (indentured servants or "Malabars," "lascars," and "coolies") began to arrive on Isle Bourbon starting in the 1670s and 1680s, respectively—the former as part of an intermarriage scheme and the latter as part of an indenture program. Like the Malagasy diaspora, they played a critical role in the peopling of Isle Bourbon.

Because it is attuned to the benefits of centering Africa in studies of the Black diaspora, this book also devotes significant attention to the early history of France's commercial outposts in Senegambia. In doing so, it offers a study of a territory where many Black-white power dynamics differed considerably from those of the French Americas in the seventeenth and early eighteenth centuries.[66]

Situating French Sovereignty

Although French officials claimed sovereignty over all those colonies and outposts, the strength of French power varied considerably from one place to another, and the question of where the limits of the French imperial formation lay was often a matter of perspective. In Senegambia and India, as was the case in North America, Europeans claimed sovereignty solely "vis-à-vis one another," to quote Kathleen DuVal's groundbreaking study of the Arkansas River valley.[67] In southern Madagascar, like in North America, the French made a particularly ambitious claim over a vast territory that remained for the most part under de facto local (Indigenous) peoples' control.[68] As legal historian Lauren Benton puts it, "Sovereignty is often more a myth than a reality, more a story that polities tell about their own power than a definite quality they possess."[69] The European representatives who made ambitious claims in North America were well aware of the tentative nature of their authority. This is why, from the start, instead of trying to achieve actual territorial sovereignties, they often made symbolic claims in strategic passages along coastal areas and water lanes to take possession of vast territories: such was the case in 1682, when the French explorer René-Robert Cavelier, Sieur de La Salle, and the few dozen Frenchmen accompanying him claimed the entire Mississippi basin for France simply by planting a French flag in the river's estuary.[70]

Like the Indigenous people of the Arkansas River valley studied by Kathleen DuVal, it was ultimately local leaders who "called the shots" in India, Madagascar, and Senegambia.[71] This is not to say that French practices and ambitions in those areas were not imperialistic. As demonstrated in Danna Agmon's excellent portrayal of imperial sovereignty in eighteenth-century French Pondicherry, notwithstanding the great power and autonomy of many local peoples, the French imperial project could still be aimed at political domination.[72] Early modern France was an imperial force, not least because its political institutions aimed to disseminate the crown's authority over colonies and outposts scattered across the Americas, Senegambia, Madagascar, the Mascarenes, and India. In vast territories where local populations had a considerable amount of power, the French tried to expand their authority beyond their strongholds, sometimes in extremely violent ways: this is illustrated by the little-known series of bloody French raids conducted in seventeenth-century Madagascar that are discussed in Chapter 2. Yet the French, in vast and densely populated continental settings like India, Madagascar, and Senegambia were also confronted by many other local groups who could hold considerable power over them.

In practice, French imperialism in vast continental settings operated *alongside* the power of local populations. As demonstrated by Allan Greer in his brilliant study of land tenure in North America and New Spain, there was a diversity of property systems in the world, beyond the "on/off binary [European] conception of property."[73] Therefore, instead of taking possession of the lands on which they established their settlements and outposts, the French in Madagascar, Senegambia, and India simply "carv[ed] out rights within [indigenous] notions of layered occupation," as they had done in multiple areas of North America—since different groups of people could have different rights over the same land in local cultures.[74] We already know of several Native American peoples—like the Quapaw at the mouth of the Arkansas River in the late seventeenth century or the Odawa at Michilimackinac—who *allowed* the French to establish forts on their territories in the hope of forming alliances with them.[75] Likewise, it was local leaders in Madagascar, Senegambia, and India who authorized the French to establish their outposts in places like the Tolagñare peninsula of Anosy,

Saint-Louis and Gorée Islands, or the Tamil country of southeastern India.[76] None of these lands were regarded as French by local populations.

French sovereignty in vast and densely populated continental settings had to be shared with local populations, and it was constrained by factors like challenging topographic terrains, the power of local people, insubordinate enslaved people, rival European powers, and limited military and financial resources. French power was weakest on vast continental borderlands where the French, few in number, faced powerful local populations. This was evident not only in North America beyond the French strongholds but also along the Senegambian coast facing Saint-Louis and Gorée following the French arrival in the 1650s as well as in Anosy, Madagascar, by the 1670s. In contrast, French control was strongest in smaller places with few local inhabitants, where most of the workforce was drawn from the slave trade and ways to evade French authorities were limited. Such was the case on the Lesser Antillean island of Guadeloupe beginning in the early eighteenth century, since the number of Kalinago (Indigenous people also called Island Caribs) had dwindled because of war and Old World diseases, while the number of enslaved Africans was increasing. This pattern of changing and uneven imperial power was in no way restricted to the French context. Lauren Benton has already pointed out how early modern European sovereignties overseas "did not cover space evenly but composed a fabric that was full of holes, stitched together out of pieces, a tangle of strings," with an "uneven configura[tion]" that was "not at all consistent with the image produced by monochrome shading of imperial maps."[77]

With a few exceptions, the French influence in the early modern period was confined to a collection of French-controlled islands; settlements and cities within vast continental frameworks; small continental enclaves made up of plantations, forts, trading outposts, or missions; and the uneven continental borderlands that lay beyond them. Beyond those borderlands lay enormous autonomous territories that had very little to do with European empires. As explained by Michael Witgen, Amy Turner Bushnell, and others, "the largest part of the New World [. . .] remained unconquered" until the nineteenth century," and "Europeans probed and traded and established coastal strongholds, but they did not manage to seize and hold very much territory."[78] Likewise, European countries had little to no control over the vast territories that lay outside the purview of their overseas empires in Africa, Madagascar, and Asia. Most local populations in those areas had little to no contact with European people, although many certainly felt or began to feel the influence of European material cultures, ideas, and so on. On the borderlands beyond those vast autonomous territories, the French would sometimes make an attempt to advance their power—for example, by seizing an opportunity when a local leader or a community appeared weakened by war, famine, disease, or other factors (see Chapter 2). However, especially in Senegambia and India, the French most often met local populations as subordinates trying to survive or make a living, and sometimes on quite egalitarian terms. To survive and succeed in their enterprises in Senegambia, Madagascar, and India, the French had no other choice than engaging in negotiations with local populations. It was typically local people themselves who set the boundaries of French influence by responding to French claims either peacefully or with violence. This is illustrated by the story of one of the first successful anticolonial uprisings in French colonial history, which took place in 1674, when a formerly allied *roandria* of Anosy essentially eradicated France's only early stronghold in Madagascar (see Chapter 2)—the French in Anosy maintained especially close relationships with Zafiraminia *roandria*, a dynasty of high-ranking nobles or princes, also called *Dian* or *grands du pays*, who ruled over small kingdoms and chiefdoms inhabited by smaller chiefs, commoners, and enslaved people.[79]

Within some of those imperial borderlands, and amid the French island colonies and several of the French cities and settlements, lay imperial centers that formed the backbone of "empire," defined by Burbank, Cooper, Havard, and Vidal as a "large political uni[t]," "expansionist or with a memory of power extended over space," attempting to subject foreign territories to "an enterprise of domination and unification."[80] French imperial centers attempted to exert their authority across much wider territories over which they had varying amounts of influence.[81] That was not only the case in America but also on the isle of Madagascar, where the French used their tiny outpost of Fort-Dauphin to lay a much wider claim to the entire region of Anosy. The French imperial centers were home to a vast network of Sovereign and Superior Councils (Conseils Souverains and Conseils Supérieurs): sovereign entities that were responsible for civil and criminal trials and also able to issue decrees, negotiate royal legislation with the king, and register regulations sent to them by the Ministry of the Marine (le Ministère de la Marine)—an institution founded in 1669 in charge of governing the French colonies and the French navy. As recently demonstrated by Laurie Wood, this large network of colonial councils formed "a large [interconnected] political unit" that spread across Quebec (starting in 1663), Martinique and Guadeloupe (1664), Fort-Dauphin in Madagascar (1669–1674), Surat (1671), Petit-Goâve and Cap Français in Saint-Domingue (1685 and 1701), Cayenne in Guiana and Pondicherry in India (1701), Isle Bourbon (1711), Louisiana (1712), Île-Royale (1717), and Isle of France (1723), as well as Saint-Louis and Gorée (foundation dates unknown).[82]

By the early eighteenth century, a French empire was slowly taking form as French authorities sought to subject foreign lands to "an enterprise of domination and unification."[83] In the past, there were claims that the early modern French colonies and outposts were too disconnected from each other and from the motherland to even constitute an "empire" capable of formulating a coherent imperial policy.[84] In keeping with the work of Nancy Christie, Michael Gauvreau, Matthew Gerber, Brett Rushforth, and others, this book illuminates important local legal particularisms throughout the early modern period.[85] Yet, beginning in the first half of the seventeenth century, French royal officials also began to devise several sets of coherent imperial policies for the French Atlantic and Indian Ocean positions, which coexisted with more specific localized laws. They did so in concert with French trading companies with which they maintained close relationships and to which the crown delegated regal power.[86]

The coherent sets of pan-imperial policies devised by the crown and the trading companies took shape in two main stages: policies of assimilation beginning in the early seventeenth century (see Chapter 1) and a body of racial policies developed starting in the late seventeenth century (Chapter 4). They were issued for all French colonies and outposts across the Atlantic and Indian Ocean worlds, targeting all overseas populations—including peoples of Native American, African, Malagasy, and South Asian descent. While assimilation policies were partly intended to advance French power by turning local populations into loyal subjects of the French king, racial policies attempted to erect racial boundaries within the socio-economic order of the colonies and outposts to advance French cultural, social, and economic domination. While policies of assimilation promoted interracial unions, racial policies prohibited both intermarriage and interracial sex: as demonstrated by Ann Stoler and other scholars, intimate domains (including interracial unions and interracial reproduction) were "critical sites for the consolidation of colonial power," because they shaped cultural formation and wealth transmission while also undermining distinctions essential to maintaining imperial hierarchies.[87]

Although most of these assimilation and racial policies failed to achieve their intended outcomes, the French colonies and outposts did come to form an empire. Most historians today agree that "colonialism is usually poorly controlled" and that "most colonies were experiments that even in their failures could strengthen the larger imperial project."[88] But if state control was limited in practice, what then enabled French authorities to keep their colonies and outposts for decades, and in multiple cases, even for centuries?[89] While French authorities endeavored to implement empire from the top down through policymaking (see Chapters 1 and 4), in practice, it was people on the ground—and especially those of non-European descent—who played the biggest role in the construction of the French empire by taking initiatives that (ironically) often contravened official policies (Chapters 1–6).[90]

Making the French Empire

How was the French colonial empire built, and what role did women and men of non-European descent and ordinary Europeans play in this story? This book answers this question chronologically. Chapters 1–3 consider the early era of French imperialism overseas, when the future of the French colonies and outposts was very uncertain and the foundations of the French empire were in the process of being laid. Although much of this early era of French imperialism was in the seventeenth century, it occurred within different time frames for each colony and outpost. For example, while the French Caribbean island of Guadeloupe moved out of this phase relatively early because it was founded in 1635, Lower Louisiana experienced this phase much later because it was only colonized from 1699.

Chapter 1, "We Shall Be One People," explores France's grand plan for assimilation, the program formulated from the early seventeenth century to integrate local populations to French society through civilization (or "Frenchification"), intermarriage and other methods, that was partly intended to advance French domination. The argument in this chapter is twofold: first, the well-known early modern French assimilation program was not restricted to seventeenth-century New France; and second, local (*roandria*) allies in Madagascar, much like those in New France, were able to shape some of its characteristics because they wielded a significant amount of influence. Recent scholarship in world history has challenged the assumption that colonial law was imposed unilaterally from the top, emphasizing instead the ways policymakers were forced to accommodate realities on the ground, including indigenous legal ideas.[91] In the French scholarship, the influence of local (Indigenous) actors in the shaping of imperial law has received relatively little attention when it comes to non-American territories and to the early period of French overseas imperialism.[92] However, these actors already informed French colonial policies by the mid-seventeenth century, and did so on a wide scale.

Chapter 2, "Shifting Strategies," demonstrates that in practice, French authorities were largely unable to implement their seventeenth-century grand plan of assimilation. Instead, France's overseas empire was unwittingly built through European and non-European peoples' attempts to survive and pursue their own interests on the ground, as well as through French officials' deliberate efforts to adapt their imperial strategies to evolving local circumstances. In the end, it was mostly the French themselves who began to embrace elements of local cultural practices in Anosy and Senegambia—a pattern mirroring forms of French cultural adaptations to Native American cultures already noted by Americanists.[93] By examining patterns of French cultural adaptation to local practices, Chapter 2 explores several understudied Malagasy and Senegambian diplomatic and military traditions. It also shows that, like their counterparts in North America, the French in Madagascar and Senegambia were forced to form diplomatic and commercial alliances with often-powerful local leaders. These local leaders formed alliances with the French because they were looking for new trading opportunities and also for ways to advance their own power and protect their peoples. Kinship in Madagascar and Senegambia never took on the same meanings and significance that it did in the context of French–Native American relations in North America. However, interracial sex facilitated commercial exchanges in Senegambia, and the *roandria* of Anosy invited the French to marry their Malagasy daughters to seal diplomatic alliances.[94]

In fact, as demonstrated in Chapter 3, "Empire of *Métissage*," sex was perhaps the most significant vector of French empire-building in the seventeenth and eighteenth centuries. This book owes much to a body of publications on other European empires (and on the later French empire) that has already called our attention to the important role of interracial intimacy in the rise of imperial power.[95] Chapter 3 demonstrates that, in the first decades of French colonization, *métissage* (defined as interracial sex in the scholarship) helped to make up for the limited arrivals of European colonists through the birth of free mixed children, and also spurred the development of some of the Caribbean's most prized slave-labor sectors.[96] By the late seventeenth century, in the French Lesser Antilles, mixed children born to enslaved women usually joined enslaved imperial workforces as a rare but particularly desirable commodity. More surprisingly, mixed children born to French-Malagasy and French-Luso-Indian couples married in the Catholic Church constituted an extremely large segment of the (pseudo) "white" free settler population of Isle Bourbon.[97] This development shaped the rise of a large and comfortable free mixed population of Bourbon Island Creoles of Malagasy and South Asian descent on the island. Similar patterns of assimilation also unfolded in places like the early French Lesser Antilles and French India, though on a smaller scale.

By the early eighteenth century, several circumstances had changed, signaling a transition out of the early era of French overseas imperialism. To begin with, during the regency of the Duke of Orleans (1715–1723), French metropolitan authorities initiated a major policy of reform that centralized official documents from and about the colonies within the Office of the Ministry of the Marine and of the Colonies (le Bureau des Archives de la Marine et des Colonies), thereby giving metropolitan policymakers a global outlook on the empire's varied jurisprudence and facilitating updates and legal unification.[98] The French Company of the Indies (la Compagnie des Indes) was also created in this period. Founded in 1719, this chartered company held trading monopolies for varying periods of time across Louisiana, the southern province of Saint-Domingue, and West Africa, but also Isle Bourbon, Isle of France, India, and China. Although scholarship has primarily focused on the Atlantic world, this company's attempt to expand plantation slavery beginning in the early eighteenth century was also extended to the Indian Ocean: in fact, it pursued *transoceanic* initiatives to develop the slave trade. Chapters 4–6 explore the consolidation of the French empire from the late seventeenth century, and especially from the 1720s, in the era of slave societies. Large numbers of enslaved laborers were by then arriving in France's slave plantation societies of the Americas and the southwest Indian Ocean. Colonial societies in Lower Louisiana, Guadeloupe, and Isle Bourbon transitioned into "slave societies," per American historian Ira Berlin's definition: hierarchical structures where whites were the ruling class, enslaved Blacks constituted a majority of the workforce, and the economy in the countryside was centered on the production of valuable export crops.[99]

Chapter 4, "Unifying Racial Policies," introduces the new stage of major pan-imperial policy formulated beginning in the late seventeenth century—one that marked a radical shift away from the grand plan of assimilation. Starting in the early eighteenth century, a unified set of racial policies, intended to advance white domination, emerged across the French Atlantic and Indian Oceans. Those policies targeted intermarriage and interracial sex, restricted inheritance rights for populations of non-European descent, and threatened free Black people with enslavement, among other discriminatory measures. In addition to very specific local circumstances in the French colonies, these policies were shaped by the centralization of colonial documents initiated during the regency, as well as by the company's initiative to expand the slave trade across the Atlantic world *and* the Indian Ocean. People of non-European descent made instrumental contributions to shaping this body of policies as well. For example, the socioeconomic success of the Bourbon Island Creoles encouraged French authorities to ban intermarriage and interracial sex and to restrict Black people's rights of inheritance on Isle Bourbon and beyond.

Ultimately, however—as Chapter 5, "Sex and Racial Power," demonstrates—mixed sexual relations between women of non-European descent and Frenchmen continued to occur, and they advanced imperial power just as much as the racial policies that sought to curtail them. This illustrates the claim that "most colonies were experiments that even in their failures could strengthen the larger imperial project."[100] In the first decades of colonization, sex had acted as a tool with which to form vital alliances with local people, grow the supply of enslaved domestic servants and craftsmen, and populate the French colonies and outposts. By the early eighteenth century, Chapter 5 argues, sex and other mixed relations were key to helping the French advance (white) racial dominion. When Catholic intermarriage—prevalent in the Indian Ocean—occurred despite legal restrictions, it often involved an underprivileged white man with a prosperous, assimilated freeborn woman of South Asian or Malagasy descent like Marianne Payet on Isle Bourbon. Her fortune allowed the man to ascend the social ladder, further advancing white dominance in the process—especially since the wife in question would often also be categorized as "white" in official documents. On the other hand, intermarriage bans dissuaded many Frenchmen from marrying enslaved Black women, blocking access to social mobility for many women and their mixed children and keeping them in a state of submission to the white class. White power was also reinforced by sexual coercion and violence, which were omnipresent across all slave societies by the first half of the eighteenth century, inflicting terror from Lower Louisiana to French India. Free and unfree women of non-European descent did not at all stay passive when facing these attempts to rape, coerce, or manipulate them. Just like white men did, some made strategic choices that could help them ameliorate their condition. Most of the time, however, mixed children born to unmanumitted women continued to join slave workforces. As their number grew, their labor increasingly fueled the colonial economy and sustained the construction of the French empire.

Indeed, as demonstrated in Chapter 6, "Empire of Labor," by the 1720s, from French Lower Louisiana to Isle Bourbon, people of African and other non-European ancestries performed most of the labor necessary to build, maintain, and exploit the settlements. Chapter 6 demonstrates the crucial role played by enslaved people in building infrastructure and producing cash crops and commodities for the financial gains of many eighteenth-century planter and merchant families. But my focus here also extends to the labor of *free* people of African (as well as Malagasy and South Asian) descent, which has attracted less attention in the scholarship. At the same time as these free people fueled the imperial economy with their labor, many challenged the rise of white dominance by making profits through their work. Some successfully manipulated the colonial legal system to protect their own business interests when dealing with greedy and bigoted people. On Isle Bourbon, a few even integrated into the political sphere after waging a remarkable—and yet completely overlooked—struggle for equal rights, many decades before the well-known Black Atlantic struggles for equality that marked the revolutionary era.[101]

Despite such parallels, there were also countless crucial differences between the French Atlantic and Indian Ocean colonies and outposts.

To name just one: Although intermarriage between white men and women of non-European descent was gradually prohibited across most French colonies and outposts beginning in the late seventeenth century, it was not directly banned in the French outposts of Senegambia.[102] However, a set of shared repertoires of empire did emerge across the French Atlantic and Indian Oceans, ranging from coherent sets of assimilation and racial policies to the formation of diplomatic and commercial alliances with powerful locals in large continental settings, and including cultural adaptation, *métissage*, and the use of slave labor. Throughout the seventeenth and early eighteenth centuries, people of African, Malagasy, South Asian, and Native American descent across the French empire grew united, as well, through their common struggles to keep their dignity, advance their interests, and seek justice and safety for themselves and for their loved ones, in many cases despite harrowing adversity.

(Re)connecting France's Transoceanic Empire

What was it that shaped the development of similar practices, policies, and ideas across the French Atlantic and Indian Ocean colonies and outposts? Often those developments were disconnected from each other but began as responses to sometimes comparable local conditions: such was probably the case for most of the struggles led by free people of non-European ancestries across the early French Atlantic and Indian Ocean worlds as they began to face similar forms of discrimination.[103] In other cases, however, the similarities among practices, policies, and ideas were clearly the result of transoceanic exchanges across the Atlantic and Indian Ocean worlds. Readers well acquainted with recent historiographical developments will not be surprised by the fact that the French colonies and outposts became significantly interconnected in the early modern period. Several Atlanticists have already discussed the mobility of white and Black mariners, enslaved people, free multiracial relatives, as well as a few French officials, merchants, intellectuals, and other individuals within the Atlantic world, while others have studied the circulation of ideas within the same region.[104] As demonstrated by a few other scholars, ideas and French people, as well as some individuals of African, Malagasy, and South Asian descent, circulated on an even wider scale that also encompassed the Indian Ocean world.[105] Further research demonstrates how officials in metropolitan France were able to obtain, analyze, and store a massive amount of information about the French colonies and outposts in both the Atlantic and the Indian oceans in order to govern them.[106] However, a clear picture of the infrastructures that enabled the transoceanic circulation of all these people, ideas, and state papers in the first place is still lacking.

Map I.1 is a first rudimentary attempt to address this absence.[107] It features hundreds of ship journeys completed by the French Company of the Indies, other French trading companies, private merchants, and the French Marine between 1713 and 1763.[108] Specifically, it draws on a computational analysis of the "Mémoire des Hommes" database of the French Ministry of Armed Forces (le Ministère des Armées), section "Compagnie des Indes," sub-section "Armements des Navires," created by Jean-Michel André, to provide a first visualization of communications between the French Atlantic and Indian Ocean colonies and outposts and between those positions and the metropole in the early modern period. It displays a total of 946 voyages conducted by 311 vessels that all departed from Port-Louis, home to the French Company of the Indies, in the French port city of Lorient. Those vessels transported tens of thousands of enslaved men, women, and children,

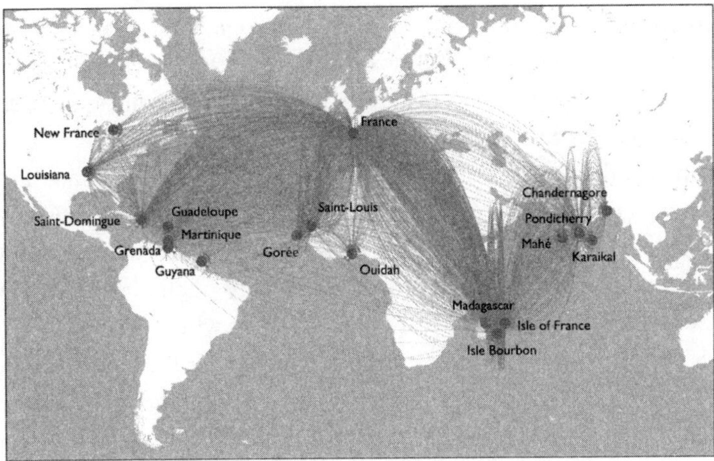

MAP I.1 *Ship Journeys in the French Empire, 1713–1763*

This map charts hundreds of large-scale maritime voyages between French colonies and trading posts in the Atlantic and Indian Oceans.

along with approximately 59,566 other free people—including tens of thousands of Europeans, and 577 (presumably free) Blacks, *mulâtres*, South Asians and Native Americans. Each arrow on Map I.1 represents one leg of a journey completed by one ship.

Map I.1 clearly demonstrates the necessity of using a wide perspective when considering the history of the early modern French colonies and outposts: between 1713 and the Seven Years' War, there were considerable large-scale maritime connections between the different French positions across the Atlantic world and the Indian Ocean. In fact, past assumptions that the eighteenth-century French positions were too disconnected to enable empire stemmed from a narrow approach to French seaborne communications.[109] Those studies primarily focused on maritime connections made by the French Marine, within the Atlantic world. It is true that Marine funding levels dropped considerably after the death of King Louis XIV, from 15,166,000 livres in 1715 to a mere 4,500,000 livres in 1718.[110] However, private ships and ships that belonged to the French trading companies completed hundreds of voyages. Throughout the early colonial era, as was the case in the British context, French colonialism was often the business of corporations—trading companies that envisioned, financed, and governed overseas expansions.[111] It was in many respects those trading companies that shaped France's colonial empire by transporting people and commodities, forging commercial connections on the ground, and using their regal power to set their own rules.[112] Between 1713 and 1763, in addition to transporting thousands of enslaved people to the colonies and outposts, the French companies carried maritime personnel (including Europeans, South Asian men and free Blacks), employees, settlers, military men, and French and South Asian indentured servants—not to mention approximately 712 French administrators.[113] They also transported official papers and orders produced by the crown.[114] The French Company of the Indies, in particular, possessed the means to assist the crown: just when the French Marine saw its funding levels drop, the French West India Company (la Compagnie des Indes Occidentales), which was integrated into the Company of the Indies in 1719, was gaining access to considerable financial resources.[115] This is why the French Company of the Indies owned more ships, with a higher tonnage threshold, than the English East India Company.[116]

While some of the connections illuminated by Map I.1 are already well known, others have not yet been explored in depth. Map I.1 supports the claim made by Atlanticists that the French Atlantic positions were particularly interconnected: in fact, 46 percent (438) of the connections displayed on Map I.1 remained within the Atlantic world. It is also clear from Map I.1 that metropolitan France maintained very close ties with the French colonies and outposts: 97 percent of the voyages displayed here passed through the metropole.[117] But most importantly, Map I.1 demonstrates that the French Atlantic and Indian Ocean positions were also interconnected, on a scale hitherto unsuspected. In fact, 52 percent (490) of the voyages displayed on Map I.1 crossed the boundary between the Atlantic and the Indian Ocean.

French Atlantic positions were connected to the Indian Ocean in multiple ways. First, many colonists, company employees, military men, and officials in the Indian Ocean—some of whom will appear later in this book—previously lived in Atlantic colonies and vice versa. Second, French ships sailing from Europe to the Indian Ocean usually stopped somewhere in the Atlantic before undertaking the perilous journey through the Cape of Good Hope, as did ships going in the other direction.[118] Ocean currents carried those ships to different places, both outside and within the purview of the French empire, including Cadix (Spain), Spanish-controlled Tenerife (Canary Islands), Portuguese-controlled Cape Verde and Brazil, and British Saint Helena, as well as French Louisiana, the French Caribbean, and Gorée Island.[119] On their way back to Europe, those ships usually stopped in French Louisiana or the French Caribbean or in Brazil, Saint Helena, or Ascension Island.[120] By the early eighteenth century, the French attempted to make the most of these transoceanic connections, building trading networks between different Atlantic and Indian Ocean colonies and outposts. In particular, they started a slave trade from West Africa (especially from Gorée and Ouidah, Dahomey) to Isle Bourbon in 1702.[121] The company abandoned its trading monopoly over Guinea in 1725, retroceded Louisiana to the crown in 1730, and gave up its monopoly over the Senegambian slave trade in 1747, partly because of its uneven financial revenues.[122] From the 1740s onward, as the company shifted its trading priorities toward more lucrative Asian markets in places like Pondicherry, Surat, Mahé, Chandernagore, and Mocha, traffic between the Americas, metropolitan France, and the Indian Ocean grew exponentially. At least 296 voyages took place between the Atlantic and Indian Oceans in the quarter century between 1731 and 1756, compared to 82 in the nearly two decades between 1713 and 1731.

Much like the Caribbean, the southwest Indian Ocean islands of Madagascar, Isle Bourbon, and Isle of France served as a crucial connection hub: this may explain their important—yet hitherto neglected—role in the pan-imperial diffusion of ideas. An enormous 50 percent (465) of the ship journeys displayed on Map I.1 converged on these islands. Located past the South Atlantic and the Cape of Good Hope—yet thousands of miles away from the East Indies—Madagascar, Isle Bourbon, and Isle of France lay at an important crossroads. This is why the French trading companies initially tried to use Madagascar and Isle Bourbon not only as agricultural colonies but also as ports of call (*escales*) on the sea route to the East Indies, supplying fresh food to passing ships, medical care to sick sailors, and storage facilities (entrepôts) for Asian merchandise.[123] Madagascar never fulfilled its intended role of port of call on the sea route to Asia, instead becoming an important nexus of the Indian Ocean slave trade and a minor source of captives for the French Caribbean.[124] However, Isle Bourbon was the only French port of call in the region until the 1720s, when Isle of France became a major new *escale* thanks to its more favorable mooring conditions.[125]

A Common Racial Culture and Nomenclature

By the late seventeenth century, the circulation of ships, people, and documents, along with officials' commitment to legal standardization, facilitated the formation of a common racial culture and nomenclature across the French Atlantic and Indian Ocean empire. This common racial culture manifested itself not only in French policies but also in racial discourse. In this book, the expression "racial discourse" refers to a pan-imperial rhetoric employed by French contemporaries that described the features of people of non-European descent as biologically inherited and immutable, as well as inferior to those of the French.[126]

The French were not the only Europeans to apply the notion of race to overseas populations. In fact, by the early seventeenth century, race had already emerged in Iberian colonies and outposts like Mexico, Chile, and Goa, where the notion of *limpieza de sangre* ("purity of blood"), initially used to discriminate against people of allegedly "impure" Jewish and Muslim ancestries, was extended to colonial populations, excluding people of African, Native American, and South Asian descent from multiple offices and professions.[127] As recently noted by literary scholar Noémie Ndiaye, those previous developments in Iberian contexts played an important role in shaping the racialization of French discourse and practices because of the "sustained exchanges between colonial powers."[128] The same culture of race crystallized across the early French world as a result of the circulation of ideas between the French and other European empires, as well as within the French transoceanic empire.

The crystallization of race in the early French empire was not limited to the colonies and outposts. In fact, we must revise the accepted timeline of the emergence of race in the political culture of metropolitan France. In the past, scholars of Ancien Régime France have dated the crystallization of racial categories in this political culture to the 1760s and 1770s—particularly when the Parlement of Paris registered a regulation denying entry to the kingdom of France to all Blacks and *mulâtres*, and when mixed marriages were prohibited in domestic France.[129] Recent historical research has begun to push the timeline for the emergence of race in metropolitan France further back in time, to the 1750s—especially toward 1762, when all free people of color were forced to register their names at the admiralty court of Paris, in an effort to protect local residents from "racial contaminants."[130] But as this book demonstrates, metropolitan officials had already begun to formulate racial policies for the French Atlantic and Indian Ocean overseas positions well before the mid-eighteenth century, as early as the late seventeenth century. This is unsurprising since, as demonstrated by recent work in the fields of French studies, Black Studies and Art history, French intellectuals and artists had already begun to racialize Black overseas populations at least since the start of the seventeenth century, in the literary and artistic spheres, and in the popular culture of the kingdom of France.[131] Additionally, although scholars have attributed the crystallization of racial policing in the kingdom of France to the arrival of several colonial officials who integrated into metropolitan political circles in the late eighteenth century, colonial officials already exerted this influence by the early eighteenth century through their correspondence with metropolitan authorities.[132] This is evident in the correspondence and legislation sent from the metropole to the colonies and outposts, which in several cases were written in direct response to colonial officials' demands for more racial policies and on occasion even repeated verbatim their language of racial purity.

The crystallization of the pan-imperial language of race and blood purity in the French colonial world is visible in state papers, imperial correspondence, and travel narratives, especially beginning in the late seventeenth century. It shows up across discussions concerning every population across the French Atlantic and Indian Oceans. French contemporaries occasionally used the word "race" (*race*) or the term "species" (*espèce*), which was commonly used to classify breeds of animals.[133] More often, they used related words like "blood" (*sang*) or "nature," evoking heredity and inalterability.[134]

Officials and other contemporary observers in the metropole and across the French Atlantic and Indian Ocean worlds also began to use a common nomenclature to categorize colonial populations. This common terminology coexisted with much more localized taxonomies, specific to one particular region or oceanic basin. Some of this language was specific to the type of populations encountered by the French in a given area. For example, French contemporaries often labeled Luso-Indian men and women in Pondicherry and Chandernagore as *Portugais* (masculine form of "Portuguese") and *Portugaises* (feminine form of "Portuguese").[135] The Luso-Indian women who were taken from India to Isle Bourbon beginning in the 1670s as part of an intermarriage scheme were also categorized as *Portuguaises* and *Portugaises des Indes* ("Portuguese from the Indies") in official documents.[136]

The French also used a religion-based terminology. In both Senegambia and India, they sometimes used the word "Moors" (*Maures*) to designate Muslim people. And whereas the word "Gentiles" (*Gentils*) was only sporadically used to designate Native Americans, it was often employed to label Hindus in India and on Isle Bourbon.[137] French contemporaries described the "Gentiles" as "idolaters" and "pagans"—by which they meant "worshiper[s] of false Gods."[138] In using the words *Gentils* and *Maures* in their Indian Ocean colonies and outposts, the French might have been following a Portuguese practice: before the arrival of other European nations, the Portuguese in India had already begun to use the words *mouros* (meaning "Moors") and *gentilos* ("Gentiles") to differentiate local populations.[139]

Alongside such localized terminologies there was a nomenclature common to the French Atlantic and Indian Oceans, with meanings that could vary from one colony to another. By the late seventeenth century, the nomenclature used to label the populations of the French Atlantic included all these categories: *Indiens* ("Indians"), *sauvages* ("savages"), *Francois* ("French"), *Blancs* ("whites"), *nègres* or *Noirs* ("negroes" or "Blacks"), *métis* ("metis"), and *mulâtres* ("mulattoes"). Except when citing primary and secondary sources, this book does not apply the misnomer "Indians" to the Indigenous people of the Americas, calling them instead "Native Americans," "Indigenous people," or by the name of their specific people when it is stated in historical documents. The French word *sauvage* (which derives from the Latin word *silvaticus,* meaning "belonging to the woods") was polysemic. While it could refer to a desirable state of nature far from the artifices of civilization, another common usage of the word *sauvage* in early modern France was derogatory—the *Dictionary of the French Academy* of 1694 defined *sauvages* as "some people who ordinarily live in the woods, with no religion, laws and fixed abode, more akin to animals than actual humans."[140] As for the "white" category, it was frequently employed in Caribbean literary sources and official documents in an attempt to clearly distinguish white Europeans or white creoles from other populations, indicating a growing yearning for a more racialized social order among French contemporaries. Some other terms derived from a vocabulary used in the Spanish colonies prior to the French expansion. The word *nègre* derived from the Spanish term *negro*, meaning "a Black person." The word *mulâtre,* which in the Atlantic world was most commonly used to designate mixed Black and white people, probably derived from the Spanish term *mulato,* which had appeared in the Spanish colonies in the sixteenth century to designate mixed Black and Spanish people. It probably originated in a zoological lexicon related to crossbreeding. According to the French missionary to the Caribbean Jean-Baptiste Du Tertre, the word *mulâtre* probably derived etymologically from the word "mule." He claimed, "These poor children are born to a white man and a Black woman, just like mules, who are born to different species of animals."[141] Meanwhile, the word *métis* was typically used to describe mixed Native American and white people, though it was also used to label the child of a white person with a *mulâtre* in Guadeloupe.[142] It probably derived from the Spanish word *mestizo,* meaning "mixed."[143] All English terms that may be considered offensive today (for instance, the word "mulatto") are used in their original French throughout this book, since they are only imagined categories with no real biological grounding, set down in historical documents by early modern people.[144] Another category occasionally used in the French Americas in the first half of the eighteenth century was *créole* ("creole").[145] The word *créole* was a Gallicized version of the Spanish word *criollo* ("creole"), pointing toward further influences from the Spanish empire. The Spanish word *criollo* probably came from the verb *criar*, meaning "to raise." Initially applied to enslaved Blacks born outside of Africa, it was then employed to designate Spanish people born in the colonies.[146]

This same terminology, with some local variations in meanings, was also used in the French colonies and outposts of the Indian Ocean. By the early eighteenth century, the word *créoles* was used more often on Isle Bourbon than it was in the French Americas to designate both free and unfree people born on the island, regardless of their origins or skin color. Moreover, by the mid-seventeenth century, the French in the Indian Ocean used the term *Indiens* to designate the people of both Madagascar and India.[147] This book avoids this word when it can lead to confusion, since scholars also use the label "Indians" to designate Native American people. Instead, the word "Malagasies" is often used throughout this book to label the people of Madagascar, while the expression "South Asian people" is used to designate the people of India, along with religious labels such as "Hindus," and regional terms like "Tanosy" (meaning "of Anosy, Madagascar"). Beginning in the second half of the seventeenth century in Guadeloupe and Isle Bourbon, and by the early eighteenth century in Louisiana, French contemporaries used the word *Francois*, as well, to designate people from metropolitan France.[148] Additionally, the words *mulâtres* and *métis* were used interchangeably on Isle Bourbon to designate people of mixed white and Malagasy, African, or South Asian descent—the word *métis* was also used in India to designate Eurasian people.[149] In using the term *métis* in the Mascarenes and India, the French might have been drawing on a terminology already used by the Dutch in the Indian Ocean: by the 1660s, the words *mesties* and *mixtiesen* were already employed in the Dutch East Indies.[150] Also from the 1660s, French observers began to use the words *Noirs* and *nègres* to describe all bonded servants on Isle Bourbon, whether they had origins in Madagascar, India, or Africa.[151] The Dutch and the British also categorized South Asian people as Blacks (*swarten* in Dutch and "Blacks" in

English) by the mid-seventeenth century.[152] Meanwhile, by the early eighteenth century, the category *Blancs* was also used on Isle Bourbon to designate white Europeans, as well as free Bourbon Island Creole people like Marianne Payet, even if they had origins in Madagascar or South Asia. The historian Alfred Rosset has referred to the assimilated inhabitants of Isle Bourbon who fit this extended definition of whiteness as *Blancs de Bourbon* ("Isle Bourbon Whites").[153] Instead of being characterized by skin color, Isle Bourbon's whiteness was achieved through social status: freedom at birth, ownership of land and enslaved laborers, and so forth.

The use of the binary Atlantic terminology "white" versus "Black" in the Indian Ocean is another testament to the circulation of ideas between the two oceans. In the Americas, skin color became closely connected to social status because of the expansion of Black plantation slavery. As demonstrated by Simone Delesalle and Lucette Valensi in their in-depth analysis of early modern French dictionaries, the words *nègres* and *Noirs* were often used as synonyms for "slaves" by the late seventeenth century.[154] This is illustrated by the definition provided for the word *nègres* in the 1671 edition of François Pomey's *Dictionnaire royal augmenté*: "Black slaves who are taken from the African coast for the farming of the land and to the [American] mainland to work in mines and sugar factories."[155] By applying parts of the racial nomenclature circulating in the French Atlantic world to the Indian Ocean, French officials attempted to emulate the binary model of slave societies in the Americas, with the schism between white slaveowners and enslaved Black people. However, in an attempt to remedy the lack of European colonists, the definition of whiteness was expanded on Isle Bourbon, allowing many free Bourbon Island Creoles of Malagasy and South Asian ancestries to enjoy the same privileges as white people.

A Note on Sources

Placing free and unfree people of African, Malagasy, and South Asian descent at the center of early modern French colonial history is a difficult task, considering the state of historical sources from this period. We are forced to rely on documents written by a white elite minority—often made of white colonists and slaveowners—because literacy rates were low among enslaved people, ordinary whites, Africans, and Eurafricans in Saint-Louis and Gorée, and people of Malagasy, African, and South Asian descent in the southwest Indian Ocean.[156] I attempt to overcome this difficulty as much as possible by drawing on a wide range of sources from thirteen archives scattered across France, the United States, and Réunion Island.

I consider the attitudes of the political and intellectual elites, as expressed in legislation, official reports, memoranda, travel narratives, and the correspondence of officials, colonists, clergymen and travelers. However, I also seek to reconstruct the experiences of free and enslaved people of non-European ancestries by examining court proceedings, parish registers, censuses, and notarial documents from several colonies and outposts. As recent groundbreaking work by Dominique Rogers, Sophie White, and others demonstrates, the court proceedings of France's colonies contain rich testimonies given by enslaved people.[157] Moreover, I draw on manumission acts, wills, donation deeds, censuses, and parish registers to uncover traces of relationships that crossed racial boundaries. Researching the relationships of enslaved women and their mixed children with white men is an arduous task because mixed relationships were usually concealed in official documents. Where census and church record keepers did not use racial labels, it is difficult to estimate intermarriage rates or the number of mixed children. In such cases, older parish registers and censuses have been combined with historical accounts to reconstruct people's genealogies and identify those with African, Malagasy, or South Asian origins. Censuses and donation deeds, as well as acts of property sales and estate inventories, serve multiple functions in this book. They are used to assess the wealth of free people of African, Malagasy and South Asian descent, and to compare it to that of whites. They are also used to assess how people of non-European descent responded to the socioeconomic discrimination against them. Specifically, this book looks at indicators of wealth, including number of enslaved people per household, real estate, furniture, livestock, cash and credit, clothing, and jewelry. The number of enslaved people per household is a reasonable proxy for overall wealth, which is why tax rates in the French colonies and outposts were based on this metric.

Although I am mindful of Jennifer Morgan's calls for an awareness of the "ideological reverberations of demographic data," I do not shy away from numbers, for two reasons.[158] First, these numbers will help us understand the demographic forces at play in empire building, which informed shifting imperial strategies on the ground. Colonial administrators themselves did not track numbers solely for capitalist purposes in the context of the slave trade, as Morgan has brilliantly demonstrated, but also because of imperialist concerns.[159] Colonial censuses reflect the preoccupations of their authors, as well as those of the local and metropolitan officials who dictated their methodology.[160] Especially in the early years of French colonization, these men were concerned with the small size of white settler populations because they could lead other European countries to question the legitimacy of French imperial claims to foreign lands.[161] These numbers could also lead foreign people to launch and win attacks against the French colonial settlements and outposts. Meanwhile, keeping track of the number of enslaved people was a way to facilitate tax collection and assess risks of slave revolts if colonists were outnumbered. Free Blacks and *mulâtres* were often counted as well, for tax collection purposes, and because their presence in the French colonies challenged the racialization of social hierarchies and raised concerns about potential alliances with enslaved people in plots and rebellions. Authorities also kept track of the numbers of *mulâtres* because they considered manumissions and wealth transmission from white fathers to their mixed children an impediment to white supremacy.

The second reason why I do not shy away from numbers is because they are strong indicators of the level of violence faced by thousands of men, women, and children who lived in slavery. The numbers of mixed children that are recorded in colonial censuses will help us realize the scope of the sexual coercion exercised by white men over thousands of enslaved women. The numbers provided for enslaved people are also useful to track the transoceanic expansion of slave labor, especially from the late seventeenth century onward. As Saidiya Hartman has pointed out, historians have long used the data of the European slave trades to engage in dehumanizing calculations and arithmetic practices "that were entrenched centuries ago." Because this approach reproduces the "devalu[ation of] [Black lives]," I always consider those numbers side by side with the complicated lived experiences of the people who were being counted.[162]

Ultimately, therefore, I am committed to embracing dual approaches to the early history of France's Atlantic and Indian Ocean empire, as well as to the archives themselves. The chapters that follow draw on an inclusive range of data from the archives while also recognizing the brutal ideologies that led European contemporaries to record them in the way they did.[163] I am committed to considering not only the perspectives of French authorities but also the experiences of the free and unfree people on the ground who faced brutal abuse, shaped their own cultures, traded, worked, tried to advance and safeguard their own interests, and sought to protect their loved ones under conditions of imperial rule. Like the stories of the two Mariannes, these dual perspectives will help us grasp the complexities of French colonialism—to acknowledge not only the scope of its violence but also the different degrees of power held by the populations of non-European descent whose desires, ambitions, and grit shaped the very contours of the French empire.

Note on Currencies in the Ancien Régime

One livre equaled twenty sols.
One écu equaled three livres.
One piastre equaled five to eight livres.[164]
One Pondicherry rupee equaled two livres, eight sols.[165]
A sailor in French colonial Louisiana earned 180 livres/year.[166]
A surgeon on Isle Bourbon earned 600 to 1,000 livres/year.[167]
A councilor on Isle Bourbon earned 2,000 livres/year.[168]

CHAPTER I

"We Shall Be One People"

In a French-Innu council that took place in Quebec in 1633, the French explorer and administrator Samuel de Champlain famously declared, "Our young men will marry your daughters, & *we shall be one people.*"[1] This same "one people" and intermarriage rhetoric became a leitmotif in Native American–French diplomacy in the American Northeast and beyond, partly because it was used in the political cultures of Native American peoples in the region.[2] We know that people in this region "interacted with one another first and most importantly as kin," forming literal bonds of kinship with strangers through intermarriage. They also used kinship metaphors (such as "one people," "brothers," or "fathers"), each of which was meant to articulate a very specific claim or relationship with strangers.[3] One known example, among others, is that of Onagan, a Mohawk representative from the Haudenosaunee (Iroquois) confederacy, who approached the French in 1641 to seal a peace treaty after years of war. He reportedly declared his own people's intent to form "*only one people* with [the French] [*plus qu'un peuple*]," by which he meant that French people would be assimilated into his big family after being turned into Iroquois.[4] Champlain strategically embraced this "one people" rhetoric during the French-Innu council of 1633, with the aim of advancing France's own diplomatic, economic and cultural interests.

While none of this will come as a surprise to scholars of seventeenth-century New France, what has not yet been fully appreciated is the scope of the influence that this same "one people" rhetoric had on early French colonial policy. Gauging the extent of this influence requires looking far beyond New France to the first colony established by the French in the Indian Ocean: namely, Anosy, Madagascar, in 1642. Twenty-three years after the Mohawk representative had approached the French to express his own people's intent to form "*only one people* with [them]," on October 26, 1664, the assembly of the French Company of the East Indies drew on the same rhetoric when declaring its intention to "eventually form *only one people* [*de ne faire qu'un Peuple*] out of the two nations" with France's roandria (noble) allies and other people in Madagascar.[5] Only three years later did the first minister of state and controller of finances, Jean-Baptiste Colbert, give his famous instruction to the intendant of New France, Jean Talon: "[You must] try to attract these people, especially those who embraced Christianity, near our habitations, and if possible integrate them so that after a time, under the same law and master, they shall become only *one people* and one blood."[6] The similarity between the company's instructions for Madagascar and Colbert's instructions for New France was no coincidence: these instructions for Madagascar and New France were both issued by Colbert himself. The document indicates that the decision to "form only *one people*" in Madagascar was made during a meeting "in which [the company] received *great assistance from the presence of Mr. Colbert*, who often came to preside over its assemblies."[7] French officials' vision of becoming "one people" with some Malagasy peoples, and with their allies in New France, was of course very different from that imagined by the Haudenosaunee: it initially entailed assimilating Christianized and Frenchified Native American women, as well as *roandria* and other manumitted Malagasy women, into French society through Catholic intermarriage.

This chapter explores the formation of France's seventeenth-century "assimilation" program across the Atlantic and Indian Ocean worlds.[8] Seventeenth-century French authorities famously promoted the conversion of allied Native American populations in New France to Catholicism, their "civilization" (or "Frenchification") and naturalization, as well as the integration of allied female Native American converts into French society through intermarriage. Scholars have referred to this body of policies collectively as "assimilation policy," though it is not to be confused with the assimilation project carried out in the nineteenth and twentieth centuries.[9] The primary claim in this chapter is that elements of this well-known seventeenth-century New France assimilation program can also be found in policies targeting local (Indigenous) populations in other seventeenth-century French Atlantic and Indian Ocean possessions. From the early seventeenth century, French authorities articulated a set of evangelization policies targeting local populations across *all French overseas positions*. They formulated naturalization policies not only for North America but also for the Caribbean, their outposts in West Africa, and all settlements and outposts in the Indian Ocean. More surprisingly, French authorities equally endeavored to "civilize" the Tupinamba of Brazil starting in the sixteenth century, as well as local women in Madagascar in the seventeenth. They also promoted intermarriage between Frenchmen and Christianized women in Madagascar, Isle Bourbon, French India, and French Louisiana. These observations challenge the idea in the historiography that the French project of "civilization" (or "Frenchification") was "exclusively reserved for New France's Indian population" and that the promotion of intermarriages was "distinctive" to New France.[10] The consistency that characterized the body of pan-imperial policies across the Atlantic and Indian Ocean worlds was the result of a royal commitment—often enforced through metropolitan officials like Colbert or his predecessor as first minister of state, Cardinal Richelieu—to apply consistent legal standards across the French colonies and outposts from their vantage point in the metropole. As Charles VII (1403–1461) and Louis XI (1423–1483) began to lay the foundations of an absolute and administrative monarchy, the crown had been trying to establish more legal uniformity across the French kingdom since the fifteenth century.[11] In the seventeenth century, the French trading companies contributed to the process of legal unification as well, since the king himself and his first minister of state had a significant influence on their policies: in addition to formulating their charters, they gave them instructions, and they presided over some of their administrative assemblies or were represented in them by several members of their patronage.[12]

There were two phases in the formulation of France's seventeenth-century pan-imperial project. During the first phase, the successive kings, along with their representatives and religious missionaries, articulated a somewhat flexible assimilation project for New France, elements of which were then extended to other American colonies and to Madagascar. During the second phase, the crown articulated a more rigid and conservative assimilation project for Madagascar, elements of which were then extended to New France and to the rest of the Atlantic and Indian Oceans. The first, more flexible iteration of the pan-imperial project, was formulated from the sixteenth century and lasted until the early 1660s, when Louis XIV began his personal rule. The second phase of the project began around this time and ended in the late seventeenth century, when French authorities began to issue a long series of intermarriage bans across the French Indian Ocean and Atlantic worlds. Americanists have mostly associated the revival of the New France assimilation project in the early 1660s with the decision by different groups of Innu, Algonquin, Wendat, Wabanaki, and Haudenosaunee in this period to form Indigenous mission settlements in the Saint Lawrence River valley, which would facilitate evangelization.[13] In reality, however, the revival of the French assimilation project in the 1660s was also intended to support the renewed French colonial expansion in the Indian Ocean, which began in 1663. This is why it initially targeted Madagascar *before* being extended to New France and to other French colonies and outposts. The 1660s were a milestone in the development of the colonial enterprise in the Indian Ocean; the French established their first permanent settlement on Madagascar's neighboring island of Bourbon in 1664, along with their first East Indian outpost in Surat in 1668. France's assimilation policies were issued from the top by French officials for strategic and ideological reasons and because those officials were committed to applying consistent legal standards across multiple territories.

However, as this chapter demonstrates, these French imperial policies were also influenced by the cultures of France's local allies on the ground. The French, few in numbers in the first decades of overseas colonization, were well aware that they could not build an empire without taking into account some of the customs, aspirations, and reactions of their local allies overseas. They thus not only tried to adapt their policies to the kinship culture of their Native American allies in the American Northeast but also adjusted them to a *roandria* tradition of intermarrying with strangers to assimilate them and form trading and military alliances with them, along with bonds of solidarity.[14] It follows that the project of assimilation in France's overseas empire should not be considered a unilateral endeavor: the local populations of Madagascar, as well as those in New France, also used an intermarriage rhetoric with the intent of assimilating foreigners, including the French, into their own communities. Strangely, therefore, France's assimilation policies were shaped not only by the colonial objectives of the French but also by local populations' own imperialist ambitions.

Origins of the First Iteration of the Assimilation Project

From the sixteenth century to the early 1660s, the French crown articulated the first iteration of its assimilation project for New France as well as Equinoctial France before extending some of its tenets to other Atlantic and Indian Ocean territories. The French became especially eager to spread the Catholic faith overseas from the early seventeenth century, partly because they had been scarred by the Wars of Religion (1562–1598). While the issuance of the Edict of Nantes by King Henry IV in 1598 had put an end to this conflict and advanced religious freedom, it had not brought religious unification.[15] By converting and naturalizing the local populations they encountered overseas, French authorities hoped to create a French empire that would be more united around the Catholic faith than the kingdom of France itself.[16] Saliha Belmessous and Gilles Havard have convincingly presented the colonies established by the Europeans overseas in the early modern period as aspirational utopias that were supposed to have none of the corruption of Western European populations—this is illustrated by the names given to the colonies, which included not only Nouvelle France (New France) but also Nueva España (New Spain), Nieuw-Nederland (New Netherland), and New England.[17]

When they began to formulate the assimilation project, French authorities could find inspiration in the ways the Spaniards, the Portuguese, and the Dutch had dealt with local populations in their own colonies since the fifteenth century.[18] French officials and missionaries were familiar with the strategies employed by these other European empires. In fact, several of the Franciscan missionaries in New Spain had close ties with France because many of them were born there. Such was the case for Jacobo de Testera, a missionary born in Bayonne, France, who spent twenty years in Spain and was sent to Mexico in 1529, where he evangelized the Maya of Yucatán (in the southeast) and the Nahua people of Huejotzinco (in central Mexico). Such was also the case for Maturino Gilberti, a missionary born in Poitiers, France, who studied theology at the University of Toulouse before traveling to Mexico in 1542, where he became an expert in the Purépecha language.[19] Moreover, many French people read about the accomplishments of the Spaniards and the Portuguese in their empires. The narratives of Spanish and Portuguese missionaries and travelers were widely translated into French and often republished in multiple editions in France.[20]

Many seventeenth-century French writers clearly knew about the Spanish and Portuguese evangelization programs, since they mentioned them in their own travel narratives. For example, in the second half of the seventeenth century, the French Dominican missionary to the Caribbean Jean-Baptiste Du Tertre discussed the conversion efforts of the Portuguese and the Dutch in the Americas, while Sieur Dellon, a French surgeon who spent time on Isle Bourbon in the 1660s, praised the progress of the Portuguese in the Christianization of the East Indies.[21]

When they formulated their assimilation project, French authorities were influenced not only by the practices of other European empires but also by the history of their own kingdom. Like Spain and Portugal, France had long considered evangelization a moral duty, as illustrated by its lengthy and violent crusades. Additionally, the French were inspired by the Roman legacy in Europe: Rome had striven to bring civilization to its provinces, including Gaul.[22] The seventeenth-century French assimilation strategy overseas was also shaped by the policies of cultural expansion conducted within the kingdom of France. In the seventeenth century, Louis XIV sought to bolster his authority by establishing political institutions, appointing local representatives, and bringing French customs to the newly conquered provinces of Flanders, Artois, Lorraine, Alsace, Franche-Comté, and Roussillon. The children of the elite of those new provinces were sent to schools where they were taught the French culture and (Parisian) French language in order to strengthen their allegiance to the crown.[23] Unlike the policies applied in the kingdom of France, however, official strategies of assimilation overseas were not limited to local leaders.

Evangelization

Especially from the early seventeenth century, French secular and religious authorities formulated foundational evangelization projects targeting local peoples in Equinoctial France and New France that they then extended to the Caribbean and Guiana, as well as to Madagascar, throughout the first half of the seventeenth century. In 1493 and 1494, the papal bulls of Alexander VI had already granted dominion of the Americas to the Catholic monarchs of Castile on the condition that they would work toward the conversion of Indigenous populations.[24] In addition to being genuinely concerned about the salvation of overseas people, French authorities themselves thus embraced the evangelization project to legitimize their own territorial claims in the eyes of Catholic leadership in Europe. Such was the case in 1665, when French secular authorities in the metropole justified the formation of the French Company of the East Indies by stressing the necessity of "let[ting] all people see the sun of faith, and let the divine light of the Gospel shine upon the most isolated nations."[25]

The stories of the evangelization campaigns launched in New France in the decades that followed the foundation of a first permanent settlement in Quebec in 1608 are well known, but they should be considered in tandem with the less familiar program formulated at the same time for Equinoctial France. As had been the case in the Spanish Caribbean, New Spain, and South America, religious missionaries were the ones tasked with the execution of the evangelization project in both New France and Equinoctial France.[26] In 1611, the start of the Jesuit missions in New France coincided with the election, in France, of a few Capuchin missionaries whose mission was to implant the Catholic faith among the Tupinamba of Equinoctial France.[27] When they returned to France in 1613, those missionaries brought six Tupinamba with them, whom French authorities attempted to turn into assimilated Frenchified Catholics in a series of propaganda events intended to motivate the French to invest in the Brazilian colonial enterprise. In a rare consideration of missionary work among the Tupinamba, Sara Melzer has convincingly described those events as "a foundational moment in the history of what would become France's most enduring stance towards the other—assimilation."[28] The Tupinamba were given French names and "dressed in a French way," according to the French poet François de Malherbe.[29] They were also asked to intone the *Ave Maria* and the *Pater Noster* in their own language before a crowd at various churches across the kingdom of France. Strikingly, they were then baptized in Paris in a major ceremony, after which three of them were married to French women in Catholic ceremonies.[30]

Following the foundational Brazilian and Canadian campaigns, the evangelization program was extended to other territories across the Atlantic and the Indian Ocean. When Cardinal Richelieu came to power in the 1620s, he even became invested in the evangelization of the Caribbean islands *before* he began to tackle Christian conversion in New France. Richelieu became Louis XIII's first minister in 1624 and remained in office until his death in 1642, when his protégé, Cardinal Mazarin, took over. It was under Richelieu's leadership that more settlements were established, not only in the Saint Lawrence valley but also in the Caribbean, beginning in 1625 on the isle of Saint-Christopher (the island was partitioned between the French and the English). Richelieu founded the Company of Saint-Christopher in 1625 (rebranded as the Company of the American Islands, ruling over the Lesser Antilles, in 1635), as well as the (New France) Company of One Hundred Associates in 1627—an imitation of the Dutch West India Company. Richelieu then formulated a series of consistent religious policies for the Caribbean *before* focusing on his well-known evangelization program for New France. In 1626, he stated his intent to send French subjects to the Caribbean to trade colonial commodities and "teach the [Indigenous/i.e., Kalinago] inhabitants of these said [islands] about the Catholic, Apostolic, and Roman religion."[31] It was only one year later, in 1627, that he famously declared—in the Act for the Establishment of the Company of One Hundred Associates—his intention to "populate [New France] with French Catholic subjects so that, through their example, [Native American] nations [may] be inclined to embrace the Christian religion."[32] In 1626, he also commanded the associates of the Company of the American Islands to maintain at least three clergymen in each Caribbean settlement to "instruct the *sauvages*" (i.e., the Kalinago) and build churches. When Richelieu formulated the Act for the Establishment of the Company of One Hundred Associates, he clearly drew on this earlier Caribbean policy: article III of the act of 1627 also put the New France company in charge of supporting at least three clergymen in each settlement and mission.[33] Those religious policies formulated for the Caribbean and for New France were echoed in following decades in policymaking for Guiana, where the French established a first permanent settlement in Cayenne in 1643. In 1651, the king issued letters patent granting the concession of Guiana to a group of men that included Lieutenant-General Balthazar Le Roux de Royville and theologian Abbé L'Isle Marivault. In those letters patent, the king stated his intention "to establish the true religion" and bring missionaries to Guiana, "[as] it [had] been done in New France, and on the islands of St. Christopher, Guadeloupe, Martinique and others."[34]

The evangelization program first formulated for the French American colonies was extended to Madagascar after the foundation of the French outpost of Fort-Dauphin on the southeastern coast of the island in 1643.

Up to forty-five Lazarist missionaries and secular priests arrived in Anosy between 1648 and 1674: this was a major effort to advance evangelization, comparable to that undertaken decades earlier in New France, where a total of twenty-nine Jesuits and a few Franciscan missionaries resided by 1640.[35] In addition to serving the Catholic population, the Lazarists of Madagascar were put in charge of converting local women and European Protestants on the island—several immigrants to the island were Huguenots, including the first French governor of Fort-Dauphin, Jacques Pronis (1642–1648).

Interestingly, one of the first Lazarist missionaries to Madagascar, Charles Nacquart, hoped to create religious missions similar to those already established in New France. He was clearly aware of the methods used by secular and religious authorities in New France. In fact, in his correspondence, Nacquart even likened his own mission in Madagascar to that of Charles de Montmagny, governor of New France from 1636 to 1648, who was a fierce advocate of evangelization.[36] Two years after his arrival on the island, in 1650, Nacquart asked metropolitan authorities to send French nuns and orphans to the colony in order to start a seminary. Nacquart intended to devote particular attention to the Christianization of local children in Madagascar, a method also employed by missionaries in New France that dated back to the establishment of a short-lived children's seminary in Quebec in 1635 by the superior of the Jesuit missions, Paul Le Jeune.[37] Nacquart proposed the creation of missions and another seminary for children north of Fort-Dauphin, in the town of Fanjahira (the royal capital of Anosy) and the region of Matataña, with six missionaries to educate the Malagasies.[38] The nuns were supposed to take care of the education of local girls and women, in particular. This focus on the conversion of girls and women echoed the approach in use in New France at least since the foundation of an Ursuline school for the education of Native American girls by Marie Guyart (known as Marie de l'Incarnation) shortly after her arrival in Quebec in 1639.[39]

Although evangelization was in the process of becoming a consistent pan-imperial project, there was always a gap between policy and implementation across the colonies, and it was blatant in seventeenth-century Madagascar. The evangelization project in Madagascar gave rise to a small group of female converts to Catholicism who later moved to Isle Bourbon with their French husbands, where their descendants came to form a considerable proportion of the free Bourbon Island Creole population in the early eighteenth century. Yet the evangelization project in seventeenth-century Anosy made very limited inroads aside from this small group of Tanosy women. Missionary work was limited to a small southeastern portion of Madagascar, and Lazarist missionaries considered the presence of Frenchmen who were not Catholic on the island a serious impediment to their evangelizing mission. Bourdaise accused the French Huguenots in Madagascar of constantly pulling local people away from the Catholic faith by giving a bad example.[40] The missionaries spent most of their time in Fort-Dauphin, where they taught a few local catechumens and officiated mass with people from surrounding villages.[41] They occasionally took trips to local villages to support the Frenchmen who lived there, evangelize local people, and baptize their children.[42] However, the *roandria* presented a major challenge for the missionaries, since most of them had no interest in becoming Catholic, and many opposed the French presence on the island. According to contemporary accounts, the fear of being punished by the *roandria* dissuaded most local subjects from approaching the missionaries.[43] Nacquart noted that few of them listened to the missionaries and warned his successors that "if any progress [was] to be made in this country [. . .] these [*roandria* needed] to be removed from the island."[44]

The Lazarists considered the power of the *ombiassa*—local "writers, doctors, priests, and diviners"—another major obstacle to their religious mission in southeastern Madagascar.[45] These religious men inspired awe in their communities because they were believed to have the power to heal and harm people through divination and making remedies and *oly*, popular charms that took the form of a small amulet filled with scriptures, roots, and other things from the natural world, which were believed to grant favors and protection to their owners.[46] The missionaries often lamented the influence of those religious men, as was the case in 1655, when the Lazarist Toussaint Bourdaise requested from his superior in France that a French surgeon be sent to Madagascar on the grounds that the *roandria* used the *ombiassa*'s healing powers "to seduce [those] poor people [of Madagascar] by making them believe a thousand superstitions."[47] One year later, the same missionary continued to lament the refusal of the local population to embrace Christianity, accusing the *ombiassa* of scaring them away by making them believe that "they could make them sick and die whenever they want[ed], and make them endure many forms of evils."[48] When the French Lazarist missionary Nacquart died a mysterious death in 1650, a bad spell cast by an *ombiassa* named Rabobe was held responsible for his passing.[49]

Although we will never know the real cause of Nacquart's death, disease was another important obstacle to missionary work in Madagascar. Most of the Lazarist missionaries and lay priests who set foot in Madagascar died of tropical diseases (including malaria) shortly after their arrival. Tellingly, Bourdaise described Madagascar as "an ungrateful land [which] ruthlessly kills its own saviors."[50] Authorities were too reluctant to invest in the colonial enterprise there, and the number of missionaries in Anosy became too small to conduct a substantial number of conversions.[51] Like his predecessor, Nacquart, Bourdaise was forced to conduct evangelization work in Anosy by himself for years because all other missionaries had died.[52] Those extreme conditions, and the limited inroads made by missionaries, may explain why French authorities did not issue a policy naturalizing Catholic converts into French subjects in the first decades of French presence in Madagascar and the Indian Ocean, whereas such a policy was issued from the 1620s for New France and rapidly extended to the Caribbean. Indeed, although evangelization yielded very few conversions among the Kalinago of the Caribbean as well, it was only around the 1660s that French authorities really came to this realization.[53]

Naturalization

In the 1620s, French authorities applied a policy of naturalization to Native American converts in New France, which they then extended to the Caribbean islands one decade later. Conversion to Catholicism was considered a stepping stone on the path toward naturalization. This is illustrated by the note that Samuel de Champlain sent to King Louis XIII in the 1610s, in which he stated, "[We will teach Native Americans] about God and the glory of His Majesty, so that along with the French language, they shall also cultivate a brave and God-fearing French heart, etched with the yearning to serve you."[54] Over a century later, a Senegal-based Spiritan priest named Jean-Baptiste Demanet was convinced that evangelization would benefit the crown "since the number of Christians and the number of good French people would [then] be one and the same.[55]

It is clear from those citations that one of the main purposes of naturalization was to turn local populations into loyal subjects of the French king.

From 1501 onward, the Spanish crown had also endeavored to turn the Indigenous people of its American empire into "subjects and vassals of the crown," bound by a duty of obedience to the Spanish monarchy and to Spanish laws.[56] By turning Indigenous people into Spanish subjects, the Spanish crown intended to populate its colonies, gain access to more laborers and soldiers, and dissuade Indigenous and European enemies from conducting raids and incursions into the Spanish empire.[57] Saliha Belmessous's work on New France has shown that the French, too, leveraged naturalization to populate their empire with loyal subjects who, they believed, would eagerly defend the colonies.[58] The seventeenth-century French Caribbean colonies had the same problem of underpopulation as New France: around the mid-seventeenth century, there were only about 1,000 whites and between 200 and 300 enslaved Africans in Guadeloupe, compared to 1,000 Kalinago.[59]

This may explain why Richelieu formulated naturalizing policies targeting the Kalinago of the French Caribbean, along with his well-known series of rulings naturalizing Indigenous converts in New France. In 1635, he issued a naturalization regulation for the Caribbean very similar to the one he had formulated in article XVII of the Act for the Establishment of the Company of One Hundred Associates of 1627, which had declared that "[Native Americans] who will be brought to the knowledge of the faith and will practice it, will be considered and known as natural-born French" and accordingly would be able to "acquire, bequeath, inherit and accept donations and inheritance like any other true French subject."[60] In article XI of the Contract for the Reestablishment of the Company of the American Islands, he also wrote, "His Majesty will allow that [. . .] the *sauvages* who convert to the faith and practice it will be considered and known as natural-born French" and would, accordingly, be "capable of all functions, honors, successions and donations like any natural French subjects."[61] This provision was then reiterated in 1642 in the king's Edict for the Formation of the Company of the American Islands.[62]

What exactly did it mean to be a naturalized French subject? As suggested by Richelieu's declaration in the New France Act of 1627 as well as the Contract for the Reestablishment of the Company of the American Islands, becoming a French subject (*un naturel*) meant being exempt from the aubaine right (*droit d'aubaine*)—the crown's right to confiscate the inheritance of nonnaturalized foreigners.[63] It was also assumed that, in acquiring French naturalization, colonial populations would bow to the crown's authority and become beholden to the same laws as natural-born French subjects. To some extent, naturalization policies were thus intended to help the crown increase the reach of its absolutist power. Gilles Havard has interpreted the second iteration of the French assimilation program from the 1660s in light of Louis XIV's "absolutist ideal," which translated into a strong impulse toward "social control."[64] Since absolutism was underway well before the reign of Louis XIV, it should come as no surprise that French authorities already endeavored to achieve strong social control over the colonies as early as the beginning of the seventeenth century.[65]

Civilization (or "Frenchification")

Alongside their naturalization and evangelization programs, French authorities were planning to "civilize" (or "Frenchify") local populations not just in New France but also in Brazil and Madagascar.[66] "Civilization" implied following certain social codes: seventeenth-century French dictionaries defined the expression "to civilize" (*civiliser*) as "to make civil and sociable; to polish the manners."[67] The word "civil" was defined as the act of being courteous and honest.[68] Being "civilized" in the eyes of the French could also have linguistic and legal ramifications. According to Sophie White in her study of the Illinois Country, "Frenchification" involved turning Native American allies "into French subjects of the king: not only Catholic but also *linguistically*, culturally, and *legally* 'French.'"[69]

The genesis of this "civilization" project went at least as far back as the French encounter with the Tupinamba of Brazil in the sixteenth and early seventeenth centuries. The famous festival that took place in the French port city of Rouen in 1550, which featured French actors performing the daily life of a Brazilian Tupinamba village, was explicitly intended to represent a journey from barbarism to civilization.[70] It praised King Francis I "for having [. . .] saved [Rouen] from barbarism" and encouraged the young King Henry II to follow his predecessor's example by assigning him the character role of the messiah bringing different peoples to civilization.[71] Over sixty years later, in addition to being given French names and French clothes, the six Tupinamba who were taken from Equinoctial France to

France by the Capuchin missionaries in 1613 received a Christian education and were taught French manners.[72]

It is only after those events that French authorities endeavored to "civilize" the local populations of New France, as well as those of Madagascar. Like the naturalization project, the "civilization" one was intended to support France's empire-building strategy.[73] By "civilizing" local people and turning them into Catholic subjects, authorities hoped to increase the number of people who could qualify as French.[74] The settlers of New France were not the only ones to have been overwhelmingly outnumbered by local populations in the first decades of French colonization. Only about 4,000 European soldiers and settlers traveled to Madagascar between 1642 and 1674, most of whom died as a result of tropical diseases and brutal conflicts with local clans: in comparison, an official document estimated the precolonial population of the island at over two million people—probably an overestimate, granted, but a valuable indicator of how outnumbered the French thought they were.[75]

French missionaries in Madagascar planned to embrace the same tactics that missionaries had practiced before them in the American Spanish colonies and New France.[76] From the early sixteenth century to 1568, the Spanish crown had encouraged the Indigenous people of New Spain to cohabitate with the Spaniards in an attempt to make them learn Spanish customs.[77] We also know that, from the early years of colonization, authorities in New France encouraged their Native American allies to move to the Saint Lawrence valley so they could be converted and "civiliz[ed]" "by [following the] doctrine and example [of the French]."[78] In 1650, just like the missionaries of New Spain and those of seventeenth-century New France, Nacquart thought that the people of Madagascar would acculturate if they were allowed to interact with French people who would set a good example. He specified that the nuns sent from the metropole to start a seminary in Madagascar should be able to read and write, to make lace and other garments "suitable for women," and to sew cotton stockings "like those made in France." Meanwhile, the orphans were to be "skilled in some form of manual labor," such as sewing. He explicitly stated his expectation that local children would "emulate these French children and these Sisters in every way."[79] There was no clear consensus on what it meant to "civilize" (or "Frenchify") a population, perhaps because there was no single definition of "Frenchness" in France. Early modern France was a very fragmented kingdom in terms of culture and language.[80] Many of the behaviors described as "civilized" or "French" in documents from the early modern period were in no way representative of commoners' practices in metropolitan France. When literate observers identified cultural features that distinguished "the French" from other populations, they did so from their own elite and idealistic perspective. Many of those cultural features were not exclusive to the French: they could be found across most Western European societies throughout the early modern period.[81] The recurring themes in plans to bring "civilization" to the populations of Madagascar and New France were religion, agriculture, craftsmanship, and clothing. Conversion to Catholicism was indeed considered central to achieving "civilization" because religion informed every aspect of society in early modern France, including moral codes, the law, and the legitimacy of the monarchy.[82] This is why local converts were initially expected not just to learn Christian dogmas and rituals but also to change their day-to-day behavior.

The objectives of the French civilizing project had a lot in common with those of the Hispanization program pursued in the Spanish colonies since the sixteenth century. The missionaries of New Spain had taught Indigenous people the basic principles of Spanish culture: they made them embrace the Spanish sartorial style, live in houses, use European tools (such as saws and chisels), and learn the Latin alphabet, Latin songs and European agricultural techniques, as well as European arts and crafts such as painting, drawing, carpentry, tailoring, shoemaking, and smithing.[83] This Spanish program was echoed in some of the language employed by the French in Equinoctial France in the early seventeenth century. Eager to lobby more support to the missionary cause in Brazil, the Capuchin father Claude d'Abbeville—who had spent time on Maranhão Island—related these words, allegedly voiced by a Tupinamba chief in 1613: "The hope that we have that our children will learn the law of God, and *your arts and sciences,* makes us believe that in the future [. . .] we will be considered French."[84] We know that religious and secular authorities in New France took those plans one step further by endeavoring to teach cultivation, as well as "different arts and trades," to Native Americans, in the words of Jesuit missionary Le Jeune.[85]

The content of the civilizing project for Madagascar was similar to that of New France, Brazil, and the Spanish Americas. French secular and religious authorities in Madagascar also planned to teach local populations about agricultural techniques, trades, and the arts. According to governor of Madagascar Étienne de Flacourt in the 1650s, France had a duty "to teach [the inhabitants of Madagascar] the right way of cultivating the land, the arts, trades and crafts."[86] Charpentier explained how the French Company of the East Indies envisioned caring for the Malagasies by "teaching them fine arts; [. . .] training them to cultivate the land that is so fertile, & enjoy the produce that Nature offers them, & of which they have been deprived by their ignorance."[87]

The practice of the "arts" and "fine arts" referred to a broad range of skills. The fine arts typically included painting, sculpture, architecture, music, and dance, while the "arts" could also encompass craftsmanship. From the point of view of French elites, these skills were supposed to distinguish "civilized" populations from the "natural" state that was often attributed to the local populations of Madagascar and New France. The *Dictionary of the French Academy* of 1694 opposed the word "art" (*art*) to the concept of "nature" (*nature*).[88] The arts-and-crafts dimension of the civilization project was extremely gendered. Girls in Madagascar were expected to engage in activities that were the preserve of women in Europe. Remember how, in 1650, Nacquart was hoping to have a group of nuns sent from the metropole start a seminary in Madagascar in order to teach local girls ways to sew lace and other garments "suitable for women," as well as cotton stockings "like those made in France."[89]

In order to "civilize" the populations they encountered overseas, French authorities also endeavored to make them change their sartorial habits, as Spanish missionaries had done years prior in New Spain.[90] This is illustrated by Nacquart's plan to teach local girls in Madagascar how to make French garments. The French preoccupation with clothing went at least as far back as 1613, when the Tupinamba brought from Equinoctial France to the French kingdom by the Capuchin missionaries were "dressed in a French way" before their baptism.[91] It was echoed in the missions and the Ursuline convent of New France, where Native American children were famously required to wear French outfits as well.[92] In Anosy, secular and religious authorities took offense at the Tanosies' nudity, although they seemed less attached to the French clothing style—perhaps due to the severe shortages of imported clothing in Anosy.[93] A regulation issued in 1665 simply instructed the colonial Council of Madagascar "to use all means to force the *nègres* to wear clothes."[94] In 1650, when discussing the dress code for children in the seminary that he intended to start in Fanjahira, Nacquart specified that while there was no need for French linen and clothes, woolen scarves would be needed to cover their naked bodies.[95] Six years later, Lazarist missionary Toussaint Bourdaise recounted explaining to a group of Tanosy women who attended church with their breasts uncovered "that it would be better to hide their breast [*sic*] and that women in France would feel ashamed to see them like this."[96] Like those in New France, missionaries in Madagascar were hoping that "civilized" and converted women would eventually be married to Frenchmen. By 1655, Bourdaise already rejoiced that several local girls who had been educated in Fort-Dauphin were now praying three times a day and waiting to find (presumably) French husbands before being baptized and married.[97]

"We Shall Be One People"—Intermarriage

Just like the French "civilization" program, the seventeenth-century French approach to intermarriage in New France was echoed in colonial policies and practices in Madagascar, mostly because the French endeavored to adapt to the wishes of the *roandria*. When they decided to promote intermarriage in their colonies, the French might have been inspired by the earlier empire-building strategies of the Spaniards, the Portuguese and the Dutch. The Spanish crown had made the decision to endorse existing mixed unions between European men and Indigenous women in the sixteenth-century Spanish Caribbean and New Spain, in order to populate their overseas positions and advance the conversion and Hispanicization of overseas populations.[98] As early as 1501, the Spanish crown had ordered the governor of Hispaniola, Nicolás de Ovando, to let those mixed relationships continue if they were consensual. This demand was reiterated in 1514, 1515, and again in 1525 on the grounds that such alliances were "useful and beneficial to the service of God and [the crown], and convenient for the populating of the island."[99] The founder of the Portuguese Indian Ocean empire, Afonso de Albuquerque, had also promoted mixed marriages between Portuguese men and local women on the other side of the globe in early sixteenth-century Portuguese India.[100] Meanwhile, a policy endorsing intermarriage with Asian women in the Dutch East Indies had been initiated shortly after the Dutch East India Company (also known as the Vereenigde Oost-Indische Compagnie, or VOC) had established a settlement in Ambon (Indonesia) in 1605.[101] Later, in 1650, Dutch officials endorsed a proposal to establish Dutch outposts in Ceylon by promoting intermarriage between Dutch men and Asian women.[102] Those precedents might have influenced French authorities when they began to promote intermarriage overseas.

The French intermarriage program appears to have first emerged over a century after Spanish authorities had explicitly endorsed mixed relationships overseas, when the six Tupinamba from Equinoctial France were taken to mainland France by the Capuchin missionaries in 1613: remember how, in this "foundational moment," three of those men who had converted to Catholicism had married French women. They had done so in Catholic ceremonies attended by the king of France himself, after they had been taught the French manners and customs and before returning to Brazil.[103] The fact that these intermarriage ceremonies involved Indigenous men marrying French women—and not Frenchmen marrying Indigenous women—may seem surprising.

The specific kind of intermarriage that was promoted in other places, including seventeenth-century New France and Madagascar, was only between Frenchmen and local women (not between local men and French women), because of political, cultural, and demographic considerations. Gender expectations in early modern Europe dictated that men should act as heads of household, and family names, property, and status were transmitted patrilineally. As a result, relationships between European women and men of non-European ancestries could be considered a threat to colonial socioeconomic orders overseas.[104] Another obvious reason why authorities promoted intermarriage with local women was the fact that there were far fewer French women than French men in the settlements. The gender imbalance was even more pronounced in Madagascar than it was in New France: only sixteen French women set foot on the island in the seventeenth century, and most of them died almost immediately after their arrival in 1674.[105] In promoting intermarriage, French authorities thus hoped to populate Anosy with subjects who could count as French. Although the gender imbalance was probably important in the European population of Equinoctial France as well, the demographic situation in the kingdom of France was radically different from that of Brazil in the early seventeenth century: most people in the metropole were Europeans, only a handful were Tupinamba, and all of these Tupinamba were men, because the journey from Brazil to France was deemed too long and dangerous for women. This explains the decision of French authorities to marry three male Tupinamba to French women: they did not have much of a choice in the absence of female Tupinamba.

The French intermarriage plan was extended from the French kingdom to North America not only as a result of a strategic adaptation to local kinship traditions—as illustrated by Champlain's declaration during the French-Innu council of 1633 that "*we shall be one people*"—but also partly because it was common practice within Europe to seal alliances with other kingdoms though intermarriage with other royal lineages.[106] To the French in North America, this convergence with Native American diplomatic practices was fortuitous and made it easier to gain the cooperation of possible high-profile allies. Intermarriages with the daughters of Native American leaders were intended to advance fur trading exchanges and sustain the formation of diplomatic alliances—for example, with the Innu, Algonquian, Wendat, and Illinois—that were vital to the survival of the French in the region.[107] As opposed to what happened in Europe, where intermarriage was mostly encouraged between royal lineages, however, with regard to New France, French authorities also promoted intermarriage between Frenchmen and non-high profile women. As had been the case in the sixteenth-century Spanish colonies, those Catholic intermarriages were meant to populate the colony and encourage local populations to convert to Catholicism and acculturate.[108]

In line with the European tradition, the practice of promoting intermarriage in New France was subsequently extended to Madagascar, in another attempt to align French policy with local tradition. Both French authorities and the *roandria* of Anosy supported intermarriage in Madagascar from the time of the arrival of the first French fleet in 1643. The *roandria* themselves encouraged Frenchmen to marry their daughters in Catholic and *local vodin'omby* (marriages *à la mode du pays*—which could be broken and could only be sanctified after the sacrifice of an ox whose best meat was offered to the bride).[109] In 1661, Governor Flacourt noted how the *roandria* would even reward the Frenchmen who "wished to marry their daughters" by giving them "everything they want[ed]," and with the opportunity to live in their villages and cultivate their land.[110] Two factors may explain why the *roandria* encouraged Frenchmen to form alliances with women in their communities. First, as demonstrated by Pier Larson, some might have strategically used intermarriage as a way to "domesticate" French colonizers and "assimilate them to island ways through dispersion away from [Fort-Dauphin]."[111] This practice echoes that of the Haudenosaunee, who—according to historian Matthew Dennis—also promoted intermarriage in order to incorporate the French into their communities.[112] It is true that the people of Madagascar had been used to assimilating foreigners—especially traders and migrants from Austronesia, East Africa, and the northern rim of the Indian Ocean—into their increasingly stratified societies through trade and marriage, since the first centuries of the first millennium.[113] By the seventeenth century, Madagascar's societies were structured around ideas of purity and rank presumably derived from Hinduism. People across most of Madagascar were divided into two social groups: the *mainty*, described as "Blacks," who formed a class of commoners or enslaved people and had African origins, and the *fotsy*—nobles of allegedly purer ancestry, often described as "whites" because of their fairer skin tones. Among the *fotsy* were the *roandria*, who claimed Arab origins, as well as the *anacandrian* and the *ondzatsi*. The *fotsy* favored endogamous marriages within their own groups since the fifteenth century. Sexual relationships with members of different groups were frequent outside of *vodin'omby* marriage, however, allowing outsiders to become allies or kin.[114] Moreover, *roandria* women were traditionally the only ones allowed to marry outside of their own group without losing their status: this might explain why most of the free women who married Frenchmen in Anosy were *roandria*.[115]

The *roandria* also supported mixed relationships with Frenchmen to get material and diplomatic support from them. This is why, in the 1640s, when the French Protestant governor of Fort-Dauphin, Jacques Pronis, married a *roandria* princess named Dian Ravellom Manor (or Andianramariuelle), the daughter of a chief named Dian Marval, and the niece of the king of Anosy (Dian Ramach), his new relatives expected that he would side with them against their Antemoro enemies (a people from the area between Manakara and Farafangana, on the southeastern coast of the island).[116] The *roandria* also expected that the

French who married women in their communities would help them raid livestock in the villages of rival clans and hand them over a portion of their booty—livestock raiding was a very important activity in Malagasy cultures (see Chapter 2).[117]

Because the French governor of Madagascar, Étienne Flacourt, knew the benefits that intermarriage could bring to the French, he, too, endorsed *vodin'omby* and Christian intermarriages between Frenchmen and local (especially though not only *roandria*) women in the 1640s and 1650s. By forming alliances with *roandria* women in *vodin'omby* and Catholic marriages, and also through extramarital sex, the French in southeastern Madagascar gained access to protection, arable land, raided livestock, enslaved captives, and trading connections—they often traded farm products, glass beads (*rassades*), mirrors, metals, firing weapons, and ammunition in exchange for enslaved captives, food, ebony, leather, wax, aloe, benzoin, wild pepper, and copper from local populations.[118] Getting food and protection was vital, given the lack of French supplies and the constant threat of attacks from local enemy clans in Anosy. This is why Flacourt rejected the idea of sending French families to Madagascar, claiming that "there [were] enough women [on the island] at the disposition of those who shall wish to marry them."[119] His position on the subject was initially endorsed by the king: The crown's letters patent of 1642 specified that all local brides had to be baptized Catholics.[120] Catholic intermarriage on the island helped the French advance their evangelization program, since the women who married Frenchmen in Catholic ceremonies converted to Catholicism. This is illustrated by the story of Dian Ravellon Manor, the *roandria* princess who married the French protestant governor Pronis: she converted to Christianity before marrying him in the Church in 1646.[121]

Shift Toward the Second Iteration of the Assimilation Project

Developments in both the Atlantic world and the Indian Ocean eventually brought the first iteration of the assimilation project to an end and led French authorities to formulate a more conservative imperial plan starting in the 1660s. Here again, local populations played a key role in shaping the content of French imperial policies: because most of them rejected France's evangelization and "civilization" project, French authorities began to issue a more restrictive series of assimilation policies. Although some dynamic indigenized Christianities did form in New France, we know that no lasting large-scale conversion and "Frenchification" took place in early North America, except perhaps in the Illinois Country.[122] In the 1630s and 1640s, this lack of progress famously led the Jesuit missionaries of New France to abandon the "civilizing" (or "Frenchification") program and to try instead to accommodate Christianity to indigenous customs—a practice that was also used by members of their order in Asia and South America.[123] Since the Jesuits had been the key drivers of evangelization in New France, their decision was effectively the final nail in the coffin of the first iteration of the assimilation project in the region. Many French officials disapproved of the Jesuits' decision, blaming them for giving up on a key pillar of the French imperial strategy.[124]

As was the case in New France, only a relatively small number of local people proved receptive to the French assimilation program in Anosy, Madagascar. On the island, however, France's so-called "civilizing" project did end up making a few inroads that proved very important in the long run. By the 1650s, in Anosy, several of the local women who had converted to Catholicism had married Frenchmen in Catholic or *vodin'omby* marriage ceremonies. Moreover, many had established slave-owning farms with their French husbands in the countryside (*la campagne*) of Anosy. The company's dream of having Malagasies "cultivate the land that is so fertile" did come true to some extent, since Malagasy women and their enslaved captives on those farms did cultivate the land and raise livestock. In doing so, they were drawing on a mixed French–Malagasy agricultural tradition: livestock raising was practiced in both Europe and Madagascar, and slavery was practiced in both the European colonies and across the isle of Madagascar since well before the arrival of the Europeans on the island. As they began to move from Anosy to colonize Isle Bourbon in the 1660s, French colonists, their Malagasy wives, and their descendants retained their tradition of Christian intermarriage and practicing subsistence agriculture, starting to form in the process one of the first "Frenchified" communities of non-European descent in the French colonial world (see Chapter 2).[125]

But despite making some consequential headway, no large-scale conversion took place in seventeenth-century Anosy. Because the French kept raiding local villages for livestock and captives, many locals just ran away at the mere sight of the missionaries, while others attempted to slaughter them.[126] Most local people were very attached to their own spiritual beliefs, and many of those who did go visit the missionaries at Fort-Dauphin lost interest and left after just a few days.[127] A few months before his alleged murder, in 1650, Nacquart noted that many of those who had been baptized had apostatized and concluded that "without a large number of priests to instruct and keep [the island Catholic], there will be no progress."[128] Nacquart's successor, Bourdaise, continued to complain about baptized locals who relinquished Christian practices "at the first opportunity."[129] By 1664, a Lazarist missionary named Nicolas Étienne lamented that "the religion has not made any progress."[130]

The perceived lack of interest in the missionaries' religious and cultural missions in North America, and probably in Madagascar as well, led French authorities to revise their initial plan.[131] In the 1660s, Louis XIV and Colbert revived the assimilation project abandoned by the Jesuits of New France, but with two important modifications: they broadened its scale and used much more restrictive and severe terms. While the first iteration of the project had only targeted the Americas and Madagascar, its second iteration was extended to all of France's positions across the Atlantic and the Indian Ocean. The second iteration of the assimilation project also made it more difficult for local Christian populations in the Atlantic and Indian Oceans to become French subjects, and it made it more difficult for mixed couples in the Indian Ocean to intermarry.

In addition to being shaped by the decision of different local allies to form Indigenous mission settlements near the French strongholds of the Saint Lawrence River valley in North America, the renewed assimilation project was partly the result of the ascent of Jean-Baptiste Colbert to the position of first minister of state, shortly after Louis XIV began his direct rule in 1661. Colbert was particularly eager to compete with other European nations already established in the Indian Ocean, especially the Dutch and the Portuguese. He was convinced that the Indian Ocean trade in textiles, spices, indigo, opium, and other goods was the most lucrative in the world and thought that the United Provinces—France's new enemy—were prosperous because of it.[132] The king had a vested interest in resurrecting the assimilation project in the 1660s for two reasons. First, he had invested an enormous amount of money in the newly founded Company of the East Indies, as well as the West India Company (both established in 1664).[133] Second, as the Company of the East Indies was expanding the scale of the French presence in the Indian Ocean, it needed a solid legal foundation to support its growth. The revived assimilation project was thus largely intended to support the renewed colonial expansion initiated in the 1660s in the Indian Ocean and the Atlantic and help make worthwhile Louis XIV's massive investment in the Company of the East Indies.

A Stricter Evangelization and Naturalization Program

Given Colbert's eagerness to compete with the East Indian trade of other European nations, it should come as no surprise that the revived French project was formulated for the French Indian Ocean colonies *before* being extended to the Atlantic world. In 1663, the king announced his intention to establish in Madagascar "a great settlement of priests and people of faith to convert and baptize most of the island's inhabitants."[134] One year later, the king's declaration for the establishment of the Company of the East Indies pledged to finance missionaries and build churches in Madagascar and to evangelize the populations of all territories that would come under the jurisdiction of the company.[135] The French Marine employee and writer François Charpentier was hired by Colbert to write an account of the foundation of this trading company for King Louis XIV. As the French began to establish their first trading outposts for textiles, spices, and other goods in India, from 1666, he discussed the company's ambition to acquire new territories in the Indian Ocean, stressing the need to "introduce Christianity among impious nations."[136] Lazarist missionaries were sent to Isle Bourbon to serve the free population and evangelize bonded laborers there.[137] Along with the Jesuits, Capuchin missionaries and the Society of the Foreign Mission were put in charge of the evangelizing mission in India.[138]

In line with the greater scale of this second assimilation project, plans to convert overseas populations were extended to the Americas and to West Africa as well. The French West India Company held a trading monopoly across all French colonies and trading stations in the Caribbean, New France, Guiana, and the West African coast until its dissolution in 1674. In 1664, article I of the king's Edict for the Establishment of the West India

Company reiterated the official intent to convert "Indians [i.e., Native Americans] and *sauvages*" in all territories under the company's jurisdiction.[139] The company's intention to also convert African people in West Africa was confirmed both in a declaration by the directors of the Royal Company of Senegal in 1688 and in a regulation issued in 1721 specifying that all white and Black children in Senegal were to attend catechism and learn Catholic prayers.[140]

In what way did the French policies issued from the 1660s onward make it more difficult for local Christian people to become naturalized French subjects? While the New France policy of 1627 had granted French naturalization to all Christian converts, the regulation of the Company of the East Indies and the Edict for the Establishment of the West India Company, both issued in May 1664, only allowed local people born to Catholic parents to become French. In other words, being a convert was no longer enough to be considered a French subject: instead of conversion, ancestry was what truly mattered. The Edict for the Establishment of the West India Company and the regulation of the Company of the East Indies still drew upon the New France policy of 1627, using the same language to describe the naturalization of local populations. However, when discussing the naturalization of local people in the Caribbean, New France, and Guiana, article XXXV of the Edict for the Establishment of the West India Company stated, "We wish that [. . .] *those born to* [. . .] *sauvages converted to the Catholic, Apostolic and Roman faith* be considered and known as natural-born French, and as such be capable of all donations, inheritance and other dispositions."[141] Similarly, article XXXVIII of the regulation of the Company of the East Indies stated, regarding the people of Madagascar and all other territories that would come under its influence, that only "those *born* Catholic" were to be "considered and known as French-born."[142]

Further French policies promoted the evangelization of enslaved populations in the Caribbean without granting them access to naturalization. In 1685, article II of the metropolitan edict known as the *Code Noir* (Black Code) of the Antilles—which contained standard rules on slavery for all French Caribbean islands—famously declared that all enslaved people "on [the] islands w[ould] be baptized and instructed in the Roman, Apostolic and Catholic religion."[143] However, naturalization for enslaved people on these islands only became a possibility if the person was manumitted. Article LVII of the *Code Noir* of 1685 declared that only "*manumitted slaves* do not need our naturalization papers to enjoy the advantages of our natural subjects in our kingdom."[144] Neither did French authorities consistently attempt to promote intermarriage between Frenchmen and enslaved Black women as they had done earlier with free Native American women in New France and with *roandria* women in Madagascar.

Intermarriage Policies and the Return of the "One People" Leitmotif

The earlier intermarriage-promotion project, which had encouraged Catholic unions between Frenchmen and local women in New France and Madagascar, was revived in more restrictive terms from the 1660s and extended to multiple other free populations of non-European descent. When the "one people" leitmotif was revived by the Company of the East Indies for the Indian Ocean in 1664, and then by Colbert for New France in 1667, it had a slightly different meaning than the one Champlain had promoted about three decades earlier. Whereas, in the first iteration of the assimilation project, the call to form "one people" essentially meant promoting intermarriage, the revived use of the phrase implied promoting "civilization," evangelization, and naturalization, in addition to promoting intermarriage in New France and cautiously endorsing it in Madagascar. On October 26, 1664, the assembly of the French Company of the East Indies declared its intention precisely, "to *make [Madagascar] entirely French* [. . .] and to eventually form only one people out of the two nations, *worshipping one same God, sharing one same religion, and recognizing one same prince*."[145] On that same day, an ordinance also declared Frenchmen on the island able to marry "women of the country," but only if the woman was Catholic and if the marriage was approved by the local commander.[146] In a dramatic turn of events, however, the company revoked this ordinance the very next day. On October 27, it formulated what seems to be the very first order of the French Atlantic and Indian Ocean worlds that prevented mixed relationships, here between Frenchmen and "women of the country" in Madagascar. This order was apparently formulated because of major public health concerns and biases against the sexuality of local women. The company issued an order to prevent Frenchmen from "giving themselves away to women of the country [in Madagascar]" on the grounds that they were "easy, incredibly lustful and carr[ied] a venereal disease that [was] usually incurable."[147] The distress caused by this venereal disease must have persisted until the 1670s. In 1670, an observer attributed high mortality rates among Frenchmen in Madagascar to a venereal disease transmitted by local women.[148]

This development did not dissuade French authorities from extending their intermarriage-promotion program to France's new colonies of Isle Bourbon and Louisiana, and to its new trading outposts in India, from 1664 until the end of the seventeenth century. The ordinance issued by the Company of the East Indies on October 26, 1664—which embraced a conservative approach to intermarriage by allowing Frenchmen to marry Catholic "women of the country" if the marriage was approved by the local commander—was extended to "all places conceded by his majesty" to the company across the Indian Ocean.[149] Then, in 1669, the king instructed the viceroy of the East Indies, de La Haye, "to find women [in India], in order [for Frenchmen] to start families."[150] This policy was no doubt intended to help the French populate and maintain their South Asian outposts: ship manifests indicate that very few French women attempted the long and perilous journey to India in the seventeenth century.[151] Many of the white women in the trading outposts of India were already married or socially outranked most European male residents. These women usually accompanied their husbands or fathers, who worked as merchants or officials.[152]

Colonial officials also promoted intermarriage with women of South Asian descent on Isle Bourbon: from 1673, they went so far as to transport Luso-Indian women from the Indian subcontinent to the island to marry Frenchmen in order to compensate for the lack of European women there.[153] In their decision to use Luso-Indian women to populate the isle of Bourbon, the French were probably drawing on an earlier Portuguese intermarriage scheme. Luso-Indian populations had already proven central to the demographic sustainability of the Portuguese empire.[154] From the sixteenth century, the Portuguese had sent female members of a Christian Luso-Indian community called the Canarins from Goa to Mozambique, Malacca, and Makassar, where they had formed a pool of prospective wives for the Portuguese, as well as for other Europeans.[155] Luso-Indian women were considered "suitable" wives for European men in the absence of European women because they were Catholic and Europeanized. The Company of the East Indies' decision to allow Frenchmen across the Indian Ocean to marry Catholic "women of the country" of 1664, the king's instruction "to find women [in India]," and the project of sending Luso-Indian women from India to Isle Bourbon roughly coincided with the plan that was revived by metropolitan authorities, and by the intendants Jean Talon and Jacques Duchesneau between 1667 and the 1680s, to "take action to support marriages between [Native American girls] and the French" in New France.[156]

This plan was echoed years later in another project formulated for the colonization of the Lower Mississippi valley, where the French were also struggling with the lack of European women—it seems that no European women resided in all of Louisiana when the French established a first outpost in the Gulf Coast area called Fort Biloxi, in 1699. The founder of French Louisiana, Pierre Le Moyne d'Iberville, was no stranger to New France's policies and customs, since he was born and raised there. He likely found it only natural to endorse mixed unions in the new colony. Given his knowledge of the North American context, he would have also anticipated the usefulness of intermarriage as a tool to advance Christianity, build diplomatic alliances, sustain the fur trade, and develop the colony. This would explain why he asked the king to "allow the French who settle[d] [Louisiana] to marry with the daughters of the [*sauvages*]."[157] In 1699, the king declared that he saw "no inconvenience [to these marriages], provided that [the brides] were Christian, in which case His Majesty [gave] his full approval."[158]

* * *

In conclusion, several elements of the assimilation project formulated for New France from the early seventeenth century were also articulated for other French overseas positions. This is true of the policy promoting intermarriage between Frenchmen and Indigenous women and also of the famous "civilization" (or "Frenchification") program. The consistency across pan-imperial policies had to do with the rise of absolutism in metropolitan France, beginning in the fifteenth century, which drove French officials in the royal administration and the trading companies to try to enforce coherent legal standards across French territories. Their commitment to legal consistency is visible in both the content and the language of these policies. By the 1660s, for example, the "one people" kinship rhetoric was employed for New France as well as Madagascar as part of a strategic attempt to adapt French policies to the political cultures of Native American allies in North America. The revived New France "one people" project formulated by French authorities in the 1660s was first articulated for Madagascar, partly as a response to the renewed French colonial expansion into the Indian Ocean beginning in 1663. This revived project was more conservative than the first one because of the perceived failure of the first iteration of the assimilation program, especially in New France.

From the start, therefore, pan-imperial policies were determined as much by circumstances on the ground as they were by the ambitions of French metropolitan officials. Local populations in both northeastern America and Madagascar, in particular, played an important role in shaping the content of France's early imperial policies. The northeastern Native American "one people" kinship rhetoric was incorporated into the French imperial project that was articulated for both New France and Madagascar in the 1660s. Similarly, the *roandria* chiefs of southeastern Madagascar were able to make their voices heard, since it is they who—in an attempt to follow their own cultural traditions, imperialist goals, and diplomatic and material interests—approached the French to ask them to marry women in their communities. The French in Madagascar adapted to local practices to survive and gain access to trading connections.

As French people grappled with very difficult realities on the ground, such as the lack of men, food, water and shelter, adaptation to local practices was not restricted to the content and language of colonial policies. These difficult realities—along with the leverage of local populations—compelled the French in several places to engage in cultural dialogue and sometimes even to integrate local communities in order to survive and trade. These patterns occurred not only in New France but across all regions where the French encountered powerful populations, including Anosy, Madagascar, and the Senegambian islands and coastal area.

CHAPTER 2

Shifting Strategies

On a winter day in 1655, Vacher de La Case, a humble French soldier, left the port of La Rochelle on a ship headed south for the island of Madagascar. Little did he know, on this fateful day, that he was embarking on a journey that would change his life forever, propelling him from the lowest echelons of the French military to the rarefied spheres of Malagasy royalty. The journey was a long one. But in the spring of 1656, after several months at sea, his ship finally arrived in Anosy, on the southeastern shore of Madagascar. La Case quickly adapted to his new life on the island: in just a few months, he learned the Malagasy language and became close friends with Dian Rassisate, the *roandria* king of the valley of Ambolo (in northern Anosy) and an ally of the French. King Rassisate put La Case in control of his large army of Tanosy warriors so that together with them and several Frenchmen he could attack one of the greatest enemies of the people of Ambolo: a chief named Dian Ramael, who lived in the valley of Mandrare in Machicore country (northwest of Anosy). La Case killed Dian Ramael with a rifle and forced his successor, Dian Dalass, to pay the *fahensa* (a local tribute) to the French. After killing Ramael and defeating his army, La Case led multiple attacks against rebellious leaders from the South using a Malagasy warfare tactic of raiding enemies for captives, grain, and livestock to subject them to French authority. Those military exploits earned La Case a reputation across southern Madagascar as an extraordinary and fearsome warrior.

Because he was repeatedly denied promotions within the French military despite his achievements, La Case left Fort-Dauphin and established himself in the village of Dian Rassisate with five other Frenchmen and 300 of his devoted Tanosy followers. There, according to French company agent Urbain Souchu de Rennefort and French adventurer Carpeau du Saussay, the villagers treated La Case "like a God" and gave him the nickname "Dian Pousse," in reference to a famous conqueror who used to rule over the entire island.[1] The French governor of Fort-Dauphin, Monsieur de Champmargou, became so jealous of La Case's popularity that he tried to have him assassinated. La Case married the *roandria* daughter of King Rassisate, a princess named Dian Nong. The couple had three children and moved to a house built on one of Nong's estates. When Dian Rassisate died, La Case—a humble French soldier no longer—became king of the valley of Ambolo.

King La Case eventually reconciled with the French governor and spent significant time and effort helping the French of Fort-Dauphin. On several occasions, he deployed his large army of 10,000 Tanosy warriors to defend his fellow countrymen against their enemies, successfully defeating the forces of an adversary named Dian Lanang. He also saved the French at Fort-Dauphin from impending famine multiple times by raiding enemies for grain and livestock. For example, in 1665, he and his Tanosy army captured 16,500 heads of livestock and stole rice from local enemies in order to feed French company employees. In November 1670, the French military finally promoted La Case, first to the rank of ensign and then to captain-commandant. La Case was so grateful that he even offered to conquer the entire island with his warriors in the name of France. Unfortunately for King Louis XIV, however, the French captain did not live long enough to carry out this plan. In June of 1671, La Case fell gravely ill and died shortly thereafter.[2]

Because French colonists were grappling with very difficult realities on the ground, French authorities were largely unable to carry out their ambitious grand plan of assimilation. Instead, this chapter argues, it was often European and non-European peoples' efforts to survive and pursue their own individual and collective interests on the ground that unwittingly shaped the contours of the early French empire—as well as French officials' deliberate attempts to tailor their imperial strategies to local circumstances. As Frederick Cooper and Jane Burbank put it, an important characteristic when we think about empire-building is "the pragmatic, interactive, accommodating capacity of empire," and "empires' durability depended to a large extent on [their] ability to [. . .] shift strategies."[3] As the story of La Case illustrates, it was often by living together with local populations, by forming alliances with them, and by adapting to their cultures and traditions that the French managed to lay the foundations of their early overseas empire in vast continental settings like Madagascar and Senegambia.

These patterns echo developments also documented in the context of the French colonization of North America: scholars have already illuminated the formation of vast kinship-based networks of alliance between the French and Native American peoples, stretching from the North American Great Lakes to the Lower Mississippi valley. These networks came to form the backbone of France's North American empire, advancing trade and supporting France's otherwise weak military defense system.[4] Although networks of alliance became especially sophisticated in North America owing to Native Americans' own strong kinship traditions, their formation was not confined to that region. Alliance formation—sometimes sealed through intermarriage—also proved indispensable to both the French and their *roandria* allies in conflict-ridden southern Madagascar. Alliances and partnerships with African and Eurafrican merchants, entrepreneurs and leaders proved vital to the success of the French enterprise in seventeenth-century Senegambia as well.

Similarly, the French adaptation to local cultural practices helped them advance their influence well beyond the Pays d'en Haut *and* the Illinois Country.[5] Consider, for example, La Case's uses of the Malagasy warfare custom of raiding. And this pattern of adaptation is also visible in French officials' decision to request that vanquished Malagasy peoples pay the *fahensa*—a local tribute that vassals usually paid to the king of Anosy and to other kings and chiefs in the region.[6] By investigating patterns of French adaptation to local cultural practices, this chapter explores several understudied Malagasy and Senegambian diplomatic and military traditions. These include the Malagasy raiding practice and the fahensa tribute tradition in Anosy, whose existences have been almost completely overlooked, as well as the Senegambia *folgars* (local festivities), whose seventeenth-century meanings have not yet been fully recognized by historians.

Shifting strategies of empire could take widely different forms, depending on the place and the time period. For example, to populate the colony of Isle Bourbon in the absence of enough European immigrants, French officials on the island resolved to let Christian Malagasy women marry Frenchmen in the Catholic Church despite the growing opposition to such relationships in Fort-Dauphin, Madagascar. They also conferred "white" statuses on Malagasy and Luso-Indian women married to European men, and on their mixed Frenchified descendants. As a result, many of these free Frenchified creoles managed to work their way up the island's socioeconomic hierarchy, and some of the women among them formed important connections with men of power. Yet the emergence of this influential and financially comfortable free population of non-European descent on seventeenth- and early eighteenth-century Isle Bourbon has attracted little attention to date.

French colonists across the Atlantic and Indian Oceans interacted with a wide variety of peoples of non-European descent, many of whom had significant influence, status, and wealth. This was most often the case in vast continental settings, where the French were largely outnumbered by local populations. As several scholars have shown, Richard White's notion of "Middle Ground"—according to which the French and Native American peoples forged common cultural grounds because they met on equal terms—did not usually apply in places like the North American western interior, the Illinois Country, the Arkansas valley, or even the Gulf South, prior to the nineteenth century.[7] This framework cannot capture the complicated nature of the relationships between the French and their allies in Anosy or Senegambia either.[8]

Like other European–African contact zones on the West African coast, Senegambia had more in common with what Kathleen DuVal has called "Native Ground": a space where local people—not Europeans—ultimately controlled the territory.[9] In the late seventeenth and early eighteenth centuries, some (especially Wolof, Lebu, and Eurafrican) peoples in the French Senegambian outposts and coastal area were very powerful indeed, and some were also quite wealthy. Several women among them acquired important influence, becoming key actors in commercial exchanges and intelligence diplomacy. The rise of this powerful and wealthy class of African and Eurafrican merchants and political elites has primarily been documented for the period beginning in the late eighteenth century, while recent scholarship on Senegambia in the earlier period has focused instead on European oppression of African men and women and African responses to this oppression.[10]

On the other side of the globe, in Anosy, throughout the period of early modern French colonization, balances of power were far too uneven and mercurial to be characterized by such stable concepts as "Native Ground" or "Middle Ground." On the one hand, some recent scholarship has described the French as "[non-]dominant players" in the story of Anosy, painting the

French presence in seventeenth-century southern Madagascar as "a non-colonial story," only to reach the conclusion that "the French colonies in Madagascar failed totally."[11] According to the late historian Pier Larson, on the other hand, approaching the French presence in seventeenth-century Anosy as a "non-colonial story" ultimately "sideline[s] Fort Dauphin's systematic, appalling colonial violence, enslavement and dispossession," carried out through a "complex and chronic cycle of [raids and] plunder."[12] In fact, as this chapter demonstrates, the cycle of colonial violence identified by Pier Larson ultimately benefited *both* the French and their *roandria* allies, one of whom ended up turning against them to lead one of the first successful anti-colonial revolts in French overseas colonial history, more than a century before the Haitian Revolution. Although balances of power in Anosy varied depending on the time period and the particular clan with whom the French were interacting, one local group did ultimately garner considerable power—enough to eradicate France's only stronghold on the isle of Madagascar and critically reshape the limits of France's seventeenth- and eighteenth-century overseas imperial formation.

Settlement in Anosy

Instead of assimilating local people into French society, the French in seventeenth-century Anosy rapidly settled in the villages of their *roandria* allies to find protection, food and economic opportunities. Arrivals of ships bringing provisions from the French kingdom, India, and Isle Bourbon were extremely rare on the island.[13] In fact, none at all came between 1648 and 1654. Although rice and other foodstuffs could be bartered with local people, the French had limited access to the goods of exchange that were popular among Malagasies, which included glass beads (rassades), manillas (used as necklaces and bracelets), pieces of iron, brandy, painted clothes, and tools.[14] As a result, most French settlers faced constant hunger and were forced to "dres[s] like the *naigres,*" without shirts and coats.[15] French hardship, along with the diplomatic and commercial interests of the roandria, thus played a critical role in shaping patterns of French settlement in seventeenth-century southern Madagascar.

Many Frenchmen left Fort-Dauphin to live in local villages, where they became full members of *roandria* families, like La Case did. This pattern of

French settlement can be traced back to the arrival of a few French adventurers in Anosy in the 1630s, among whom was the explorer François Cauche. Cauche's party was hugely weakened when most of his French companions left the island to return to France, leaving him alone in Anosy with only four Frenchmen.[16] Incapable of feeding and protecting themselves against potential enemy attacks, the remaining Frenchmen established themselves in allied villages.[17] One Frenchman named Jacques Du Val went to live in the capital of Fanjahira, the place of residence of the king of Anosy, Dian Ramach. Another moved in with one of Dian Ramach's relatives, in a village named Razeme.[18] Cauche and his two French companions accepted an invitation from chief Dian Machicore—Dian Ramach's son-in-law—to relocate to his village at Mannhale. From there, the three Frenchmen explored the island and traded French merchandise for livestock with the peoples of Fanjahira and other places, under the protection of some of Machicore's servants.[19] The French maintained this tradition of living in local villages for years to come. When commander-governor Jacques Pronis arrived in Anosy with forty sailors and settlers in 1642, he rapidly sent twelve Frenchmen to live in allied villages in Matataña country (north of Anosy).[20]

Although this practice of cohabitation allowed Frenchmen to secure food, shelter, and trading opportunities, letting them live in local villages did not come without risk: a few Frenchmen who were fully assimilated into local communities ended up turning against the French. Pronis' successor as governor, Étienne Flacourt, mentioned two Frenchmen in particular who had joined local villages and plotted against the French of Fort-Dauphin.[21] One of them was Flacourt's former interpreter, a man nicknamed Ranicaze, who had mastered the Malagasy language, embraced the local lifestyle, and become familiar with some of the island's best trading places.[22] Flacourt lamented Ranicaze's desire "to stay in Madagascar his entire life and to live in the manner of these barbarians [i.e., Malagasies]." After he was caught stealing goods from the French, Ranicaze sided with France's enemies in Anosy to avoid punishment.[23] In 1650, in Manafiafy (a subregion of Anosy), he assisted a *roandria* named Dian Tallach in his attempt to kill two Frenchmen named la Vigne and Imbert Garnier, along with the French crew who came to rescue them.[24] Ranicaze also incited another *roandria* named Dian Tserongh to try to murder Flacourt and attack the French. Ranicaze had reportedly told Tserongh that "he would not rest until he had massacred the French, and that he [had] himself renounced France, and would do anything he could to serve him."[25] The other Frenchman who also turned against the French was said to be the reincarnation of Ranicaze. After he had joined a local village-community, this man was reportedly given the name Dian Marououlle by his new people.[26] He even sent an emissary to Governor Flacourt to let him know that Ranicaze was not dead "but instead resurrected in the person of Marououlle."[27]

In addition to living in local villages like Ranicaze and Dian Marououlle, beginning in the 1650s, Frenchmen in Madagascar would often stay on after their contracts with the company ended and build farms in the countryside (la campagne) surrounding Fort-Dauphin to survive. According to one estimate, Frenchmen established as many as fifty to a hundred farming households across Anosy, where they lived together with their *roandria* (or other Malagasy) concubine or wife.[28] Missionary Nacquart noted in 1650 that Frenchmen "who marr[ied] the women of the country will choose far off and out of the way places" to settle and grow food.[29] These French-Malagasy homesteads established in the countryside of Anosy played a key role in the defense of Fort-Dauphin, alerting the French in the event of enemy attacks.[30] Several of those French-*roandria* households were formed in an attempt to seal alliances with local kings and chiefs.[31]

Alliance Formation and *Souvou* Raiding in Madagascar

Rather than assimilation, it was by building a fragile network of alliances with some *roandria* and by conducting joint raids with them in accordance with a local tradition that the French in Anosy were able to advance their own power. Those alliances fueled the rise of powerful allies, one of whom ultimately turned against the French, essentially ending their seventeenth-century colonial enterprise in Anosy. Southern Madagascar was a very complicated world filled with many independent kingdoms and chiefdoms, which were constantly at war with each other, engaging in conflicts over land acquisition, thefts of livestock and captures of war prisoners. This significantly weakened the influence of local kings and chiefs, making it crucial for them to forge alliances to defend their peoples and prevail in attacks against their enemies. Possible allies included kinsfolk and other local chiefs and kings, as well as European people who possessed sought-after military skills and firearms. The French needed to form alliances with local leaders, too, to get captives, food, and export goods—the main export commodities included ebony, leather, wax and gum.[32] They also needed to form those alliances to secure local warriors who could help them expand the reach of their power and defend their very weak position at Fort-Dauphin. In the first decades following the arrival of the French, in 1650, a Frenchman described the fort at Fort-Dauphin as a mere "fortress whose walls are a hedge" and whose "houses are like small barns covered with leaves and walls of reeds or sticks."[33]

In order to get food and expand their respective power, the French and their *roandria* allies practiced a Malagasy warfare tradition of raiding enemies called "doing the *souvou*" (*faire le souvou*) together. As Sieur Du Bois, a French administrator who spent time in Madagascar, explained, "*Souvou* is a group of *nègres* who launch assaults at night and plunder [the villages of their enemies]."[34] He also wrote, "[The *nègres*] conduct many small wars against each other, which they call *souvou*, traveling through their enemies' land at night, killing, plundering, and taking whatever they can."[35] The most important booty was livestock, which could include oxen, cows, sheep, goats, and pigs.[36] The plunderers also took enemy captives (especially women and children) whom they would either keep or sell. It was customary for local societies to enslave their enemies, which is why the French who arrived in Madagascar in the seventeenth century found a large preexisting population of war captives.[37] Raids of livestock and captives played a key role in the bloody conflicts between the different kingdoms and chiefdoms of southern Madagascar. Livestock raiding was a very important activity in seventeenth-century Malagasy cultures, not only because livestock were a source of sustenance and acted as a form of currency on the island but also because they were a symbol and source of power.[38] Sacrificing animals (or *mitaha*, in local parlance) was believed to influence supreme beings able to control things in the world. According to the French explorer François Cauche and to Flacourt, Tanosy people would frequently make sacrifices of animals to thank *zanhar* (god). They would also sacrifice animals to appease *diambiliche*—a devil held responsible for all the bad things in the world.[39] Animal sacrifices were also deemed necessary to control one's *oly*, the powerful charms made by the *ombiassa* that could protect and grant the wishes of their owners.[40] Malagasies would also sacrifice animals when any major life event took place. They would ritually slaughter oxen, chicken, sheep, and other animals to bless a marriage, bring a bountiful harvest, cure someone from a disease, protect a pregnant woman, or bury a loved one.[41]

The *roandria* initiated the French to this Malagasy warfare custom before the establishment of Fort-Dauphin in 1643, at a time when the French had a negligible influence over the region of Anosy. As a result of their decision to move to the village of Dian Machicore to get food and shelter, Cauche and his party had already become entangled in multiple local conflicts. One of those conflicts was with the people of Machicore country. Because those people had attacked the village of Dian Machicore, killing nine villagers and stealing 400 oxen—some of which belonged to the French—Cauche and his party had had no other choice than to accompany Dian Machicore and his people in their retaliatory raiding campaigns. Cauche ended up giving military advice to Dian Machicore and accompanying his army on multiple raids across Machicore for oxen and captives.[42] The French in this period also accompanied Machicore's father-in-law, Dian Ramach, the king of Anosy, in his campaign against his enemies in the valley of Manampanihy, north of Anosy.[43]

Following the establishment of Fort-Dauphin, the French used the knowledge they acquired through their interactions with the *roandria* to conduct more raids that allowed them to procure much-needed grain and livestock, enslave thousands of war captives, and subject peoples to their influence. It is the French themselves who initiated many of the *souvou* raiding campaigns conducted together with their local allies inland and as far as the northeastern coast of the island between the 1640s and the 1670s. Those episodes are recounted in multiple French accounts from the period.[44] While we must be cautious when interpreting the documents because their French authors were likely to exaggerate the extent of their influence to impress their superiors and garner support in metropolitan France, there is no doubt that the French in southern Madagascar succeeded in spreading terror and affliction, and extracting a considerable amount of local resources, by using the local raiding tradition.[45] They were able to do so as a result of three main factors: local people's limited access to firearms, especially in the first decades of French colonization; complex conflicts between local chiefdoms and kingdoms that weakened them considerably; and the fact that Fort-Dauphin and its surroundings lay at the periphery—not at the center—of the island's major kingdoms and chiefdoms.[46] The raids conducted by the French in this period were extremely violent, leaving a path of utter devastation in their wake. In total, between the 1640s and 1670s, the French and their allies captured and enslaved over 10,000 Malagasies, killing another 10,000 in the process, and raided about 350,000 heads of livestock across southern Madagascar.[47] In addition to Cauche's raiding experiences in Machicore country and the valley of Manampanihy, the French had multiple opportunities to learn *souvou* raiding techniques while fighting alongside their allies. For example, under the rule of Governor Pronis, in 1648, forty-five Frenchmen accepted an invitation from the *grands du pays* of Betsileo (northwest of Fort-Dauphin in the highlands of south-central Madagascar) to go raid and burn their neighboring enemies for 1,000 heads of livestock.[48] This episode was a turning point in France's relationship with the king of Anosy, Dian Ramach, who did not approve at all of this new alliance. Several Frenchmen were murdered while trading rice in Matataña, in a retaliatory move orchestrated by some of Dian Ramach's relatives.[49]

Although the real extent of the French influence in Madagascar cannot be established with certainty, it clearly peaked on two occasions as a result of French use of the local *souvou* raiding tradition: once under the rule of Étienne de Flacourt (1648–1655) and then again under his successor, Champmargou (1659–1668). In 1651, the French plundered Fanjahira, murdered its villagers, stole their livestock, and burned their houses to the ground. In an astonishing turn of events, they also murdered king Dian Ramach with a rifle to avenge an attempted attack on Fort-Dauphin.[50] The French also assassinated Dian Ramach's son, decapitated him, and placed his head on a stake for everyone to see.[51] Flacourt's lieutenant, a man named Sieur Angeleaume, conducted a series of additional raids against the *Lohavohits*, free people who lived in neighboring mountains.[52] After burning their villages, stealing their livestock, and taking war captives, the French forced over forty of them to renounce their allegiance to the *roandria* and to formally recognize the king of France "as their lord sovereign and master, whom they w[ould] always obey wherever they are. In addition to having to formally declare their allegiance to King Louis XIV, the vanquished were forced to pay an annual *fahensa* to the French established at Fort-Dauphin.[53]

Taking the form of a gift of livestock and crops, the quantity of which depended on the means of each individual chiefdom or kingdom, this tribute was vital to the survival of the French in hunger-ridden Anosy.[54] The *Lohavohits* were not the only ones who were forced to pay the *fahensa* to the French: Flacourt also pressured several *roandria* and *anacandrian* into paying them a tribute.[55] To maximize profits, he even put in place an organized tribute collection system, selecting one *roandria* and one anacandrian to become his *omänghais*—local agents in charge of making a king's subjects pay their tribute and stay obedient to him.[56] Probably because he had a lot of enemies, a king named Dian Manangue was among the *roandria* who reportedly came to Fort-Dauphin to officially recognize King Louis XIV as his "lord."[57] Although he had married the daughter of Dian Ramach, Dian Manangue was a humble king at the time, ruling over the territory between the south of Anosy and the valley of Mandrare in Machicore country. Even Dian Rassisate, the king of the valley of Ambolo and Vacher de La Case's father-in-law, eventually began to pay his own tribute to the French.[58] The French influence weakened considerably toward the end of Flacourt's governorship and into the early 1660s, because war and diseases considerably reduced the number of French colonists in Anosy.[59]

Especially from 1663 onward, however, Governor Champmargou used his alliances with king Dian Manangue and king Dian Rassisate, along with the military skills of the legendary Vacher de La Case, to reconsolidate the power of the French by renewing France's brutal raiding campaigns across southern Madagascar.[60] That year, the French and their allies conducted multiple raids against several *grands du pays* of the valley of Mandrare in Machicore country because they had refused to pay their tribute to Fort-Dauphin.[61] The French appear to have considerably expanded the reach of their authority during this period. While this is almost certainly an exaggeration, by 1664, Souchu de Rennefort mentioned "over two hundred thousand men" who had been forced to pay a tribute to the French and came from dozens of small chiefdoms scattered between Matataña and the Bay of Saint-Augustin, in the West of the island.[62] More raids were conducted by the French and their allies, including one in 1665 against a chief named Dian Ravarasse and another into Matataña country.[63] Given the very small number of Frenchmen on the island, it was chiefly France's *roandria* allies who enabled the success of all those souvou raids. For example, when Governor Champmargou launched yet another attack—against an enemy of the French named Rajessaf in 1668—he was accompanied by only 145 Frenchmen and as many as 5,000 or 6,000 allied Malagasies. That year, the French and their allies captured an astonishing amount of livestock, even if the reported total of 40,000 oxen and cows is likely exaggerated.[64]

In addition to becoming a major source of food, those raids also provided crucial economic opportunities for Frenchmen and their families. Along with their tribute, the French would also get their share of the spoils after each raid—the rest was split between their allies or kinsfolk.[65] Enslaved captives, along with some of the grain and livestock, were taken to the French-Malagasy farming households outside of Fort-Dauphin to be managed by Malagasy women there.[66] Some captives were used to tend livestock and cultivate food crops, while others were sold at Fort-Dauphin for the benefit of the French. All remaining livestock was sold or slaughtered in order to feed the French.[67] Such was the case in 1667, when Carpeau du Saussay sold captives, along with 160 heads of livestock he had captured during a raid, to a group of French colonists who had just arrived on the island.[68] In 1668, an alleged 50,000 heads of livestock that were captured in northern and western Madagascar were also taken to Fort-Dauphin to feed the French there.[69] Meat became a very important part of the French diet in Anosy. The French on the island ate large quantities of oxen and cows, whose flesh was described as being "just as tasty as that of [European beasts]" by Sieur Du Bois.[70] They ate that meat with European vegetables and indigenous yams, beans, roots, and rice—the latter was described by Flacourt as "very nice to eat and tasty."[71] Sheep, goats, poultry, and pork—also captured in *souvou* raids—were another important source of protein.[72]

At the same time as they benefited the French, however, these *souvou* raids also precipitated the staggering political ascent of king Dian Manangue.[73] According to Souchu de Rennefort, the French delegated considerable authority to Dian Manangue, granting him power over "the conquered territories [. . .] on condition that he would keep acting with deference, following the wishes of the French Governors."[74] For each of the raids conducted by the French with his warriors, Dian Manangue not only acquired his own share of the stolen livestock and enslaved war captives; he also acquired new territories and became entitled to a tribute from many southern chiefs.[75] Most of the power of the French in Anosy soon hinged on Dian Manangue's willingness to remain an ally (and, according to French accounts, a vassal) of the king of France. As he began to expand his influence, his incentive to do so diminished. Blinded by their imperialist ambitions, however, the French failed to fully understand the situation in which they found themselves.

In the end, the zealous evangelization strategy of French missionaries in Madagascar triggered the collapse of the vital coalition between the French and Dian Manangue. Although Dian Manangue did eventually learn to speak the French language "very well," he showed no interest in the Catholic faith, despite French missionaries' multiple threats and persistent efforts to convert him.[76] Dian Manangue became very suspicious of the missionaries' intentions after seeing his own son die almost immediately after his baptism.[77] The Lazarist missionary Nicolas Étienne became so frustrated that he eventually ripped away Dian Manangue's beloved *oly* (charms) from his neck and threw them into a fire.[78] Infuriated by Étienne's disrespect, Dian Manangue subsequently killed the missionary.[79] The French retaliated by burning over 150 villages; killing over 1,000 children, women, and men; and stealing at least 4,000 heads of livestock across the valley of Mandrare.[80]

This response was a major strategical error, since the balance of power had shifted considerably in favor of Dian Manangue by 1674. Governor Champmargou and the famous Frenchman-turned-*roandria* conqueror La Case were both dead by then.[81] Dian Manangue had mastered the military techniques of the French, and he had also learned to use their powerful weapons.[82] Inside his expanded kingdom, the *roandria* of the valley of Mandrare hated the French for their constant attempts to meddle in local politics and for the many raids they had conducted on their western chiefdoms.[83] It is in this context that Dian Manangue launched his anti-colonial revolt.[84] On August 27, 1674, with the assistance of his *roandria* vassals, he conducted a brutal attack against the French at Fort-Dauphin, killing over half of its remaining population. The sixty-three people who survived the massacre were forced to escape the island for Mozambique, Surat, and Isle Bourbon.[85] Of the 4,000 French people who had been sent to Madagascar since the 1640s, none remained, except perhaps for a few Frenchmen who had shifted their loyalties and were now fully assimilated into local communities.

Gift-Giving Traditions and *Folgars* in Senegambia

The French embraced elements of local customs in politics and warfare in Madagascar, as illustrated by their adoption of the *fahensa* and *souvou* raiding practice in the south of the island. But they did not stop there: in Senegambia, they also resolved to embrace local diplomatic customs, some of which they clearly regarded with contempt, to form alliances and partnerships that were vital to the success of their local enterprise. Since the French in Senegambia were largely outnumbered, and because they needed to defend their weak military positions, they had no choice but to try to form peaceful relationships with local leaders and workers. The fact that the French military position in Senegambia was weak is illustrated by a comment made by the director of the Company of Senegal, Michel Jajolet de La Courbe, when he arrived in the outpost of Saint-Louis. After noting the vulnerability of the French fort on the island, which according to him was poorly built and wide open to potential enemy attacks, he concluded his observations with these words: "If the *nègres* were bad, they would have easily butchered white people already."[86] This situation was echoed in most other contact areas of the Atlantic coast of Africa where Africans also remained in "full control" of their territories, which have been studied by Mariana Candido, Robin Law, Patrick Manning, Rebecca Shumway, Randy Sparks, John Thornton, and others.[87] Trading made the necessity of forming alliances with local leaders especially pressing. The French Company of Cape Verde and Senegal had established outposts off the west coast of Africa primarily to procure enslaved captives for the Americas, in addition to commodities including leather, gum, gold, wood, beeswax, and ivory.[88] Only African and Eurafrican kings, merchants, and businesspeople possessed the connections, skills, and knowledge necessary to acquire those captives and local goods.

To be successful in their commercial and diplomatic exchanges with these kings, merchants, and businesspeople, French officials in Senegambia were forced to adapt to local diplomatic gift-giving practices. French officials ended up practicing gift giving with most of their local allies across the Atlantic and the Indian Ocean worlds. This practice of offering gifts to allies overseas went as far back as the French encounter with the Tupinamba in sixteenth-century Brazil.[89] We also know how important gift giving was in the French colony of New France, partly because of its centrality to Native American diplomatic cultures.[90] Gift giving was a practice common to many diplomatic cultures worldwide—most importantly on the American continent but also in other places including Europe, Senegambia, and India. Offering gifts would have come rather naturally to the French in West Africa, India, and North America because European officials had made gifts to other European nations for centuries to thank or reward them for a service, to advance their interests in the course of diplomatic negotiations, or to display their power and prestige.[91]

When engaging in gift-giving rituals in Senegambia, the French were also adapting strategically to local practices with the goal of keeping their outposts and retaining permission to trade. It was local African chiefs who explicitly requested that the French pay a tribute called *la coutume*—which took the form of gifts or money—in exchange for land grants, protection, and trading agreements.[92] This request echoed a more familiar practice in India, where the French also paid a tribute to the nawabs (governors of the Mughal empire) and *faujdars* (local heads of tributary military or police force) for their *farman* (grant or charter), which also took the form of payments in gifts and money.[93] The *coutume* of Senegambia had its roots in a well-established local tradition: African kings had begun to request tributes from their own subjects well before the arrival of the Europeans on the West African coast. Tributes of various types were paid to the king of the kingdom of Ghana as early as the ninth century.[94] Before the arrival of the Portuguese, the ruler (*Bour ba* or *Buurba*) of Jolof—an empire that stretched from Senegal to the Gambia and lasted until the mid-sixteenth century—requested quarterly tributes from the rulers of the kingdoms of Waalo, Kayor, Baol, Siin, and Saloum. Then, when the Portuguese began to sail down the west coast of Africa in the fifteenth century, they began to pay an annual tribute to local rulers in exchange for the right to trade.[95] Such was also the case with the French by the late seventeenth century. For example, in June 1685, the French director La Courbe paid his tribute to the heir of the kingdom of Waalo (on the lower Senegal River), a Wolof prince whom the French called Brac, on a boat off the coast of a village named Montaubé, located about three miles away from Saint-Louis.[96] Brac also made the French director promise that he would bring him a justaucorps and a jacket for purchase.[97]

Not only did the French adopt local gift-exchange customs, but they also catered to local people's tastes.[98] Scholars have shown how the French in New France ended up adapting their presents to Native American preferences: this is illustrated by their numerous gifts of wampum—seashell beads especially prized among the Ottawa, the Iroquois and the people of Green Bay as a means of communication, as a symbol of peace, and as material reminders of diplomatic agreements.[99] In Senegambia, paper and cloves took on an outsized importance in French-African diplomatic exchanges as a result of another adaptation to local predilections. Paper was a popular good of exchange in Senegambia because it was needed by local marabouts (Muslim religious leaders) to make gris-gris—African charms or amulets used among Africans in Senegambia as "a protection against all sorts of accidents."[100] As for cloves, they were coveted by local African women for their fragrance: La Courbe explained that "women w[ore] [them] around their necks to smell nice." Brandy was another important item in French-African diplomatic exchange rituals in Senegambia: La Courbe generalized that local Africans "loved [brandy] very much."[101] Therefore, by the 1690s, upon the departure of the convoys that went up the Senegal River from Saint-Louis to Galam (where the French trading fort of Saint-Joseph de Galam was established), it was customary for African chiefs from villages on the coast to come and offer gifts of brandy, cloves, gris-gris paper, and beads to African and European travelers before they boarded their boats every year in June; those convoys returned in October with enslaved captives, gum, gold, wax, ivory, hides, and food.[102] It was also customary for French authorities to offer those popular items to African rulers: as a case in point, when La Courbe paid his tribute to Brac in June 1685, he also gifted him a barrel of brandy, cloves, and paper intended to craft African gris-gris.[103] Six months later, in December 1685, when La Courbe left Saint-Louis to attend a *folgar* hosted by Jean Barre, the chief of the island of Sor (east of Saint-Louis), his men were also carrying brandy for the chiefs they were going to meet, as well as gifts of gris-gris paper.[104]

The *folgar* was a crucial site of French-African diplomatic exchanges, as well as another important locus of cultural adaptation for the French. It provided an opportunity for Frenchmen not only to form commercial relations and affectionate bonds with local women, as already noted by the scholarship, but also to meet prospective commercial male allies and strengthen their bonds with existing local male partners.[105] The French word *folgar* probably came from the Portuguese cognate *folgar* (meaning "rejoicing") and meant "festivities." It might have been a European translation for the Wolof word *sabar*, used in Senegambia to describe African balls.[106] Europeans used the term *folgar* more often than Africans to describe festivities shaped by local cultures and, to a lesser extent, by European influences.[107] According to the French naturalist Michel Adanson, who spent time in Senegambia between 1749 and 1753, and to a French official named Pruneau de Pommegorge, *folgar* attendees would dance to the beat of drums, coming in close contact with each other and pressing their thighs against those of the person in front of them—a practice that was almost certainly African in origin. They would also drink a local beer made of millet (called *pitot*), with locally produced palm wine, as well as European brandy and "even wine from France."[108] Scholars have described the *folgars* as feasts organized by local African and Eurafrican women to attract European suitors.[109] Attendees would indeed congratulate the best female dancers by throwing handkerchiefs at them, after which the women would bow before their admirers to thank them—a practice that, according to Senegalese historian Aissata Kane Lo, "belongs to the African cultural patrimony, and is typically Senegalese in origin."[110]

However, in the seventeenth and early eighteenth centuries, male African and European leaders alike also organized and attended *folgars* to advance their own diplomatic and economic interests. Male African leaders traditionally used the *folgar*s to celebrate religious events, find new trading partners, and form and maintain peaceful relationships with old and new allies. This is illustrated by a description of a *folgar* in La Courbe's account of his 1685 voyage to Senegal. The African chief Jean Barre invited La Courbe to a big ceremony in his village, attended by over 2,000 people, in which all boys over fifteen or sixteen were to be circumcised.[111] Barre promised La Courbe that this event would give him the opportunity to "meet quantities of high-ranking people from the interior, who had never seen white people before and could not wait to meet some."[112] La Courbe, who was critical of those gatherings for bringing disorder and conflict, was reluctant to accept this invitation at first. But, in order to strengthen his alliance with Barre, he eventually accepted it and left Saint-Louis on December 31, 1685, accompanied by several officers and *habitants* (free African and Eurafrican residents of the French outposts). La Courbe reached Jean Barre's village in the evening and was taken to a cabin near Barre's residence. While the *folgar* was taking place, several high-ranking African chiefs came to visit La Courbe in his cabin, one by one. Those chiefs were formally introduced by a *maître de langue* (interpreter) and were served brandy while several villagers were eagerly watching the scene from the windows.[113] The next morning, more than twenty griots (musician-entertainers) surrounded La Courbe's cabin, playing the tambourine and singing for eight hours to thank the French for their presence. Despite being horrified by this unfamiliar spectacle and excitement—he scorned the performance as "a diabolical sabbath" in his writings—La Courbe remained very polite and did not attempt to put an end to this lengthy display.[114] The circumcision ceremony took place in a field near the village and was followed by another *folgar,* which lasted the whole day and night.[115]

Although they did not necessarily enjoy the merriment of the *folgars,* French officials strategically began to organize such festivities as well because they understood their diplomatic and commercial potential. By the late seventeenth century, they invited the kings and chiefs of nearby kingdoms and villages to come together to Saint-Louis once a year for festivities. La Courbe explained that these festivities were intended "to maintain a peaceful alliance with [the Blacks]."[116] The (male) *maîtres de langue* and *laptots* (Wolof word for sailors) who served the French trading companies were also invited to attend since it was vital for the success of the French enterprise in Senegambia not only to form alliances with local leaders but also to maintain strong partnerships with skilled male African workers. The region of Gajaaga, where the French trading outpost of Fort Saint-Joseph de Galam was established, was only accessible by boat when the river's waters were high enough, during the rainy season.[117] Yet even then, crossing the Senegal river was notoriously difficult and dangerous because it was shallow and filled with sandbars, often requiring sailors to disembark and drag their boats through the river.[118] River convoys were initially led by Frenchmen and consisted of French sailors and soldiers. However, French authorities were forced to shift their strategy by the early eighteenth century because many of them died in drowning accidents and of tropical diseases such as malaria and yellow fever—La Courbe complained of the fever afflicting Europeans in Senegambia, as he himself had become very sick after his arrival in West Africa in 1685.[119] The French thus increasingly relied on the *laptots* to run the convoys going upriver.[120] La Courbe explained that "without these people, it is impossible to go up the river; because it is they who, when we face headwinds, tow the boat with ropes and sometimes get neck-deep into the water when the river is blocked."[121] The French also needed the services of *maîtres de langue* who could act as guides and translators in their interactions with the *laptots* and local leaders.[122] Such was the case in November 1685, when La Courbe left Saint-Louis to trade ivory, feathers, and amber in the kingdom of Cayor, southeast of Waalo: he was accompanied by six white men, ten *laptots,* and one *maître de langue.*[123]

When hosting local *maîtres de langue, laptots,* and leaders in *folgars,* the French embraced multiple local cultural elements to make those events enjoyable for their guests. For example, one year, in 1686, La Courbe invited a group of griots to come entertain his hosts in the festivities he organized in Saint-Louis. The guests were served beef with palm wine purchased at a local market in the coastal town of Bieurt, along with an African dish of couscous. Everyone danced the whole day and the whole night. The event was evidently a success since an African king named Bourguyolofe seized the opportunity to invite La Courbe to send French representatives to his kingdom further inland, to "establish trade in his country," by purchasing enslaved captives, ivory and leather. He even gifted four young enslaved captives to the French to give them a taste of the perks this new alliance could bring.[124] In January 1686, La Courbe sent a French clerk, along with two *laptots* and two interpreters, to the kingdom of Bourguyolofe, with orders to purchase captives, leather and ivory. Although the Bourguyolofe expedition ended up being very costly, the party returned safe and sound, with captives and leather, after a successful trading voyage.[125]

African Power in Senegambia

The balance of power between French people and Africans or Eurafricans in Senegambia varied depending on the category of locals with whom the French interacted: Africans of a low social standing (including enslaved people) had a lot less power over the French than those with connections and other resources. Ordinary people were more likely to face thefts and other assaults by French company employees. This is illustrated not only by the sexual violence perpetrated by Frenchmen on low-ranking (free and enslaved) African women, which has been studied by Jessica Johnson, but also by an offensive that took place in 1685 at a place named Biffeche (northeast of Saint-Louis), in which a French plunderer named Sieur de la Marche brutally targeted a community of villagers.[126]

On the other hand, many African and Eurafrican merchants and businesswomen had more power, simply because the French depended on them to secure food and water, keep their outposts, and trade various goods. West African gender norms dictated the kind of interactions in which the French had to engage to survive and prosper in their commercial enterprises in Senegambia. The French in Senegambia lacked the manpower, financial means, and connections to fulfill their trading agenda on their own. They needed the support of different groups of African and Eurafrican women because it was customary in many West African cultures for women to handle trade and run businesses. There were many examples of women well versed in commercial matters in West African societies. Local women on the Gold Coast ran biweekly town markets that were attended by thousands of people. It was also women who traditionally traded rice in Sierra Leone and Liberia.[127] Elite Wolof women often conducted trade within and outside of their large households. Among them were the wives and mothers of wealthy estate owners, as well as the *lingers* (queens and relatives of kings), who used royal enslaved people as field laborers and domestics to produce and sell goods. In polygynous Wolof, Pulaar and Lebu communities, wives traditionally managed their household together, which allowed many to gain managerial and collaborative skills that they could use in their commercial ventures.[128]

Many African and Eurafrican women, merchants, and businesspeople in the seventeenth-century French outposts and coastal areas wielded authority in their relationships with the French. Without local assistance, the French in Saint-Louis would have been forced to live in the uncomfortable French fort, and they would have struggled to feed themselves because there were no farmers among them.[129] Luckily, many Wolof, Pulaar, Serer, Soninke, Mande Bamana, and Lebu women traveled to Saint-Louis from the countryside and coastal villages in order to sell them necessities and export goods.[130] Shortly after his arrival in Saint-Louis, La Courbe met several women from Bieurt and other villages on the coast, who were bartering local goods for European commodities in the company's store. These women traveled by foot, carrying the merchandise on their heads and on the backs of donkeys. They then used canoes to reach the French outposts. In exchange for

French merchandise, they provided the French in Saint-Louis with millet, as well as loincloths, cotton fabrics and pieces of leather purchased inland by their enslaved servants.[131] Another group of African and Eurafrican businesswomen invited Frenchmen to live in their straw cabins around the island of Saint-Louis, which were much cooler than the French fort.[132] These women also supplied French company employees, officers, soldiers, and merchants in Saint-Louis with precious food and hides.[133]

Some belonged to a distinguished community of people (sometimes labeled *Crioulos, Portugais,* or *Portingalls*) descended from female African traders (the Senhoras) who had begun to build wealth and influence by playing a central role in Atlantic commerce and by engaging in exchanges with the Portuguese, Dutch and British men who had arrived on the West African coast starting in the fifteenth century.[134] Mixed relationships between African women and Portuguese men had been common in West Africa since the beginning of the Portuguese presence in the region—as was also the case between Asian women and Portuguese men in Portuguese India.[135] By the 1440s, the Portuguese had begun to trade captives and gold between the Senegal River and Sierra Leone. They were followed by the Dutch and the English. Their Eurafrican descendants formed important trading communities in the region. Although some lived on the islands of Saint-Louis and Gorée, most were established at the mouths of the Senegal and Gambia Rivers and in Sierra Leone.[136] By the 1720s, the French would sometimes call African and Eurafrican businesswomen among them *signares*—a derivation of the Portuguese word Senhoras.[137]

Since the Europeans depended on them for vital necessities and access to strategic information and commercial networks on the continent, some of these businesswomen became very powerful. Some Frenchmen leveraged these women's skills to sell and purchase goods on behalf of the companies, while many others traded with them for their own individual benefit, in violation of the companies' trading monopolies.[138] Some women in Saint-Louis and on the coast helped facilitate the entry of the French into preexisting trading networks, including Wolof and Lebu circles.[139] In the mainland town of Albreda, in the late seventeenth century, one African princess and merchant named Senhora Belinguere was famous for her trading relationships with the French, Portuguese and English companies, as well as with the royal court of the kingdom of Niumi, near the Gambia River. She was at some point married to a Portuguese man and spoke perfect French,

Portuguese, and English.[140] It was probably not unusual for influential African leaders or businesspeople on the coast like her to play different European nations against one another, influencing European politics in the process.[141] Senhora Belinguere gave secret information about the dealings of other European nations to the directors of the French company. She also gave important advice to, and traded with, several French company agents.[142] Several businesspeople on the coast had excellent relationship-building skills, which they used to secure advantageous deals for themselves at the expense of the Europeans. One historical account noted that Senhora Belinguere "is polite and cheerful, enough to let many people fall into her traps, and she has a wonderful talent to ruin those who deal with her; their number is not small."[143]

The power of these women was amplified by the fact that the French also depended on them to hire enslaved workers. European men in Saint-Louis and Gorée were few and unskilled: in the late seventeenth century, most of them spent their days curing leather and making bricks and lime for the construction of houses and other structures.[144] By 1685, La Courbe counted only sixty Europeans in Saint-Louis, "most of whom [did] not know any trade."[145] The French in Senegambia thus relied on enslaved Africans and free laborers in the spheres of housekeeping, agriculture, trade, transportation and more. They were not allowed to own enslaved workers, presumably because authorities wanted to keep their focus on trade and also perhaps to maximize the number of enslaved people who could be sent to the Americas.[146] As a result, especially in the eighteenth century, local African and Eurafrican women would often lease their own enslaved workers to the companies.[147] Enslaved people working at the service of African women in Saint-Louis and Gorée were called *captifs de case* (or *Jaam-juddu*). They had a different status than the *captifs*, who were purchased specifically to be sold in the Americas and were held in cages in the *captiveries* of the French outposts before being forced aboard slave ships.[148] While most enslaved people sent to the Caribbean by the early eighteenth century were destined to work the land on plantations, *captifs de case* often ran commercial errands in the outposts and on the mainland on behalf of their African mistresses. They were given some level of autonomy and could sometimes own property. Some of those on the mainland cultivated food crops, while many of those inside the French outposts worked as domestic servants for their African mistresses.[149] Others navigated the Senegal River to facilitate French trade.[150]

Thanks to their dealings with the French, the Portuguese, the English, and the Dutch, many African businesspeople had already become quite rich by the late seventeenth century, at a time when most French company employees were living in penury.[151] Some Senegambian African and Eurafrican businesswomen, in particular, owned multiple *captifs de case,* as well as solid houses made of mud, bricks and tiles. They also wore lavish jewelry and clothes, including *pagnes* (African skirts), headwraps and eventually *indiennes* (printed and painted clothes from India), as well as European shirts, dresses, and shoes.[152] It was common for African and Eurafrican businesswomen and merchants in Senegambia to embrace some material indicators of European culture to position themselves more advantageously in the sphere of Atlantic commerce and differentiate themselves from other local people.[153] One of the African and Eurafrican businesswomen who had already become quite rich and embraced elements of European material cultures in seventeenth-century coastal Senegambia was Senhora Belinguere, the African princess and merchant of Albreda. Belinguere lived in a large Portuguese-style home with white mud walls that was filled with furniture and servants. When she received André Brue, the future director-general of the French company in Senegal, she was wearing a shirt adorned with buttons of gold, topped with a Portuguese corset made of satin. Her waist was wrapped in luxurious *pagnes altes* from Cape Verde—commonly worn by the female West African elite. On each of her fingers was a beautiful ring, while her head was covered with a gold-striped cotton turban. She also wore an elaborate necklace made of amber, gold and coral (another popular French trading good in the area) around her neck.[154]

Some African men were also able to accumulate significant wealth, and a few held considerable power over the French, even though power dynamics were fluctuating. All this is illustrated by La Courbe's account of his tribute and gift-giving visit to Brac, the Wolof heir to the kingdom of Waalo, off the coast of Montaubé, in June 1685. Brac arrived at the seashore on a horse, surrounded by his entire court. He boarded the canoe that was sent to carry him to the boat with three other African leaders and several griots. On the boat, a *maître de langue* introduced the guests formally, and La Courbe presented his numerous gifts to Brac: the brandy, the gris-gris paper and cloves, along with a red linen cover for his horse, sewing equipment, and coral.[155] Then, astonishingly, after he had received all his gifts, Brac swiftly grabbed La Courbe's white feather hat and placed it on his own head, asking everyone jokingly if it would fit him well. Such an act would have been deemed completely unacceptable in early modern Europe and the Americas.[156] Several months later, Brac kept his own hat on when saluting La Courbe: this behavior shocked the French director because it was customary for Europeans to remove their head coverings as a mark of respect toward their peers or superiors.[157] After he had placed the white feather hat on his own head, Brac casually lay on La Courbe's bed, requested a drink, and asked the French if he could borrow a few scarves and silver ornaments from them, to which La Courbe agreed.[158]

Although French officials like La Courbe did endure such displays of power on the part of African leaders, they did not hesitate to seize the opportunity to assert their own authority over high-ranking locals when the circumstances were right. As a case in point, just a few months after the tribute and gift-giving visit of June 1685, the balance of power began to shift between the French director La Courbe and the Wolof prince Brac. A conflict arose after a French beef trader accidentally shot his rifle through the wall of an African villager's cabin while hunting in the region of Biffeche. The beef trader was arrested, and a local chief named Guiobo decided to force his French superior, a man named La Jeunesse, to pay a fee of thirty-six leather pieces (or thirty-six livres) to repair the cabin.[159] In retaliation, La Jeunesse captured an enslaved Black man from the village, whom he took to Saint-Louis. La Courbe worried, initially, that this incident would anger Brac, which is why he imprisoned La Jeunesse and took good care of the captive. He also forbade all whites from traveling to African villages on the coast, "[for] fear that such incidents may happen again."[160] But La Courbe's efforts were in vain, for not long after, the abovementioned French plunderer Sieur de la Marche attacked this same Biffeche village, leading Brac to gather an army of 500 men.[161] Interestingly, however, while La Courbe agreed to return the stolen captive to the Biffeche village, he refused to give the plundered goods back to Brac.[162] He was probably aware by then that Brac could not really dispense with the French alliance because he wished to maintain access to European trade and needed to avoid making more enemies: Wolof leaders, including Brac, were now in the middle of a major conflict with the Moors of Morocco.[163] Brac eventually resolved to make peace with the French and even asked

La Courbe if he could assist him in the event of an attack by his Moorish enemies. After the relationship was normalized, an African interpreter explained Brac's decision in these terms: "I think that Brac is quite pleased, because he did not wish to break with whites."[164] African leaders like Brac valued their relationships with the French because they and their people developed a taste for European merchandise, including firearms, tools, and *indiennes,* along with other clothes and fabrics. In another case in point, one year after La Courbe's tribute and gift-giving visit to Brac, the king of the kingdom of Cayor resolved to reallow the French to enter his territory after a conflict, invoking his intent "to grow the commerce of his country."[165]

This African demand for European goods gave the French some leverage that they used to assert their authority: after Brac had reconciled with the French, La Courbe no longer displayed the deference and respect that he had shown to him in June 1685. During another tribute and gift-giving boat visit, La Courbe attempted to humiliate Brac by telling him that he would not let him drink any brandy on his boat because he did not want him to get drunk and behave "like a master." La Courbe then informed Brac that he would not give him any more gifts beyond his tribute because he had already given him enough.[166] Brac did not complain of La Courbe's changed attitude because he wanted his military support and probably because he wanted to secure more trading agreements with the French. Of course, this does not mean that the African prince had entirely lost his power: in fact, he still very much had the upper hand over the French, since they agreed to pay him their tribute. Although power dynamics were unstable at times, the French in Senegambia were ultimately subject to the whims and choices of local kings, chiefs, merchants, and businesspeople.

The Rise of Isle Bourbon's Creole Society

Many free people of non-European descent also garnered status and wealth, and probably some political influence as well, on late seventeenth-century Isle Bourbon because French authorities endeavored to assimilate them to "white" society to populate the colony in the absence of enough European immigrants. A total of only 180 Europeans arrived on Isle Bourbon between 1663 and 1695.[167] Some did not stay, and the majority (121) were men. Initially uninhabited, seventeenth-century Isle Bourbon was a less desirable destination for aspiring French settlers than its Caribbean counterparts because it was located far from the French kingdom and thousands of miles away from both the Americas and the East Indies. French officials ended up populating the island by promoting migration from Europe, Madagascar, and India, as well as East and West Africa, and by letting Frenchmen engage in Catholic intermarriages with Malagasy, Luso-Indian, and African women whose Frenchified mixed descendants were then integrated into the island's free settler society.[168]

Instead of finding more European volunteers for immigration, authorities turned the difficulties experienced by the French in Madagascar into an opportunity to lay a solid colonial foundation on Isle Bourbon. Two Frenchmen had already left Madagascar in 1663 to establish a first permanent settlement on Isle Bourbon with ten Malagasies.[169] By the early 1670s, French authorities were beginning to question the sustainability of France's colonial enterprise in Madagascar following major human and economic losses.[170] These setbacks led the French viceroy of the Indies, Jacob Blanquet de La Haye, to start evacuating several French soldiers, settlers, their Franco-Malagasy families, and their Malagasy bonded servants to Isle Bourbon starting in 1671. (French officials at the time initially labeled bonded Malagasy workers as "servants" (*domestiques*) instead of "slaves" (*esclaves*) because a 1664 ordinance—whose goal was to maintain peaceful relationships with France's *roandria* allies—made it illegal to trade any locals as captives.[171] Following the anti-colonial revolt of Fort-Dauphin in 1674, a total of twenty-one French refugees reached Isle Bourbon with their free Malagasy spouses, joining those who had already begun to arrive since the 1660s.[172] All those Frenchmen and Malagasy women who had left Madagascar for Isle Bourbon since 1663 were labeled "the remnants of Madagascar" (*les débris de Madagascar*) in contemporary sources.[173] Those remnants came to form the core of Isle Bourbon's original settler society. It was also around this period that the French company began to bring free Luso-Indian women from India to the island so that they could marry Frenchmen.

Due to the small number of white women on Isle Bourbon, officials also decided to let French colonists on the island marry freeborn and manumitted Christian women of Malagasy and African ancestries, which helped accelerate demographic reproduction in the free population.[174]

These intermarriages were not officially endorsed by French authorities: since 1673, officials on the island had only promoted Catholic intermarriages between Frenchmen and Luso-Indian women. The order issued by the French Company of the East Indies on October 27, 1664 had in fact prohibited mixed relationships with "women of the country" in Madagascar.

But French authorities on Isle Bourbon were immediately forced to shift their strategy because the number of white women on the island rose only negligibly between 1676 and 1690—from eight to just thirteen. A ship officer who spent time on Isle Bourbon in the 1670s, Chevalier de Ricous, described the consequences on European men on the island in those terms: "Those miserable men are desperate for women; most of them having been forced to marry *négresses,* their own slaves."[175]

This tradition of intermarriage became the primary vector in the colonization of Isle Bourbon in the seventeenth century. The arrival of the Christian and Europeanized Luso-Indian women from India in the 1670s marked what was probably the last influx of free women on the island until 1718, with the exception of a few French women. Scholars have described the following decades as a period of "incubation" for Bourbon Island's creole society. The population of Isle Bourbon tripled between 1689 and 1714, mostly because of mixed unions.[176] By 1690, the proportion of free people of Malagasy and South Asian ancestries on the island equaled that of Europeans and white creoles whose ancestors all came from Europe (*créoles blancs*): *métis* or *mulâtres* of Eurasian and French-Malagasy origins that year amounted to 46 percent of the free population of Isle Bourbon (94 people) and free Malagasies or Blacks to 6 percent (12 people). Meanwhile, white settlers whose ancestors all came from Europe amounted to only 47 percent of the free population (97 people).[177] Reconstructing the racial makeup of the island in following decades is very difficult because census makers began to classify all people born on the island as creoles regardless of their ancestry.[178] By 1709, many free people were categorized as creoles or had at least one parent from India or Madagascar.[179] A study tracing the origins of 201 free adults recorded in a 1711 census of Isle Bourbon found that 52 percent had at least one grandparent of Malagasy or South Asian descent.[180] As a result, it is safe to assume that an extremely large proportion of the free population of Isle Bourbon had non-European origins by the early eighteenth century.

Many of those free *métis* or *mulâtres* practiced respected and profitable European skilled trades, and French officials could envision assimilating them into the colonist population because they were described as successfully Frenchified in early eighteenth-century documents. Although governor of Madagascar Étienne de Flacourt's old dream of having the people of Anosy educated in "the [French] arts [and crafts]" never materialized in Madagascar, it did make considerable inroads on Isle Bourbon. The Bourbon Island Creoles were gradually Europeanized through their contact with European missionaries, settlers, company employees, and others on the island—and also back in India, in the case of the Luso-Indian people. Some must have received apprenticeships in European craftsmen's workshops on the island, while others had probably already been taught several European crafts by the Portuguese back in India. In 1711, the storekeeper and upcoming governor of Isle Bourbon Antoine Desforges-Boucher (1723–1725), usually a cynical and scornful man, praised *mulâtre* blacksmiths on Isle Bourbon for their ability to repair firearms and forge knife blades "almost as good as those of France's [blacksmith] masters."[181] According to Boucher, those same *mulâtres* produced different iron and steel objects so perfect that "all Europeans agree[d] that they could not look any better."[182] Others played European musical instruments like the violin "with great natural talent." Boucher also noted the presence on the island of "very good" *mulâtre* carpenters and joiners, who made musical instruments and built houses.[183] Among those men was a Luso-Indian man named Emanuel Tixere.[184] Boucher described Tixere as an excellent carpenter and surgeon. He was also an educated man, able to read, write, draw and speak Latin. By the early eighteenth century, Emmanuel and his Black wife owned four enslaved people, one house, a large plot of cultivated land, and a highly frequented tavern located halfway between the parishes of Saint-Paul and Saint-Denis.[185] Boucher described Tixere as a "very comfortable man and well-dressed," who had a lot of money (1,500 écus).[186]

Many women of Malagasy and South Asian ancestries practiced respected skilled crafts as well, using European skills. Although the Lazarist missionary Nacquart's old dream of having Tanosy women sew clothes "like those made in France" never materialized in Madagascar, it did come true on Isle Bourbon. According to Boucher, many *mulâtresses* who worked as dressmakers on Isle Bourbon were able to sew corsets, skirts, and caps "with dexterity," and they also made spectacular shirts, which even France's most esteemed dressmakers were unable to reproduce.[187] He claimed that the Europeans who stopped at the island on their way to the East Indies "admired [these products] for their designs and for the shape of the buttonholes," agreeing that "such clothes could not look any better, even in Paris."[188]

The Frenchification of the Bourbon Island Creoles was not limited to the arts and crafts. The French company's ambition to "trai[n] [Malagasies] to cultivate the land," which had yielded its first results in Anosy, also materialized on Isle Bourbon. Many free Blacks and *mulâtres* there became successful farmers, having already acquired agricultural skills on the French–Malagasy slave-owning farms of Anosy or through their French and Malagasy parents. Those people began to form creole village communities organized according to Tanosy, French metropolitan, and French colonial agricultural models, where they raised cows and sheep and cultivated French crops such as wheat and grapes, along with exotic products like potatoes, banana, rice, sugarcane, and tobacco.[189] Among those who prospered as farmers and livestock breeders were Anne Caze, a Malagasy woman, and her French husband, Gilles Launay, both residents of the parish of Saint-Paul. By 1690, they owned twelve enslaved people, at a time when the average household on the island owned fewer than three. By 1708, Launay had willed half of his property to his French–Malagasy daughters Anne Jr. and Marguerite. Yet Anne Caze still owned fourteen enslaved people, a house and five plots of land cultivated with food crops and small quantities of sugarcane, as well as hundreds of livestock. Boucher praised Anne for being "an exemplary woman, devout and charitable" and hardworking.[190] Meanwhile, a Franco–Malagasy *mulâtre* named Gilles Fontaine accumulated a considerable 2,000 écus through his activities as a pirate, which he then used to purchase an estate in Saint-Paul.[191] By 1708, he was farming food crops and livestock on the estate of his mother, a Malagasy woman named Marie Anne.[192] Gilles Fontaine married a Luso-Indian woman named Françoise Lauret and eventually turned his own estate into a coffee plantation, with the assistance of his four enslaved laborers. When Gilles and Françoise died in 1729 in a smallpox epidemic, their inheritance was estimated at a significant 3,587 livres.[193]

Like Anne Caze, Gilles Fontaine, and Françoise Lauret, many free people of Malagasy and South Asian ancestries embraced the slave-owning practices in use in Tanosy societies and other European slave plantation colonies.

As a result of the company's decision in the 1670s to use Isle Bourbon as a replacement for Madagascar as a port of call provisioning ships with fresh food, the bonded population of the island grew fivefold between 1689 and 1714.[194] Enslaved laborers amounted to 42 percent of the population of the island (311 people) by 1704, and this proportion grew to 50 percent in 1715 (736 people).[195] The ordinance of 1664, which prohibited the Indian Ocean slave trade, fell almost completely into oblivion during this period: by the 1680s, bonded "servants" were increasingly labeled *esclaves* ("slaves") instead of *domestiques* ("domestic servants").[196] By 1709, 39 percent of this enslaved population (150 people) was born on the island, 24 percent came from Madagascar (95 people), 23 percent came from India (90 people), and 13 percent came from East and West Africa (55 people).[197]

Although all bonded laborers on Isle Bourbon had non-European origins, there was no strong correlation between race and socioeconomic status on the island because many white Europeans and white creoles were poor, while many free *mulâtres* and *mulâtresses* lived comfortably. Because they did not own any land they might live off of, some European colonists were described as being "just as miserable as their own slaves."[198] Such was the case of Lezin Rouillard, a company employee from the French city of Angers and a father of four. He was eventually granted a few plots of land in the parish of Saint-Paul, which his wife, a woman from Lyon, cultivated on her own after he died.[199] In a memorandum he wrote in 1709, Boucher described white European and white creole colonists on the island as a miserable and pitiful lot. He claimed that Gilles Dugains, a Frenchman from Saint-Malo, was "as poor as a church mouse, with nothing to cover [himself]."[200] Dugains was married to a creole woman of Malagasy ancestry whom Boucher—drawing on a growing hypersexualizing trope about Black women that I discuss later—described as a corpulent and libidinous "saddle for all horses," nicknamed "the great mare."[201] The rope maker Samson Le Beau, another Frenchman—this time from the city of Tours—was, according to Boucher, a miserable uneducated fool, married to a woman from India. Boucher explained, "He is starving to death, has nothing to cover himself up, and he is forced to travel to the town of Saint-Paul from time to time, to go begging for a shirt."[202] French officials regularly criticized the white population of the island for their complete lack of skills.[203] Strikingly, Boucher even claimed to have more regard for the colony's *mulâtres* and *mulâtresses* than he did for white creoles and white Europeans, attributing his disdain for white people to their incompetence.[204] By the early eighteenth century, white women on the island had no sewing skills—which, according to Boucher, forced them to rely on *mulâtresses* to take care of their households.[205] Boucher addressed this startling rhetorical question to white creoles on the island:

> Please tell me, dear white creole people [. . .]: what are you good for? [. . .] This question must embarrass you, except for a few of you who can barely chop wood [. . .]. The *mulâtres* are not like you [. . .] they are more skillful and few of them are incapable of doing things [. . .]. Messrs. white men: [. . .] you do not have their talents. Listen to me and let go of your pride: let us not pretend that you are superior [. . .] to the *mulâtres* just because you are white.[206]

Patterns of wealth distribution show that, on average, free people of Malagasy and South Asian ancestries on Isle Bourbon were not poorer than French people. An assessment of the number of enslaved people per household for the year 1690 does not show any significant difference between white, mixed, and non-European households. In fact, the island's largest slaveholders in 1690 were the Malagasy woman Anne Caze and her French husband, Gilles Launay. Wealth distribution patterns remained roughly similar in the early eighteenth century. By 1704, there was an average of four enslaved people per Malagasy, French–Malagasy, and creole–Malagasy household. A full 33 percent of these mixed households owned more than three enslaved people. The largest slave-owning household on the island was headed by a white man and a woman of Malagasy ancestry—this couple owned twenty-three captives. Fifty percent of all Malagasy, French–Malagasy, and creole–Malagasy households owned more than one plot of land and 25 percent owned more than one house. Meanwhile, South-Asian, mixed French–South Asian, and creole–South Asian households owned an average of two enslaved people or more. All of these mixed households owned land and houses. In comparison, that same year of 1704, French households owned an average of five enslaved people, but the most prominent French slaveowners owned no more than fourteen enslaved people. In addition, 67 percent of all French households owned more than one plot of land, but only 22 percent owned more than one house.[207]

Patterns of wealth distribution remained steady into the 1710s. By 1719, in the parish of Saint-Paul, non-European, mixed French–non-European, or creole–non-European households owned over nine enslaved people on average. One household, headed by a Malagasy woman, owned twenty-eight enslaved people—more than any of the three French households recorded in the census that year. Among those French households, two were single men who each held fifteen enslaved people, while the third household owned twenty-five.[208]

Some of these free people of Malagasy and South Asian ancestries on Isle Bourbon must have wielded political power since they maintained very close ties with colonial officials. The story of the island's Council of the Six Seniors of Saint-Paul (the Conseil des Six Anciens de Saint-Paul, also known as the Directoire de Saint-Paul) is a case in point. This council ruled over the island from 1692 to 1696, after the French governor Sieur Henry Habert de Vauboulon had been imprisoned as a result of his unpopular reforms.[209] Among the Six Seniors ruling over the island, three had formed close bonds with women of non-European descent: Athanase Touchard from Paris, who acted as president of the council, Louis Caron from Brittany, and Antoine Payet.[210] Antoine Payet was none other than the grandfather of Marianne Payet, the successful coffee planter of French–Malagasy ancestries whom we encountered earlier in "A Tale of Two Mariannes." Antoine had married a Malagasy woman named Louise Siaram in 1677. Although he was just a humble carpenter before his departure from Dauphiné in southeastern France, his relocation to Isle Bourbon had allowed him to climb the social ladder: in 1696, Antoine and his wife acquired a residence with several profitable tobacco and food crop farms in the parish of Saint-Paul.[211] By the time his wife died in the 1710s, in addition to being a prominent slaveowner, he owned over a hundred heads of livestock and the considerable sum of 3,080 écus.[212] Meanwhile, councilor Louis Caron had married a Luso-Indian woman from Daman named Monique Pereire in 1679, with whom he had six children. Louis and Monique farmed livestock, tobacco and food crops with their enslaved laborers on their estate of Saint-Paul.[213] Finally, Athanase Touchard, the director of the Council of the Six Seniors, had married a woman named Elisabeth Houve, described as a "*négresse* from Madagascar" in 1710, and together the couple had five children.[214] Touchard's alliance with a Malagasy woman did not prevent him from becoming the most powerful man on the island, nor did it tarnish his reputation. In fact, even the scornful Boucher had nothing but praise for him. Boucher portrayed Touchard as a remarkable man who "live[d] more like a Saint than a man." Despite being impaired by a severe case of gout, he took great care of his family, raising his children "in the most inspiring manner," allowing them to be "a model of wisdom for all creoles on the island."[215] According to Boucher, Touchard's Malagasy wife, Elisabeth, was also "acclaimed by all" for the education she gave her children.[216] Together, the couple owned two houses in the parish of Saint-Paul, several heads of livestock, and multiple plots of land on which their enslaved laborers cultivated food crops.[217] In the words of Boucher, this agricultural venture allowed the couple to be "very comfortable" financially.[218] Boucher's interest in the Touchard family probably went far beyond the description he provided in his memoir: by 1709, he had by all evidence started an out-of-wedlock relationship with one of Athanase and Elisabeth's children, a *mulâtresse* named Marie Touchard, with whom he probably had a son named Antoine.[219]

* * *

In conclusion, French policymakers often found it necessary to adapt their strategies to local circumstances. These policy accommodations—along with European and non-European people's attempts to survive and pursue their own economic and diplomatic interests in each context—helped lay the foundations of the French empire in the early modern period. To look beyond France's North American colony is to see just how far certain patterns extended. From New France to Senegambia to Anosy, the French sought food and shelter in local people's homes and villages and also formed diplomatic and commercial alliances with local kings, chiefs, merchants and entrepreneurs. In order to advance their commercial and wider imperial ambitions, French colonists across the empire also embraced different elements of local cultural practices—from the Malagasy *souvou* raiding tradition, to the custom of requesting the *fahensa* tribute from vanquished people in southern Madagascar, to the male practice of using the Senegambian *folgars* as diplomatic gatherings.

Like the Indigenous peoples of North America, many people of non-European descent in the French Atlantic and Indian Ocean worlds wielded considerable power over the French. Some populations in coastal Senegambia—especially Wolof, Lebu and Eurafrican people—were already wealthy and powerful by the late seventeenth century. And while the French in Madagascar were certainly able to advance their own power over multiple villages, they dealt with powerful locals on that island as well. Peoples of Malagasy and South Asian descent could also wield significant power on early Isle Bourbon because they formed the core of the island's population of free colonists, partly as a result of French officials' resolution to unofficially allow Catholic intermarriages with Malagasy women to populate the colony.

In fact, the most important shifts in French imperial strategy during this time period were probably in the domain of *métissage* (intermarriage and mixed sexual relationships). In order to populate Isle Bourbon, French authorities on the island ended up not only turning a blind eye to officially unendorsed mixed Catholic marriages, but also literally assimilating the children born to early mixed unions into "white" society, by categorizing them as "whites" in early eighteenth-century official documents. In other places where intermarriage was not endorsed by French authorities, officials also resolved to let European men form relationships with women of non-European ancestries. Such was the case in Senegambia, partly because mixed relationships became deeply entangled with the commercial exchanges that sustained the European presence in the region. These practices in Senegambia and on Isle Bourbon were not isolated cases. In fact, they indicated the crystallization of a wider repertoire of empire spanning the Atlantic and Indian Oceans, marking the transformation of the French imperial formation into an empire of *métissage*.

CHAPTER 3

Empire of Métissage

A few years after marrying the French carpenter Antoine Payet in the Catholic Church, on January 30, 1681, in Saint-Paul, Isle Bourbon, the free Malagasy woman Louise Siaram gave birth to a *mulâtresse* baby girl named Louise Payet.[1] Louise's childhood was cut short abruptly in 1692, when, at age eleven, she was married to a twenty-one-year-old French-Malagasy creole *mulâtre* named François Cauzan in the Catholic Church.[2] But despite the hardships entailed in such an early marriage, she grew up to become one of the most admired women on Isle Bourbon. By 1709, Boucher described her as "a model for all women of the island."[3] Louise never had children of her own, but she took in several little girls from her neighborhood and made it her mission to raise them to become the "wisest and most educated" ladies of the island, teaching them to perform European domestic tasks like sewing and washing the laundry.[4] Louise and her husband François worked so hard to make a living for themselves that they became one of the island's wealthiest couples.[5] By the early eighteenth century, they owned nine enslaved people, many heads of livestock, and several parcels of land.[6] Louise and François also embraced some elements of French material culture: for example, records of public sales and other documents indicate that—in addition to cultivating crops favored in early modern Europe, such as wheat and wine grapes—they wore silk stockings as well as shirts made in France.[7] By 1709, Louise and François were described as "the most fashionable and best lodged of all the settlers" and had saved up 2,000 écus—a significant amount of money.[8] François passed away on June 7, 1715.[9] His death turned Louise into one of the most eligible widows of Isle Bourbon.

It took only a few months for Jacques Macé, a thirty-two-year-old white army surgeon from Brittany, to propose to Louise. She accepted, and they married on January 14, 1716, in the church of Saint-Paul.[10] Ancien Régime patriarchal customs gave Jacques some control over Louise's estate, and he could also count on her generosity.[11] Louise Payet was an extraordinarily generous woman indeed, as suggested by the many gifts that she made to the Church and to her family and friends. For example, in 1714, she donated a plot of land in the mountains to the incoming governor of Isle Bourbon, Henry de Justamond, who was from Languedoc and also the husband of her youngest sister, another *mulâtresse*, named Luce Payet.[12] A devout Christian, Louise also maintained close ties with the Catholic Church throughout her life. In 1696, she became the godmother of a little girl named Marie Grondin, to whom she gave an enslaved six-year-old Malagasy girl as a Christmas gift in 1714.[13] In 1715, she also made a donation of 200 écus to Lazarist missionaries on the island, "to provide for two female schoolteachers who should educate the girls of the parishes of Isle Bourbon."[14]

In 1729, Louise Payet fell gravely ill and died shortly thereafter. She had so many personal effects that it took three days to complete the postmortem inventory of her estate. This inventory listed many plots of land, seven residences and cabins, a pharmacy cabinet worth 400 livres, countless furniture, clothes, shoes, jewelry, and tools for dressmaking, construction, and gardening, as well as kitchenware, including China dishes. By the end of her life, Louise owned thirty enslaved people and several hundred heads of livestock worth over 3,681 livres. She also had over 30,146 livres in savings—an enormous sum of money.[15]

This chapter demonstrates that *métissage* (interracial sex) was instrumental to the establishment of France's colonial empire. In remote places where European women were especially few in number, such as Isle Bourbon, mixed children born to early Catholic unions between white men and freeborn or manumitted women of non-European ancestries like Louise Siaram furnished the fledgling French settlements and outposts with free Christian colonists, planters, farmers, artisans, and other free workers, offsetting limited arrivals of people from Europe. Some of these mixed people, especially in isolated places with restricted metropolitan oversight like Isle Bourbon, French India and early Guadeloupe, were assimilated into white settler societies by being classified as "whites" in local official documents—because they were Christian, and often Europeanized and well-off financially.[16] Meanwhile, other mixed children on Isle Bourbon and the French Caribbean islands, who were born to enslaved women who had sexual relationships with white men, began to grow slave workforces as a relatively rare, yet especially coveted commodity. In vastly larger territories with much more powerful local populations—like Louise's mother's homeland in Madagascar, or Senegambia—mixed relationships (including Catholic unions, intermarriages *à la mode du pays,* and casual sex) between Frenchmen and local freeborn women helped the French forge many of the diplomatic and commercial alliances that proved vital to the endurance and commercial success of the French empire.

In the end, the sexualities of both unfree and free women of non-European ancestries were harnessed in the making of France's early overseas empire. Only a few French officials, most of whom lived overseas, foresaw how some of these widely different mixed relationships could solidify the foundations of empire. Even when these relationships were not endorsed, or when they were outlawed, they often turned a blind eye to them and even leveraged them in order to grow local populations and protect the French colonies and outposts.

Most of the ordinary men and women who engaged in these relationships were probably unaware of the ways their day-to-day sexualities advanced the formation of empire. Some of the free women of non-European descent who formed relationships with white men might have wanted to escape difficult matrimonial practices in their own cultures or increase their influence, for example, by becoming Christian leaders in their societies or diplomatic mediators between the French and their own community. Some were almost certainly hoping to advance their own socioeconomic interests. Many others—both free and unfree—were brutally coerced and violated by European men. The early modern French imperial formation was grounded in sexual violence and coercion because all enslaved women, and many free women of non-European ancestries, did not have the freedom to refuse European men's sexual advances. In Madagascar, for example, several free *roandria* women were presumably pressured by their own kinspeople to marry or live in concubinage with Frenchmen to advance their clan's military and economic interests, while hundreds of female captives were also coerced into forming such relationships.

This chapter addresses important gaps in the rich literature on the exploitation of enslaved Black women's wombs.[17] In the French colonial historiography, literature on this topic tends to focus chiefly on the Caribbean islands in the late eighteenth and the nineteenth centuries, giving less attention to the earlier period and to other French colonies.[18] Most importantly, although scholars have already focused on the instrumentalization of enslaved Black women's wombs in the rise of slave reproduction, they have paid less attention to the role played by the sexualities of both unfree and free women of non-European ancestries in the growth of *free* settler populations across early European empires.[19] In the Illinois Country, Catholic intermarriage between Frenchmen and Frenchified Illinois (especially Kaskaskia, but also Tamaroa and Peoria) women famously minted new subjects who were categorized as "French" in official documents, thereby helping the French to populate their settlements.[20] Americanists often cite the Illinois Country as "the exception to the rules" for having "managed to incorporate Native and *métis* people as subjects in the French empire" through widespread Catholic intermarriage—which itself has been described as "a practice unique to the Illinois Country."[21] Yet even more Frenchmen entered Catholic marriages with women of non-European ancestries in the remote outposts and settlements of seventeenth- and early eighteenth-century French India and Isle Bourbon.

In addition to growing colonial populations, mixed Catholic marriages, marriages "in the manner of the country" (*à la façon du pays* or *à la mode du pays*) and casual sex with local women facilitated the formation of essential diplomatic and commercial alliances in vast continental arenas well beyond North America.[22] In particular, like their counterparts in North America, Frenchmen in Senegambia and Anosy understood very well the opportunities that flexible (breakable) unions "in the manner of the country" could give. They leveraged those marriages in both regions to multiply alliances with local populations. Well beyond North America, too, in places like Madagascar and Isle Bourbon, Catholic intermarriage also advanced French colonization by encouraging female converts and their female descendants to serve as models or spread Christianity in their communities. Many of the women of non-European descent who formed relationships with Frenchmen entered these relationships as agents in their own right, hailing from widely different cultures that gave them significant sexual freedom.

The question of whether *enslaved* women could have some agency as well when having sex with a free man is a more complicated and delicate one. Some scholars hypothesize that some enslaved women used their relationships with white men to improve their own living conditions and those of their mixed children.[23] According to other scholars, this perspective runs the risk of minimizing the violence of the slave system "by turning the trauma and coercion enforced by enslavers into narratives of power wielded by the enslaved."[24] As Walter Johnson puts it, the agency of the enslaved is "thick with the material givenness of a moment in time."[25] This is why this book approaches the agency of enslaved women as a "historically confined" process—to use the words of Marisa Fuentes.[26] It does so by offering an in-depth study of the "thickness" of the adversity within which these women's agency existed while also recognizing the possibility that some of these women who improved their conditions may have done so as a result of their own strategic actions. In particular, this chapter seeks to recover the "thickness" of the adversity faced by enslaved women by questioning the notion of "consent" within the context of slavery, and by exposing the hitherto unacknowledged breadth of the sexual violence they faced across the French Atlantic and Indian Ocean worlds.[27]

Sexual Abuse and Slave Reproduction in the Caribbean

From the onset of French colonization in the seventeenth century, the sexual coercion and rape of enslaved women by white men, when resulting in pregnancy, helped reproduce enslaved workforces in the nascent Caribbean slave societies. Ownership gave slaveholders unlimited power over the bodies of enslaved men, women, and children, allowing them to act with impunity whenever they wanted to.[28] For this reason, I agree with Saidiya Hartman, Tiya Miles, Jennifer Shaw, and other scholars that real "consent"—defined in the *Oxford English Dictionary* as "voluntary agreement to sexual intercourse or other sexual activity by a person *who has the (legal) freedom and capacity to make such a choice*"—could not exist between an enslaved person and their owner.[29] Instead, Sharon Block usefully employs the expression "coerced sex" to describe sexual relations between slaveowners and enslaved people that cannot be neatly categorized as "rape" defined as "the act or crime, committed by a man, of forcing a woman to have sexual intercourse with him against her will."[30] This does not necessarily mean that mutual fondness and desire did not exist and complicate the dynamic in those relationships.[31] However, these affective ties—real though they sometimes probably were—did nothing to free enslaved people from their owners' control when they did not result in a manumission. Affection could even reinforce an enslaved woman's subordination when a white man used it to his own advantage to further exploit her or when he made her jealous by forming relationships with other women: as Hartman puts it, "sentiment, enjoyment, affinity, will, and desire facilitated subjugation, domination, and terror [. . .] by preying upon the flesh, the heart, and the soul."[32]

While many scholars have already theorized slaveowner–slave relationships, less attention has been paid to sexual relations between enslaved women and white men other than their owners. Those men could also act with impunity because French slaveowners were not inclined to defend their enslaved women against abuse, especially if they were not so injured that they became unable to serve them. Some slaveowners gave very little value to their enslaved servants' lives and well-being, especially when doing so could come at the expense of another white person. This is illustrated by an incident that took place in 1752 involving the Ursuline nuns of New Orleans: when asked if they wanted to press charges against a French soldier named Pochenet for wounding their captive, Louison, in what looked like a probable attempt at sexual assault, the Ursulines responded that "they would prefer losing their *négresse* rather than doing anything uncharitable to their fellowmen."[33]

Cases of sexual coercion and rape of enslaved women appear only sporadically in early French legal records because authorities never criminalized sexual abuses perpetrated against enslaved people in the French colonies.[34] The Edict of Blois of 1580 defined rape in the kingdom of France as the enticement of a woman under the age of twenty-five, which was punishable by death.[35] However, enslaved women remained unprotected by this regulation because of their special nonhuman status as property.[36] Instead of trying to dissuade slaveowners from abusing their own female captives, article IX of the *Code Noir* of the French Antilles (issued in 1685 to regulate slavery) merely condemned freemen who had children with enslaved women outside of Catholic wedlock to pay a fine of 2,000 livres of sugar and ordered the confiscation of their enslaved concubines and mixed children except if "the man [. . .] were to marry the aforementioned slave in the Church."[37] Enslaved people were not even allowed to appear as plaintiffs in civil and criminal courts.[38] When a case involving a sexual assault against an enslaved woman did reach a court, it was because a white person had also been injured in the process or because the trial focused solely on the resulting loss of or damage to "property" on the part of the owner (if an enslaved person had been murdered or wounded in the process).[39]

For enslaved Africans bound for the Americas, sexual abuses began in Africa. African women, girls, men, and boys in the context of the Atlantic slave trade faced humiliating physical examinations in which merchants and buyers evaluated their beauty as well as their physical and reproductive capacities.[40] Marine personnel sometimes purchased women and girls with the sole intention of abusing them during their long transatlantic voyage, like the French ship captain who acquired an enslaved woman from the *damel* (king) of Kajoor in 1715, reportedly "for his own lecherous abuse."[41] Several ship captains and sailors also abused women and girls in cargo holds during the Atlantic crossing. Women and girls amounted to about one-third of the captives sent from Senegambia to the Caribbean between 1701 and 1807.[42]

Once in the French Caribbean, many enslaved Black women were raped and sexually coerced in their owner's households, on their owner's plantations, and outside their owner's estate, from the very beginning of African slavery in the region. After spending time in the French Caribbean in the 1640s, Du Tertre explained that "there are some colonists who have abused their *négresses*."[43] He also lamented that many enslaved women and girls in the Caribbean were forced into submission by "[their] fear of bad treatment, the terrifying threats of [their masters], and the force used by these passionate men to corrupt them."[44] Such relationships were not unusual as suggested by the French crown's decision to punish slaveowners who had fathered a child with their female captives in the *Code Noir* of 1685. In 1695, the missionary Jean-Baptiste Labat mentioned several (allegedly jealous) white mistresses who had denounced their own husbands to religious authorities because they had fathered a child with their enslaved servant. One of those white mistresses was married to a mysterious Monsieur ***, who was described as a rich planter established in Fort-Royal, Martinique. Labat lamented that several white men had even promised freedom to their Black concubines on the condition that they would not mention their names to French authorities.[45] He recounted how one of these white slaveowners went so far as to induce his Black partner to falsely accuse a priest of being the real father of her *mulâtre* child, insisting—amid general courtroom laughter—that her baby really resembled the missionary.[46]

Plantation overseers in the Caribbean also often used their positions of authority to abuse enslaved Black women. A regulation issued in the French Caribbean in 1672 condemned "the vicious actions of plantation overseers with the *négresses*."[47] Du Tertre noted in 1667 that "a plantation overseer sometimes abuse[d] a *négresse*," who would then give birth to "a *mulâtre* child."[48] Those abuses were frequent enough to prompt Labat to advise plantation owners to hire Blacks or elderly whites instead of young white men as plantation overseers, "so that they would be less inclined to cause [those] disorders with the *négresses*."[49] He also advised plantation owners that "as soon as one realizes that white men at our service are doing things with the *négresses*, the best response is to fire them immediately."[50]

The status of children born from sexual relations between freemen and enslaved women in the French Caribbean changed in the second half of the seventeenth century. Before 1674, the *mulâtres* were, it seems, not subject to the Roman legal principle *partus sequitur ventrem* ("that which is born follows the womb"), according to which the slave condition was literally transmitted to children through their enslaved mothers' womb. Du Tertre explained that "the governors [in the Caribbean] do not follow that legal principle giving the condition of their mother to the child, *partus sequitur ventrem*, and [therefore] [the *mulâtres*] have been declared free."[51] It is unclear at which point in their lives the *mulâtres* became able to enjoy this freedom. According to Labat, they were only considered free after reaching twenty-four years of age, and only so long as they had serviced their owner for eight years to compensate for the loss of labor incurred when their mother raised them.[52] French authorities initially approved of the manumission of the *mulâtres* not only because of their paternal parentage but also because of their Europeanized upbringing. The French governor-general of French Antilles, Charles de Courbon, count of Blénac, advocated for the systematic manumission of the *mulâtres* on the grounds that they were Christian and Frenchified. He explained that: "they take our manners, our language, and they rise up in our religion."[53]

The relatively flexible practice of letting the *mulâtres* become free at some point in their lives began to disappear in the 1670s as the result of a change in their legal status. The king decided in 1674 that all *mulâtres* born to an enslaved mother and a free father in the Caribbean would inherit the condition of their mother, in accordance with the Roman law principle *partus sequitur ventrem*. Labat explained that "the king [. . .] reinstated the Roman law principle according to which children follow the condition of the womb that bore them [. . .], and as a consequence, *mulâtres* born to slave mothers will also be enslaved."[54] The Council of Guadeloupe officially confirmed the enslavement of the *mulâtres* born to unfree women in 1680.[55]

In applying the principle *partus sequitur ventrem* to all children born to enslaved women, the French had aligned their legislation not only with Roman law but also with existing Iberian and British legal practices. As early as the thirteenth century, the *Siete Partidas* (a famous Castilian statutory code) had already determined that "he who is born of a slave mother is also a slave."[56] The practice of hereditary slavery was also inscribed in the slave code of Virginia since 1662, on the basis of this same *partus sequitur ventrem* Roman legal statute.[57] As shown by Camillia Cowling, Jennifer Morgan and Sasha Turner, among others, the *partus sequitur ventrem* principle applied across all other early modern British, Spanish, and Portuguese Atlantic colonies.[58]

As was the case in other European empires, hereditary slavery was above all else a way for authorities to perpetuate slavery and help European slaveowners maximize their wealth.[59] Buying enslaved people was initially considered more cost effective than relying on slave reproduction, due to high infant mortality rates, the labor loss incurred when an enslaved woman was pregnant or nursing, and the cost of raising enslaved children into their adulthood.[60] Because fertility rates were low and infant mortality rates were high, slavery in the seventeenth-century French colonies was essentially maintained through the slave trade.[61] Yet French officials and planters began to take a few measures to advance slave reproduction as early as the late seventeenth century because, as Jennifer Morgan puts it in her study of the early British American colonies, "high mortality rates and decreased fertility rates [among enslaved women] did not remove childbirth from the equation"; on the contrary, "if anything, the rarity of surviving infant births may have further highlighted the pragmatic and symbolic value of African women's reproductive potential."[62]

French contemporaries clearly understood the possible advantages of hereditary slavery from the beginning of French colonization in the

Caribbean. As a case in point, here is what Du Tertre explained to his readers after he had spent time in Guadeloupe between 1635 and 1647:

> The power that masters have over their slaves is so complete, and they enjoy such a full ownership over them, that they do not only own them as they do purchased goods: they also have the same right over the unfortunate children who are born to their marriages [. . .]. It is for this reason (that the *nègres* make the strength and wealth of their masters [. . .]) that our Frenchmen marry [their Black slaves] to each other as soon as they can: to acquire children who then replace their own fathers, doing the same work, and serving them in the same way.[63]

Even King Louis XIV recognized the possible economic benefits of hereditary slavery: in 1680, he complained of the lack of marriages among enslaved Blacks in the Caribbean, lamenting that such conduct "prevented [slave] women from becoming pregnant, thereby depriving him of the support that he could get from *nègres* who could be born in the country."[64] The French began to explicitly promote Christian marriages among enslaved people as early as the late seventeenth century, in order to increase enslaved labor forces and advance Christianity.[65] According to the Jesuit missionary Jean Mongin, who spent time in Martinique and Saint-Christopher between 1676 and 1682, a few French slaveowners even went so far as to pay enslaved men from other plantations to breed with their enslaved women "in order to acquire the children who always belong to the master of the mother."[66] A similar practice was recorded on Isle Bourbon where, in 1704, a slaveowner gifted a twenty-year-old Black woman named Isabelle Moine to another slaveowner, in order to force her to copulate with a twenty-two-year-old enslaved Black man named Maximin, in exchange for "a little six-year-old *négresse*," as well as "the first two children to be born to said Black and *négresse*."[67]

By applying the Roman legal principle *partus sequitur ventrem* to the *mulâtres*, French authorities ensured that coerced sex and rape by freemen against enslaved women would further expand enslaved workforces. The number of *mulâtres* recorded in Guadeloupean censuses rose from 47 in 1671 to 282 in 1696. It reached 290 in Martinique by 1688.[68] Those numbers were admittedly small. However, planters in the seventeenth-century French Caribbean particularly valued enslaved *mulâtre* workers. Because of their mixed origin and creole upbringing, the *mulâtres* were typically assigned the most desirable positions within Caribbean enslaved communities, instead of being asked to do field work, which was considered especially demeaning. By the late seventeenth and early eighteenth centuries, several *mulâtres* in the Caribbean were trained as artisans, while others worked as domestic servants.[69] The *mulâtres* thus became a highly marketable commodity in the eyes of many slaveowners.

As is to be expected, Black women reacted to the commodification of their children with ineffable grief and despair. Since the 1940s, considerable research has been produced on instances of "gynecological revolt" by enslaved women in the Americas, who dared to defy sexual exploitation through infanticide and the use of herbal remedies as contraceptives or abortifacients.[70] In the French Caribbean, the missionary Labat lamented "the frequent abortions" performed by enslaved women when they became pregnant with mixed children. He described these women as "very skillful" in their use of herbal remedies to terminate their pregnancies without suffering medical complications.[71] He also accused their white abusers of encouraging them to do so.[72]

Recent work by Jennifer Morgan, Sasha Turner, Rhaisa Kameela Williams and others has also moved beyond historiographical narratives of resistance by approaching motherhood among enslaved women as a site of trauma—attributed to their inability to "convey kinship," or "to have family represent something other than the expansion of someone else's estate."[73] Black women in the French world were no strangers to this unbearable suffering. In the French Caribbean, Du Tertre even dedicated a special section of his book to the love that enslaved Blacks had for their children. He explained, "The *nègres* love their children with such intensity that [. . .] they can't bear the thought of seeing them being punished, or to hear them scream [. . .] I have never seen a slave as unable to control their anger as when the interest of their poor children is in question."[74]

French contemporaries in the Atlantic and Indian Ocean worlds sought to morally dissociate themselves from the sexual exploitation of the enslaved by spreading representations of Black women as extraordinarily resilient mothers. Much like British observers, they depicted those Black mothers as nonhumans who could not be descended from the biblical figure of Eve since they were not subject to the curse that made her feel the pain of childbirth. In order to make the commodification of mixed children more acceptable and to justify horrible postpartum treatment, French observers, like their British counterparts, described those Black women as extremely fertile mothers who were so unaffected by the difficulties of childbirth that they could go back to work immediately afterward.[75] Du Tertre described enslaved Black women as "naturally hugely fecund." He added: they "give birth with a lot of ease; most don't even need a midwife to help them do it." "They are so untouched by childbirth that I have seen some work right after for two or three hours in the cabin, as if nothing had happened."[76] Frenchmen in the Indian Ocean made very similar remarks regarding Black women. Here is what Carpeau du Saussay said about Madagascar: "It seems that the punishment imposed on Eve by God after her sin, in condemning her to give birth in pain, does not apply to women of this country; indeed, the easiness with which they give birth is unimaginable [. . .] a woman giving birth in the morning returns to her usual business in the afternoon, as if she had never been interrupted."[77] As opposed to what happened in the French Caribbean from the late seventeenth century, many of the mixed children born to white men and unfree Malagasy women in Madagascar and Isle Bourbon were free, since their mothers had been manumitted before they had married European men. Those mixed couples minted more colonists who came to play a vital role in the progress of the colonization of Isle Bourbon.

Assimilation and the Peopling of Imperial Margins

French officials instrumentalized the sexualities of free and manumitted women of non-European descent by assimilating mixed children born to their Catholic marriages with Frenchmen to "white" society in an attempt to populate the French settlements and outposts. This pattern of assimilation through Catholic unions occurred on multiple French imperial margins, including the Illinois Country, but also early Guadeloupe, Isle Bourbon, and French India. Assimilation in the Illinois Country was largely the result of consistent campaigns of Christianization, Frenchification and Catholic intermarriage that had begun in the first half of the seventeenth century in New France. French authorities had also promoted intermarriage between Frenchmen and Christianized women of South Asian descent on Isle Bourbon and in French India. By contrast, they had shifted their policy regarding Malagasy women when they prohibited relationships between Frenchmen and "women of the country" in Madagascar, starting in 1664. Intermarriage in the Caribbean was not supported by any official policy either, except, some may argue, for article IX of the

Code Noir of the Antilles of 1685, which condemned freemen fathering mixed children with their enslaved servants to pay a fine and have their concubine and mixed children confiscated, except if they were "to marry the aforementioned slave in the church."[78] Yet colonial officials often turned a blind eye to *inter*marriages when they were unendorsed by French authorities or even when some began to be prohibited from the 1660s. They also allowed some of the mixed descendants of Christian unions to be integrated into "white" society, no matter their (Malagasy, African, South Asian, or Native American) origin(s), well into the early eighteenth century.

The practice of assimilation was not limited to the French colonies: it was a common pattern across many other European colonies and outposts, from the Spanish Americas to Dutch Batavia.[79] An official form of whiteness grounded in wealth, instead of being inscribed in skin color, was made accessible to people of non-European descent in the Spanish Americas as early as the sixteenth century.[80] By the 1770s, children born to Portuguese men and Christian Asian women in Portuguese India were officially granted white status, too, in accordance with an earlier order that had declared the "Christians of Portuguese India [to be] equal in every respect to the Portuguese."[81] Similar assimilationist practices were recorded more sporadically in the English-speaking world. By 1707, several people of non-European descent in Jamaica were able to claim white status at colonial assemblies. People of African ancestries were able to claim "white" status in Barbados, as well, after four generations of intermingling with Europeans.[82]

The most important step toward assimilation in the French context was the formation of Catholic unions between white men and freeborn or manumitted women of non-European descent, whose Catholic mixed offspring were then integrated into the settlers' class. French authorities in the Caribbean initially turned a blind eye to the practice of assimilation partly because they needed whites to control growing enslaved workforces and defend the colonies against enemy threats.[83] Recounting the history of this practice in 1842, the French abolitionist and politician Victor Schoelcher explained, "When we ask the reasons for this [. . .], they retort that we probably needed white people at the time!"[84] Frenchmen in the early period of colonization in the Caribbean were especially likely to seek out relationships with non-European women, since there were very few female European colonists on the islands. By 1686, there were more than two white men per white woman of marriageable age in Guadeloupe (1,899 men for 788 women), and some of these women were already married.[85]

Few European men in Guadeloupe ended up marrying Indigenous women because contact with the Kalinago was limited. As early as 1636, authorities in Guadeloupe implemented a segregation policy, confining the Kalinago to an area in the Southeast of the island, which was labeled "the home of the *sauvages*."[86] By 1671, only fifty-one Indigenous people (categorized as *sauvages*) were recorded in the census of Guadeloupe because many had died of Old World diseases or been removed from the island in the aftermath of the Franco-Carib Wars (1654–1660).[87] With the rapid decline of the Kalinago population, only a few Frenchmen married Indigenous women in the Catholic Church. Among them was Charles des Champs, a man established in the southern parish of Capesterre. He married Susanes Belamée, a woman categorized as a *sauvagesse,* with whom he had twin boys who were baptized in 1648.[88]

Other French men and women in Guadeloupe married people of African ancestry. Some of these unions were between white women and men of African descent. Here is what Du Tertre noted in 1667: "There are many [. . .] *mulâtres* on the islands, who are free; I have seen some of them, who have married French women. This disorder was more common in the past than it is today: but at the beginning of the establishment of the colonies, it was dreadful and almost without remedy."[89] The first census of Guadeloupe, taken in 1664, listed Manuel Vaze, a thirty-five-year-old "free *nègre,*" married to a (presumably white) "Marie Blanche," with whom he lived in Capesterre.[90] But most intermarriages in Guadeloupe were between white men and women of non-European descent, owing to the challenges posed to both gender and racial hierarchies by alliances between white women and men of African descent and because men outnumbered women in the French population.[91] In 1669, governor of Guadeloupe Claude-François Du Lyon wrote that "there [were] many more men and boys than girls of marriageable age, which is why [. . .] some masters have married their *négresses*."[92] For example, the census of 1671 listed Mathieu Pasquet, a white slaveowner married to a Black woman named Marie, with whom he had a *mulâtre* son. That year, another white man named Florent Commère was married to a Black woman named Luce Sarisse, who came from the parish of Goyave, in the East of Basse-Terre. One Jacques Cramilly was married to a Black woman named Suzanne in Grande-Terre.[93] Some of the white men who married women of African descent in Guadeloupe came from the upper strata of French society. For example, Jacques Valette, a Frenchman listed as a "Cabin Master, Bourgeois and Merchant" in the Guadeloupean census of 1671, had married a woman named Marie Mamachou, categorized as a *négresse* and a "domestic servant."[94] Another Frenchman named Sieur Antoine Lietard, described as a lieutenant in the militia of Pointe-Noire (on the western shore of the island), married a Black woman named Barbe in 1673.[95] The missionary Labat described Barbe Lietard as "a very beautiful *négresse*" and her mixed children as "handsome little *mulâtres*."[96]

While Labat's comments seem rather supportive, by the late seventeenth century, many local colonists looked unfavorably on those mixed alliances. According to the parish registers of Pointe-Noire, no banns were published to announce the marriage between Antoine and Barbe, "for very grave reasons."[97] Authorities in Guadeloupe had already expressed their objection to such alliances six years before Antoine had married Barbe. In 1667, a Flemish settler named Jacob Michel had been taken to the court of the Council of Guadeloupe by relatives who wanted to exclude his Black wife, Marie Läcotti, from a family inheritance. Strikingly, the council had agreed to annul this marriage, invoking "the shame [*la honte*] on the family"—we will see later how this notion of familial shame was brought up again several times across the empire.[98] This sentiment of shame arose as settlers in the Caribbean increasingly relied on enslaved Africans, causing Black identity to become increasingly associated with the debased status of the enslaved. The Council of Guadeloupe had also issued an edict after the trial, which in the end was never ratified by the crown, that prohibited clergymen from officiating weddings "between a white man and a Black woman, and a white woman and a Black man" without the approval of the governor or the commander of the island.[99]

But despite growing opposition to intermarriages, some of the *mulâtres* born to mixed Catholic unions in the French Lesser Antilles were assimilated into the "white" population of the islands. This practice was apparently less frequent in Martinique than it was in Guadeloupe, for several possible reasons. The first of these is that Black plantation slavery was more developed in Martinique than in Guadeloupe: there were 11,476 enslaved people in Martinique in 1688, compared to 5,347 in Guadeloupe in 1687.[100] Martinique may have exhibited heightened prejudice as a result, with colonists on that island being more committed to protect the slave system.

Importantly, colonists in Guadeloupe experienced less oversight from metropolitan authorities than their counterparts in Martinique owing to the island's isolation: beginning in the 1660s, the port of Saint-Pierre in Martinique exercised a monopoly that prevented direct exchanges between France and Guadeloupe.[101] According to historian Jessica Pierre-Louis's study of the parish registers of Fort-Royal, Lamentin, Marin, Rivière-Pilote, La Trinité, Sainte-Marie, and Le Prêcheur, the number of people of African descent who were assimilated into white society in Martinique grew from thirteen in the period between 1674 and 1683 to fifty-two in the period between 1714 and 1723.[102] A higher proportion of people of African descent might have been able to cross the color line in Guadeloupe: this is suggested by Frédéric Régent's study of the story of the 1,400 members of the Caniquit family, who were all descended from two Black women named Marguerite Maignan and Isabelle Galande and from a Brazilian man named François Caniquit. Because all the female descendants of the Caniquit family married white men, only one was classified as a *mulâtre* in parish registers.[103] According to Régent, the process of assimilation that took place in the seventeenth century played a significant role in the formation of the (pseudo) "white" planter class of Guadeloupe.[104]

But of all French colonies, Isle Bourbon was probably the one where the practice of assimilation was the most widespread. To trace the history of assimilation on Isle Bourbon, we must first go back in time and return to Madagascar for a moment. Since the 1640s, many Frenchmen in Anosy had married local women in both *vodin'omby* ceremonies *à la mode du pays* and the Catholic Church, often after establishing a farm with them in the countryside of Anosy.[105] While some of these unions, between Frenchmen and *roandria* women, were intended to seal or strengthen diplomatic and commercial alliances with *grands du pays*, others were to enslaved captives captured in raids since the 1630s. Many of these mixed marriages to manumitted captives started off as relationships of concubinage.[106] Johannes Swarts, a traveler from Batavia, noted sarcastically in 1661 that every French colonist in Madagascar "openly [kept] a concubine in his house to serve him, like a nobleman [served] by a slave."[107] Because unfree and free Malagasy women in those relationships with European men in Anosy faced sexual coercion and abuse, the French Company of the East Indies resolved to take measures to protect them: article III of the "Statutes, Ordinances, and Regulations" issued by this company in 1664 prohibited Frenchmen from raping and mistreating local women in Madagascar. It explicitly declared, "Whoever takes a woman or girl by force will be punished."[108] Although this ordinance did not target enslaved women specifically, article XIII of the same document did enjoin Frenchmen to treat enslaved servants "humanely without molesting or outraging them, under pain of corporal punishment."[109]

Because no parish registers have survived, the precise number of Catholic intermarriages officiated between manumitted or freeborn women and Frenchmen in seventeenth-century Madagascar cannot be assessed, nor can the number of mixed children born from them. Over two dozen French–Malagasy Catholic intermarriages are documented, however, and dozens more probably took place.[110] As early as 1648, the missionary Nacquart reported that some of the Malagasy women who had been baptized in Anosy had been married to Frenchmen.[111] Then, in 1656, the missionary Bourdaise officiated the marriages of ten Frenchmen (and one English Catholic convert) to Malagasy women.[112] Over a decade later, Sieur Du Bois noted the presence of 250 Frenchmen in Madagascar, who "for the most part [had] married women from this island," although probably not all of those marriages were Catholic.[113] Most Catholic marriages celebrated in Madagascar were between a Frenchman and a Malagasy woman who were already married in the manner of the country, or already living in concubinage.

The Tanosy tradition of intermarriage was subsequently transported to Isle Bourbon by the French–Malagasy couples and other evacuees who began settling on the island from 1663, helping authorities to remedy the lack of European settlers in the colony. Reflecting on the history of Isle Bourbon in 1717, the French traveler Guy Le Gentil de La Barbinais recounted how some of the mixed couples on the island had come from Madagascar, fleeing the French outpost of Fort-Dauphin after the anticolonial revolt of 1674. A group of European pirates had also settled on Isle Bourbon, where, in his own words, "they [had] married Black women out of necessity."[114] European sailors had then married the mixed girls born to those earlier alliances. La Barbinais claimed that these mixed girls were "neither Black nor white, but rather had something of both colors."[115] By 1690, an astounding 70 percent of all free couples recorded in the census of Isle Bourbon consisted of a European man and a woman of non-European descent (twenty-eight couples). Of these European men, 39 percent had married Christian Luso-Indian women (categorized as *métis des Indes* or *Indo-Portugaises*), 32 percent had married Malagasies, and 21 percent had married mixed women of Malagasy, South Asian, or other non-European ancestries born on Isle Bourbon (labeled *métis* or *mulâtresses*).[116] Most of these mixed unions were celebrated in the Catholic Church because those women had been converted by European missionaries in India, in Madagascar, or on the island itself. Many manumitted women of Malagasy, South Asian, and African descent on Isle Bourbon also married Frenchmen in the Catholic Church after they were baptized by the Lazarist priests.[117]

This is how mixed children born to Catholic unions between Frenchmen and women of non-European ancestries came to form the bulk of Isle Bourbon's free settler society through the late seventeenth century and into the beginning of the eighteenth. Among the dozens of evacuees from Madagascar, there were already at least four mixed French–Malagasy children (categorized as *métis*).[118] Sieur L'Huillier even claimed (by mistake) that "the first people who [settled] on [Isle Bourbon] were [mixed French–Malagasy] *métis* who had found refuge [on the island] after they had been expelled from Madagascar," following the anti-colonial revolt of 1673.[119] Among these immigrants, Malagasy women married to European men had at least 97 children (amounting to 37 percent of the first generation of settlers born on Isle Bourbon). Meanwhile, Luso-Indian women had 109 children (42 percent), and Frenchwomen had only 55 (21 percent).[120] The number of mixed people on Isle Bourbon (initially labeled interchangeably as *mulâtres* or *métis*) grew from only 3 people in 1667 (4 percent of the population) to 106 in 1686 (30 percent).[121] Most of these *métis* or *mulâtres* were of mixed French–Malagasy and Eurasian ancestries.

French metropolitan authorities rapidly began to look unfavorably on these mixed alliances. Many colonial officials on the island clearly supported intermarriages, since they engaged in them. Remember the story of the Six Seniors of the parish of Saint-Paul who ruled over the island from 1692 to 1696: half of them—Touchard, Carron, and Payet—had married women of Malagasy or Luso-Indian ancestries. Yet, from the 1670s, metropolitan authorities began to issue the very first consistent series of intermarriage bans of the French empire, for Isle Bourbon. Ten years after the Company of the East Indies had expressed its intent to prevent mixed relationships between Frenchmen and Malagasy women in Madagascar, in 1674, while visiting Isle Bourbon, the viceroy of the

East Indies, Jacob Blanquet de La Haye, issued an ordinance whose article XX stated, "We forbid Frenchmen from marrying *négresses* [. . .] and we forbid Black men [*Noirs*] from marrying white women [*Blanches*]."[122] This ban clearly targeted unions between Frenchmen and Malagasy or South Asian women since the labels "*négres*[*ses*]" and "Black" were commonly employed to designate free and unfree people of South Asian and Malagasy ancestries on the island at the time.[123] Metropolitan authorities thereafter repeated on multiple occasions La Haye's intermarriage prohibition of 1674 for Isle Bourbon, first under governor Sieur de Vauboulon in 1689 and then under his successor, Sieur de Villiers, in 1701 and yet again in 1709.[124]

How can we explain this decision by metropolitan officials to prohibit intermarriage on Isle Bourbon? When they made their decision to ban intermarriage, metropolitan authorities might have been influenced by ideas from other European colonies and outposts in the Atlantic and Indian Ocean worlds. To better understand La Haye's decision to issue the original intermarriage ban of 1674, we must look at his prior travel experiences. When visiting the French outpost of Fort-Dauphin while on his way to India in 1671, La Haye might have heard about the local ban of 1664, which prohibited Frenchmen from "giving themselves away" to "women of the country." Then, when he finally reached India in 1672, La Haye traveled to Portuguese Daman, San-Thomé, and Goa, where he also witnessed growing opposition to intermarriage, in this context between the Portuguese and South Asian women.[125] When issuing the intermarriage bans of Isle Bourbon, French officials might have also been influenced by ideas from the Atlantic world. In fact, the rhetoric employed by French authorities to justify the issuance of the intermarriage ban on Isle Bourbon in 1709 echoed the language of "shame" already used by the Council of Guadeloupe decades earlier: its authors described intermarriages between whites and Blacks on Isle Bourbon as "indecent and shameful [*ignominieux*]."[126]

But the series of intermarriage bans issued for Isle Bourbon from the 1670s was, above all else, a response to local circumstances. These bans were clearly intended to protect the emerging bonded labor system on the island, since article XX of La Haye's ordinance explicitly stated that mixed marriages would "divert Blacks from [their] duties."[127] Colonists on Isle Bourbon initially engaged in subsistence agriculture to become self-sufficient and supply fresh food to passing ships en route to Asia.[128] Because they relied on a bonded workforce, bonded laborers on Isle Bourbon already amounted to 45 percent of the population by 1674.[129] Preventing intermarriage in this context thus seemed necessary to avoid manumissions and protect the local economy.

Despite prohibitions, however, the tradition of *métissage* on Isle Bourbon remained alive and well throughout the early eighteenth century. The number of mixed couples on early eighteenth-century Isle Bourbon cannot be evaluated with precision, though, because census makers in 1704 and 1705 began to group all island-born free men, women and children under the undifferentiated categories "creoles of the island" (*créoles de l'isle*) and "from Mascarin island" (or *de Mascarin*, which was the other name given to Isle Bourbon).[130] Only four French married couples were recorded in 1705, amounting to just 5 percent of all free households on the island. Eight free mixed white-Malagasy married couples were also recorded that year (amounting to 10 percent of all free households), as well as five free white-Luso-Indian married couples (6 percent). It is reasonable to assume that many of the free men and women categorized as "creoles of the island" or "from Mascarin island" by the early eighteenth century had origins in Madagascar and South Asia, since most were born to earlier mixed unions. Therefore, as many as sixty other free married couples in 1705 might have been mixed or nonwhite (78 percent).[131]

The story of the Fontaine family illustrates how *métissage* became entrenched in the local tradition of Isle Bourbon. The French carpenter Jacques Fontaine married Marie Anne Sannes "from the Matataña [province], on the Island of [. . .] Madagascar," in 1671.[132] Together the couple had five children, whom Boucher labeled "creole *mulâtres*" in 1710.[133] Hervé, their fifth son, married Thérèse Damour—the daughter of Georges Damour from Paris and Marie Toute from Madagascar—in 1696. Marie Anne Sannes and Marie Toute were close friends, which probably brought the two families together. In 1698, Jacques and Marie's third child, Jacques Fontaine Jr., married the daughter of a Frenchman and a Malagasy woman. Their second child, Marie Anne Jr., married a Frenchman named Jacques Lauret a year later and had three children with him.[134] The Fontaine family ended up building kinship networks that extended far beyond Isle Bourbon: in 1702, Jeanne, another of Marie Anne and Jacques's children, married a white sailor named Eustache Le Roy from the Caribbean island of Martinique.[135]

Mixed French–Malagasy and French–Luso-Indian children born to early intermarriages were assimilated into the "white" population of Isle Bourbon, eventually forming the bulk of the island's "white" planter class, which by the 1720s played a key role in France's colonial coffee economy.[136] These mixed children probably amounted to a majority of the free population of Isle Bourbon by the 1710s: in a random sample of 201 free adults studied by historian Nathan Marvin, as much as 52 percent had at least one parent of Malagasy or Asian ancestry by 1711.[137] The assimilation of these *mulâtres* into the "white" population of the island was progressive, as reflected by the evolution of the lexicon used in local censuses to describe them. Until the 1690s, local census makers employed racial labels to classify free people on the island—such as "white woman" (*femme blanche*), "*négresse* woman from Madagascar" (*femme negresse de Madagascar*), "*métis* woman from the East Indies" (*femme des indes mestice*), or "*négresse* woman from the East Indies" (*femmes des indes negresse*).[138] Those racial labels began to fade around 1704 and 1705, when local census makers began to use the labels "creoles of the island" and "from Mascarin island."[139] Then, finally, the census of 1713 lumped together all white Europeans and white creoles with free creole people of Malagasy and Luso-Indian descent under the label "white males and females" (*Blancs mâles et femelles*).[140]

French officials' practice of assimilating populations of Eurasian descent into the "white" category was not limited to Isle Bourbon: Eurasian people were also classified as "whites" in the censuses of French India, as a result of an attempt by local officials to populate their commercial outposts with white-passing residents.[141] With the near-absence of European women, Frenchmen in the remote South Asian outposts were especially inclined to associate with local women: this applied to men from all strata of society, from soldiers and gunners to high-ranking officials.[142] Many of these women were Luso-Indians, while some were Indian Hindus (labeled as *Gentils*), Muslims, and *topas*—the *topas* formed a community of Indians who had been Christianized and exposed to European cultural practices during the earlier period of Portuguese presence.[143] While some were economically comfortable, most came from the lower strata of society: in 1702, Louis-Estienne de Pilavoine, the director-general of the company, told company officials that "those of your employees who die in the [East] Indies are typically married to a woman of the country, who is often of low birth."[144] Marriage, even to a low-ranking Frenchman, could bring some economic benefits to an Indian or Luso-Indian woman and to her family. Such was especially the case when the man died because widows in French India were entitled to a pension that was paid to them by the company.[145]

Many mixed marriages took place in the French outposts of India. Around 1690, the French traveler Robert Challe noted that most of the 200 Frenchmen who resided in Pondicherry had married "Indian women or Portuguese girls, who are not Black, but rather *métis* or *mulâtre*."[146] In 1693, Pilavoine mentioned several company employees "with families in Surat."[147] Although parish registers from the outposts of French India do not usually state people's origins, it is reasonable to assume that many of the women with Portuguese names in these records had South Asian origins, since the populations labeled as "Portuguese" (*Portuguais[es]*) in India usually had mixed ancestries.[148] An official document from Pondicherry, dated 1716, presented most members of the so-called "Portuguese race" of India as "*mulâtre*s" (Eurasians).[149] According to officer Mathieu de Gennes de la Chancelière, who spent time in Bengal in the 1740s, the "Portuguese" were "mainly descended from the families of Portuguese *métis* (*or mulâtres*), widespread in Bengal."[150] Thus, as many as 89 percent of the marriages (93 out of 104) recorded in the parish registers of Pondicherry between 1687 and 1719 might have involved a European man and a woman of South Asian descent. Seven of these unions involved women labeled as *métis* or "creole" or women whose parents were labeled as *Gentils*. The rest involved women born in South Asia or Africa, with creole origins on Isle Bourbon—or who had a Portuguese name and/or at least one parent with a Portuguese name.[151] In the same Pondicherry registers, only seven unions can be identified with near certainty as involving two Europeans.[152] Because they were Christian, Europeanized and often comfortable financially, Luso-Indian women and their mixed children in Pondicherry and Chandernagore were either not assigned a racial label at all in official documents or lumped together with white Europeans under the "white" label. In fact, Luso-Indian people lived together with the French in the "white town" (*la ville blanche*) of Chandernagore.[153]

How did the process of assimilation work, exactly, across the French Indian Ocean and Atlantic positions? Multiple factors determined who could be assimilated into the "white" population. To start with, assimilated people had to be Catholic, married in the Catholic Church, Europeanized, and/or born to Catholic parents. According to historians Adrian Carton and Leonard Hodges, being "white" in Pondicherry and Chandernagore depended on one's style of dress and religious practice rather than skin color.[154] Similarly, the Bourbon Island Creoles of Malagasy and Luso-Indian ancestries were classified as "whites" because they were Catholic and embraced European fashion conventions, as well as other elements of French material culture, such as farming European crops with axes and spades, drinking wine, cooking in iron pots, or using European silverware.[155] But other factors also determined who could be considered "white," including social rank, wealth, profession, education, reputation, and social networks.[156] In fact, social status was probably the most important criteria for assimilation.[157] In 1804 and 1805, looking back at the history of Guadeloupe, a Frenchman stressed the importance of reputation. He claimed, "There are some whose African origin did not even go back three generations when they were incorporated into the white class! The virtues of these families made them deserve to pass into the superior class."[158] This same Frenchman emphasized the importance of social connections as well: "protections also brought this surprising privilege," he claimed.[159]

Phenotype—especially white-looking skin acquired through generations of intermixing with white people—also allowed many to integrate into the "white" category. By the late seventeenth century, French observers began to notice the presence overseas of several communities of non-European ancestries able to blend into the white population because they had literally become "whitened" by successive generations of intermixing with white Europeans. This rhetoric had already surfaced in the Indian Ocean by the 1690s. One of the Frenchmen who articulated this idea of skin "whitening" through *métissage* was Robert Challe—a French globetrotter who spent time in New France before traveling to Pondicherry in the 1690s and spent time in the Antilles while on his way back to France. Like several French observers after him, Challe recounted with both fascination and contentment his encounter with one of those "whitened" populations. In 1690, he reflected on the impact that mixed alliances had on the skin color of Eurasian children. He claimed that the children of Luso-Indian women and Frenchmen in Pondicherry were "light-haired, and with a skin color *as white as that of the finest Europeans.*"[160] The French traveler Guy Le Gentil de La Barbinais reached a similar conclusion while spending time on Isle Bourbon, suggesting that this kind of rhetorical gesture was probably not uncommon in the Indian Ocean. He explained in 1717 that, through sustained association with white men over generations, mixed Bourbon Island

Creole women "purif[ied their] blood" and "their complexion "bec[ame] whiter step by step," to the point that three generations later, the child was "blond-haired, and as fair-skinned as an Englishwoman"—a visual experience which in his own word "made him feel admiration."[161]

By the end of the seventeenth and early eighteenth centuries, French observers in the Americas drew on this same "whitening" rhetoric that had emerged in the Indian Ocean by 1690. Only five years after Robert Challe had noted the presence of Eurasian people with a skin "*as white as that of the finest Europeans,*" the missionary Labat had reached a similar conclusion concerning the children born to Caribbean *mulâtres.*[162] He claimed, "If we marry male or female *mulâtres* to white people, *their children will become whiter* [. . .]. A color becomes stronger step by step, by merging with a color of the same species."[163] A few years later, after spending time on Isle Bourbon between 1698 and 1702, Henri Roulleaux Sieur de La Vente, the vicar-general of Louisiana and one of the most fervent proponents of Native American–French intermarriage, also invoked the skin "whitening" effect that intermarriages could have on mixed children.[164] Here is what he wrote about Illinois converts to Christianity in 1708, perhaps after hearing similar language used with respect to Bourbon Island Creole people while he was sojourning in the Indian Ocean: "We do not see that the blood of the *sauvages* will have any prejudicial effect on the blood of the French. As we see, the whiteness of the children of French men married with the *sauvagesses* is equal to that of the French themselves."[165] It should be noted that not everybody agreed with La Vente that the process of amalgamation through skin whitening could ever be complete. Back in the Indian Ocean, La Barbinais felt compelled to specify that the women who had become "blond-haired" and "as fair-skinned as Englishwom[e]n" on Isle Bourbon "though they had changed their [skin] color, never lost a certain smell (which may be called *fumet* [game meat smell], which betrays their origin."[166]

Women's Role as Christian Leaders Advancing Evangelization

In addition to enabling assimilation, Catholic intermarriage also advanced the French colonial enterprise by encouraging local female converts and their descendants to set a good example and become evangelizing leaders in their communities. Scholars have already brought to light the stories of several Illinois women who endeavored to evangelize their communities after they had married Frenchmen in Catholic ceremonies.[167] The story of Marie Rouensa, an Illinois woman who took it upon herself to Christianize both her family and her community in Kaskaskia after she married a French *voyageur* named Sieur Michel Accault in the Catholic Church, is well known.[168]

Several Christian women of non-European descent played a similar role in the Indian Ocean after they had married Frenchmen in the Catholic Church. This is illustrated by the story of Louise Payet, the French-Malagasy *mulâtresse* of Saint-Paul, Isle Bourbon, who educated several little girls from her neighborhood and also made a donation to Lazarist missionaries so that they could appoint two female schoolteachers who would instruct young women across the island. Recall also how Malagasy women had been encouraged to take on a key role in the French evangelizing project around the mid-seventeenth century, in the context of the French colonial enterprise in Anosy, Madagascar. As early as 1655, the missionary Bourdaise had praised several Malagasy female converts who had just been married to Frenchmen for their virtue and devotion to the Catholic faith, describing them as "a model for all other women to follow."[169] One year later, in the valley of Ambolo, Father Mousnier baptized three Malagasy women who had also married Frenchmen.[170] He rejoiced that these women had relinquished their old ways and were now "living righteously, setting an example for other Malagasy women."[171] Bourdaise hoped that the daughter of a village chief named Dian Ramouse would encourage members of her community to convert to Christianity. She had gotten married to a Frenchman described as "a very honest man, and especially a good Catholic."[172] At least one Malagasy woman did convince members of her community to convert. Bourdaise praised the *roandria* daughter of a *grand du pays* who had married a Frenchman named Balar for her wisdom and devotion to the Christian faith. Like Marie Rouensa, she had managed to convince her entire family to convert to Catholicism. She also frequently brought new converts to Bourdaise so they could be baptized.[173]

Mixed Christian marriages had another unforeseen positive effect on the progress of the religious missions: they turned insubordinate Frenchmen into compliant Christians. Catholic intermarriage in the Illinois Country famously encouraged unruly French itinerant *coureurs de bois* and *voyageurs* to become devout Christians, settle down, and cultivate the land.[174] The story of Accault, Marie Rouensa's French husband, who was "famous in [the] Illinois Country [for all his debaucheries]," is well known. Accault was transformed by his marriage to the devout Marie Rouensa: he purchased half of the Illinois concession, stopped traveling, and embraced a righteous Christian lifestyle.[175] His story echoes that of another Frenchman who lived in Madagascar in the second half of the seventeenth century, whom Bourdaise described as a drunken scoundrel "ruder and more barbaric than [Malagasy] islanders." He portrayed his Malagasy wife as "the strongest woman that God made [him] find in this corner of the world." Although she was brutally battered by her French husband, this woman still took good care of him when he fell sick, eventually nursing him back to health. Bourdaise claimed that this woman "touched the heart of this barbarous Frenchman [. . .] who [began to] love her deeply and [. . .] abandoned his debaucheries." He described this Frenchman as "an unbeliever [who had been] sanctified by his devout wife."[176]

What led those Malagasy women to embrace Christianity and to marry Frenchmen? Imbalanced sex ratios caused by endemic male-led warfare in Anosy might have been an important factor. Some might have also wanted to stay away from the difficult realities of polygamous life. According to Flacourt, women within the same polygamous household in Anosy called each other *mapirase,* which meant "enemy," because these "wives who share only one man hate[d] each other to death."[177] Many were also looking for security, food, foreign goods and connections for themselves and their kinspeople.[178] Conversion to Catholicism and marriage to a European man also allowed a few to garner influence in their patriarchal communities as evangelizing agents but also as diplomatic intermediaries. Some, on the other hand, were pressured into marrying Frenchmen by members of their communities because they were eager to form advantageous military and commercial alliances with the Europeans.

Métissage and Alliance Formation

As was the case in North America, Frenchmen in Anosy and the Senegambian coastline utilized intermarriage to multiply alliances with powerful locals.[179] Catholic marriage and marriages *à la mode du pays* with *roandria* women helped the French form vital diplomatic and military alliances with several kings and chiefs in Anosy. Marriages in the manner of the country in Anosy were almost certainly more widespread than Catholic unions, partly because of the lack of missionaries on the island. This would explain why, in 1656, the missionary Bourdaise rejoiced that Malagasy women on the island were finally asking to be "properly married, like the [wives] of the French."[180]

Accounts of wedding ceremonies *à la mode du pays* in seventeenth-century Madagascar vary. Flacourt mentioned a blessing said by an *ombiassa,* after which the newlyweds would tie their hair together while holding hands and press against one another's knees.[181] The marriage was sealed with the sacrifice of an ox or a sheep, intended as a gift to the ancestors to attain their blessing. Then the blood of the sacrificed animal was mixed with red coal to form a paste (*aringelo* or *arimbelona*), which was applied to the faces of the newly wedded couple. The best part of the sacrificed animal's meat (*vodin'omby* for cow's rears and *vodiondry* for sheep's rears) was offered to the wife's family.[182] The ceremony was followed by a feast and a dance.[183]

Several *roandria* explicitly supported marriages between women in their communities and Frenchmen. Despite the fact that they favored endogamy, they sometimes let *tha-vinany* intermarriages ("across the lagoon") take place in order to find new allies who were obligated to give them food, livestock and military support after being integrated into their family.[184] The *roandria* had very high expectations from their kinfolk indeed. After they married a *roandria* woman, Frenchmen were expected to feed their new relatives and share with them a portion of the livestock that they captured in raids.[185] This is illustrated by the story of Governor Jacques Pronis. Pronis married the *roandria* princess Dian Ravellom Manor, the niece of the king of Anosy, in a ceremony "following Malagasy precepts" in 1643.[186] His subsequent decision to support his new *roandria* relatives occasioned a major mutiny in Fort-Dauphin: in 1646, a group of hungry French soldiers threw the governor in prison for having used the company's meager food supplies to feed his new kinfolk.[187]

On the other hand, marriage to a *roandria* woman also allowed the French to strengthen their military power and be given new land. Remember how, after marrying the daughter of King Rassisate, the French soldier La Case became the king of the valley of Ambolo and acquired an army of 10,000 Malagasy warriors, which he used to defend and feed the French at Fort-Dauphin. La Case was not the only Frenchman positioned to inherit a local kingdom as a result of marrying into a local royal lineage. After marrying Dian Ravellom Manor, Jacques Pronis joined the line of possible heirs to the entire kingdom of Anosy and was given the new name Ra[/]jac (which meant *grand Jac*) by his new people. Pronis's brother-in-law, another pretender to the throne named Dian Tsissei, even attempted to murder the man in order to improve his chances: he plotted an attack on Fort-Dauphin that was eventually thwarted in 1648.[188]

Like their counterparts in the early eighteenth-century Illinois Country, many of the Frenchmen who formed alliances with local women in Anosy acquired a plot of land that they could cultivate.[189] The French administrator Sieur Du Bois counted hundreds of Frenchmen in Madagascar who had acquired agricultural estates after marrying local women.[190] It was customary for the future husband in a marriage *à la mode du pays* to pay a dowry to the wife's family, which usually consisted of livestock, jewelry, furniture and other valuables. The groom would traditionally receive a dowry from his wife's family, too, that could include livestock and household goods.[191] He would also be granted privileges and land by the chief of his wife's village. Remember when governor Flacourt reported that the masters of the villages offered to French grooms the opportunity to cultivate their land.[192]

Local wives and consorts in Anosy acted as diplomatic intermediaries between their communities and the French at Fort-Dauphin.[193] Such was the case of queen Dian Nong after she had married La Case, the legendary French soldier who became king of the valley of Ambolo. She came to the fort bearing gifts as a testimony to the continued friendship between the French and the people of Ambolo.[194] In 1671, another Malagasy woman, who was married to a French lieutenant named Thomaspin, was sent as an emissary to negotiate an important peace deal with a *grand du pays* from southern Madagascar named Rafelle, who had plundered the French outpost at Fort-Dauphin and kidnapped a Frenchman.[195] Other local women alerted French authorities at the fort of impending enemy attacks.[196] In fact, it was Pronis's own spouse, Dian Ravellom Manor, who had allowed the French to thwart the 1648 attack of the other pretender to the throne of Anosy, Dian Tsissei, by sounding the alarm.[197] That same year, Dian Ravellom's own nursing mother also alerted the French at Fort-Dauphin of an impending attack by king Dian Ramach after he had turned against them.[198]

In addition to helping them protect their fragile position on the Tolagñare peninsula, intermarriage and relationships of concubinage enabled the French in Anosy to advance their commercial and wider economic interests. Those who married high-ranking *roandria* women in Catholic and *vodin'omby* ceremonies *à la mode du pays* gained membership in both a local clan and trading networks.[199] Those who farmed the land across the countryside of Anosy often formed business partnerships with their Malagasy wives and consorts, managing the land, livestock, and human captives together with them and using their own houses to store their farm products before they could be sold.[200] The women drew on their own connections to find buyers, selling the farm's products on their husbands' behalf.[201] According to a French settler named Degrandmaison, by 1670, individual Frenchmen effectively controlled the French trade in Madagascar because they—unlike the Company of the East Indies—had intimate access to "Blacks" able to find outlets for their merchandise.[202]

Intermarriage *à la mode du pays*, along with casual sex, played a similar role on the islands and in the coastal areas of Senegambia. French authorities repeatedly complained of high-ranking company agents and ordinary employees in the region who broke the company's monopoly by trading with African and Eurafrican women. Looking back at the history of Saint-Louis while on his mission to Senegambia in 1758, the French botanist Michel Adanson explained that, in the past, "these women [. . .] traded on behalf of the employees with whom they partnered, at the expense of the company, and they obtained [. . .] fine and precious merchandise from the director or commandant [. . .]."[203] The evidence suggests that some European men had sex with some of these African and Eurafrican merchants. When he met several women from coastal villages in the company's store in 1685, La Courbe claimed that "there are many of them who, on the pretext that they come to sell merchandise, debauch our white men to get merchandise in return."[204] He eventually resolved to expel these women from Fort Saint-Louis in 1686 in an attempt to prevent French company employees from having sex with them.[205] Some of the relationships between Frenchmen and female merchants were in all appearances formed in the context of the *folgars*. An adventurer named Sieur Mathelot accused Frenchmen in Senegambia of wasting "the most beautiful and precious merchandise of the company to please and satisfy the luxurious aspirations of those indecent women" during festivities.[206] A few of the female merchants who formed relationships with French company agents and employees in Senegambia were high ranking. For example, La Courbe described Senhora Belinguere, the merchant princess who hosted him in Albreda in 1685, as a "famous *courtesan* of this country [. . .] beautiful, tall, and with a nice body, although a little old."[207]

Casual sex, along with the regularity of divorce and remarriage in marriages *à la mode du pays* with local women, must have played a critical role in sustaining colonial trade in both Senegambia and Anosy.[208] Back in Madagascar, Carpeau du Saussay noted that "polygamy, which is in use among many populations, is also practiced among [Malagasies]."[209] Sieur Du Bois also specified that "men [in Madagascar] ha[d] as many women as they want[ed] as long as they ha[d] the means to feed them."[210] French observers also commented on the reversibility of marriage in Anosy: as Carpeau du Saussay explained, "Men and women [were] allowed to remarry whenever they want[ed]." In an attempt to satisfy his readers' craving for sensationalism, he added that "many use[d] this freedom to change wives almost every day."[211] According to Sieur Dellon, "[Malagasies] accept[ed] each other without demanding reciprocal promises, and they le[ft] each other whenever they want[ed] to" as well.[212] Sieur Du Bois agreed that "men [were] allowed to leave their wives when they want[ed], and women c[ould] leave their husbands [. . .]." He explained that "they live[d] together as long as they like[d] each other, otherwise they le[ft] each other and [found] someone else."[213]

Although many people in early modern Christian Europe would have disapproved of divorce and polygamy, many Frenchmen in Anosy embraced those practices out of personal preference—and probably out of economic self-interest as well. In 1642, so many Frenchmen had already separated from their spouses in Anosy that Governor Flacourt was forced to stipulate in letters patent that "a Frenchman married to a girl or woman from the island shall not leave or abandon his wife under any circumstances."[214] Unaware of the existence of this ban, the missionary Bourdaise wrote a letter to his superiors in 1655, explaining that "we need a law here, among the French and the *nègres,* compelling men to only have one woman, and to stay with her."[215] Neither Flacourt's letters patent nor Bourdaise's complaint succeeded in convincing the French in Anosy to abstain from polygamous practices. By 1664, the French Lazarist missionary Nicolas Étienne literally complained of the numerous Frenchmen on the island who were in the habit of "maintain[ing] several wives."[216]

Divorce and remarriage were common practices in Senegambia as well, allowing Frenchmen to form alliances with local African and Eurafrican merchants and businesswomen. Most of the Frenchmen who married local African and Eurafrican women in Saint-Louis did so through Lebu and Wolof ceremonies *à la mode du pays.*[217] Intermarriage between local women and European men was hardly new in the region: African women had begun to marry Portuguese traders on the west coast of Africa beginning in the late fifteenth century.[218] Jean Barbot, a French Huguenot who spent time in West Africa in the 1670s and 1680s, explained that marriages *à la mode du pays* were "not unbreakable [. . .] but rather [lasted] as long as the parties ha[d] no reason to complain about each other, or until they [were] separated forever."[219] The French medical doctor and explorer René-Claude Geoffroy de Villeneuve, who traveled to Senegambia in the 1780s, also explained that free African and Eurafrican women "freely contract a type of limited marriage with Europeans, regarding themselves as legitimate wives [. . .]. The departure of the white [man] to Europe, with no expectation of returning, breaks the ties of matrimony, and [the woman] soon after enters a new contract."[220] Those unions could be advantageous for local African and Eurafrican women if the Frenchman had access to European merchandise. They were especially advantageous for Frenchmen when the woman had access to inland connections that could allow her to secure trading opportunities across Wolof, Lebu, and Pulaar circles.[221]

Although those mixed relationships turned out to be crucial to the commercial exploitation of the French outposts in Senegambia, French authorities had divided opinions about them. Several French officials clearly approved, since they were willing partners in such unions. Sieur Mathelot noted in 1687 that French "*superiors,* residents and sailors [in Senegambia], freely formed relationships with the *négresses,* and for all to see, as if they were their legitimate wives."[222] Yet other French officials loudly disapproved. Because these interactions facilitated illicit trading exchanges, the Royal Company of Senegal took measures to prevent them in an ordinance issued in January 1688. Articles III and IV of this ordinance prohibited Frenchmen in Senegambia from "support[ing] any *négresses*, go[ing] to their cabins, or let[ting] them enter their own, under any circumstances [. . .] under penalty of paying a fine of six livres for each time" or "go[ing] to the villages of the *nègres* without orders from the commandant."[223] These regulations were clearly intended to prevent illicit trade between French employees and African women: their authors explicitly complained of "abuses and disorders sustained by [. . .] Directors, Captains, Clerks, Sailors, Soldiers and other employees, who only think about their own profit and will bring about *the ruin of [the company's] business*."[224]

* * *

Métissage helped the French lay the foundations of their early colonial empire overseas in many different ways. Some women engaged in sexual relationships with Frenchmen as powerful (though most of the time unwitting) agents themselves, while others faced brutal sexual exploitation, coercion and violence. The French began to exploit slave reproduction as early as the seventeenth century in the hope of improving their revenues. They established hereditary slavery and on occasion even engaged in brutal human breeding practices. Though mixed children born in slavery were relatively few in number, they were considered a particularly desirable commodity in the eyes of French colonists. *Métissage* also facilitated the populating of France's most remote overseas colonies and outposts. Well beyond the Illinois Country, French authorities endeavored to assimilate many freeborn and manumitted Christianized and Europeanized people of non-European descent into "white" society. This pattern of assimilation was most widespread on Isle Bourbon, though it also existed in places like French India and the early French Caribbean. Similarly, the practice of forming alliances with powerful locals through intermarriage or sex advanced empire building not only in North America but also in Anosy and Senegambia. From North America to Senegambia and Madagascar, many Frenchmen embraced local matrimonial practices, using intermarriage "in the manner of the country" to form vital alliances.

Despite the role it played in empire building, not all French officials viewed *métissage* positively. Biases against local women, along with public health preoccupations, led the French Company of the East Indies to issue a first order prohibiting mixed relationships in Madagascar in 1664. Then, as Black people's identity became associated with the debased status of the enslaved, the Council of Guadeloupe issued the unratified edict of 1667 that prohibited clergymen from officiating marriages "between a white man and a Black woman, and a white woman and a Black man." A few years after this, between 1674 and 1709, colonial officials on Isle Bourbon enacted a consistent series of intermarriage bans, citing concerns that such unions would "divert Blacks from [their] duties" and were "indecent and shameful." This series of bans was followed by the decision of the Royal Company of Senegal, in 1688, to prohibit Frenchmen from associating with African or Eurafrican women, in order to curb illicit trade. Opposition to intermarriages was also on the rise in North America by the early eighteenth century.[225] There were concerns that the Frenchmen who had married Native American women in ceremonies *à la façon du pays*, along with their mixed children, were becoming *ensauvagés* ("savage") by staying in Indigenous villages. At the same time, the Christian missions of New France were failing to deliver their expected outcomes. These factors, along with the staggering expansion of plantation slavery across the eighteenth-century French Atlantic and Indian Oceans, brought a very important shift in the content of imperial policy during the 1720s. This shift marked the end of the early era of French imperialism overseas, whose hallmark was the assimilation project, and ushered in a new era of stringent racial policing.

CHAPTER 4

Unifying Racial Policies

Henri Roulleaux de La Vente was ordained a priest in France around the year 1688. After joining the Paris Seminary of Foreign Missions, he went on his first overseas mission in 1698 to Isle Bourbon. For six years, he worked in Saint-Paul, Isle Bourbon, preaching and baptizing the children of the parish and serving his parishioners "beyond duty's call, manifesting unusual interest in their public as well as private affairs."[1] La Vente must have known everyone in Saint-Paul, since it was a very small parish, home to only fifty free adults by 1690. He certainly met many mixed couples, since eleven of the eighteen free couples living there in 1690 were French/Malagasy or French/Luso-Indian.[2] His mission on Isle Bourbon lasted at least until 1701.

In 1704, La Vente was sent on another mission, to the other side of the world—in Mobile, French Louisiana—where he was appointed vicar-general of the colony.[3] Soon after his arrival in the Mississippi valley, La Vente reportedly told missionaries to officiate "many marriages between Frenchmen and *sauvagesses,*" which angered Louisiana governor Jean-Baptiste Le Moyne de Bienville.[4] Then, in 1710, La Vente—who had become one of the most zealous proponents of intermarriage in Louisiana—tried to convince authorities to promote intermarriage between Catholic Native American women and Frenchmen as a means of turning the locals into "good Christians and good subjects of the king" who could populate the colony.[5] La Vente's endorsement of intermarriage could be attributed to his status as a missionary concerned with the rising incidence of relationships outside of Catholic wedlock in Louisiana. But it is also likely that he was drawing upon his experience on Isle Bourbon, where Catholic intermarriage had allowed the French to populate the island with many Christian colonists.[6] Nearly half of La Vente's free parishioners in Saint-Paul (52 out of 121 in

1690) had been mixed-race people born to parents who were married in the Catholic Church.[7]

As a result of his proposition to promote intermarriage, La Vente became involved in a policy debate that lasted until 1716. This debate pitted him against two other colonial officials who opposed such unions: the *commissaires-ordonnateurs* Jean-Baptiste-Martin d'Artaguiette and Jean-Baptiste Duclos. Like many French officials in North America, these two rejected as a failure the assimilation project that French authorities had formulated in the early seventeenth century, which had aimed to convert, "Frenchify," and naturalize Native Americans before integrating their female converts into French society through intermarriage.[8] In the end, La Vente was not successful in implementing his intermarriage agenda in Louisiana. Instead, in 1716, the Ministry of the Marine chose to follow the advice of d'Artaguiette and Duclos, forbidding Frenchmen in Louisiana from marrying Native American women.[9]

La Vente, Bienville, d'Artaguiette, and Duclos were all part of a group of well-traveled Frenchmen who spread (sometimes conflicting) ideas across oceans, thereby taking part in a pan-imperial conversation that ultimately shaped the formation of a coherent set of racial policies throughout the empire. Like La Vente, Bienville had arrived in Louisiana with prior experience in another French colony, which probably informed his views on intermarriage. Born in Montreal, he had spent most of his life in New France, where authorities had tried to prevent mixed marriages between Native Americans and French people since the late seventeenth century.[10] After spending time in Louisiana, Duclos moved to Saint-Domingue, where he became *commissaire-ordonnateur* and intendant, and d'Artaguiette went to metropolitan France, where he took up the positions of director (1717–1721) and syndic (1723–1731) in the French Company of the Indies (la Compagnie des Indes).[11] In these roles, d'Artaguiette sat on the company's assembly in Paris, an administrative body that oversaw all territories under the company's influence, including Louisiana, Senegal, Isle Bourbon, Isle of France and India.[12] Shortly after he joined the company, the assembly began issuing policies consistent with the plan he had pushed for in Louisiana a few years earlier, which attempted to dissuade Frenchmen across the empire from marrying local women of non-European descent. Unsurprisingly, given d'Artaguiette's previous experience in the Mississippi valley, the first of these policies, formulated in 1726, targeted Louisiana.[13]

Starting in 1728, the company's assembly attempted to prevent intermarriage between Frenchmen and local women on Isle Bourbon and in French India, as well.[14]

The story of these intermarriage policies illustrates this chapter's primary argument: beginning in the late seventeenth century, a coherent body of racial policies began to emerge across the French Atlantic and Indian Oceans, shaped by actors in the French colonies and the kingdom of France. This coherent body of racial policies was issued as a response to an emergent vision among French officials of how empire building should be achieved. With the previous body of assimilation policies issued from the early seventeenth century, officials had intended to integrate colonial populations into French society through conversion to Catholicism, "civilization," naturalization, and the promotion of intermarriage, in order to populate their colonies with new French subjects and better justify France's imperial claims in the eyes of other European countries. By contrast, with the new body of policies issued from the late seventeenth century, French domination was to be achieved through the erection of racial boundaries within the socioeconomic order of the French colonies and outposts. Racial policies thus targeted mixed marriages and sexual relations between white people and those of non-European descent, as well as the latter's inheritance rights and socioeconomic statuses.

In addition to very specific local circumstances in the colonies, two factors shaped the unification of French colonial policies. First, authorities such as the Company of the Indies' assembly in the 1720s attempted to standardize policies across the Atlantic and Indian Oceans. Second, official correspondence and people such as La Vente and d'Artaguiette circulated ideas across oceanic basins. A secondary claim in this chapter is that racial policies in the Atlantic world were shaped by developments in the Indian Ocean—and vice versa—because of transoceanic standardization and pan-imperial circulation. The coherent transoceanic body of racial policies and the circulations and standardization efforts that contributed to their formation have received little attention because the historiography on race in the French colonies is largely compartmentalized into smaller geographic units.[15] In particular, little work has been produced on race and racial policies for the French Indian Ocean, and the vast majority of publications on this topic have so far been produced by Atlantic specialists.[16] Using the Atlantic approach, these historians have already identified similarities in the content of racial discourse and policies within the North Atlantic, which they have attributed to the circulation of ideas through correspondence and people's travels in the region.[17] The French Atlantic colonies were no doubt particularly interconnected, which shaped the formation of a coherent set of racial ideas in the region. But just as it did within the Atlantic, the circulation of people and state papers between the Atlantic and the Indian Oceans also drove the circulation of racial ideas.

Recognizing the existence of both the previous seventeenth-century pan-imperial assimilation program and the coherent body of racial policies brings nuance to recent claims in the field of early modern French colonial legal history that "a unified body of law did not apply" and that "the Bourbon monarchy showed little interest in establishing uniform legislation across its colonial empire."[18] In fact, multiple clusters of identical and semantically similar assimilation and racial policies emerged across

TABLE 4.1.

Clusters of French Policies Targeting People of Non-European Descent, 1603–1758

CLUSTER NAME	ATLANTIC POLICIES	INDIAN OCEAN POLICIES
Baptizing the enslaved	2	2
Sending priests to the colonies	4	3
Converting local people	5	2
Prohibiting the practice of religions other than Catholicism	2	1
Civilizing local people	1	1
Naturalizing baptized local people	2	0
Naturalizing children born to baptized local people	1	3
Encouraging intermarriage between the French and local women	2	2
Limiting mixed relationships	1	1
Prohibiting intermarriage between Black and white people	3	2
Naturalizing manumitted people	2	1
Limiting intermarriages with local women	4	5
Forbidding donations from whites to Black people	3	1
Career penalties for Frenchmen who marry local women	1	2
Forbidding local women from inheriting from Frenchmen	1	1
Enslaving free Black people caught sheltering maroons	2	0
Enslaving free Black people caught sheltering maroons should they fail to pay fine	3	1

the Atlantic and Indian Ocean colonies from the early seventeenth to the mid-eighteenth centuries, targeting people of non-European descent. Table 4.1 identifies seventeen of these clusters, fifteen of which contain policies formulated in identical or similar terms before 1758 for France's Atlantic and Indian Ocean colonies—the Appendix details individual policies in these clusters.

This being said, just because there was a significant degree of coherence in racial policies does not mean there was no legal pluralism. Another important claim in this chapter is that the coherent bodies of racial policies coexisted with a constellation of regulations that were unique to each French colony or outpost: though French officials aspired to standardization, they also understood very well the importance of adapting their policies to local circumstances. This is illustrated by French officials' tailored approach to intermarriage in Senegambia.

By the early eighteenth century, French officials justified their decision to issue this coherent body of racial policies by drawing on a racial discourse influenced by pre-existing ideas from the kingdom of France and other European empires. As Guillaume Aubert has shown in his work on the French Atlantic, the notion of race had already surfaced in metropolitan France by the sixteenth century in discussions concerning the nobility. Several political theorists and literary figures described the alleged vices of commoners as immutable features passed down through blood (*sang*) from generation to generation, thereby corrupting the "purity of blood" of the allegedly superior old nobility (*noblesse de race*).[19] The same notion of race was then extended to overseas populations. Though the current historiography only documents how French racial discourse targeted the populations of the Atlantic, the semantic shift toward race is visible in discussions about all populations of non-European descent: Native Americans, Africans, Malagasies and South Asians, as well as their descendants. Both the formation of a coherent set of racial policies and the crystallization of this language of race on an imperial scale challenge the previous scholarly consensus that early modern French colonies and outposts were too disconnected to form an "empire." In fact, a French "empire" that was unified by a coherent set of racial discourse and policies had come into existence by the 1720s.

Origins of the Shift toward Racial Policing

What brought about the rise of racial policing beginning in the late seventeenth century? Authorities began to issue a body of racial policies as a response to the actions of ordinary people on the ground, who shaped local cultural, social, and economic developments and brought their own cases to court. Atlanticists have already shown how Native American people's rejection of the assimilation program in New France, and European planters' determination to build profitable slave plantation economies in the Atlantic world, shaped the making of racial policies.[20] But other important developments have been overlooked. The arrival of hundreds of bonded laborers from Madagascar, India and Africa on Isle Bourbon beginning in the second half of the seventeenth century also played an important role in the formation of racial legislation in the southwest Indian Ocean and the Americas. In this context, some officials deemed intermarriage bans necessary to prevent manumissions, protect the slave economy, and safeguard the reputation of white families from the purported "stain" attached to Blacks. Frequent sexual relations between European men and free and unfree women of Malagasy and South Asian ancestries on seventeenth-century Isle Bourbon encouraged further racial policing. As many free Bourbon Island Creoles accumulated substantial wealth, some officials also deemed it necessary to prevent people of non-European descent from inheriting from whites and climbing the socioeconomic ladder. Bans on mixed sexual relations and intermarriage were also aimed at protecting white families' patrimonies. Indeed, as noted by Ann Stoler, Julie Hardwick, Sarah M. S. Pearsall, Karin Wulf, and others, officials across European overseas empires attempted to control sexual relations and family formation because of genealogy's role in transmitting culture and wealth.[21] The issue of inheritance shaped opposition to intermarriage because marriage was the primary vector for the transmission of wealth and social status (including surnames and honorifics) in France.[22] In trying to prevent intermarriage, authorities thus hoped to avert the diversion of white families' property and titles and help whites achieve social and economic domination. Attempts to control family formation and inheritance were not at all new in the French context: since the sixteenth century, the "family-state compact" (an alliance between the king and a group of legists whose political standing rested on strategic family formation) had already taken measures to regulate marriage and inheritance practices in the kingdom of France, in order to protect family interests from misalliances. Among many other measures, from 1639, priests in metropolitan France were asked to start requesting proof of parental consent and social status from prospective spouses.[23]

Back in the colonies and outposts, legal action taken by ordinary European people over inheritance concerns across the Caribbean, French India, and the Illinois Country furthered opposition to intermarriage. Recall how, in 1667, after they had annulled the marriage of the Flemish settler Jacob Michel to his Black wife, Marie Läcotti, members of the Council of Guadeloupe had then issued the unratified edict prohibiting clergymen from officiating weddings "between a white man and a Black woman, and a white woman and a Black man," without the approval of the governor or commander of the island.

Because French officials had already begun to formulate a few isolated racial policies in the second half of the seventeenth century, we must repeatedly go back in time to the late seventeenth century and the first few years of the eighteenth in order to identify each of the foundational policies echoed in the coherent set of pan-imperial racial policies. A few years after the formulation of the unratified Guadeloupean edict of 1667—in 1674, 1689, 1701, and again in 1709—the viceroy of the East Indies, Jacob Blanquet de La Haye, and other colonial officials had issued their series of intermarriage bans for Isle Bourbon, intended to prevent the "divert[ing of] Blacks from [their] duties" and shield white families from the alleged "shame" brought by alliances with Blacks. From the first decades of the eighteenth century, this series of intermarriage bans issued for Isle Bourbon was used as a model to create a coherent set of racial policies for the French Atlantic and Indian Ocean worlds.

There was an inflection point in the volume of racial policies issued beginning in the late 1710s and early 1720s that was brought about by three developments. The first was demographic: assimilation policies were no longer deemed as necessary to populate the colonies because of the arrival of important waves of European immigrants. From the late 1710s and early 1720s, the French trading companies took measures to send European men and women to Louisiana and Isle Bourbon.[24] Along with demographic reproduction, this development caused the "white" population of Isle Bourbon to expand sixfold between 1713 and 1758 (from 633 people to 3,762).[25]

Thousands of other European recruits were also sent to Louisiana between 1717 and the early 1720s. Among them were French and German families, *engagés*, craftsmen, merchants, and French and Swiss soldiers.[26] They were joined by hundreds of forced European migrants, including convicts, vagabonds, military deserters, poor women and prostitutes.[27] In multiple places, the proportion of white women to white men became more even. There were 3,887 free white women in Martinique and 4,323 in Guadeloupe by 1719 and 1724, respectively, amounting to approximately 40 percent of these islands' free settler populations.[28] By 1732, European women amounted to 40 percent (169 people) of the free adult settler population in New Orleans.[29] In 1731, 626 women were categorized as "whites" in the census of Isle Bourbon (44 percent of the white population), although many of those women were no doubt of non-European ancestries.[30]

The second major development, which took place in the late 1710s, was the foundation of the French Company of the Indies, which brought the staggering expansion of transoceanic Black plantation slavery. This episode marked a turning point in the expansion of French racial capitalism—defined as the exploitation of racialized groups for economic profit.[31] The Scottish economist John Law merged multiple Atlantic and Indian Ocean trading companies into the new Company of the Indies from 1717 to 1719, during the regency of Philippe II, Duke of Orleans (1715–1723), selling company shares to reduce the crippling national debt caused by Louis XIV's protracted warfare.[32] As demonstrated by Malick Ghachem, the foundation of this company marked a critical moment in the development of capitalism and plantation slavery because it was intended to rescue the French monarchy through massive public investment in the slave trade, whose effects persisted even after the Mississippi Bubble burst in 1720.[33] This company expanded plantation slavery not only in Louisiana but also on Isle Bourbon, which became an important coffee provider for Europe.[34] The proportion of enslaved people of Malagasy, Indian, and East and West African descent on Isle Bourbon grew from 46 percent of the population in 1713 (538 people) to 82 percent of the population by 1731 (6,587 people).[35] The arrival of thousands of enslaved captives in the southwest Indian Ocean and the Americas ushered in a new era, in which France's American and southwest Indian Ocean colonies began to form slave societies. Given the massive public and private investments in the Atlantic and Indian Ocean slave trades that were channeled through the company in the late 1710s and 1720s, it is no coincidence that French authorities began to devote more energy to pan-imperial racial laws during that time period.

The third development that took place between the late 1710s and early 1720s was administrative. The ongoing process of legal standardization intensified beginning in the 1720s because of the crown's major policy of administrative reform initiated during the regency of the Duke of Orleans. Increased centralization within the Office of the Ministry of the Marine and of the Colonies from this period onward allowed royal policymakers in the kingdom of France to often take a policy already in place in one colony and apply it to another colony's legal corpus.[36] They did so either because they considered it a good fit or in an attempt to comply with the crown's old standardizing ambitions—in some cases, this latter scenario created a situation in which a transplanted policy was shoehorned into another colony's socioeconomic mold. The Ministry of the Marine in Versailles, in particular, ingested jurisprudence sent from the councils of the colonies and used it to broadcast both specialized and standardized directives across the empire. Several officials in the colonies were also committed to the standardizing effort, some of whom represented the French Company of the Indies. The composition of this company's leadership was hardly distinguishable from the crown: the king selected its syndics and directors and was represented in its metropolitan administrative assembly by a royal commissary who, in the words of Philippe Haudrère, was "the real master of the company."[37] As a result, royal officials and representatives of the Company of the Indies in the colonies and the metropole all worked in tandem to fulfill the crown's standardizing aspirations, shaping the emergence of the coherent set of racial policies.

Prohibiting Unions between "Whites" and "Blacks"

From the 1720s onward, as a result of standardization and the circulation of official papers, the series of intermarriage bans that was issued for Isle Bourbon starting in 1674 was echoed in a coherent body of policies that targeted intermarriage between Blacks and whites across the Atlantic and the Indian Ocean. Although scholars have attributed the issuance of this body of laws solely to Caribbean developments, they were first issued for Isle Bourbon, and their repetition from the 1720s onward was initially prompted by developments that took place on Isle Bourbon.[38]

French authorities had issued a couple of restrictions before 1674 that had not directly prohibited intermarriage between Black and white people. The first restriction on mixed alliances within the French empire, which had been formulated by the Company of the East Indies for Madagascar in 1664, had prohibited Frenchmen from forming relationships with "*women of the country*" rather than *Blacks*.[39] The edict then issued by the Council of Guadeloupe in 1667 was never ratified by the crown, and it was intended only to *restrict, not ban,* interracial marriages by prohibiting clergymen from officiating marriages between whites and Blacks *without the approval of the governor or commander* of the island.[40] This restriction might have been inspired by a practice in place in the Dutch empire, where Dutchmen were also asked to request prior consent from their local governor before they could marry a non-European woman.[41]

By contrast, the multiple regulations issued for Isle Bourbon from 1674 to 1709 to protect the emerging bonded labor system and the reputations of white families had directly prohibited all interracial marriages between Blacks and whites. Remember how La Haye's ordinance of 1674 had directly prohibited "Frenchmen from marrying *négresses*" and "Blacks [*Noirs*] from marrying white women [*Blanches*]."[42] In 1701, the order issued by the directors of the French Company of the East Indies had then enjoined the governor of Isle Bourbon, Jean-Baptiste de Villers, "[not to] allow a white man [*Blanc*] to marry a négresse."[43] Their subsequent ordinance of 1709 directly prohibited interracial marriages on Isle Bourbon as well, stating: "We forbid any white man [*Blanc*] to marry a négresse, and likewise white women [*Blanches*] from marrying Blacks [*Noirs*]."[44]

For decades, this consistent series of bans issued for Isle Bourbon remained the only regulations of the French empire prohibiting unions between Blacks and whites. Remember how, in 1685, article IX of the *Code Noir* of the Caribbean had instead *encouraged* freemen who had children with their captives in the Caribbean to marry them in the Catholic Church or else pay a fine of 2,000 livres of sugar and see their enslaved concubine and mixed children confiscated. Unlike previous bans issued for Isle Bourbon, article IX of the *Code Noir* of the Antilles had focused on social status rather than race: it prevented "*freemen* [*libres*]" (not "whites") from living in concubinage with "*slaves* [*esclaves*]" (not "Blacks").[45]

When the French crown formulated a more explicitly racialized version of this *Code Noir* of the Caribbean for Isle Bourbon and Isle of France in 1723 (known as the Letters Patent of Isle Bourbon and Isle of France) and for Louisiana in 1724 (known as the *Code Noir* of Louisiana), these new slave codes likely drew upon the consistent series of intermarriage bans issued for Isle Bourbon beginning in 1674. Scholars have not yet been able to determine how these two documents were produced and by whom, perhaps because no historical sources documenting their production have yet been found. Both were issued just a few months after Jean-Frédéric Phélypeaux, Count of Maurepas, took over the position of Marine secretary in August 1723. In this role, Maurepas must have played an important part in crafting these two new slave codes: his predecessor as Marine secretary, Jean-Baptiste Colbert (1669–1683), had overseen the creation of the *Code Noir* of the Antilles of 1685.[46] Moreover, there is no doubt that, when making his decisions, Maurepas was heavily influenced by preexisting colonial rules, for two reasons. First, he was exceptionally well versed in colonial politics, having been trained from a very young age by his father, the former Marine secretary Jérôme Phélypeaux (1699–1715), and by his cousin, Louis Phélypeaux, the acting head of the Ministry of the Marine from 1715 to 1717.[47] Second, he had direct access to the body of laws issued for the French Atlantic and Indian Ocean colonies beginning in the 1660s. Indeed, as part of their efforts to centralize colonial documents during the regency period, from 1716, metropolitan authorities endeavored to compile all legal documents that had been used for all colonies from this date onward.[48] It is probably no coincidence that this inventory was completed in 1722, just a few months before the issuance of the Letters Patent of Isle Bourbon and Isle of France of 1723 (or Letters Patent of the Mascarenes) and the *Code Noir* of Louisiana of 1724—the new Black Codes that came after the *Code Noir* of the Antilles of 1685, containing standard rules on slavery.[49] The knowledge Maurepas acquired through those colonial documents and inherited from his mentors served as inspiration for the racialized directives he gave for several colonies beginning in 1723. In fact, as soon as he took up the position of Marine secretary, Maurepas appears to have made a consistent effort to prevent intermarriages in the Mascarenes and Louisiana through the Letters Patent of the Mascarenes and the

Code Noir of Louisiana, as well as in the Caribbean islands, through directives he gave to the intendant of the *Îles du Vent* (Lesser Antilles), Charles-François Blondel.[50]

The *Code Noir* of Louisiana of March 1724 matched, almost verbatim, the Letters Patent of the Mascarenes of December 1723, which means one of two things: either the *Code Noir* of Louisiana was a copy of the Letters Patent of the Mascarenes or the two slave codes were formulated together prior to their respective publications. French officials either formulated the two documents synchronously or within an interval of just a few months because of the company's simultaneous initiatives, beginning in the late 1710s, to develop slave plantation agriculture on Isle Bourbon and Louisiana. Just like article V of the Letters Patent of the Mascarenes of 1723, article VI of this *Code Noir* of Louisiana stated, "We forbid our white subjects, of both sexes, to marry Blacks under penalty of punishment and arbitrary fine."[51] All the other details of the intermarriage ban of Isle Bourbon and Isle of France also appear in article VI of the *Code Noir* of Louisiana (see Table 4.2). Both articles prohibited white subjects, manumitted people, and freeborn Blacks from living in concubinage with enslaved people, under penalty of a 300 livres fine for both the transgressor and the slaveowner. In both cases, too, slaveowners who had children with their own captives would also see their concubines and children confiscated, with no possibility of manumission. However, both articles contained an identical amendment, which specified that free Blacks were still allowed to marry their enslaved concubines and in the process manumit them and their children. Article V of the Letters Patent of the Mascarenes and article VI of the *Code Noir* of Louisiana both stated, "The present article shall not be enforced if the Black man, freed or free, who was not married [. . .] during his concubinage were to marry the aforementioned slave in the church."[52]

Although few Americanists have noted the connection between article VI of the *Code Noir* of Louisiana of 1724 and article V of the Letters Patent of the Mascarenes of 1723, awareness of their coincidence seems indispensable to understanding why article V of the *Code Noir* of Louisiana existed in the first place and how it came to be. Preventing mixed marriages in Louisiana made little sense because Black plantation slavery was still in its infancy in the Mississippi valley in the 1720s. Although settlers in Louisiana asked for enslaved Africans as early as 1706, the crown and the financier and investor Antoine Crozat, who obtained a monopoly on Louisiana's

TABLE 4.2.

Comparing Article V of the Letters Patent of the Mascarenes to Article VI of the *Code Noir* of Louisiana

"Lettres Patentes En Forme d'édit, concernant les esclaves nègres des îles de France et de Bourbon [1723]," in *Code des Îles de France et de Bourbon*, 2nd ed., ed. M. Delaleu (Port-Louis, Mauritius, 1826), 248. Source: gallica.bnf.fr / Bibliothèque nationale de France	**"Edit du roi Touchant l'Etat & la Discipline des Esclaves Négres de la Loüisiane [. . .] 1724," in *Recueil d'Edits, Declarations et Arrests de sa Majeste, Concernant l'Administration de la Justice & la Police des Colonies Françaises de l'Amérique*, 2 vols. (Paris, 1744–1745), 2:138–139. Source: gallica.bnf.fr / Bibliothèque nationale de France**
V. Défendons à nos sujets blancs de l'un et de l'autre sexe de contracter mariage avec les noirs, à peine de punition et d'amende arbitraire, et à tous curés, prêtres ou missionnaires séculiers ou réguliers, et même aux aumôniers des vaisseaux de les marier; défendons aussi à nosdits sujets blancs, même aux noirs affranchis ou nés libres, de vivre en concubinage avec des esclaves; voulons que ceux qui auront eu un ou plusieurs enfans d'une pareille conjonction, ensemble les maîtres qui les auront soufferts, soient condamnés chacun en une amende de trois cents livres; et s'ils sont maîtres de l'esclave de laquelle ils auront eu lesdits enfans, voulons qu'outre l'amende ils soient privés tant de l'esclave que des enfans, et qu'ils soient adjugés à l'hôpital des lieux, sans pouvoir jamais être affranchis; n'entendons toutefois le présent article avoir lieu lorsque l'homme noir affranchi ou libre qui n'était pas marié durant son concubinage avec son esclave, épousera, dans les formes prescrites par l'église, ladite esclave, qui sera affranchie par ce moyen, et les enfans rendus libres et légitimes.	VI. Défendons à nos Sujets blancs de l'un & de l'autre sexe, de contracter mariage avec les Noirs, à peine de punition & d'amende arbitraire; & à tous Curés, Prêtres, ou Missionnaires séculiers, ou réguliers, & même aux Aumôniers des Vaisseaux, de les marier. Défendons aussi à nosdits Sujets Blancs, même aux Noirs affranchis, ou nés libres, de vivre en concubinage avec des Esclaves. Voulons que ceux qui auront eu un, ou plusieurs enfans d'une pareille conjonction, ensemble les Maîtres qui les auront soufferts, soient condamnés chacun en une amende de trois cens livres; & s'ils sont Maîtres; de l'Esclave de laquelle ils auront eu lesdits enfans, voulons qu'outre l'amende, ils soient privés tant de l'esclave que des enfans, & qu'ils soient adjugés à l'Hôpital des lieux, sans pouvoir jamais être affranchis. N'entendons toutefois le présent Article avoir lieu, lorsque l'homme Noir, affranchi, ou libre, qui n'étoit point marié durant son concubinage avec son Esclave, épousera dans les formes prescrites par l'Eglise ladite Esclave, qui sera affranchie par ce moyen, & les enfans rendus libres & légitimes.

trading activities in 1712, did not respond to their demands because they lacked the financial resources.[53] In 1706, no enslaved Blacks whatsoever were recorded in the census of Louisiana.[54] Only ten enslaved Blacks had been transported to the colony by 1710, and the number of enslaved people of African ancestry remained very small until the arrival of the first slave ship from Africa in 1719.[55] In 1721, a couple of years before the issuance of the *Code Noir* of Louisiana, there were only 533 enslaved people in all of France's positions across the vast Mississippi valley.[56] Moreover, no mixed Black and white intermarriages were recorded in the parish registers of New Orleans, Biloxi, Yazoo, or Natchez for the entire period preceding 1724.[57] Lawmakers were no doubt aware of this when they formulated the *Code Noir* of Louisiana: in fact, a note added to the margin of article VI claimed that "there are no instances of such marriages in the colony."[58] Article VI of the *Code Noir* of Louisiana was thus an instance of legally shoehorning a transplanted regulation as part of the crown's broader standardization efforts.

Although scholars in the field of Atlantic history have attributed article VI of the *Code Noir* of Louisiana to Caribbean influences, there were major discrepancies between the way it dealt with intermarriage and the legislation in effect in the French Caribbean by 1724.[59] The most recent regulation addressing the question of intermarriage in the Caribbean at that time was in the *Code Noir* of the Caribbean of 1685, which *encouraged* intermarriage as an alternative to concubinage instead of prohibiting it as the *Code Noir* of Louisiana did.[60] As Guillaume Aubert puts it, the provision concerning intermarriage in the *Code Noir* of Louisiana of 1724 was thus "a dramatic departure from the Caribbean Code [of 1685]."[61]

So how did the intermarriage ban in the *Code Noir* of Louisiana come into being in the first place? Since the *Code Noir* of Louisiana was either a copy of the Letters Patent of the Mascarenes or formulated together with it, it is very likely that the concerns that led to the issuance of both regulations originated on Isle Bourbon. In fact, the intermarriage bans of 1723 and 1724 encapsulated the many decades of existing jurisprudence issued for Isle Bourbon. By prohibiting intermarriage for whites of both sexes, article V of the Letters Patent of the Mascarenes and article VI of the *Code Noir* of Louisiana echoed the ordinance of Blanquet de La Haye from 1674 and the prohibition issued in 1709 by the directors of the Company of the East Indies for Isle Bourbon. And by prohibiting marriages between "white subjects" (*Blancs*) and "Blacks," it also echoed the intermarriage ban issued by the Company of the East Indies in 1701. While the *Code Noir* of the Caribbean of 1685 focused on status rather than race by punishing "free men" who had children with "slaves," the authors of the Letters Patent of the Mascarenes and the *Code Noir* of Louisiana were preoccupied with race, just like La Haye when he issued the Isle Bourbon intermarriage ban of 1674. This is demonstrated both by their use of the labels "Blacks" and "white subjects" and by the fact that—despite preventing unions between whites and all Blacks—they still allowed free Blacks to marry enslaved Blacks (within their own alleged "race") in the special penalty exemption. The intermarriage bans of 1723 and 1724 were also intended to respond to recent developments on Isle Bourbon: namely, the expansion of coffee plantation agriculture and slavery from the 1720s and the many intermarriages that had been celebrated in the colony since its establishment in the 1660s, despite the bans of 1674, 1689, 1701, and 1709.

Although French officials did attempt to inhibit intermarriage in the Caribbean, it seems that no intermarriage ban was ever issued for the French Caribbean islands until the second half of the eighteenth century.[62] How can we explain this Caribbean divergence? Intermarriages with women of African ancestry were common practice in Saint-Domingue by the early eighteenth century, amounting, for instance, to over 30 percent of marriages by the 1720s in the parish of Léogane and to 40 percent by the 1760s, partly because of the gender imbalance in the free white population of the island.[63] Many of the women of African descent who engaged in relationships with white men in Saint-Domingue came from the free population. Many owned properties, businesses, and enslaved people, making them desirable partners for many.[64] This helps explain why French authorities produced no explicit intermarriage ban for that island, until the second half of the eighteenth century.[65]

With regard to the Lesser Antilles, there was no need to prohibit intermarriage in the eighteenth century because the governors and intendants of the French *Îles du Vent* of the Caribbean could already keep a close eye on intermarriages through a practice that has been almost completely overlooked in the historiography: beginning in 1645, they were allowed to prevent any marriage they disapproved of in Martinique and Guadeloupe.[66] The French missionary Jean-Baptiste Du Tertre commented on this practice in the 1660s and 1670s, arguing, "One does not get married on the islands without having requested the authorization of the governor."[67] When the governor of Martinique, Jacques Dyel du Parquet, initiated this practice in 1645, he did not do so because he was preoccupied with the question of intermarriage. He only wanted to prevent a Frenchman named Sieur Saint-André from marrying a white woman named Marie Bonnard because he intended to marry her himself.[68] However, by the early eighteenth century, this practice was used almost exclusively as a tool to prevent whites from marrying people of African descent. In particular, beginning in 1725, Blondel, intendant of the *Îles du Vent*, systematized the practice of authorization requests for marriage. In doing so, he was following a directive from Maurepas, who was responding to the staggering expansion of Black plantation slavery and sugarcane plantation agriculture in the Caribbean, beginning in the early eighteenth century.[69] As planters began to use the vacant fertile lands of the Grande-Terre, stolen from the Kalinago after the Franco-Carib Wars (1654–1660), the proportion of enslaved Black people grew from 59 percent of the population of Guadeloupe in 1699 (6,185 people) to 82 percent in 1753 (41,026).[70] In Martinique, too, the proportion of enslaved Blacks grew from 61 percent of the population in 1670 (6,183) to 82 percent by 1755 (64,827).[71]

Even then, however, not all officials in the French Lesser Antilles systematically opposed intermarriage to all women of African descent. This is illustrated by a trial that took place in Guadeloupe in 1727, reminiscent of the Jacob Michel inheritance court case of 1667. Here, too, a French relative, Jacques Huard, wanted to exclude Magdelon, the Black widow of his French brother-in-law Gilles Petit, from his legitimate heirs by nullifying their marriage. Magdelon and Gilles had gotten married in the parish of Pointe-Noire before they moved to Grand Cul-de-Sac, where they reportedly had "many *mulâtre* children."[72] The French attorney-general, Mr. Dorillac, recommended that Magdelon and Gilles's marriage be declared null and void, owing to "the considerable inequality between their status."[73] He drew on the same rhetoric of shame as that applied on Isle Bourbon, labeling their union as "scandalous," "infamous," and "shameful [*honteux*]."[74] He insisted that such mixed unions were no longer justifiable because the colony no longer lacked European women and also drew on a racial rhetoric to ask that such marriages be banned. He claimed that "there is [now] a proportionate number of people of all *colors* and all *species* [*espèces*]" and "no shortage of men and women of *equal blood*" on the island.[75] Strikingly, however, in the end, seven council members declared the Petit marriage legally valid, while only four members voted to invalidate the union. While the outcome of this trial is unknown, the Council of Guadeloupe did not ultimately prohibit unions between Blacks and whites.[76]

Thirty years after the Gilles Petit trial, two lawyers based in Guadeloupe tried to impose the intermarriage ban of Isle Bourbon, Isle of France, and Louisiana onto the Caribbean *Îles du Vent*. These two lawyers, one named Marin and the other Charles François Emmanuel Nadau du Treil (the latter was also Guadeloupe's governor), proposed in 1758 to allow the governor-general and the intendant to forbid marriages between white and Black people on the *Îles du Vent*, arguing that with "article 6 of the Edict [*Code Noir*] of March 1724 [. . .] His Majesty [. . .] prevented the inhabitants of Louisiana of both sexes from marrying Blacks."[77] Although this attempt was unsuccessful, it is noteworthy because it explicitly invoked the legal code of a different colony, which itself was either a copy of, or formulated in concert with, the Letters Patent of the Mascarenes of 1723, as a legal precedent to standardize colonial legislation. Such explicit influences confirm that representatives of the crown in the colonies, of whom Du Treil is one example, were committed to carrying out the crown's standardizing ambition. Since the intermarriage ban in the Louisiana *Code Noir* echoed decades of jurisprudence initiated in 1674 by La Haye on Isle Bourbon, the Marin and Du Treil Caribbean proposal is further evidence of the circulation of ideas regarding racial policies between the French Atlantic and Indian Oceans.

Prohibiting Intermarriage with Local People

From the late seventeenth century onward, the failure of the assimilation project in North America prompted the crown and the French Company of the Indies to formulate another coherent body of intermarriage policies for various positions in the French Atlantic and Indian Oceans. These policies targeted unions between local (Indigenous) women and white company employees, and they were shaped both by standardization and by the pan-imperial circulation of correspondence and officials. While several Americanists have studied their issuance for New France and Louisiana, none have noted their subsequent extension to Isle Bourbon and the French outposts in India.[78] Yet this particular kind of intermarriage prohibition shows us that racial policies formulated for the French Indian Ocean, too, could be shaped by ideas and precedents from all across the empire, including the Atlantic.

A first directive targeting marriage between French employees and local women was formulated around 1693 in India by the Company of the East Indies: it does not appear to have been connected to the body of intermarriage bans subsequently issued for North America and other colonies and outposts, and it was issued in response to local concerns about the economic costs of intermarriage. Of particular concern were the wages or pensions granted by the company to the Indian or Luso-Indian widows of deceased employees, which French officials considered a drain on French resources. In a letter dated 1693, the director-general of the company in Surat, Louis-Estienne de Pilavoine, recounted a case in which the Indian widow of a French clerk named Coquelu threatened legal action against the company for refusing to pay her pension or late husband's wages.[79] While the company eventually agreed to pay, Pilavoine complained that it could not afford to keep supporting the families of its employees, and he blamed intermarriage for "always [causing] trouble among employees."[80] He had previously decided to forbid all marriages in the Surat outpost, declaring, "I will not consent to letting any of your employees commit to marriage unless he agrees to leave your service."[81] Even though he did not mention it explicitly, this directive targeted intermarriage in particular, as most French marriages in India were de facto mixed.[82]

A few years after Pilavoine had forbidden company employees from getting married in Surat, royal officials in New France, Louisiana and the French kingdom began to target marriage between Frenchmen and Native American women with a well-known body of policies whose coherence was the result of more pan-imperial connections. Those North American policies were intended to protect France's cultural influence in the face of Native Americans' rejection of the assimilation project and reports that many Frenchmen in New France were becoming *ensauvagés* ("wilded") and lived in Native American villages.[83] Officials in New France famously began to embrace a racial rhetoric to describe Native American people's alleged incapacity to become "civilized," and they also issued a series of bans prohibiting marriage with Native American women. Those intermarriage bans resonated with each other because the people who made them circulated across the North Atlantic, as did their letters. As early as 1696, the governor-general of New France, Louis de Buade de Frontenac, recommended sanctions against Frenchmen who married Native American women without prior approval from the governor or the king.[84] Then, in June 1706, his successor, Philippe de Rigaud de Vaudreuil, ordered the commandant of Detroit, La Mothe Cadillac not to permit "any Frenchman, whatever, either soldier or otherwise, to marry [a Native American woman] *until such time as we have received orders from the Court on this matter.*"[85]

This shift in intermarriage policy in New France in turn shaped decisions and discourse concerning intermarriage for the Illinois Country and the Mississippi valley. The Canadian-born governor of Louisiana, Bienville, was familiar with the conversation happening in New France, since he received regular correspondence from the colonies there, where he had spent most of his life. Therefore, it is probably not a coincidence that, only four months after Vaudreuil had told Cadillac to prohibit French–Native American intermarriage in New France, Bienville made the same decision for Louisiana. Just like Vaudreuil in 1706, he proposed the prohibition of such unions until metropolitan authorities made a final decision, declaring, "Those marriages should be pronounced null if the Prince does not approve them," and they "will not be approved *until the Court has made known what is to be done.*"[86] This is when the policymaking debate discussed earlier, in which the missionary La Vente was opposed by Bienville and the *commissaires-ordonnateurs* d'Artaguiette and Duclos, began. D'Artaguiette justified his opposition to intermarriage by arguing that Native American women were too libertine to be faithful wives, while Duclos portrayed mixed French–Native American children as "very *swarthy* [*extremement Bazanées*] [*sic*]." The latter also drew on a racial rhetoric, describing those children as "*naturally* lazy, libertine and [. . .] rogues [*naturellement faineants, libertins, et* [. . .] *fripons*]."[87] Back in New France, in 1709, Philippe de Vaudreuil reiterated his opposition to intermarriages and also drew on racial rhetoric in a letter he sent to the Council of the Marine (Conseil de Marine)—the metropolitan institution in charge of the colonies during the regency—claiming, "One should *never mix bad blood with good blood* [*mesler un mauvais Sang avec un bon*]."[88]

Strikingly, when they finally responded to Bienville's question regarding intermarriage in Louisiana in 1716, metropolitan officials merely paraphrased the letters they had received earlier from New France and Louisiana: this is direct evidence that official correspondence acted as an important vehicle for the circulation of racial ideas. Members of the metropolitan Marine Council used Duclos's exact words, describing mixed children as "extremely *swarthy* [*extremement basanés*] and "*naturally rough* and *lazy* [*d'un naturel dur* et *faineant*]."[89] They also repeated d'Artaguiette's claim that Native American women were too libertine and quick to leave their husbands for other men.[90] Still in 1716, members of the Council of the Marine parroted the claim Vaudreuil had made in New France in 1709 about mixing "*good blood with bad blood*," this time when discussing intermarriage between Frenchmen and Native American women in Louisiana, writing that "there is a reason to fear *the mixture of good blood with bad blood* [*mesler le bon Sang avec le mauvais*]."[91] The Council of the Marine eventually commanded colonial officials in Louisiana to "prevent these sorts of marriages to the full extent of their power."[92] Five years later, in 1721, the same metropolitan council took measures to prevent these intermarriages in New France as well, requiring the colony's bishop to get the approval of the governor-general before officiating the marriage of any French soldier or officer.[93]

Finally, beginning in the 1720s, the metropolitan assembly of the Company of the Indies began to issue a bevy of policies targeting intermarriage between its employees and local women across multiple territories under its purview, in what looks like an effort to follow the crown's standardizing ambitions. These policies followed directly on the heels of the appointment to the company assembly of d'Artaguiette, the *commissaire-ordonnateur* who had opposed intermarriage while still in Louisiana.[94] The policy issued in 1726 by the metropolitan company assembly, which was probably shaped by d'Artaguiette, threatened the career advancement prospects of company employees who wished to marry Native American women in Louisiana. The company asked the Council of Louisiana to provide "clarifications" regarding the marriages of several of its employees.[95] A Frenchman named Texier was subsequently denied a promotion within the company for having "married the bastard daughter of Sieur de Mandeville, the daughter of an enslaved *sauvagesse*."[96]

Not long after this, the metropolitan company assembly began to take measures to stifle the careers of other employees in similar relationships across the Indian Ocean. In 1728, it issued a law for Isle Bourbon that prevented settlers from marrying without the governor's approval. This law drew on the same rhetoric of "blood mixing" that had emerged in French North America and mainland France: it was explicitly intended "to prevent the *mixing of French blood* [*le Meslange du sang français*], which becomes weaker, corrupted, and degraded after engaging with sluggishness."[97] Then, in 1734, the company denied admission to the Council of Isle Bourbon to "any employee who should marry a creole woman."[98] The company reiterated this ban in 1736, 1738, 1740, 1742, 1743 and again in 1754, these times threatening members of the council, soldiers, officers, and sailors with removal from their positions if they married a "creole woman." A document explicitly stated that all these policies targeting "creole women" applied only to "mixed-blood people [*sang mêlés*]."[99] Eventually, the company began to follow a policy closer to the one it had previously adopted in Louisiana, based on career hindrance rather than direct dismissal. As in the Texier case in Louisiana, a document indicates that most employees on Isle Bourbon were allowed to keep their jobs and were instead denied promotions at work.[100] Also as in the Texier case, in 1755, officials on the island launched an investigation to determine if a man named Deheaulme could be promoted to commandant in the parish of Saint-Paul. They eventually approved his promotion, after being "very much assured that Deheaulme's wife was born to a white man and a white woman."[101]

The Company of the Indies implemented similar policies in its South Asian outposts. In 1730, it had already commanded company employees in Bengal to "marry the daughters of Frenchmen" as much as possible.[102] Joseph Dupleix, the famous French administrator who at the time was the governor of Chandernagore, had then prohibited priests from officiating unions between Frenchmen and "bastards, or country women who are not descended from Europeans" in 1732.[103] But mixed unions in India persisted, leading the company to take measures consistent with its previous strategies for Louisiana and Isle Bourbon. In 1743, the metropolitan company assembly declared that no employee or officer in India could marry without an authorization from the council.[104] Five years later, still in the metropole, the company decided to adopt a strategy akin to the one it had applied earlier to adjudicate the Texier case in Louisiana. It declared "that every employee [in the East Indies] who should marry a woman of Indian *blood* [*une fille issüe de sang Indien*] [. . .] will only be able to reach the rank of under-merchant [*sous-marchand*]," one of the company's lowest positions.[105] According to the company, this directive was intended to "extinguish the Indian *blood* [*éteindre le sang Indien*] among employees," which was deemed "too prejudicial to [the company's] interests in every way."[106] Here, the company appealed to the global rhetoric of blood purity to prevent the transfer of power and resources into Indian hands. In addition to considering the financial support of Indian widows a great burden, French officials feared that Indian women would eventually go back to their communities if their French husbands predeceased them, effectively diverting the inheritance away from French control, which brings us to the topic of inheritance.

Inheritance Bans

Beginning in 1702, the chartered companies, colonial officials, and the crown formulated two series of policies for the French Indian Ocean and the Atlantic that restricted the rights of non-Europeans and their descendants to receive bequests and donations from whites. The French Indian Ocean once again played a critically neglected role in shaping at least some of those policies because of transoceanic standardization and the large-scale circulation of ideas. Inheritance bans were partly intended to override the Paris Custom on inheritance (*la Coutume de Paris*) initially followed overseas, which granted a widow half of her late husband's estate, with the remainder being divided among children if they were born in Catholic wedlock.[107] The preoccupation with inheritance was already evident in several lawsuits filed across the Atlantic and Indian Oceans starting in 1667. Recall how, that year, in Guadeloupe, relatives of the deceased Frenchman Jacob Michel had already demanded to have his Black widow cut out of his will. In Surat, India, over a quarter of a century later, the director-general of the company, Pilavoine, had prohibited all marriages in his outpost in 1693 after the Indian widow of the clerk Coquelu had threatened legal action against the company for refusing to pay her pension or late husband's wages. Much later, in 1727, again in Guadeloupe, Jacques Denis Huard attempted to have his brother-in-law's Black wife excluded from the family inheritance by annulling their marriage.

The first series of inheritance policies targeting the rights of local widows was formulated in India about a decade after the Coquelu complaint. The issue of inheritance was already a central preoccupation in the region, as demonstrated by Pilavoine's complaint in 1693 that the company could not afford to support the families of its employees. In Surat in 1702, Pilavoine eventually refused to apply the Paris Custom on inheritance in order to protect French economic interests in the region.[108] He decried the diversion of French wealth that resulted from inheritance, explicitly expressing concerns about Indian widows who remarried "with God knows whom" (presumably Indian men). He complained that in such cases "the assets [that the widow had inherited from her French husband] were lost."[109] To justify his concern about inheritance, Pilavoine invoked stereotypes concerning South Asian women, describing Indian widows as wastrels incapable of managing their own estates.[110]

Twenty-six years after Pilavoine wrote those words, local authorities in Louisiana began to reject the Paris Custom on inheritance as well. This shift in inheritance practices in Louisiana was pushed by a man named Étienne Périer the Elder, whose backstory is worth mentioning here, intertwined as it is with the broader narrative of global circulation and the formulation of racial policies. Périer pursued a military career in Senegal, Peru, and Chile from 1714 to 1724 and later in the French outpost of Mahé (south of Surat) in 1724–1725.[111] While in India, Périer no doubt met many of the European men stationed there who had married women of South Asian descent. As a military man well versed in politics, he might have heard about Pilavoine's 1702 decision in Surat to revoke South Asian widows' inheritance rights after the deaths of their French husbands.

After spending a year in India, Périer became governor of French Louisiana and, in 1728, imposed a restriction on inheritance that echoed the measure taken more than two decades earlier in Surat. Périer and other members of the Council of Louisiana declared that all Native American women who had married Frenchmen in Louisiana would be "excluded from the successions of the French."[112] Instead, the company would seize their estates, with the exception of real estate holdings, which were to be controlled by guardians. A widow was only entitled to a pension amounting to one-third of the estate's revenue, and only on the condition that she stayed among the French. The remaining two-thirds would go to her children, if she had any. If a Native American widow died childless, however, the assets were to be handed over to the company instead of being given to her relatives.[113]

When advocating in favor of this drastic solution for Louisiana, Périer might have been emboldened by what he had seen and heard in India. Indeed, the Louisiana inheritance restriction of 1728 was formulated after yet another legal dispute, which this time took place in Kaskaskia, Illinois Country, where a Jesuit missionary named Jean-Baptiste Antoine Robert Le Boullenger requested that only one Illinois woman, named Marie Achipicourata, be disinherited because she had cheated on her French husband. Echoing Pilavoine's earlier argument, authorities sought to justify Périer's decision in Louisiana by claiming that it was "not agreeable that the *sauvages* take the goods of the French among their nations."[114] Authorities eventually enforced the Louisiana inheritance regulation in 1745, when a guardian was chosen for a Native American widow named Françoise to manage the estate of her deceased French husband, Charles Egron, "because of her status as an Indian [Native American] woman." Just like Pilavoine, who had portrayed Indian widows in Surat as irresponsible wastrels, colonial administrators in Louisiana described Françoise as "an imbecile," unable to manage her own estate.[115] Such stereotypes were thus used to justify the dispossession of these women on both sides of the globe.[116]

The second series of pan-imperial inheritance bans was issued by the crown for Isle Bourbon and Isle of France in 1723 before being extended to Louisiana and the Caribbean. Initiated as a response to developments that took place on Isle Bourbon, it was intended to prevent free Blacks from receiving any form of donations from whites. The first ban targeting donations from whites to free Blacks appeared in the Letters Patent of the Mascarenes of 1723 and then in the *Code Noir* of Louisiana of 1724. The articles that dealt with donations and inheritance from whites to Blacks in those two slave codes matched each other word for word (see Table 4.3). Article LI of the Letters Patent of the Mascarenes and article LII of the *Code Noir* of Louisiana of 1724 both stated, "We forbid [. . .] manumitted slaves as well as free *nègres* from receiving any donation from whites, neither inter vivos, nor after death or for any other reason."[117]

Here, too, being aware of the connection between the *Code Noir* of Louisiana of 1724 and the Letters Patent of Mascarenes of 1723 is vital to fully understanding why and how article LII of the *Code Noir* of Louisiana came to be. There is little doubt that, in their decision to prevent Blacks from inheriting from whites in the *Code Noir* of Louisiana, metropolitan authorities

TABLE 4.3.
Comparing Article LI of the Letters Patent of the Mascarenes to Article LII of the *Code Noir* of Louisiana

"Lettres Patentes En Forme d'édit, concernant les esclaves nègres des îles de France et de Bourbon [1723]," in *Code des Îles de France et de Bourbon,* 2nd ed., ed. M. Delaleu (Port-Louis, Mauritius, 1826), 251. Source: gallica.bnf.fr / Bibliothèque nationale de France	**"Edit du roi Touchant l'Etat & la Discipline des Esclaves Négres de la Loüisiane [. . .] 1724," in *Recueil d'Edits, Declarations et Arrests de sa Majeste, Concernant l'Administration de la Justice & la Police des Colonies Françaises de l'Amérique,* 2 vols. (Paris, 1744–1745), 2:154. Source: gallica.bnf.fr / Bibliothèque nationale de France**
LI. Déclarons les affranchissemens faits dans les formes ci-devant prescrites, tenir lieu de naissance dans nosdites îles, et les affranchis n'avoir besoin de nos lettres de naturalité pour jouir des avantages de nos sujets naturels dans notre royaume, terres et pays de notre obéissance, encore qu'ils soient nés dans les pays étrangers; déclarons cependant lesdits affranchis, ensemble les nègres libres, incapables de recevoir des blancs aucune donation entre-vifs à cause de mort, ou autrement; voulons qu'en cas qu'il leur en soit fait aucune, elle demeure nulle à leur égard, et soit appliquée au profit de l'hôpital le plus prochain.	LII. Déclarons les affranchissemens faits dans les formes ci-devant prescrites, tenir lieu de naissance dans notredite Province de la Louisiane, & les affranchis n'avoir besoin de nos Lettres de naturalité, pour jouir des avantages de nos Sujets naturels dans notre Royaume, Terres & Pays de notre obéissance, encore qu'ils soient nés dans les pays étrangers; Déclarons cependant lesdits affranchis, ensemble les Nègres libres, incapables de recevoir des Blancs aucune donation entre-vifs, à cause de mort, ou autrement. Voulons qu'en cas qu'il leur en soit fait aucune, elle demeure nulle à leur égard, & soit appliquée au profit de l'Hôpital le plus prochain.

were echoing concerns from other parts of the empire, since there were very few free Blacks in Louisiana in the 1720s. Although some enjoyed a more informal and unofficial form of freedom as *libres de fait*, there are only 146 petitions for manumissions in the Louisiana archives for the entire French period, and only fifty-five enslaved people were clearly manumitted.[118] While there is evidence that some did receive inheritance or donations from their white relatives, lovers, or friends, few were very comfortable financially.[119] No policy targeting the rights of free Blacks to receive inheritance and donations from whites was issued in the Caribbean before the crown issued the Letters Patent of the Mascarenes in 1723.[120] The most recent regulation addressing the question of such donations in the Caribbean was to be found in the *Code Noir* of 1685, which in fact *allowed* enslaved people to be made "universal heirs by their masters" and in this way to acquire their freedom.[121] It makes sense that the first rule restricting the inheritance rights of free Blacks was formulated for Isle Bourbon, since many free people with origins in Madagascar and South Asia on the island had climbed the socioeconomic ladder.[122]

The inheritance ban of Louisiana, which was either a copy of, or formulated together with, article LI of the Letters Patent of the Mascarenes, in turn influenced policymaking for the Caribbean and Guiana. A royal decree issued in 1726 for the Caribbean and Guiana stated that "*in conformity with article LII of our edict of March 1724*, all manumitted slaves as well as free *nègres* will be forbidden from receiving any donations from whites in the future, neither inter vivos, nor after death or for any other reason."[123] Though nothing on the scale of what was happening on Isle Bourbon occurred in the Caribbean before the 1720s, French authorities had some reasons to be concerned about the right of inheritance of free Blacks there, too. By 1712, free Blacks amounted to 17 percent of the free population of Saint-Domingue (1,189 people), and this proportion rose to 25 percent (4,861) in 1754.[124] Some were quite comfortable financially: a few became landowners and slaveowners, though a majority cultivated food crops and coffee on small estates in the mountains, where the land was less fertile and coveted than on the sugar plains.[125] Most importantly, as was the case in 1758 when Marin and Du Treil proposed to forbid marriages between whites and Blacks on the *Îles du Vent*, metropolitan authorities issued the royal decree of the Caribbean and Guiana of 1726 in an explicit attempt to standardize colonial legislation.

Tackling Legal Particularities: Intermarriage and Inheritance in Senegambia

The standardized body of racial policies that took shape across multiple French positions by the early eighteenth century coexisted with myriad legal particularities intended to address local circumstances. An example of this can be found in Senegambia, where French officials embraced a different approach to intermarriage than the ones in the Caribbean, Louisiana, Isle Bourbon and Isle of France, because several Africans and Eurafricans in West Africa wielded particular power and influence. Despite claims to the contrary, French authorities did not explicitly prohibit intermarriage in Senegambia in the early modern period, as they did for other French colonies.[126] Rather, officials' positions regarding intermarriage in Senegambia were divided. On the one hand, several French officials in the region explicitly endorsed such marriages. On the other, the Royal Company of Senegal took measures in 1688 to prevent the French from *associating* with women of African descent in Senegambia—a decision that would admittedly have made it difficult for them to marry local women. Remember how, in January 1688, in order to end illicit trade, the directors of the Royal Company of Senegal had issued their ordinance prohibiting Frenchmen in Senegambia from "go[ing] to [the *négresses*'] cabins, or let[ting] them enter their own [. . .] under penalty of paying a fine of six livres for each time" or "go[ing] to the villages of the *nègres* without orders from the commandant." Although the director of the company in Saint-Louis, Louis Moreau de Chambonneau, did propose "to prohibit [Frenchmen] from marrying the *négresses*" a few months later, his proposal was not accepted.[127]

As a result of Frenchmen's continued engagement in illicit trade with female African and Eurafrican merchants and entrepreneurs, the Royal Company of Senegal issued more regulations that reiterated those made in the 1688 ordinance and also did not prohibit intermarriage. In 1721, the director-general of the Royal Company of Senegal, Julien du Bellay, issued a regulation whose article XIV prohibited settlers from "going to the villages of the *nègres* [. . .] without prior authorization from the commandant." In article IV of the same regulation, he also forbade settlers from "supporting a *négresse*, entering her cabin, or allowing her in [their] own home."[128] The penalty for breaking the rule decreased from six livres to about two livres (40 sols) in the 1721 regulation. However, the 1721 rule was no more lenient, since it included an additional provision expelling from the colony any company employee who might "live a life of debauchery or give a bad example."[129] Just like the ban of 1688, the regulation of 1721 was clearly intended to protect the company's trading interests. Article VII of the 1721 regulation stated, "We forbid [all those who will be at our service, and even the captains, officers, sailors, and soldiers on board our ships] to do any trafficking for their own profit."[130] By the mid-eighteenth century, French officials portrayed female African traders in Senegambia as "leeches," sucking the most precious merchandise away from the company.[131] Just like the rule of 1688, that of 1721 deplored "abuses [. . .]

sustained by our [. . .] employees, who only think of their own profit and will bring about the ruin of our business."[132] Du Bellay also added new provisions to the 1721 regulation. Article XXVI forbade the director-general, commandants, and clerks to "support women openly [. . .] or to indulge in any debauchery that might give a bad example to employees," under penalty of losing their salary.[133]

Article XXV of the same regulation rescinded French officials' initiative to invite Africans to the Senegambian *folgars* organized in Saint-Louis for diplomatic and other purposes. It instructed the director-general and commandants not to admit any Black people or African leaders to such feasts or celebrations.[134] Those provisions were clearly intended to prevent the depletion of company resources: when referring to colonial feasts and celebrations, article XXV accused the company's directors and commandants of squandering rations in wine and brandy. It also deplored "the unfortunate consequences and the losses suffered by the company through these sorts of *debaucheries*"—at the time, the term "debauchery" (*debauche*) was defined as "disorder, excessive drinking and eating" as well as "incontinence."[135]

But despite those prohibitions, most French officials in Senegambia do not appear to have rejected intermarriage between Frenchmen and women of African descent. Even Du Bellay himself did not reject those marriages, though he clearly considered white unions more desirable since he proposed sending young women from the Children's Hospital in Paris (Hôpital des Enfants Trouvés) to Senegambia to marry French sailors and other employees stationed there. Yet, in a letter addressed to the company in 1724, he complained of "having *only* five young *mulâtresses* [in Saint-Louis], which *is insufficient* for the establishment of the number of inhabitants in this settlement"—suggesting that he was in fact wishing for the arrival of more Eurafrican women to marry Frenchmen.[136] Strikingly, members of the Council of Senegal even rejected Du Bellay's decision to bar Frenchmen from associating with Black women as a strategy to curb illicit trade. In 1737, they explicitly supported intermarriage, declaring, "We believe that the root cause of [illicit] trade is that we have not acted firmly enough against the transgressors."[137]

Why did French officials decide not to directly prohibit intermarriage between Frenchmen and women of African descent in Senegambia, as they did elsewhere? Officials in Senegambia were unlikely to want to end mixed relationships, since they took advantage of them themselves to engage in illicit commercial exchanges: this is illustrated by the aforementioned company's complaint in 1688 of "abuses and disorders sustained by [. . .] *Directors,* Captains, Clerks [etc] [. . .] who only think about their own profit and will bring about the ruin of [the company's] business."[138] This is also suggested by the Royal Company of Senegal's decision in 1721 to forbid the *director-general, commandants,* and clerks to "support women openly." French officials identified other unanticipated advantages in those mixed relationships: another argument used to overturn the decision of Du Bellay of 1721 was that mixed unions would in fact help the company "retain good and wise workers who will grow attached to the country."[139] Some officials supported Catholic intermarriage in Senegambia also because they were clearly concerned about the prevalence of concubinage and extramarital sex in the area: when members of the Council of Senegal declared their support for intermarriage in 1737, they invoked "a more Christian motive," claiming that "several women and girls would remove themselves from the crime that they commit."[140]

Taxing Blackness in the Lesser Antilles

Another example of a local legal particularity in the French Atlantic world is that of the *capitation* policy—a rule that might have been both French metropolitan and Spanish inspired—which, by the 1660s, forced free Blacks (*Noirs libres*) and *mulâtres* in the French Lesser Antilles to pay a tax. Designed in France to finance Louis XIV's protracted warfare, the *capitation* was a poll tax—a flat tax levied on individuals. In the Lesser Antilles, it was first levied by the French trading companies in charge of establishing colonies on some (but not all) whites, free people of non-European descent and enslaved people.[141] The application of the *capitation* in the Lesser Antilles was intended to create a racial divide in emerging slave societies through a set of carefully chosen exemptions: this is illustrated by a claim made by the lawyers Marin and Du Treil that French authorities were using this tax "probably to establish a difference between whites and [free Blacks]."[142] French policymakers made it compulsory for manumitted and freeborn Blacks and *mulâtres* in the French Lesser Antilles to pay this tax for themselves, as well as for each of their enslaved workers (if they owned any). By contrast, exemptions were aimed to facilitate the socioeconomic ascension of many white families. This practice was intended to undermine the legal, social and economic status of free Blacks compared to whites.

Discriminatory applications of the *capitation* were limited to the French Lesser Antilles: neither free people of non-European descent nor white colonists were asked to pay this tax for themselves in Saint-Domingue and the Mascarenes. A possible explanation for this difference that has been given by historian Auguste Lebeau is that Saint-Domingue and the Mascarenes did not come under the authority of the trading companies that ruled over the French Lesser Antilles when the tax was first levied overseas. Instead, applications of the *capitation* in Saint-Domingue and the Mascarenes were restricted to enslaved people.[143]

French officials might have gotten the idea for the discriminatory application of the *capitation* from the Spaniards, who themselves borrowed the idea of levying a special tax on people of non-European ancestries from the west coast of Africa, where kings had been requesting tributes from their own subjects since the ninth century.[144] As early as the 1570s, Spanish authorities had already started to force multiple *castas* (castes of African and Indigenous descent) in Guatemala, Mexico, Peru, and the Spanish Caribbean to pay a similar discriminatory tribute. When justifying their decision to require this tribute from the *castas* in 1574, Spanish authorities explicitly invoked the fact that Africans were already "accustomed to paying tributes in great quantity to their kings."[145]

By 1665, authorities in Guadeloupe exempted "gentlemen," "white women" and "white children of the islands, as well as their descendants" from paying the *capitation,* but made no exemptions for free Black women and Black creoles, even if they were born on the island.[146] As a result, free Black women and Black creoles were still forced to pay the *capitation* on their own behalf and that of their captives, as were white colonists from Europe who were not categorized as "gentlemen." In a possible attempt to facilitate tax collection, the Guadeloupean census of 1664 utilized the label "free *nègres*" (*nègres libres*) to differentiate free Blacks from whites.[147] A brief interlude followed, during which all Blacks were exempt from paying the *capitation* alongside white women and white creoles: in 1671, the governor and lieutenant-general of the American islands (French Lesser Antilles), Jean-Charles de Baas, issued an ordinance exempting "white women and girls whatever their country of origin," "creole males and females, born on the island[s]," and "*nègres* above fourteen years of age, along with whites above sixty years," from paying the *capitation*.[148]

All this changed in 1683, however, when local authorities reinstated the *capitation* for free Blacks and free *mulâtres* in the French Lesser Antilles, even if they were born on the islands. That year, the intendant of the *Îles du Vent*, Jean-Baptiste Patoulet, reported that he "had [those people] pay [the tax] without any resistance."[149] He justified this decision by invoking the *mulâtres'* origins as children born outside of Catholic wedlock. He explained, "I have decided that the *mûlatres*, *born out of vice*, should not enjoy the exemption, and that with regard to the *nègres*, their masters can give them their freedom but not the exemption from the tax paid by white people from France." Patoulet's successor as intendant of the *Îles du Vent*, a man named Michel Bégon, confirmed in 1684 that "creole *nègres* and *négresses*, *mulâtres* and *mulâtresses*" had to pay the tax.[150] In another possible attempt to facilitate tax collection, census makers in Martinique began to record "free *mulâtres*, *nègres* and *sauvages*" separately from whites, beginning in 1694.[151]

Only a few people of African descent in the Lesser Antilles obtained tax exemptions for themselves, either thanks to their respectable status in society or because the French relied on them to grow and protect their colonies. In 1688, the intendant of French Saint-Christopher, Gabriel Dumaitz de Goimpy, declared free men and women born to *mulâtres* or *mulâtresses* exempt from the *capitation*, on the grounds that they were creole, few in number, and important to the well-being of the colony. He also invoked his "fear of seeing in Saint-Christopher people whose loyalty was never in doubt go find refuge among the English [on their side of the island]," where they would not have to pay the *capitation*.[152] Metropolitan authorities rejected this change, forcing all people of African descent on the French side of the island to pay the *capitation*.[153] Subsequent exemptions were only granted on a case-by-case basis. One exemption, in particular—to a free Black woman named Magdeleine Berne and her mixed children—was granted in 1696 in Martinique by intendant François-Roger. The latter justified his decision by stressing Magdeleine's status as a woman "born free [. . .] of free parents."[154] Magdeleine's marriage to a Frenchman from Dieppe in 1679, along with her parents' condition as comfortable slaveowners, probably influenced François-Roger's decision as well.[155]

Despite Patoulet's claim that free Blacks and *mûlatres* in the Lesser Antilles agreed to "pay [the tax] without any resistance," many did refuse to pay the *capitation*. A tax collector named Joyeux complained in the 1680s of several free Blacks and *mulâtres* who refused to pay the tax "even if they [were] without a doubt subject to it."[156] In 1738, the enforcement of the *capitation* even prompted a group of free Blacks and *mulâtres* in Guadeloupe to revolt against French authorities. Local officials complained of "the spirit of rebellion at the Grande-Terre, among free *mulâtres* and *nègres*, regarding the *capitation*."[157] Several Guadeloupean *mulâtres* were subsequently imprisoned at Fort-Royal in Martinique for refusing to pay the tax.[158]

Enslavement: A Punishment for Free Blacks

French colonial and metropolitan officials issued a further set of laws establishing yet another difference between whites and free Blacks by threatening only the latter with enslavement if they committed a crime. Initially issued for the Caribbean islands from the 1670s, this set of laws in turn inspired metropolitan officials to apply similar enslavement laws in the Indian Ocean as part of their standardization efforts. The first laws threatening free Blacks with enslavement originated in Martinique when, in 1678, the council of that island issued a first edict forbidding "both free *nègres* [*nègres libres*] and *sauvages*" to give asylum to maroons. This law stated that "*in the event of a second offence*, they will be deprived of the liberty that they are enjoying."[159] This law exacerbated the racial divide in French colonial law and society by targeting all free people of African descent (*nègres libres*), regardless of their status at birth. The standard rule formulated by the crown in the *Code Noir* of 1685 for the Caribbean islands was narrower and less draconian, targeting social status rather than race: article XXXIX of the *Code Noir* of 1685 condemned *manumitted* people (*les affranchis*) who sheltered enslaved people to pay a fine of three hundred livres of sugar per day of protection.[160] Twenty years later, however—upon the request of the governor-general of the French American islands, Charles-François de Machault—the king amended this provision to make it more severe, lamenting that article XXXIX did not dissuade free Blacks from "hosting [maroons], and even from concealing and sharing their stolen goods."[161]

In 1705, he issued an ordinance condemning *all* "free *nègres* [*nègres libres*]" (not just manumitted people) who offered shelter to maroons and kept or shared their stolen goods to *immediate* enslavement, along with their families.[162]

As much as they were intended to diminish the status of free Blacks in relation to white colonizers, these enslavement laws were also aimed at preventing marronage in the Caribbean and dissuading free people of non-European descent from fraternizing with enslaved people. In the first decades of French colonization in the Caribbean, Kalinago communities occasionally offered food and refuge to enslaved maroons in their villages and sometimes partnered with them in raids against French colonists.[163] Free Blacks were also likely to want to assist those of their relatives and friends who remained in captivity. The urge to prevent free Blacks and *mulâtres* from associating with enslaved people became all the more pressing when Black plantation slavery and marronage developed in the Caribbean, along with conspiracies in slave communities. Seventeenth- and eighteenth-century court records, correspondence and travel accounts from the Caribbean are rife with reports of marronage and slave revolts.[164]

Metropolitan authorities drew on these legal precedents from the Caribbean to formulate a standardized body of rules threatening free Blacks with enslavement across Isle Bourbon, Isle of France, and Louisiana (see Table 4.4). Article XXXIII of the Letters Patent of Isle Bourbon and Isle of France of 1723 condemned "manumitted and free *nègres* [*negres affranchis ou libres*]" sheltering maroons to pay a fine and stated that "if [they] fail to pay the fine, they will be reduced to slavery."[165] This article clearly drew on article XXXIX of the *Code Noir* of the Caribbean of 1685, which required manumitted people sheltering enslaved people to pay a fine.[166] Unlike the *Code Noir* of 1685, however, the Letters Patent of Isle Bourbon and Isle of France of 1723 applied to *all* free Blacks, whether or not they were born free. Therefore, it might have been influenced by the 1678 ruling issued in Martinique, which also prescribed the enslavement of all "free *nègres*" in the event of a second offence. Since article XXXIII of the Letters Patent of Isle of France and Isle Bourbon only applied to those free Blacks who were unable to pay the fine levied for sheltering maroons, it did not target comfortable Bourbon Island Creole people of Malagasy or South Asian ancestries.

The 1723 regulation was established in response to marronage, slave rebellions, and the expansion of coffee plantation slavery on Isle Bourbon

TABLE 4.4.
Comparing Article XXXIII of the Letters Patent of the Mascarenes to Article XXXIV of the *Code Noir* of Louisiana

"Lettres Patentes En Forme d'édit, concernant les esclaves nègres des îles de France et de Bourbon [1723]," in *Code des Îles de France et de Bourbon,* 2nd ed., ed. M. Delaleu (Port-Louis, Mauritius, 1826), 250. Source: gallica.bnf.fr / Bibliothèque nationale de France	**"Edit du roi Touchant l'Etat & la Discipline des Esclaves Négres de la Loüisiane [. . .] 1724," in *Recueil d'Edits, Declarations et Arrests de sa Majeste, Concernant l'Administration de la Justice & la Police des Colonies Françaises de l'Amérique,* 2 vols. (Paris, 1744–1745), 2:148. Source: gallica.bnf.fr / Bibliothèque nationale de France**
XXXIII. Les affranchis ou nègres libres qui auront donné retraite dans leurs maisons aux esclaves fugitifs, seront condamnés par corps, envers le maître, en une amende de dix piastres par chacun jour de rétention; et les autres personnes libres qui leur auront donné pareillement retraite, en trois piastres d'amende aussi pour chacun jour de rétention; et faute par lesdits nègres, affranchis ou libres, de pouvoir payer l'amende, ils seront réduits à la condition d'esclaves et vendus; et si le prix de la vente passe l'amende, le surplus sera délivré à l'hôpital.	XXXIV. Les affranchis, ou Nègres libres, qui auront donné retraite dans leurs maisons aux Esclaves fugitifs, seront condamnés par corps, envers le Maître, en une amende de trente livres par chacun jour de retention; & les autres personnes libres qui leur auront donné pareille retraite, en dix livres d'amende, aussi par chacun jour de retention; & faute par lesdits Nègres affranchis ou libres, de pouvoir payer l'amende, ils seront réduits à la condition d'Esclaves & vendus; & si le prix de la vente passe l'amende, le surplus sera délivré à l'Hôpital.

beginning in the 1720s, when the island began to transition to a slave coffee plantation economy.[167] By 1729, the Superior Council of Isle Bourbon had created white militias whose sole purpose was to capture enslaved maroons, and it later formed a Black militia tasked with the same mission.[168] The frequency of marronage on Isle Bourbon increased after a series of droughts, hurricanes, and heavy rains, which resulted in severe food shortages in the 1720s, 1730s, and 1750s. Authorities complained in 1721 that the lack of food "turns [the *nègres*] into fugitives, leads them to plot" and to steal.[169] Between the 1720s and the 1750s, in particular, the records of the Council of Isle Bourbon are rife with mentions of maroons assaulting and murdering colonists for food, weapons, tools, and clothes.[170]

Article XXXIV of the *Code Noir* of Louisiana of 1724 reiterated word for word article XXXIII of the Letters Patent of Isle Bourbon and Isle of France of 1723, subjecting all free Blacks to enslavement if they failed to pay the fine for sheltering maroons.[171] When they formulated article XXXIV, French officials intended to follow in the footsteps of Isle Bourbon and Isle of France. They were also motivated by the emergence of a slave plantation economy based on tobacco, indigo, and rice in the lower Mississippi valley and especially by the rise of marronage and slave rebellions in the region.[172] The penalty for free Blacks sheltering enslaved fugitives in Louisiana became even harsher in 1751, when local authorities issued a regulation echoing the metropolitan ordinance applied to all free Blacks in the Caribbean in 1705. Although the Louisiana regulation of 1751 only applied to *manumitted* people, it likewise prescribed the *immediate* enslavement of freed people who had sheltered maroons and their stolen goods.[173] The Superior Council of Louisiana declared that "all *nègres* and *négresses* having obtained their freedom [. . .] who will receive slaves in their home, to seduce them and incite them to steal from their masters and lead a scandalous life [. . .] will lose their freedom."[174]

Article XXXIV of the *Code Noir* of Louisiana, in turn, inspired metropolitan authorities to revise their punishment for free Blacks sheltering maroons in the Caribbean. The ordinance of 1705 condemned all free Blacks caught sheltering maroons and their stolen goods in the Caribbean to *immediately* lose their freedom.[175] The 1726 royal declaration for the *Îles du Vent* of the Caribbean revised these conditions so that immediate enslavement was no longer the rule for free Blacks sheltering maroons. Rather, the royal declaration for the *Îles du Vent* stated, "In accordance with the edict of March 1724 which acts as law for slaves in our province of Louisiana, should manumitted *nègres* or freemen who have sheltered fugitive slaves be unable to pay the fine of 300 livres of sugar due for each day of shelter, they shall be reduced to slavery."[176] This legal document thus, once again, recycled a Louisiana rule from the *Code Noir* of 1724 (itself based on the Letters Patent of Isle Bourbon and Isle of France), thereby creating a coherent network of racial laws across the empire.

* * *

In conclusion, a pan-imperial and transoceanic approach to the French colonies and outposts is indispensable for fully grasping the origins of racial discourse and policies in the first half of the eighteenth century. France's Indian Ocean colonies and outposts played an important role in shaping racial policies in the Atlantic world due to standardization, the circulation of colonial officials, and the centralization of state papers, which gave metropolitan officials a global outlook on the legal landscape of the French empire. The *Code Noir* of Louisiana of 1724 was the product of this standardizing impulse and global perspective. Since it was a copy of the Letters Patent of the Mascarenes of 1723 (or was formulated together with them), it also reflected concerns that had emerged on Isle Bourbon since the seventeenth century. In fact, the architect of the *Code Noir* of Louisiana and the Letters Patent of the Mascarenes was most likely Marine Secretary Maurepas, who found inspiration in the jurisprudence and other colonial documents thoroughly gathered in metropolitan France during the regency era and counted among his mentors two administrators well versed in colonial politics.

Indian Ocean developments influenced Atlantic policies, and reciprocally, Atlantic developments shaped rulings issued for the French Indian Ocean colonies and outposts. In the 1720s, a set of North American policies intended to prevent intermarriage between Frenchmen and local women was extended to Isle Bourbon and French India by members of the metropolitan assembly of the Company of the Indies because they, too, were committed to standardization and one of their members had spent time in Louisiana. A coherent body of racial policies gradually formed across the empire, coexisting with a constellation of much more localized French policies adapted to local circumstances. Although prohibitions did dissuade many Frenchmen in the colonies from marrying women of non-European descent, however, it was often by transgressing these policies that ordinary people on the ground ended up unwittingly advancing the consolidation of empire. Indeed, whether they took place inside or outside of Catholic wedlock, continuing interracial relations between white men and women of non-European descent turned out to be a very effective instrument of racial power.

CHAPTER 5

Sex and Racial Power

André was born around 1708 in the city of Basse-Terre in Guadeloupe to a white Englishman named Richard and a *mulâtresse* named Jeanneton. Jeanneton was enslaved, and she belonged to Richard's wife, a white woman named Elisabeth. André became Elisabeth's captive at birth, in accordance with the Roman legal principle *partus sequitur ventrem* ("that which is born follows the womb").[1] The precise nature of Richard and Jeanneton's relationship is forever lost to history. Was it an ongoing love story, or did Richard violate Jeanneton? No matter the nature of their relationship, Jeanneton was unable to refuse Richard, since she was apparently never manumitted by Elisabeth. The latter did approach a notary before she died in 1716 with the intention of freeing André, reportedly because of "the friendship that [she and her husband felt] towards [him]."[2] Unfortunately for André, however, the manumission act was deemed invalid because it did not comply with an ordinance issued in 1713, which prevented slaveowners from manumitting their captives without permission from the governor and the intendant of the island.[3]

As a result of this oversight, André spent most of his life in slavery. Following Elisabeth's death, he lived with his father, Richard, according to Guadeloupean authorities, "as if he were his own child, and as a free man."[4] Then, in 1720, Richard made a secret agreement with a Capuchin priest named Ambroise to have him take André to France so that he could be free.[5] The priest took André under his wing, teaching him to read and write and treating him as a free man. However, Ambroise and Richard both died before André could be taken to France.[6] After the two men's passing, the Capuchins did not honor the promise made to Richard. They had André trained as an artisan, allowing him to become "a skillful carpenter, of considerable value."[7] They treated him like their captive, forcing him to work in the city of Basse-Terre where he reportedly built "a church and other remarkable buildings" for them.[8] When in 1738, André petitioned members of the Superior Council of Guadeloupe to obtain his freedom, they rejected his request, declared his freedom papers invalid, and confiscated him from the Capuchins.[9] Although André's market value as a captive was appraised at a considerable 5,000 livres, the Marine Secretary ultimately decided to keep him in the king's estate. In the end, André spent the rest of his life in slavery, building infrastructures for the French crown, including a major bridge in the city of Basse-Terre.[10]

André's story illustrates the main claim of this chapter: although French officials sought to prevent sexual relationships between women of non-European descent and Frenchmen during the first half of the eighteenth century, the continuation of these relationships played an integral role in advancing white people's domination throughout the French empire. Mixed relations within and outside of Catholic wedlock remained widespread across the French empire in this period, contrary to past claims in the scholarship that the French Americas and Indian Ocean were home to a "small number of mulattoes" and that "racial and ethnic boundaries remained largely distinct" in the French context.[11] Although several scholars did note the pervasiveness of *métissage* in these contexts, it was often interpreted as the hallmark of a "lenient racial regime."[12] Interracial sex in the French colonies has been considered a signal that "racial openness" prevailed and that French contemporaries "exhibited no embarrassment at [the] mixing of blood."[13] However, as this chapter demonstrates, interracial relations often contributed to fostering racial regimes by advancing white people's socioeconomic domination. This argument aligns with recent work on race, empire, and slavery in other European imperial contexts.[14] As these publications have shown, in the context of slavery, "the institutional dominance of white [people] had to be translated into personal dominance," and such relations could "reinforc[e] the sexual, gendered, and racial orders of colonial societies."[15]

Sexual coercion and violence, in particular, played an important role in advancing white domination. By the first half of the eighteenth century, they both acted as large-scale instruments of subjugation through the terror they inflicted on now-sizable enslaved communities in the slave societies of the Caribbean, Isle Bourbon and Lower Louisiana. Even in the Mississippi valley, the number of enslaved Black people rose from 533 in 1721 to 4,730 in 1746, and the bulk of this population concentrated in the Gulf Coast region, especially in the New Orleans and Mobile areas.[16] Spurred by the influx of thousands of new enslaved captives in the colonies, white colonists tried to find ways to subjugate expanding slave populations: sexual coercion and violence helped them achieve this goal. Their scope has yet to be assessed, especially because their development in the Indian Ocean has received relatively little attention.[17]

Interracial relations outside of Catholic wedlock between Frenchmen and enslaved women also helped shape white dominion by reducing access to social mobility for enslaved Black women and their mixed children. Especially in Louisiana and the Lesser Antilles, these out-of-wedlock relationships became widespread, partly because of official attempts to prevent whites from marrying Blacks. Unlike marriage—which necessitated the approval of a priest and the publication of public banns—interracial relationships outside of Catholic wedlock could flourish because they were relatively easy to hide. Unlike marriage, however, relations out of wedlock did not permit enslaved women and their mixed children to inherit, nor did they allow them to systematically achieve manumission. Their fate in such situations usually remained under the control of their white partners or owners: consider Jeanneton, who was never manumitted by Elisabeth, and André, who could never be free because of his mistress's negligence. Access to patrimony for these people was further blocked by a slew of—largely overlooked—Atlantic policies that prohibited white fathers from acknowledging their mixed children in parish registers.

When Catholic intermarriage did occur despite legal restrictions—as was frequently the case in the Indian Ocean—it was often between an underprivileged white man and a prosperous, assimilated freeborn woman of Malagasy or South Asian ancestry whose fortune allowed the man to ascend the social ladder. This further advanced white socioeconomic dominion, especially since the woman was often categorized as "white" in official documents. Because French inheritance customs and household financial practices were patriarchal, these alliances conferred substantial advantages on underprivileged Frenchmen.

However, free and unfree people of non-European descent refused to stay passive when confronted with manipulation or coercion. This chapter is premised upon Vincent Brown's interpretation of Orlando Patterson's notion of slavery as "social death," not as the actual outcome of bondage, but rather as a constant threat that drove the enslaved to fight against alienation.[18] Enslaved women resisted their aggressors as best as they could, for example, by running away or by using self-defense, and they (along with enslaved men) also attempted to protect girls and women in their communities. Other enslaved women, as well as their mixed children, like André, strove to free themselves from enslavement or to ameliorate their socioeconomic condition.

Sexual Violence: A Large-Scale Weapon of Domination in Slave Societies

With the rise of Black slavery in the eighteenth century, sexual coercion and violence became a defining feature of all French slave societies, acting as a large-scale instrument of subjugation not only insofar as it boosted slave reproduction but also by terrorizing large enslaved communities across the Atlantic and Indian Ocean worlds. Black feminist scholar Angela Davis has convincingly presented sexual violence and coercion as a way for white men to assert their sovereignty by spreading affliction and fear—not only among enslaved Black women but also across enslaved Black communities at large, given the depth of kinship and friendship bonds.[19] We know how enormous the impact of sexual violence was on enslaved people's experience in other (especially Anglo-American) slave societies for which we have firsthand slave narratives. It is very clear from those accounts that the emotional and physical toll of sexual abuse on enslaved communities cannot be sidestepped, even if the evidence documenting it in the French context is scarce.[20]

Sexual violence was not solely the preserve of white men over women of non-European descent. Same-sex sexual abuses and sexual abuses perpetrated by white women on Black men were also an important reality. Same-sex sexual abuse is much less visible in French historical documents partly because the French did not have access to an archive-keeping institution like the Spanish Inquisition, whose role was specifically to combat religious irreverence, as in cases of sodomy.[21] Moreover, most European contemporaries would have found the idea of a white woman abusing an enslaved woman or man unfathomable: chastity was too central to gender ideals imposed on European women, and any assault by a woman against a man would have upended established European gender hierarchies.[22] This is not to say that such abuses did not take place: in fact, there is no doubt that white women also engaged in acts of sexual violence against enslaved men and women. This is illustrated by the story of a white creole woman on early eighteenth-century Isle Bourbon named Gabrielle Bellon, who was said to commit horrible acts of sexual mutilation against her captives. The storekeeper and upcoming governor of Isle Bourbon Antoine Desforges-Boucher described Bellon as "the devil incarnate" because she was known for punishing her captives by attaching them to a pillar, burning their intimate parts, and placing iron plates into their mouths to prevent them from eating.[23]

By the first half of the eighteenth century, multiple cases of sexual violence were being recorded in the court registers of the now flourishing French slave societies of the Americas and the Indian Ocean. In 1733, on Isle Bourbon, for example, a French carpenter named Rochefort was fined and imprisoned because he had attempted to rape a pregnant enslaved Malagasy woman named Nanon, causing the death of her unborn baby.[24] About ten years later, French officials lamented the presence of colonists on this island who did not hesitate "to resort to violence against [the *négresses*] who resist[ed] their criminal desires."[25] In 1744, in Guadeloupe, a merchant named Antoine Thuillon, who was awaiting his trial for unpaid debts in prison, was accused of having entered the cell of an enslaved Black woman named Marie Anne in order to sexually assault her.[26] We only know of this story because Thuillon also attacked the white jailer who came to Marie Anne's rescue. In the end, Thuillon was not punished for his assault on Marie Anne: he was only sentenced to spend a month in prison and pay a fine of 200 livres for his attack on the jailer who tried to intervene.[27]

Enslaved victims behaved with incredible dignity, fighting back against their oppressors and attempting to protect members of their communities. This is illustrated by the story of Louison, an enslaved Black woman cook who belonged to the Ursuline nuns of New Orleans. On a rainy afternoon in June 1752, Louison was washing linen with other enslaved women by the Mississippi River, near the Ursuline nuns' convent-hospital, when she spotted a drunken French soldier named Pochenet. Pochenet's face looked familiar, for she had taken care of him at the hospital. Pochenet walked toward the river and requested that the women wash his dirty handkerchief, which they refused to do. Infuriated, Pochenet threw himself at Babet, one of the other laundresses, and stabbed her to death with his bayonet. Louison immediately ran toward Babet to rescue her, putting her own life at risk. In an attempt to assert his control over Louison's Black body, Pochenet forced her to her knees, hit her with his bayonet, and demanded that she beg for his forgiveness. Louison apologized, but only after defying Pochenet by saying, "It is only from God that one ask for forgiveness."[28] The whole incident no doubt had a sexual undertone: when the case went to court, one of the first questions that the French commissioner Jean-Baptiste Raguet asked Pochenet was whether he had intended to "seduce the *négresses*," to which the soldier answered that he did not remember because he was too drunk at the time.[29] The victims and witnesses' testimonies in this court case shed light on the spirit of mutual aid and community among enslaved people. After hearing the women scream, many enslaved people ran to their rescue, along with a Frenchman and other people from the hospital. They were eventually able to stop Pochenet and take him away. Louison's husband, who was an enslaved surgeon's aide at the hospital, even wounded his hands while trying to protect the women.[30]

Sexual violence and coercion by white men caused widespread emotional and physical suffering in enslaved communities. This is illustrated by a series of sexual assaults that took place on a plantation in the environs of New Orleans in 1730. That year, a plantation owner and member of the colonial council named Sieur Raymond Amyault d'Ausseville filed a civil claim against his plantation overseer, a Frenchman named Jacques Le Roy Charpentier, for engaging in horrible acts of cruelty. Le Roy created a climate of terror on d'Ausseville's plantation, keeping enslaved people severely overworked and underfed. In addition to having killed a captive, he repeatedly tried to form "scandalous relations" with enslaved women in the fields, mistreating those who rejected his sexual advances. Le Roy had also caused a series of miscarriages among enslaved women on the plantation, killing several unborn babies who might have been his own. An enslaved woman named Suzanne gave birth to two stillborn babies, one of whom had reportedly had "its head crushed," as a result of "a violent blow." Suzanne's husband, an enslaved man named Lafleur, was devastated and inconsolable: "[He] does not want to eat nor drink, all he does is cry, he complains that [Le Roy] ha[s] beaten his wife even though she is pregnant," d'Ausseville explained.[31] D'Ausseville's position as a colonial councilor did not help him win this case in the end, since the court decided not to rule against Le Roy: the French overseer was allowed to keep working on the plantation until the end of his contract.[32]

Like Jacques Le Roy, many white plantation overseers and other white staff on Atlantic and Indian Ocean plantations abused enslaved women, causing such turmoil that officials and several slaveowners were forced to take matters into their own hands to protect French financial interests. Such was the case with a planter named Sieur du Buisson, who lived in Martinique: in 1717, he made the decision to fire his white sugar refiner "for having pressured a *négresse* instead of having her work like he should have done."[33]

Sexual abuse against enslaved women by plantation overseers was especially common on Isle Bourbon. This development even prompted the French Company of the Indies to write a letter to the Superior Council of Isle Bourbon in 1729, complaining that "disorder persists [. . .] with the *négresses*, and [yet] you allow young soldiers to become plantation overseers, and don't attempt to curb their debauchery."[34] Several Frenchmen described as "young libertine soldiers [. . .] unable to restrain their amorous desires" were imprisoned on Isle of France because they had had sex with enslaved people on plantations. After they were released from prison, one of these soldiers took a married enslaved Black woman away from her cabin, and another abducted a domestic servant described as a "*négresse*" belonging to one Madame Dhauterive.[35] Because of those developments, authorities on Isle of France and Isle Bourbon declared in 1729 that "we must ensure that no soldier will abduct any *négresse*, that all the *négresses* have cabins where they can lock themselves while their husbands are away, and which are kept separate from soldiers' cabins."[36] This declaration did not, however, deter French soldiers and plantation overseers on Isle Bourbon from trying to have sex with enslaved women. In 1736, three white men were expelled from the island because they had had sex with an enslaved Black woman. One of them was a plantation overseer named Joseph Pascal, who used to work for a female planter named Catherine de Justamond in the parish of Saint-Denis. Pascal had reportedly "developed a habit with a married *négresse* with whom he was apparently caught in the act several times" and who worked as a nurse on Justamond's estate.[37] Members of the Council of Isle Bourbon lamented that "most plantation overseers," of whom Joseph was a prime example, were becoming "insolent, arrogant and libertine."[38] Another one of the expelled men was a plantation overseer accused of "leading a scandalous life devoted to wine and *négresses*" on the plantation estate of one Mr. Villarmoy.[39]

Although some refused to let plantation overseers abuse their enslaved property, many slaveowners did not hesitate to assert their own sovereignty over their captives' bodies, by coercing and violating them. It has been argued in recent work on French New Orleans that, in contrast to what happened in the Caribbean, "white men who did not have a white woman (mother, spouse, or daughter) to take care of their house did not rely on a free or enslaved *ménagère*"—a housekeeper who lived with a white man, often having sexual relations with him, and sometimes acting as his business partner.[40] A close look at city census data nuances this assumption: by the 1720s and 1730s, a substantial number of single white men and white women in the city cohabited with an enslaved Black domestic servant.[41] By 1721, almost 20 percent of all slave-owning households in New Orleans were home to one single white male or female who lived with only one enslaved Black housekeeper or domestic servant.[42] Additionally, three out of ten slaveowners in the village of Tchoupitoulas that year cohabited with only one enslaved Black domestic servant.[43] In 1731, thirty-nine of the slaveowners who lived by the river right outside of the city also lived together with one Black domestic servant.[44]

Coerced sex must have been a widespread occurrence in this context, reinforcing white dominion in the process: this is suggested by the fast-growing number of *mulâtres* born to enslaved Black women who were baptized in and right outside of New Orleans, most of whom officially spent their life in slavery. The New Orleans census of 1732 listed only six "*mulâtres* or *mulâtresses*," and only two *mulâtres* were baptized in New Orleans between 1731 and 1733.[45] However, over the course of the short period between 1744 and 1759, as many as 184 *mulâtres* appeared in New Orleans' parish registers, most of whom were born outside of wedlock and few of whom were officially manumitted. This is an enormous figure when considered in context, since there were only 759 white people living in New Orleans by 1737.[46] Priests over this period also baptized eleven children described as *quarterons* ("quadroons"), or born to white men and *mulâtresses*.[47] *Métissage* in French New Orleans eventually peaked at the end of the French period: 124 other *mulâtres* and 3 *quarterons* appeared in the city's parish registers between 1759 and 1762, most of whom were not manumitted.[48] This remained a proportionally large figure, since only 1,284 white people lived in New Orleans by 1763.[49] Several of these mixed children were explicitly described as being born to "an unknown white father," "an unknown father," "a businessman," or "a master." A baby girl named Marie-Françoise, who was baptized in December 1752 in New Orleans, for example, was described in church records as a *mûlatresse* born to a Black woman named Angelique and as "the product of her master."[50]

Cases of sexual coercion by white slaveowners against their enslaved properties were not restricted to New Orleans and its surroundings: many *mulâtres* were baptized in the northern parish of Pointe Coupée as well, most of whom also remained in slavery. Located about 150 miles north of New Orleans, Pointe Coupée was an isolated frontier settlement surrounded by a U-shaped lake now known as False River.[51] French colonists there purchased a growing number of enslaved people in order to expand tobacco and indigo plantation agriculture, as well as farming. This is why the census of Pointe Coupée of 1731 listed thirty-seven white men, twenty-five white women, and seven *engagés* for seventy enslaved Blacks.[52] Because those enslaved people were spread quite evenly across all estates, most were forced to live in very close proximity with whites: a majority of white estates in Pointe Coupée owned up to five enslaved people, whereas only six households owned no enslaved people at all.[53] Many enslaved women must have faced sexual coercion as a result. This would certainly explain why fifteen *mulâtres* were recorded in the census of Pointe Coupée in 1745, none of whom were officially manumitted, as well as twenty-three others, most of whom were born to enslaved Black women and "unknown father[s]" between 1756 and 1763.[54] These numbers are significant since Pointe Coupée was home to only 259 white residents by 1745.[55]

Because the French in the Caribbean also lived in very close contact with some of their captives, many enslaved women in the Antilles also faced sexual abuse from their owners or from men in their owner's family. It became a notoriously common practice among white men in late eighteenth-century Saint-Domingue to live in concubinage with an unfree or free Black *ménagère*.[56] The practice of living in concubinage with a female Black housekeeper already existed in Martinique decades earlier. This is why, in 1722, the Dominican missionary Father Mane criticized white men on the island "who [were] not ashamed to stay and live with *négresses* and *mulâtresses* as their concubines, as if they were their legitimate wives."[57] Father Mane blamed Blacks and *mulâtresses* for "easily ced[ing] to the seduction and threats, gifts and solicitations of those who want to debauch them"—who, according to him, included "their masters, very often the children of the house, and almost always white domestic servants."[58] He explained that "there [were] almost no plantation[s] [in Martinique] left where there [were] not many [*mulâtres*]" as a result.[59]

In the eighteenth-century southwest Indian Ocean, many slaveowners also asserted their authority by forcing enslaved women in their households into concubinage. A Lazarist priest lamented in 1740 that "most [settlers on Isle Bourbon] have a large number of bastard children born to their *négresses*."[60] According to the French writer, engineer, and botanist Bernardin de Saint-Pierre, who spent time in the Mascarenes, few settlers on Isle Bourbon were willing to get married "because of how easy it [was] to find concubines among Black slaves."[61] He claimed that "men far too often neglect[ed] [European and creole women on the island] in favor of enslaved Black women."[62]

The practice of keeping enslaved concubines was not restricted to France's slave societies in the Americas and on Isle Bourbon: in seventeenth-century Pondicherry, for example, the French traveler Robert Challe noted the presence of several very young enslaved Hindu girls whom he branded *filles de mauvaise vie* (prostitutes) because they were hired out by European men for sex and domestic services. He advanced the commodification of these enslaved little girls by describing them as sexually available and consumable, explaining, "There are many Europeans who maintain [them] [. . .]. They cost the same price as *valets* and domestic servants, a *roupie* [local currency] each month is enough."[63]

Enslaved women's sex work was a very important site of enactment of white supremacy. Marisa Fuentes has already shown how brothels and other such institutions, in particular, were places where "degrading and violating racia[l] and [gender] inequalit[ies]" were replicated, since they reproduced the power relations "owner and owned; patriarch and submissive female" and confined enslaved women and Black procurers to "a particular economic function." White men's control over enslaved women's bodies was so complete in this context that powerless women were forced to perform the illusion of "mutuality," given the "performative nature of such [economy]."[64] All this is best illustrated by Challe's extremely troubling account of the prepubescent enslaved Asian girls forced into sex work in

Pondicherry.[65] He catered to his male readers' appetite for exoticism by bragging about his own sexual adventure with eight of these girls, who according to him had nothing to cover their bodies "except for some bracelets around their arms and legs."[66] He explained, "Don't be surprised if I am so knowledgeable and confident when I talk about this subject: [. . .] I was there, my eyes have seen, my hands have touched: I have satisfied my curiosity, and that is all."[67] Challe's account is appalling. He claimed that the oldest girl in the group was only twelve years old and that the two others he touched "weren't even ten years old, having no pubic hair on their intimate parts."[68] French Caribbean cities were home to a particularly large number of brothels, as well as other such institutions where enslaved women were also forced into sex work. According to a Guadeloupean legal document written in 1711, many enslaved people in Caribbean cities acted as procurers, "gathering women, and conducting their business in manumitted people's homes, managing cabarets, even in white people's homes."[69]

Especially in the Caribbean, many white contemporaries attempted to displace the responsibility for sexual contacts between white men and enslaved women onto enslaved women themselves by describing them as dissolute temptresses responsible for their own victimization. This is manifest in the language employed by members of the court in Guadeloupe in 1738, after they refused to manumit the aforementioned *mulâtre* carpenter André, the son of the Englishman Richard and the enslaved Black woman Jeanneton. They invoked a "need to dissuade those masters who are weak enough *to succumb to the lubricity of their négresses*" from manumitting their children.[70] Many scholars, including Saidiya Hartman, have already discussed this rhetoric in British American and US slave societies.[71] In 1722, a priest in Guadeloupe even began to encourage acts of public penance for enslaved Black women who had had sex with white men, forcing them to wear iron collars "in order to make the public sanction more glaring."[72]

Out-of-Wedlock Relations and White Social Dominion in Slave Societies

Out-of-wedlock relations between white men and unfree and free women of non-European descent also helped shape white supremacy by narrowing the path to upward mobility for these women and their mixed children.

Because these relationships, unlike marriage, did not necessarily result in the manumission of enslaved women and their mixed children, white men in this context retained complete power over the fate of their enslaved partner and mixed children.[73] They were the ones deciding whether they would receive gifts or whether they would be manumitted and under what terms. And even when the white man did take measures to manumit a woman, a nonmarital relationship did not normally enable her and her mixed children to inherit: the Paris Custom only allowed widows to have a claim to the estate if the couple had been married in the Catholic Church.[74] Nonmarital relationships between white men and enslaved women thus helped keep patrimony in white hands.

Relatively few Frenchmen across the French Atlantic slave societies defied intermarriage restrictions in the first half of the eighteenth century, favoring out-of-wedlock relationships instead. In the Lesser Antilles, intermarriage became increasingly rare when the practice of requesting marriage authorizations was normalized after the 1720s.[75] This period also coincided with the prohibition of intermarriage by the *Code Noir* of Louisiana of 1724, which—according to historian Léo Elisabeth—had an enormous impact on marriage practices in the Lesser Antilles.[76] The governors and intendants of Martinique only occasionally allowed intermarriages from the 1720s onward.[77] While a total of twenty-four mixed marriages had been celebrated in Fort-Royal, Martinique, in the thirty years between 1679 and 1709, only eleven were celebrated between 1710 and 1739 and only five between 1740 and 1769.[78] In Guadeloupe, too, authorities appear to have sanctioned only a few of these unions. When they did so, it was often because the relationship was already happening out of wedlock. As a case in point, for the period between 1700 and 1759, the well-preserved parish registers of Le Gosier, Guadeloupe, mention only one mixed marriage, which took place in 1757. This marriage was between a white creole woman named Marie-Madelaine Delbourg and a "free *mulâtre*" named François Taouïra, with whom she already had two mixed children born out of wedlock, named Charles and François.[79] Marie-Madelaine's own father, Nicolas Delbourg, already had a mixed-race boy out of wedlock with a free *mulâtresse* named Marie Rose Taouïra, who was probably a relative of François.[80] This family connection may have encouraged him to approve of his daughter's union with a man of African descent. The parish register in which Marie-Madelaine and François Taouïra's marriage is recorded specified that "the marriage was celebrated with the consent of the parents."[81] This was unusual: relations between white women and Black men provoked even greater opprobrium than those between white men and Black women because they challenged race and gender hierarchies and threatened to give Black men control over white patrimony.

Intermarriages between whites and Blacks, prohibited by the *Code Noir* of 1724, were even rarer in Lower Louisiana than they were in the Lesser Antilles, with Frenchmen preferring out-of-wedlock relationships that offered fewer social advantages to enslaved women and their mixed children. There are no records of mixed marriages celebrated between whites and Blacks in the parish registers of Mobile for the period between 1724 and 1763 or in the records of Natchitoches from 1729 through 1763.[82] The same is true for the parishes of Pointe Coupée from 1756 to 1768 and Biloxi, Yazoo, and Natchez between 1720 and 1730.[83] In the parish registers of New Orleans for the period between 1720 and 1763, only two mixed marriages between a Black person and a white person were recorded. The first one, which took place in 1725, was between a white woman named Marie Gaspart and a free Black man from Martinique named Jean-Baptiste Raphaël. The priest sought the permission of the commandant-general, Pierre du Gué de Boisbriant, before performing the ceremony, probably because of the *Code Noir* prohibition of 1724.[84] The second mixed marriage recorded in the archives of New Orleans took place more than two decades later. A woman named Christine Chovin, who was listed as a "free *mulâtresse*," gave birth to a child named Jean-Paul in 1747.[85] A New Orleans–born man named Jean La France (or La Flot), whom we may assume was white, acknowledged being the father of Jean-Paul and "having the intention to marry the *mulâtresse* Christine, the mother of the child."[86] Christine was born to a Frenchman named Delerÿ and a woman named Françoise, who was identified as an enslaved *négresse*. Jean eventually married Christine in 1748, and the couple had another son named Jean-Baptiste in 1754.[87] Jean-Paul and Jean-Baptiste were lucky because most white fathers in French Louisiana did not usually recognize their mixed children.

Since one of the few scenarios in which a mixed child born outside of Catholic wedlock could inherit was if their father recognized them in official documents and gave his consent, most mixed children born outside of Catholic wedlock faced social inertia.[88] It has been argued that, "as a general rule, white fathers remained silent [in the parish registers of

New Orleans, Louisiana], not deigning to publicly acknowledge their sexual partners or mixed-race children."[89] In making this choice not to record the names of the white men who had fathered those mixed children, however, Louisiana priests might have also been complying with a series of policies imposed by French authorities in the Caribbean and metropolitan France.[90] A judgment issued after a white father refused to have his name listed next to his *mulâtre* son in a church register of Martinique in 1670 stated, "We prohibit priests as well as all other clerics, to baptize any child *and to name the father* without having obtained the explicit consent of the man who fathered [said child]."[91] Then, in 1734, an ordinance issued in the kingdom of France forbade priests from inquiring about the names of the fathers of all children born outside of wedlock.[92] Finally, the practice of requesting the names of white fathers who had had mixed children outside of wedlock was targeted by a series of policies formulated in the French Caribbean.[93] In 1752, the French intendant of the *Îles du Vent*, Charles-Martin Hurson, opposed the practice of letting mixed children bear the names of their white fathers and requested that priests use the idiom "unknown father" (*père inconnu*) instead.[94] The Council of Martinique issued another judgment six years later, which reminded priests that, for children who "are not born to a legitimate marriage, there will be no mention of the father" in the records.[95] This partly explains why 45 percent (228 out of 501) of all free children of non-European descent born between 1763 and 1767 in Martinique, many of whom were mixed, were listed as the progenies of "unknown father[s]" (*père[s] inconnu[s]*) in the records.[96]

A very small proportion of white fathers had their names recorded next to their free and enslaved *mulâtre* sons and daughters in the parish registers of Lower Louisiana, suggesting that few mixed children of African descent in the region were able to enjoy their male progenitor's patrimony and relative social status. Priests in the Mississippi valley employed the exact same expression as that used in the French Caribbean, labeling the fathers of mixed children "unknown." Of the fifty-one *mulâtres* baptized between 1744 and 1753 in New Orleans, thirteen were recorded as born to an "unknown father," and thirty-eight others did not have their father's name listed in the registers. Only four were born to a white father identified by a name.[97] Ninety-six of the *mulâtres* baptized between 1759 and 1762 were also born to "unknown father[s]," and only a handful of mixed children bore their white father's name: the *mulâtre* Joseph La Combe, the presumed son of the French pitch-and-tar manufacturer whom we encountered earlier in the opening of this book, is one such example.[98] Another young *mulâtre* of Louisiana, Mathias Forcade, also bore the name of his white father, Jacques Forcade. Mathias was born to Jacques and to an enslaved Black woman named Manon, who belonged to a resident of the German Coast, west of New Orleans. After purchasing Mathias from his owner, Jacques officially acknowledged him as his own son by calling him "Mathias Forcade" in the documents that he drafted to secure his freedom. After moving to Saint-Domingue, in 1745, Jacques enlisted a New Orleans-based woman named Anne Galbreon to help him get Mathias's freedom.[99] Since out-of-wedlock relationships, unlike marriage, did not bring manumission, enslaved Black women and their mixed children only became free when their white partners or fathers took the necessary steps to manumit them, as Jacques did.

This dynamic reinforced white men's authority over enslaved women and their mixed-race children. Some slaveowners might have manipulated their female captive's hopes of manumission in order to sexually exploit them.[100] The records of a New Orleans court case point toward one probable example of such manipulation. Sometime before 1736, a white slaveowner named Pierre Garçon L'Eveillé promised freedom to his enslaved Black house servant Jeanneton. However, L'Eveillé changed his mind after Jeanneton ran away, told authorities that she was pregnant with his child, and asked to be taken away from him.[101] Others only manumitted their captives under certain conditions, perhaps to keep their leverage over them. Such was the case in 1762, in the parish of Pointe Coupée, Louisiana, when a white man named Alexandre Chenet used the services of a notary to manumit his captive Hypolite, classified as a "*négresse*," and her six-year-old *mulâtre* son, Isidore. Perhaps because Chenet wanted to dissuade Hypolite from leaving him, he added a provision to the manumission act specifying that she would only become free after his death and that she should continue to serve him until then.[102]

Since very few white men in Lower Louisiana took the necessary steps to officially manumit their mixed children or Black sexual partners, most Black concubines and mixed children in the region had no path to getting freedom papers.[103] According to Cécile Vidal, half of the manumission deeds recorded in New Orleans during the French period involved enslaved women and their mixed children, suggesting that some white men did emancipate their Black partners and mixed offspring.[104] Manumission records point toward a few cases in which a white man appears to have freed his Black partner and mixed children. For example, in 1735 in New Orleans, one Sieur Pierre de Saint-Julien mortgaged all his enslaved servants and property to manumit Marie Charlotte and Louise, the two daughters of an enslaved Black woman named Gaigne. Saint-Julien claimed to want to manumit those girls to thank Gaigne "for specific reasons, to ease his conscience," without further explanation.[105] Some fathers used intermediaries to free their mixed children, presumably because they wanted to avoid paying the fee prescribed by the *Code Noir* of 1724 for free men fathering children with enslaved women. I already mentioned Jacques Forcade, the Saint-Domingue-based white man who enlisted Anne Galbreon to help him get his son's freedom in New Orleans in 1745. A few years earlier, prior to his departure for the Chickasaw Wars (1721–1763) with little hope of return, a Marine troop captain named Sieur Jacques de Coustillas officially manumitted Pierrot, Françoise and Marianne—three captives described as "*mulâtre*" and "*mulâtresse[s]*" in one document. Pierrot was born to a white man who might have been no other than Jean-Baptiste Martin Diron d'Artaguiette—Coustillas's army fellow and the *commissaire-ordonnateur* of Louisiana turned director of the French Company of the Indies who opposed intermarriage between Frenchmen and Native American women. Manumission records explicitly described Pierrot as "the *mulâtre* son of D'Artaguette [*sic*]."[106] A few years later, in 1745, in Pointe Coupée, another white man, Vincent Le Porche, manumitted a *mulâtresse* named Marie Louise on the grounds that she should "enjoy full and complete liberty, being the daughter of a Frenchman," though he did not identify this man.[107]

Although more white slaveowners took the necessary steps to free their Black partners and mixed children in the French Caribbean than in French Louisiana, such manumissions were slightly less common in Martinique and Guadeloupe than on the isle of Saint-Domingue. Saint-Domingue developed a large free population of non-European descent as a result of *métissage* and manumissions through self-purchase, military service, and other accomplishments.[108] Colonists on the island developed a flexible approach to manumissions, perhaps because the island's sizeable dimensions made it more difficult for authorities to control mixed relationships, and the colony also shared a porous border with a Spanish colony—where manumissions had long been common practice.[109] Although Blacks, *mulâtres*, and people of Indigenous descent amounted to almost 18 percent of the free population in Saint-Domingue (2,525 people) by 1740, they only amounted to 14 percent of the free population in Guadeloupe by 1731 (1,332) and to 13 percent of the free population in Martinique as late as 1764 (1,846).[110] At least some white men in the Lesser Antilles must have manumitted their enslaved female partners: this is suggested by the fact that women outnumbered men in the free population of African descent of Martinique.[111] Women amounted to 63 percent of the free adult population of non-European descent in Martinique in 1726 (422 people) and to 54 percent in 1742.[112] Some white fathers must have manumitted their mixed children, as well, since mixed people (categorized as *mulâtres* or *métis*) amounted to a majority within the population of free children of non-European descent on both Martinique and Guadeloupe.[113]

Once freed, however, those people saw their social mobility restricted by the slew of racial policies issued beginning in the late seventeenth century. The provision of article LII of the *Code Noir* of 1724, which banned endowments from whites to Blacks "[neither] inter vivos, nor after death," was applied on at least two occasions in Louisiana.[114] Such was the case in 1728, in New Orleans, when a ship captain on his deathbed granted all his personal possessions and all the money owed to him by the French Company of the Indies to an enslaved woman described as "Mr. Larou's [*négresse*]," reportedly to reward her for "her faithful care of him while [he was] sick."[115] Colonial authorities refused to honor this section of his will invoking "said *négresse's* incapacity to receive donations."[116] The provision banning donations from whites to Blacks was then used a second time to disenfranchise a Native American woman. One year after the Larou case, in Natchitoches, an enslaved Osage woman was also denied a donation from her owner on the grounds that "said *sauvagesse* cannot enjoy [the legacy] in accordance with article fifty-two of the *Code Noir*."[117]

Some other Blacks in Louisiana, who had been manumitted, were even reenslaved following court sentences for crimes. These reenslavement cases did not fully align with article XXXIV of the *Code Noir* of 1724, which subjected free Blacks to enslavement if they had failed to pay the fine for sheltering maroons: there is evidence that two manumitted Blacks were reenslaved for other reasons.[118] One of them was a twenty-year-old free man of African ancestry named Jean-Baptiste (or Baptiste) Coustillas, who had been manumitted with his family in the 1730s by his owner and possible father, the aforementioned Marine troop captain Jacques de Coustillas.[119]

Jean-Baptiste only enjoyed his freedom for a few brief years until he was accused of theft by one Sieur Fabry in 1743. Although Jean-Baptiste denied the accusation, he was convicted for robbery, reenslaved, and sold for the benefit of the hospital of New Orleans.[120] Jean-Baptiste's sister Jeanne (or Jeannette) was also reenslaved four years later in 1747 for theft and unpaid debt.[121]

Although some enslaved Black women and their mixed children did obtain their freedom and retain it, the vast majority remained subject to their white owner's yoke. When a Frenchman wanted to free a Black female partner whom he did not possess, there was no guarantee that her owner would agree to sell her. Still in New Orleans, a militia officer named Sieur André Jung succeeded in convincing one Monsieur Benoît Payen de Chavoye to sell him his probable Black partner, Jeanne, in 1763 for the exorbitant sum of 17,500 livres. He also convinced Chavoye to sell him Jeanne's *mulâtresse* daughter within four years for an additional 4,000 livres.[122] However, another enslaved woman in Louisiana, named Catherine, was not so lucky. We only know of Catherine's story because she ran away when her owner, a man named Sieur François Henry Duplanty, refused to sell her to her presumed partner, Louis, in 1767, and she found refuge in a cabin belonging to one of her friends. Catherine and Louis continued to see each other in this cabin and in Louis's bedroom at the inn where he had been staying. When Catherine was arrested, Duplanty requested from Louis that he pay a fee of ten livres for each day that she had been away.[123]

There were also several cases in which a child was manumitted while the mother was not. In New Orleans, this is what happened to a woman named Marie-Jeanne, categorized as a "*négresse* slave." Although her sexual partner, a French merchant named Louis Rançon, secured the freedom of their *mulâtre* son, Louis-François, in 1751, he did not free her and eventually married a more "acceptable" (white) woman, Marie Françoise Gallot, in 1762.[124] Another woman of African descent from New Orleans, Jacqueline Lemelle, also remained enslaved after a man named Gardelle Gaspard spent 800 livres to purchase and manumit her six-month-old so-called "*quarteron*" ("quadroon") in 1765. Gaspard also agreed to pay an extra twenty sols per day to allow this infant to stay with his mother for another year. He may have acted on behalf of a man named Joseph Dusuau de La Croix, who later admitted being the father of one of Jacqueline's children, a boy named Louis.[125]

Even when the child and the mother were both freed, it could take years before their freedom was officialized or before they could leave their owner's estate. Remember Marianne, the Black house servant who likely engaged in a relationship with Claude Vignon La Combe, with whom she cohabited and probably had two mixed children. It turns out that La Combe's business partner at the pitch-and-tar factory on Lake Pontchartrain, a Paris-born Frenchman named Chavannes, also had a relationship with his house servant. In 1732, in New Orleans, Chavannes requested an authorization from the governor and *commissaire-ordonnateur* of Louisiana to manumit his Black or mixed-race housekeeper, Isabelle.[126] Yet it took Chavannes another six years to finally have her freedom recorded at the clerk's office, on the grounds that she had "contented him through her loyalty and services."[127] Chavannes appears on several occasions in historical documents because of his activities as a planter and a secretary at the Council of Louisiana.[128] He may have fathered a daughter with Isabelle and allowed her to live as free without freedom papers. Strikingly, however, Isabelle and her daughter continued to work for Chavannes, even after their manumission. The couple eventually moved to the northern shore of Lake Pontchartrain, where Chavannes ran the pitch-and-tar factory with La Combe.[129] When he died in 1752, Chavannes designated Isabelle and her daughter as his sole heirs "as a payment for their salary for when they worked for him."[130] The council agreed to deliver Chavannes's belongings to Isabelle despite article LII of the *Code Noir* of 1724 (which prevented Blacks from receiving such donations from whites), but only because of "their limited value."[131]

Like Isabelle's daughter, several mixed children in the Americas were allowed to enjoy an informal and incomplete form of freedom, without official documentation, and which forced them to remain under white people's yoke. There were different paths to freedom for enslaved people. A few white men in the French Americas used church registers to manumit their mixed children. Such was the case of the abovementioned French merchant Louis Rançon: he had his *mulâtre* boy Louis-François recorded as a "free *mulâtre*" in 1751 in a baptism record of New Orleans, acknowledging his paternity and claiming to have "procured [his] freedom" from his owner beforehand—though there is no evidence that he actually did so.[132] The practice of recording enslaved mixed children as free in church records was not limited to French Louisiana. The crown protested in 1736 that several white men in the French Caribbean "have children whose mothers are slaves baptized as free, in order to have them identified as manumitted slaves." As a result, the king enjoined priests not to baptize any children as free unless their mother was clearly manumitted.[133] Scholars have called the people in this state of limbo in between slavery and freedom the *libres des savanes* or *libres de fait,* though neither of these expressions was used before the late eighteenth century.[134]

As shown earlier by the story of the carpenter André in Guadeloupe, informal manumissions created a group of second-class subjects of non-European descent whose freedom was entirely dependent on white people's intentions. The story of Charlotte, an enslaved *mulâtresse* from New Orleans, also illustrates this point well. Charlotte was born to an enslaved Black woman named Jeanneton and a white infantry captain named Pierre-Henri Derneville. Although Charlotte was by all evidence allowed to live as free in her father's household, he never formally manumitted her. As a result, Charlotte was rumored to be working as a prostitute in the city to make enough money to purchase her own freedom. It seems that she was pushed to do so by her father's wife, Mrs. Pelagia Fleuriau, who happened to be the daughter of the attorney-general of Louisiana.[135] Around 1754, Charlotte had a son named Charles, who was probably raised alongside Derneville's children. Charlotte was only able to purchase her own freedom, and that of her son, years later, in the 1770s, under the Spanish regime.[136]

The archives contain some evidence of white men attempting to afford more protection and care for their mixed children and Black partners than Pierre-Henri Derneville did. Some even took measures to transmit patrimony to them. Recall Chavannes, the secretary at the Council of Louisiana who made his former enslaved housekeeper, Isabelle, and her mixed daughter his sole heirs in 1752. Three years later, in Saint-Claude, Guadeloupe, a white man on his deathbed named Michel Antoine Bourdaise Demontérant manumitted his enslaved house servant Roze, as well as her children and grandchildren, bequeathing them a plantation named Petite Place.[137] In 1758, still in Guadeloupe, another Frenchman named Sieur Duchesne confessed to having murdered an enslaved man named Pierre to steal the cassava that he was carrying. Members of the Guadeloupean court accused Duchesne of having fabricated his confession to protect his own son, the real murderer—a *mulâtre* named François. In the end, François was sentenced to be whipped and pilloried, and his father was condemned to pay a compensation along with a fine of 300 livres for his false confession.[138] Other white fathers took measures to provide for the education of their mixed children, though this did not always lead to freedom, as the Guadeloupean story of the *mulâtre* carpenter André demonstrates. Some mixed children really took advantage of the educational opportunity that was given to them. The story of the Guadeloupean *mulâtre* Joseph Bologne, born in the mid-eighteenth century to a wealthy planter named Georges Bologne and one of his Black captives, is well known.[139] Georges sent Joseph to France so he could be educated at the Collège Saint-Louis of Angoulême.[140] Joseph then became a renowned composer, conductor, violinist, and fencer, taking the name of Chevalier de Saint-Georges.[141] Other white men also made arrangements for the education of their mixed children in Lower Louisiana. Such was perhaps the case with a merchant of New Orleans named Sieur Henry Decours, who manumitted an enslaved *mulâtresse* named Rosette in 1757 on the grounds that he was "much attached to her as she [was] good-natured, and he wish[ed] to take care of her education."[142]

Marriage and White Men's Social Mobility

Like enslaved women and their mixed children, white men, too, found some opportunities for upward mobility through their relationships with affluent women of non-European ancestries: such alliances could therefore advance white dominion, especially since French authorities often classified these women as "whites" in state papers.[143] It was in the Indian Ocean world that intermarriages could be most advantageous for Frenchmen.[144] In India, Catholic intermarriages took place throughout the eighteenth century, partly because of the persistent gender imbalance in the French outposts.[145] Intermarriage in India involved Frenchmen from all strata of society, from soldiers and company employees to merchants and high-ranking officials.[146] Several Frenchmen in India achieved social mobility by marrying affluent women of South Asian descent in the Catholic Church. Probably less than half of the twenty-three wedded European merchants employed by the company in Pondicherry in 1727 were married to French women.[147] Moreover, out of the 306 marriage ceremonies involving a European groom that were celebrated between 1720 and 1750 at Notre Dame des Anges in Pondicherry, only 35 were to European brides.[148] Many of these marriages were to Christian Luso-Indian women, as suggested by their Portuguese names, while others were to other Eurasian and Indian women.[149] According to a French navy officer named Louis de Granpré, only two European families in Pondicherry had not "allied to Indian families" by the late eighteenth century.[150]

Not all South Asian brides and concubines in India came with wealth and prestige. In fact, many French company employees and soldiers continued to form relationships with Hindus, Muslims and low-ranking *topas*, both inside and outside of Catholic wedlock.[151] The founder of Pondicherry and first governor-general of French India, François Martin, told the story of a Frenchman named Lafleur who had murdered his wife—a woman described as a "Muslim or Gentile"—for adultery and had run away to Bengal with their children to escape punishment.[152] Officials in India could not prevent French deserters, mercenaries, company employees, and other adventurers from marrying low-ranking and non-Christian Indian women because many of them lived beyond the reach of French authority. Members of the Superior Council of Pondicherry complained in 1731 of several Portuguese monks in Bandel, near Chandernagore, who had agreed to marry several French deserter soldiers to local women "without any formalities" and without the approval of the governor.[153] Because French authorities in Chandernagore disapproved of his union with an Indian woman named Manique, one former French company employee named Zacherie Piget had found refuge in a Danish outpost. He was sentenced to be burned in effigy in 1729 because he had murdered the French shipmaster who tried to arrest him.[154] By 1737, the upcoming governor of Pondicherry, Joseph-François Dupleix, lamented that "most [company] employees [were] married to creole women of obscure origins."[155]

However, several other Frenchmen in India—including Dupleix himself—also formed alliances with affluent and high-ranking Christian women of South Asian descent. Financially comfortable Christian Luso-Indian women were desirable matches for low-ranking company employees and soldiers eager to marry up.[156] Many employees and soldiers in Bengal had fled severe financial hardship in France only to survive on low wages in Asia.[157] Only a few privileged company employees could afford a wealthy European lifestyle, with a large residence, European commodities, enslaved people, and domestic servants. Marrying a Luso-Indian woman with a significant dowry could give low-ranking Frenchmen access to this kind of fortune.[158] Wealthy Luso-Indian women also formed a pool of desirable brides for high-ranking French officials and for merchants and employees seeking socially suitable spouses.[159] For example, a French surgeon in Pondicherry married an affluent Luso-Indian woman named Dona Rose de Castro in 1705 and had eight children with her. One of these children, a girl named Jeanne, married a French councilor in 1719. After she became a widow, she married the soon-to-be governor of Pondicherry, Dupleix, in 1741 in Chandernagore.[160] Jeanne Dupleix, also known as Joanna Begum, received a substantial inheritance from her Luso-Indian mother, which included an estate in Pondicherry, furniture, jewelry, and multiple domestic servants.[161] Still in Bengal, the nephews of the renowned Scottish-French financier John Law, two high-ranking company employees named Jean and Jacques Law de Lauriston, also married into a wealthy Luso-Indian family called the Carvalhos.[162] Jean's Luso-Indian wife came with a considerable dowry of 17,000 rupees.[163]

Because these relationships could help European men climb the social ladder, French officials did not target mixed marriages to Catholic, Europeanized and financially comfortable Luso-Indian women with their prohibitions. This is illustrated by the language employed by the French governor of Chandernagore in 1732 when he banned unions between Frenchmen and "bastard or country women *who are not descended from Europeans* or French."[164] This language was meant to allow Frenchmen to keep marrying Luso-Indian women born to European men. In fact, Dupleix is not the only French official to have married a Luso-Indian woman himself. Born in 1697 in Châtellerault (a city near Poitiers in France), the director of the Company of the Indies, Pierre Mathieu Renault de Saint-Germain, also married a Luso-Indian widow, named Claire Splanger d'Aranha. Although Renault de Saint-Germain did not get the approval of the Council of Pondicherry, this alliance did not preclude his being promoted to governor of Bengal in 1755.[165]

Many other European men formed advantageous alliances with women of non-European descent on the isle of Bourbon. Intermarriage rates cannot be measured with precision for eighteenth-century Isle Bourbon because clergymen stopped recording people's origins on a systematic basis in parish registers. In 1717, however, La Barbinais claimed that "among free people, there [were] only six families without mixed blood who have been careful enough not to associate with families of *mulâtres* and *métis* [on the island]."[166] About ten years later, the Company of the Indies described the number of mixed marriages between whites and free people of non-European descent on Isle Bourbon as "disproportionate."[167] Lineages on the island can sometimes be inferred by cross-referencing parish registers with census data and other sources. Through this method, it becomes clear that many white men on the island continued to marry free women of non-European descent in the first half of the eighteenth century.

In particular, just like their counterparts in India, many Frenchmen on Isle Bourbon formed alliances with financially comfortable or affluent women of Eurasian descent. Such was the case of a former pirate from La Rochelle named Jacques Bouyer. In 1707, Jacques married a creole woman of Eurasian descent named Jeanne Wilmann, whose grandmother, Françoise Royer Des Rosaires, was a Christian resident of Daman in India. Jeanne must have come with a generous dowry since her parents, Jeanne Royer and Henri-Guilbert Wilmann, a German man, were prosperous landowners. By 1708, they owned a residence in Saint-Denis, with two plots of land where they raised livestock and cultivated food crops and sugarcane.[168] Jacques Bouyer's union with a woman of Eurasian descent evidently did not compromise his career, since he eventually became a member of the island's council.[169]

Even the governor of Isle Bourbon and Pondicherry, Pierre-Benoît Dumas, married a high-born woman from Nagapatnam (on the Coromandel Coast of India) in the 1720s, whose name was Marie-Gertrude.[170] Governor Dumas was a low-ranking and penniless man who brought very little to this marriage, as illustrated by a dispute that took place after the couple's wedding. The controller-general of Isle Bourbon, Mr. Orry, recorded this dispute in a memorandum written around 1731.[171] While traveling at sea, presumably somewhere between Isle of France and Pondicherry, the Dumas couple became friends with a Frenchman named Sieur Marion, a major on Isle of France formerly stationed in Guiana, where he had worked as an infantry captain.[172] Dumas soon became suspicious of the relationship between his wife and their new friend, accusing her of "making love to Sieur Marion."[173] The controller-general of Isle Bourbon promptly came to Marie-Gertrude's defense, describing her as "a very friendly Indian woman," "young and amiable," "virtuous and austere," and "innocent." He accused Dumas of slander, adding that "nothing is more hurtful for a virtuous lady than to feel dishonored."[174] He also recounted Marie-Gertrude's disenchantment after realizing that she had married a penniless man "with no name and no family," which she reportedly experienced as a "cruel betrayal."[175] This union to Marie-Gertrude must have been hugely advantageous for Dumas: by 1732, the pair had become the most successful slaveowners on Isle Bourbon.[176]

Many other mixed marriages on Isle Bourbon were to financially comfortable women of Malagasy ancestry. In addition to being successful professionally, some of these women had accumulated significant wealth through successive marriages. Many had outlived their husbands because they had gotten married at a particularly young age, due to the scarcity of women on the island in the early years of colonization: remember, for example, Louise Payet, the affluent and devout *mulâtresse* slaveowner of Saint-Paul who married a creole *mulâtre* named François Cauzan at age eleven in 1692, became a widow in 1715, and married a French army surgeon a few months later (see Chapter 3).[177] In accordance with the Paris Custom, a widow retained half of her household's estate after her husband's death, with the other half being divided between the children if they were born inside of Catholic wedlock.[178]

This is why several Frenchmen were able to climb the social ladder by marrying Bourbon Island Creole widows.[179] This is illustrated by the stories of both Louise Payet and her niece, Marianne Payet—the wealthy creole woman of French-Malagasy ancestry whom we encountered in the introduction to this book. After inheriting from her late French husband in 1742, Marianne married Joseph Choppy Desgranges, a French army captain and the soon-to-be commander of Saint-Pierre and Saint-Louis. The story of another one of Marianne's aunts (one of Louise Payet's sisters), Luce Payet, and her French husbands, Pierre Boucher and Henry de Justamond, is also worth mentioning here. By 1705, when Bourbon Island households possessed an average of three enslaved people, Luce's parents, Antoine and Louise, owned more than ten, as well as several plantations and food crop fields, and two residences.[180] Pierre Boucher, a former pirate from Nantes, must have received a generous dowry before marrying Luce in 1707.[181] Antoine Boucher described the man as "a hard-working [person]

[. . .] [who] purchased several plots of land when he settled on Isle Bourbon."[182] By 1709, the couple owned a residence in Saint-Paul, eight enslaved people, nine farms and plots of land, and almost 200 heads of livestock.[183] Luce was the sole beneficiary of Pierre's sizable estate when he passed away on June 22, 1710. This might explain why Mr. Henry de Justamond—an ambitious Frenchman from Languedoc who was the former tax collector and warehouse keeper of Isle Bourbon, as well as the soon-to-be governor of the island—rushed to propose to her only a few days after her husband's passing.[184] Luce and Justamond went on to amass a considerable fortune in the parish of Saint-Denis that by 1732 included dozens of heads of livestock, a coffee plantation, and close to a hundred enslaved people.[185] Although the couple's five children inherited a significant portion of the estate after Henry's passing in 1763, seventy-one-year-old Luce still owned more than fifty enslaved people and a plantation.[186]

In 1715, another former French pirate, Jean-Baptiste de Laval, also married a comfortable creole woman of Malagasy descent, Louise Aubert. Born in 1696, Louise was the daughter of a French-Malagasy *mulâtresse* named Anne Launay and a Frenchman named Jacques Aubert.[187] Marrying Louise would have earned Jean-Baptiste some prestige, since her French father was a prominent political figure on the island: Jacques had worked as the commander of the parish of Saint-Paul.[188] Louise would have also come with a generous dowry, since her parents were among the wealthiest inhabitants of Isle Bourbon: by 1709, they owned hundreds of heads of livestock, ten farms and plantations, and a total of fourteen enslaved people.[189] One year before she married Jean-Baptiste, Louise was also gifted a large estate in the mountains by her friend Louise Payet.[190] Jean-Baptiste enjoyed a comfortable life in the parish of Saint-Paul thanks to his enslaved workers and spouse's estate.[191]

* * *

In conclusion, mixed relations between white men and women of non-European descent remained widespread across the eighteenth-century French empire, acting as a key instrument of racial power. Especially in the Indian Ocean, mixed marriages to assimilated, financially comfortable, or affluent freeborn women of non-European descent helped many white men improve their socioeconomic standing, further advancing white dominion in the process. At the same time, many enslaved Black women across the

French Atlantic and Indian Ocean worlds faced sexual coercion and violence. Those abuses helped white men subjugate the by-now-sizable enslaved Black communities in these regions by spreading fear and affliction among them. Sexual coercion and violence affected many enslaved people in the city of New Orleans, where a substantial number of white slaveowners kept an enslaved domestic servant in their homes. Colonial policies furthered the subjugation of enslaved and manumitted Black women and their mixed children by denying them the financial security marriage could provide and by discouraging white fathers from acknowledging their own mixed children.

French racial policies attempted to erect socioeconomic boundaries in colonial societies not only by prohibiting intermarriage but also by targeting the social mobility of people of non-European descent. Yet, as the story of the Bourbon Island Creoles suggests, many people of non-European descent still managed to accrue wealth and prestige, through the profit they made from both inheritance and their labor. This labor helped challenge the formation of strict socio-racial hierarchies across the empire at the same time that it helped France build, maintain, and exploit its colonial possessions in ways that proved hugely beneficial to many French people throughout the eighteenth century.

CHAPTER 6

Empire of Labor

Mulâtresse *Louise Nativel was born in* Madagascar in 1669 to a Malagasy woman named Thérèse Varach Solo and a Parisian candlemaker named Pierre Nativel. She left Madagascar for Isle Bourbon with her parents when she was still a child as part of the relocation program created in 1671 by the French viceroy Blanquet de La Haye.[1] At the age of fourteen, Louise married a Frenchman, Antoine Cadet, with whom she had six children. Like many mixed couples on Isle Bourbon, Louise and Antoine worked diligently to support their family, which enabled them to enjoy a comfortable lifestyle. They eventually acquired a coffee plantation in the parish of Saint-Paul.[2] It is unlikely that they performed much of the demanding physical labor in the fields themselves. Instead, this burden was probably shouldered by the fourteen enslaved people who lived on their estate by 1719. A captain's report written in 1722 described Louise and Antoine's plantation as the most prominent estate visible offshore when approaching the island from the west.[3]

Antoine passed away in 1726, after which Louise began to run the plantation on her own. By 1732, she had expanded her holdings, acquiring three additional plots of land where her twenty-seven enslaved laborers tended livestock and cultivated coffee beans intended to satisfy the growing demand of consumers in Europe. In 1733, Louise inherited land and captives that her Malagasy mother had acquired over the course of several decades of hard work in the farming sector. When Louise passed away in 1735, her estate was divided into several "very fine properties" that became home to multiple families all descended from her and Antoine.[4]

As this story illustrates, people of non-European descent in eighteenth-century French slave societies could challenge the advancement of white dominion by making profits through their labor, even as this labor became essential to the functioning of the French empire. From Isle Bourbon to the Caribbean to Lower Louisiana, enslaved Black people performed the bulk of the roughest labor necessary to build, maintain, and exploit the French settlements. Skilled and unskilled captives planted, harvested, and processed most of the crops; built infrastructure; cared for the colonists; defended the colonies; and also helped develop them by laboring in the transportation, military, medical, leisure, metalworking, construction, and agricultural sectors of the economy. Their labor allowed the crown, the trading companies, and thousands of slaveowners to make profits that could then be reinvested in the French colonial enterprise. Slaveowners used these profits to expand their colonial holdings, pay the *capitation* (used to fund wars), and acquire more captives who could perform vital construction work under the French *corvée* system (official levy on labor).[5] *Free* people of Malagasy African, and South Asian descent also helped maintain and exploit the French colonies through their labor, as plantation or farm owners (as in the case of Louise Nativel and her mother) but also as craftsmen, builders, sailors, and even active participants in imperial politics.[6]

As all these people began to face the rise of French racial capitalism, they also challenged emergent socio-racial hierarchies in a variety of ways, beyond the many acts of marronage and revolt already considered by historians: people of non-European descent also challenged those hierarchies by learning skilled trades, turning a profit from their labor, and using the judicial system to protect their own socioeconomic interests when dealing with greedy and bigoted people. The prospects of socioeconomic ascension for the enslaved were very limited across all French slave societies. Yet some did succeed in competing with whites for economic opportunities by acquiring desirable skills or by working independently in their free time for their own profit as part of "the slaves' economy"—the autonomous organization of slave communities with respect to the production and consumption of goods and services for their own gain.[7] Especially on Isle Bourbon, other people of non-European descent who were free became very successful professionally.

Relatively little attention has been given to the labor of free people of non-European descent in the early French empire, despite the vital role they played in shaping, sustaining, and exploiting the colonies. While existing work has illuminated the presence of substantial and relatively affluent free populations of African descent in the late eighteenth-century

French Caribbean—especially in Saint-Domingue—there is a noticeable lack of research on such populations in the earlier period of French colonization.[8] The labor of free people of African, Malagasy and South Asian descent on early eighteenth-century Isle Bourbon, in particular, has received little attention, especially in the English-speaking scholarship. This gap is especially salient given that Isle Bourbon was home to one of the largest populations of free people of non-European ancestries within the French empire—many of whom achieved economic success and some of whom accessed political offices decades before their counterparts from other colonies.

In addition to exploring this little-known history, this chapter is partly intended to bring the labor of enslaved people of African, Malagasy and South Asian ancestries in the French colonies emphatically to the fore, in response to a growing body of French works that runs the risk of obscuring their important contribution to French history. These works examine the impact of French colonial trade (including the slave trade and slave-produced commodity trade) on economic development only to come to the sweeping conclusion that "France is a long way from having been transformed by its colonial possessions" and that "the existence of slavery probably did not shape European culture in major ways."[9] These publications do not engage with a robust and still vibrant body of works that demonstrates how central the "bent and broken backs" of enslaved Black people were to building up "[the wealth,] world power and universal dominion" of Europe, the United States, and Latin America.[10] Most importantly, they use a macroeconomic approach completely detached from the realities of slave labor. This perspective runs the risk of perpetuating the abstraction of production, which, according to Elizabeth Heath, became second nature in modern capitalist societies as Europeans were looking for ways to make the growing consumption of slave-produced commodities "acceptable" in Europe.[11] In this chapter, I follow the path of a few scholars before me in seeking to do justice to the role of enslaved people's labor in French history.[12]

Instead of focusing only on cash crop production, this chapter gives particular attention to other forms of slave labor, such as building infrastructure or laboring in the transportation sector—what historians John Donoghue and Evelyn P. Jennings have called the "constructive labor" of empire. Unlike the "productive labor" of empire, which can easily be quantified because its end product had a market value, the value and productivity of empire's "constructive labor" are harder to measure. This may explain why, as noted by Donoghue and Jennings, "studies of Atlantic economic and labor history [at large] have focused more on the work of colonial subsistence and market production than the work necessary to establish and defend colonies, and build imperial infrastructure."[13] Yet the contribution of this labor to the construction and endurance of empire makes it just as important to French history and the history of French slavery. By shifting the focus onto the enslaved's various work activities, I also seek to illuminate their (often quite extraordinary) grit and resourcefulness, under the most dire circumstances.

Assigning the Dirty Work of Empire to Enslaved Blacks

By the 1720s, unskilled enslaved Black people in the Caribbean, the New Orleans area and Isle Bourbon performed much of the roughest labor in French slave societies, generating returns that supported the growth, upkeep, and protection of the French colonies. This included field work, which was considered one of the most taxing and degrading activities in slave societies. The low regard for field labor in slave societies is illustrated by the story of an enslaved Black domestic servant named Saint Louis, who worked on an indigo plantation near New Orleans in the mid-eighteenth century. Saint Louis formed a close relationship with his owner, Jean Charles Pradel, who at one point demoted him to field labor as a punishment for stealing from him. Mocking the despair of his Black servant after this had happened, Pradel reported euphemistically that "Monsieur St. Louis" "[did] not like that very much."[14]

Soon after the foundation of the first French Caribbean colonies, a consensus took hold that enslaved Black people should be tasked with the roughest kinds of work. The origins of this consensus can be traced back to the seventeenth century, to the failure of French attempts to use—beginning in the 1620s—workforces of European indentured servants (*les engagés*) as artisans, farmers, and field workers, alongside enslaved Indigenous people (especially Arawaks, Brazilians, and Kalinago).[15] As was often the case, Caribbean colonists were quickly cornered into shifting their strategy. The indentured program was never cost effective, since most indentured servants ran away, eventually returned to France, or died of tropical diseases (especially yellow fever and malaria), against which Africans possessed better immunity.[16] It was also during this earlier period that French colonists in the Caribbean came to believe that Indigenous people were less suited to slavery than Black people.[17] This is illustrated by a statement made by the missionary Du Tertre in 1654: "Regarding *sauvage* slaves," he claimed, "they are not usually fit for hard work [. . .]. They are usually so melancholic that we can get no work out of them, except perhaps if we flatter them. There is a proverb in this country which says 'beating a *nègre* means feeding him [. . .] but beating [a *sauvage*] means killing him.'"[18] Du Tertre advised French Caribbean planters to assign Indigenous men to less demanding tasks such as fishing or hunting and women to housekeeping duties.[19] He explicitly advised slave-owners to treat enslaved Indigenous people "as if they were free," describing them as "only quasi-enslaved."[20] The French missionary Jean-Baptiste Labat drew on a similar rhetoric in 1700, arguing that "our Caribs have always been a proud and untamable people, who prefer death to servitude."[21]

The rhetoric stressing Black people's alleged better suitability for hard labor was disseminated by Indigenous people in the Caribbean in a calculated attempt to shield themselves from difficult work in the field. There were complaints that they refused to do field work because agricultural labor was the preserve of women in their own cultures.[22] Du Tertre explained how, when asked to perform hard labor, Arawak and Kalinago peoples responded that "these sorts of tasks are only good for the *nègres*."[23] Labat advised Caribbean planters not to use Indigenous servants, on the grounds that there was "a strong dislike between them and the *nègres*." He concluded, "[The Kalinago's] pride has led them to believe that they are far superior to the *nègres*."[24]

By the late seventeenth century, French observers in the Caribbean contrasted the rhetoric of Indigenous untamability with a discourse depicting Blacks as unintelligent people particularly fit for slave labor. Here is what Du Tertre said about Black people: "They are so stupid that they do not even resent their enslavement, as if they never had any knowledge of what kind of happiness freedom can bring."[25] "These *nègres* have the qualities required by Aristotle to be a good slave," pontificated another missionary, Jean Mongin: "body strength and heaviness of spirit, because the *nègres* can work a lot and they do not think very often."[26] By the late seventeenth century, French Caribbean planters thus increasingly relied on Black workforces to satisfy the rising demand for sugar in Europe.[27] Thousands of enslaved Black people in the Caribbean were forced to plant, harvest, and process large quantities of sugarcane under inhumane conditions. This led to a significant increase in the number of sugar factories between 1700 and 1788: from 73 to 300 in Guadeloupe, from 183 to 324 in Martinique, and from 18 to 793 in Saint-Domingue, which became the world's leading producer of sugar by the 1730s.[28]

The Caribbean rhetoric of Indigenous "untamability" and Black fitness for hard work was echoed in French North America by the early eighteenth century. According to Governor Périer enslaved Native Americans in Louisiana were "of very little use" and "not suited for anything other than fishing and hunting."[29] The French commissary Nicolas de La Salle concurred with him in 1709, describing enslaved Indigenous people in the Mississippi valley as "unfit for hard work, unlike the *nègres*."[30] Forty years later, the governor-general of New France, Jacques-Pierre de Taffanel de la Jonquière, and the intendant of New France, François Bigot, opposed the idea of sending enslaved Native Americans to Martinique, claiming, "The Indian [i.e., Native American], although a slave, does not work, [. . .]. He is not like the *nègre*. He is lazy and cannot be kept indoors however well or badly treated. [. . .] They cannot breathe unless they are returned to the woods, and it is nearly impossible for them to learn a trade."[31]

The thousands of European recruits sent to French colonial Louisiana between 1717 and the early 1720s, to work in all sectors of the colonial economy, further fueled the rhetoric stressing Black people's alleged superior capacity for strenuous work. Echoing the situation in the early Caribbean islands, many of those European immigrants died of tropical diseases, tried to escape, or simply refused to work, which led French authorities to the conclusion that most were unfit for hard labor.[32] François Fleuriau, the attorney general at the Superior Council of Louisiana in 1720, described those European recruits as "lazy, with wicked manners, unfit to work but able to corrupt other colonists and even the natives of the land."[33] Four years later, the ecclesiastical director of the company, Gilles Bernard Abbot Raguet, deplored the "libertinage and poor conduct" of the new European recruits, especially in New Orleans and Mobile. Describing those Europeans as "lazy and unskilled people," he advised the council of Louisiana to expel them from New Orleans.[34] According to the *commissaire-ordonnateur*

Edme Gatien Salmon, enslaved Blacks in French Louisiana were forced to perform "all the vile tasks that whites refuse[d] to accomplish." These included "clean[ing] and clear[ing] the ditches, latrines, [and] wells."[35]

Like their counterparts in the Caribbean, enslaved Blacks in mid eighteenth-century Lower Louisiana were given the most difficult assignments in colonial society. As a case in point, in 1752, a white servant in Louisiana who was asked to go chop wood by the river retorted that "this [was] the job of the *nègres* of this country."[36] French Louisiana colonists increasingly favored enslaved Blacks to perform all kinds of difficult tasks, including working in the fields. From the 1720s onward, thousands of enslaved Blacks were forced to labor on tobacco and indigo plantations, concentrating around the New Orleans, Natchez, Pointe Coupée, Bayagoulas, and Natchitoches areas.[37]

Meanwhile, thousands of miles away, on Isle Bourbon, Africans *and Malagasies* were both considered especially suited to hard labor. As opposed to what happened in the Caribbean, Africans did not form a majority of enslaved labor forces in the first half of the eighteenth century on Isle Bourbon. By 1735, 59 percent of the enslaved population of the island came from Madagascar (3,855 people), 23 percent were creoles (1,503), 7 percent were from India (480), and only 11 percent came from East and West Africa (725).[38] The French rhetoric regarding Malagasy and African people on Isle Bourbon mirrored the language used on the Caribbean islands to describe Black people. In 1705, a French traveler named Sieur L'Huillier described Malagasies as "robust and tireless at work," mirroring the claim by Caribbean missionary Jean Mongin about Black people's purported "body strength" and capacity to "work a lot."[39] Twenty years later, a French official and lieutenant named Sieur Jean Feuillet compared South Asian people to Malagasies, only to come to the conclusion that "Blacks from Madagascar are big and strong, sturdy at work, while those from India are effeminate, frail and weak."[40] A French official advised planters on Isle Bourbon to use enslaved East Africans, on the grounds that they were "well-built, strong, hard-working," and more obedient than Malagasy workers.[41] Bourbon Island's planters thus increasingly relied on both enslaved Africans and Malagasies to cultivate the land on coffee plantations, as well as tend livestock.[42] As a result, coffee bean production on Isle Bourbon grew from 180,000 livres in 1726 to 2,500,000 livres by 1744.[43]

On the other hand, the language used to describe enslaved Indians (South Asians) on Isle Bourbon echoed the rhetoric about Indigenous peoples in the Americas. In 1710 and 1734, two company employees on Isle Bourbon referred to enslaved people from South Asia as "lazy."[44] Other French officials echoed this sentiment, describing enslaved people from India as "weak and lazy," though more robust after their arrival on Isle Bourbon because of the climate. A memorandum written shortly after 1763 described enslaved South Asian people as "witty, adroit but usually shy, weak, and prone to sluggishness."[45] Perhaps because Europeans in India primarily encountered enslaved people in an urban setting, slaveowners on Isle Bourbon preferred enslaved Indians to work as domestic servants, maids, nurses, cooks, and gardeners, rather than cultivating plantations.[46] Echoing Du Tertre's recommendation regarding Indigenous women in the Caribbean, French officials described South Asian enslaved people as "fitter for household duties" than field work.[47] Out of the twenty-one domestic servants owned by the French governor of Isle Bourbon and Pondicherry, Pierre-Benoît Dumas, for example, as many as fifteen came from India.[48] Because French colonists considered enslaved creoles and South Asian people "able to learn and practice a trade," others labored as apprentice artisans as well as in the maritime sector as sailors and fishermen.[49] The Council of Isle Bourbon claimed in 1733 that most of the crew members aboard company's boats were "creoles or Indians raised at sea from a tender age.[50]

Skilled Slaves and the "Constructive Labor" of Empire

Enslaved people with specialized skills competed with whites for skilled employment in the transportation, construction, metalworking, and medical sectors of the economy, supporting the operation of empire by moving people, goods, and state papers; building infrastructure; healing people; and more. Beginning in the 1720s, the French Company of the Indies initiated an important project, whose transoceanic scope has so far been overlooked, to replace skilled whites with enslaved Black people.[51] This project was applied to Isle Bourbon before being extended to Louisiana in an attempt to reduce the company's expenses and maximize profits—illustrating, once again, French authorities' stances toward policy unification. In the 1720s and 1730s, the company deplored the "great expenses in wages and rations" stemming from the employment of skilled whites in Louisiana and also complained about white "craftsmen from France" being "immensely costly" on Isle Bourbon.[52] Members of the Council of Isle Bourbon agreed with the company's assessment, lamenting "the exorbitant amounts of money" requested by those artisans.[53] The company ultimately came to the conclusion that it was "of the utmost importance to train Blacks" to replace skilled whites in both Louisiana and Isle Bourbon.[54]

Measures were taken to teach skilled trades to enslaved Black people, ultimately allowing some to compete with whites for artisan positions. Some enslaved people had prior craftsmanship experience from their homeland, while others were trained as apprentices in France and in the colonies.[55] White craft-masters agreed to apprentice enslaved people in the colonies because the Company of the Indies promised to compensate them.[56] The company first enacted its project of replacing white artisans on Isle Bourbon from the early 1720s. In 1723, its directors ordered authorities on the island "to place young Blacks for apprenticeship with craft-masters who c[ould] train them in their own trades and instruct them well" for a period of three years.[57] In 1724, many enslaved people on Isle Bourbon were placed in the workshops of sawyers, gunsmiths, blacksmiths and locksmiths for apprenticeship, reportedly to "serve them as companions and spare the salaries of the [white artisans] that [the company was] support[ing]."[58] This initiative was renewed in 1734 and 1741. The company wrote, "Nothing is more rewarding than [. . .] to have allocated Blacks to serve [craftsmen on Isle Bourbon]. We must continue to replace [artisans from France] with Blacks."[59]

The French company later enacted the same project for French colonial Louisiana.[60] In 1726, forty enslaved Blacks were placed on the company's boats and ships in Louisiana to receive sailing training from whites, and a French locksmith was later asked to apprentice a company-owned captive in exchange for a compensation.[61] Many slaveowners followed the example of the company, training their captives in reputable skilled crafts to improve their finances. In New Orleans, in 1763, for example, a priest named Dagobert placed his Black captive Antoine in a white blacksmith's workshop for a three-year apprenticeship.[62] Slaveowners would sometimes hire out their own enslaved skilled men to other colonists, to either pay their debts or increase their revenues. In 1744, in New Orleans, such was the case of a widow named Francoise Hubert who owed 4,500 livres to one Sieur Brosset. Instead of paying him the money, she offered to give him an enslaved man of hers, described as "a [*nègre*] joiner named George." One year later, a slaveowner named George Cappo hired out one of his enslaved men, described as a Black cooper, to one Sieur Germain, to help him in his work for a period of two years.[63]

Before the retrocession of Louisiana to the crown in 1731, most company-owned captives practiced respected skilled trades rather than cultivating the land on plantations. The Company of the Indies became one of the largest slaveowners in Louisiana, owning a total of 148 men and 68 women, as well as many children. Most enslaved men under the company's purview labored in construction and maritime sectors, with a focus on renovation, shipbuilding, woodworking, metalworking, and transportation across Louisiana, the circum-Caribbean, and the wider Atlantic world.[64] A document written in 1729 listed many enslaved people who belonged to the company as carpenters, blacksmiths, sailors and boat captains.[65]

Enslaved people in Louisiana and Isle Bourbon maintained and operated the many ships and boats that connected the French settlements and outposts to each other and to other places. When measures were taken to replace whites with Black sailors in Louisiana in 1726, enslaved Blacks were tasked with transporting commodities up and down the Mississippi River because travel by boat was the only viable option in the valley.[66] Similarly, enslaved people on Isle Bourbon were in charge of transporting officials, settlers, and food supplies in boats around the island because travel between parishes rarely happened overland.[67] Most of the enslaved sailors staffing these boats were either creoles or from India.[68] Around 1724, the Company of the Indies endeavored to train more enslaved men in the maritime sector on Isle Bourbon until they amounted to at least one-quarter of all crew members working on the boats and ships that serviced the Mascarene Islands.[69] Enslaved men in Louisiana and Isle Bourbon also worked at major harbors, loading and unloading vessels at the docks, repairing passing ships, and working in warehouses.[70]

The crown disapproved of the practice of replacing skilled whites with captives, considering it a potential threat to white dominion. Concerned with the risk of slave revolts and the reduction of employment opportunities for whites, the king lamented in 1765 that "the navigation of the colonies is almost entirely in slaves' hands."[71] Royal officials also criticized the practice, widespread among slaveowners, of replacing white overseers, domestic servants, and artisans with enslaved Blacks to reduce their expenses. Here is what Marine Secretary Maurepas wrote in 1737: "I am very upset to learn that colonists continue to use Blacks instead of whites to direct their estates and work as their domestic servants. This stubbornness may one day cause great disorder on the islands."[72] Seventeen years later, the Council of Martinique and the crown both explicitly expressed their concerns that "the multitude of *nègre* craftsmen working in the colony [were] a great evil, because they t[ook] away white people's livelihood."[73]

The presence of enslaved people in the medical professions was also a source of concern, despite their important role in healing people. There were fears among French Caribbean colonists that Black people would use their skills to harm white colonists and try to overthrow them. The techniques used by African healers and soothsayers were often misunderstood as well.[74] In 1674, authorities in Guadeloupe accused African healers of "communicat[ing] with the devil or engag[ing] in magical and diabolical arts," ordering them to cease their activities.[75] But a few other Black practitioners got a lot more recognition for their medical skills. In 1743, in Louisiana, three enslaved people belonging to a man named Dubreuil were imprisoned on suspicion of theft. When questioned in court, one of them, an eighteen-year-old Black man named Louis, claimed to be a professional surgeon trained at the king's hospital.[76] Dubreuil demanded Louis's immediate release from prison because he needed him to treat the sick on his estate.[77] As another case in point, one of the two enslaved witnesses in another trial discussed earlier, which took place in 1752 in New Orleans, was an enslaved Black man in charge of making herbal remedies at the Ursuline convent's pharmacy, while another was a surgeon's aide at the hospital.[78]

Enslaved people could turn significant profits by using their medical skills to work independently in their own free time. This is illustrated by a story that was recorded in Guadeloupe many years before the 1752 New Orleans trial. An enslaved Black woman on the island, Jeanne Fary, who worked as a midwife, was reportedly allowed by her owner "to enjoy the profit that she made by delivering the babies of the women of this country."[79] Jeanne's nephew, a freeman named Jean, eventually inherited her entire estate, which he owned until 1716, when he died without having an heir. That estate was large enough to catch the attention of Jeanne's former master, a white man named Sieur Houel: it included a farm, a residence, and a lot of furniture. Houel went so far as petitioning the king to be allowed to seize the property.[80]

The Slaves' Economies

Enslaved people often competed with whites for job opportunities when working autonomously for their own profit. From the Caribbean to Louisiana and Isle Bourbon, enslaved men and women engaged in independent or semi-independent economies that helped the French reduce their expenses, grow their incomes, get food, and find domestic services, among other benefits. While many works have been published on slaves' economies in other European empires and the United States, those in the French colonies have received relatively little attention.[81] Many enslaved people in the French colonies produced and sold foodstuffs and handiworks or hired themselves out on a freelance basis, keeping some or all their profits for themselves. Slaves' economies were the most developed in Caribbean cities that were highly frequented by European merchants, sailors, filibusters, and other travelers in need of services.

The idea that enslaved people could earn money for themselves may seem surprising because enslaved people were, by definition, someone else's property. Any money or personal effects possessed by an enslaved person would have, in theory, belonged to their owner. Yet, in practice, most slaveowners allowed their captives to keep their own savings and belongings. They were allowed to do so by yet another body of standardized policies that targeted the Atlantic and the Indian Ocean. Article VI of the *Code Noir* of the Caribbean of 1685, article IV of the Letters Patent of the Mascarenes of 1723, and article V of the *Code Noir* of Louisiana of 1724 all designated Sundays and holidays as days off for enslaved people.[82] A legal document written in 1731 in Louisiana confirmed that "celebration days and Sundays are holidays for [the *nègres*]," which meant that "they [were] free to work for themselves."[83] In addition, many planters in the French Caribbean allowed their captives to work independently on Saturdays.[84] This allowed enslaved people to accumulate savings and material possessions. The *Code Noir* of the Antilles of 1685, the Letters Patent of the Mascarenes of 1723, and the *Code Noir* of Louisiana of 1724 all declared enslaved people unable to own property. However, they also allowed the enslaved to have a *peculium* (savings), which they could earn by performing paid assignments for their owner.[85]

Independent work could bring hardship to the enslaved, since slaveowners often used it to free themselves from the burden of having to feed and clothe their captives, forcing them to cater to their own needs instead. The missionary Du Tertre explained that "when new ships arrived [in the French Antilles], [the *nègres*] s[old] to the captains (who [were] at this time craving fresh meat) pieces of chickens or capons, which are four times more expensive than usual." He continued, "This small business helps [the *nègres*] a lot, *allowing them to provide for their own needs, and not to depend on their masters for necessities.*"[86] By 1673, instead of providing rations to their captives, slaveowners in the Caribbean had become accustomed to giving them Saturdays (or another day of the week) off to get food on their own. That year, a regulation prohibited slaveowners from granting days off to enslaved people in place of food.[87] This provision was reiterated in 1682 and again in 1685, when the *Code Noir* of the Caribbean also instructed slaveowners to provide weekly rations of two and a half cups of manioc flour to enslaved people, along with two to three livres of salted beef or fish.[88] The provision of the *Code Noir* of 1685 was reiterated in 1697 in Guadeloupe because many slaveowners continued to instruct their enslaved laborers to find food on their own.[89] In 1720, a French official in Martinique complained of "some colonists who fail to provide food to their slaves as required by the king's ordinance, instead giving them a few hours of free time to make up for the lack of food."[90] According to an anonymous memorandum from 1728, "settlers [in Guadeloupe] d[id] not feed their Black slaves, asking them to provide for their own sustenance through their diligence and their work."[91] Authorities continued to complain of the practice among slaveowners in the Caribbean of giving Saturdays off to their captives as a substitute for food at least until the 1740s.[92]

Independent work provided a solution to French colonists looking for ways to maximize their profits, not only by freeing them from the responsibility of providing necessities to their captives but also by allowing them to hire other enslaved people on Sundays and Christian holidays to work on their plantations and in their factories, stores, households, and so on.[93] The French Louisiana archives are rife with contracts detailing activities performed by captives for hire on behalf of colonists. Several enslaved men in the French American colonies were hired as construction workers—especially as carpenters or roofers. Others worked as game hunters.[94] Some Louisiana colonists, either because they did not own enslaved people or because they needed more, hired captives for extended periods of time to work as sailors or to transport flour to Lower Louisiana from the Illinois Country—colonists in the Mississippi valley imported growing quantities of crops and flour from the Illinois Country (an important wheat producer), beginning in the 1710s.[95]

The lease system was an income source for both slaveowners and enslaved people.[96] Some slaveowners in Guadeloupe allowed enslaved people to work in the cities for long periods of time, provided that they agreed to share their earnings with them. By 1749, authorities in Guadeloupe complained that "masters leave their slaves to their own devices [in the cities], as long as they consistently pa[id] the required amount for a day or a month." These urban captives reportedly hired themselves out "as sailors, porters, domestic servants, or for travels, behaving as if they were independent."[97] French officials described them as "almost free" because they enjoyed unrestrained freedom, being able "to practice any trade or profession."[98]

Enslaved people's involvement in the leisure and entertainment sectors of the economy, in particular, contributed to making Caribbean cities especially attractive to travelers and colonists. Several enslaved people in Guadeloupean cities rented taverns and cabarets in which they served food and drinks and where some free and enslaved Black women were forced into sex work.[99] Others worked as musicians. Labat claimed that "several slaves play[ed] the violin quite well, and earn[ed] money by playing for gatherings, feasts, and weddings."[100]

Other enslaved people in the Caribbean, Louisiana, and Isle Bourbon produced and sold oft-vital foodstuffs and handicrafts. Authorities in the colonies often complained about the lack of food. In the Caribbean, in particular, the emphasis on sugarcane cultivation—at the expense of subsistence farming—resulted in severe food shortages that affected both colonists and enslaved people. Between 1703 and 1740, authorities in Guadeloupe and Martinique complained about the lack of food on multiple occasions, urging colonists to cultivate cassava, bananas, potatoes, and other essential foodstuffs.[101] Yet the problem persisted until the 1760s. In 1748, officials lamented that "bad weather, hurricanes and war, instead of encouraging colonists to cultivate foodstuffs, have only led them to focus even more on sugarcane."[102] Authorities in Martinique continued to complain, as late as 1750, of colonists disregarding the directive to cultivate edible crops, thereby exposing "many settlers and all domestic servants, both white and Black," to the threat of starvation.[103] The lack of food was also a problem in the Mississippi valley, where French soldiers were scarred by chronic food shortages and the lack of support from France.[104] In 1712, Louisiana's commissary reported, "The distress is great; [. . .] It is pitiful also to see them as they are all naked and most often living on crushed and boiled Indian corn with a piece of meat."[105] Louisiana experienced major food shortages due to war and repeated crop failures between the 1720s and 1763. The colony was struck by famines in 1722, 1733, and again in 1738.[106]

Enslaved people in Louisiana, the Caribbean, and Isle Bourbon helped colonists cope with these food shortages by growing crops in their own provision gardens on plantation estates, raising poultry and livestock, and going fishing or hunting in their own free time.[107] The practice of letting enslaved people cultivate their own plots of land also existed in Africa, Brazil, and the British Caribbean.[108] Since a lot of time could be invested in these gardens, they were an efficient way for slaveowners to attach enslaved people to plantations. The garden practice had spread to Isle Bourbon by the early eighteenth century. A French traveler named Sieur Durot, who spent time on the island in 1705, noted that "when [slaves] work with affection for their masters, they receive[d] a small land parcel as a reward, which they cultivate[d] for their own profit."[109] In addition to raising poultry and hogs, the enslaved on Isle Bourbon used their gardens to cultivate manioc, corn, potatoes, yam, squash, fruits, tobacco, and cotton.[110] It was also common for enslaved people in the Lesser Antilles to raise poultry in their gardens, as evidenced in a document written in Guadeloupe in 1735.[111]

Enslaved people found different ways to market the produce from their private gardens, along with their handicrafts, which included indispensable carpentry items and tools, as well as sought-after objects like baskets, pots, and ceramics, which could be made of wood, clay, or other materials.[112] Those in Guadeloupe and Louisiana were allowed to sell goods independently provided that they carried a written authorization from their owners to do so.[113] Such was also the case on Isle Bourbon until 1715, when a regulation issued by colonial authorities barred colonists from trading with the enslaved.[114] The slave codes of the Mascarenes and Louisiana both allowed enslaved people to sell their products in town markets on Sundays and Christian holidays.[115] Enslaved plantation workers would often purchase manioc, poultry, eggs, game, fish, and vegetables from enslaved city workers, to then resell these products at city markets. By 1749, enslaved city workers and servants were largely overrepresented in Caribbean city markets, in comparison to their plantation counterparts.[116] Many other enslaved people in Caribbean cities worked independently as merchants, bakers, confectioners, and grease sellers.[117] French authorities lamented in 1749 of Guadeloupean cities' streets being "full of stalls where slaves s[old] [goods]." Those same enslaved people were reportedly able to rent houses and stores "just like white people, with the same freedom."[118] Despite a decree issued the same year to prohibit enslaved people from renting stores and stalls, slaveowners were still allowed to lease commercial facilities on behalf of the enslaved.[119]

Because the slaves' economies were considered a growing threat to white people's economic prosperity, further regulations targeted enslaved people's commercial activities. Local decrees issued in 1666, 1734, 1735, and 1749, along with the *Code Noir* of 1685, prevented enslaved people in the Antilles from selling wood, sugarcane, syrup, rum, cotton and coffee beans.[120] These prohibitions were clearly intended to limit economic competition and dissuade enslaved people from stealing food and goods from colonists to resell them.[121] According to a legal document, partly because of enslaved merchants, "traders in [Guadeloupean] cities suffer[ed] great prejudice since the sale of their merchandise [had] stopped."[122] Prohibitions were reiterated on multiple occasions because enslaved people flouted them.

Some enslaved people were able to challenge socio-racial boundaries by making substantial profits through their independent work. Some must have used this opportunity to enact their position of strength over underprivileged whites. As a case in point, in 1698, in the Caribbean, the missionary Labat reported owning a young enslaved Black man who decided to give his own savings to a white beggar just "to have the pleasure of calling him 'poor white man.'"[123] Other enslaved people used their earnings to improve their wardrobes. Many observers in the French Americas noted the lack of adequate clothing among enslaved people.[124] According to the missionary Du Tertre, the luckiest enslaved men only wore "bad pants made of thick canvas," while enslaved women wore "skirts made of the same fabric."[125] He added, "If we ordinarily judge the status of people by looking at their clothes, we can conclude when seeing the rags of the *nègres* that [slaves] occupy the lowest condition on earth."[126] Yet many enslaved people in Guadeloupean cities began to use their own earnings to purchase luxurious items of clothing. As early as the 1720s, authorities complained of enslaved people in Guadeloupean cities "w[earing] apparels which [were] well above their rank [. . .] and often above those of [French colonists]."[127] That same year, a regulation made it obligatory for enslaved people on Guadeloupean plantations to wear cheap fabrics, threatening them with a prison sentence if they failed to comply. The same regulation forced domestic servants to only wear poor-quality fabrics or "similar old clothes." Depending on the status of their owners, they could wear silver or crystal bead jewelry, but no gold or precious stones, and hats, caps, or turbans, but with no gold effects, lace, or ribbons.[128] These prohibitions must have been ineffective: as late as 1749, Guadeloupean authorities complained that "[they could not] recognize the slaves anymore [because of] their apparel well above their rank, their bold and insolent attitudes, and their jewelry."[129]

A few other enslaved people in the French Caribbean used independent work to try to purchase their own freedom from their owners. This is why regulations issued in 1711 and 1713 prevented slaveowners on the islands from manumitting enslaved people without the consent of local authorities. Both legal documents lamented "the ease with which settlers grant[ed] freedom to [their slaves] in exchange for sums of money."[130] In another possible attempt to unify legislation, the *Code Noir* of Louisiana of 1724 also prohibited owners from manumitting enslaved people without the consent of local authorities, claiming that "some masters may want to sell their freedom to their slaves."[131] Once freed, manumitted people procured access to a wide range of socioeconomic opportunities that could further competition with whites.

The Danger Posed by Free People of Non-European Descent

Free people of non-European descent usually posed a far greater threat to socio-racial orders than enslaved men and women because of the wealth they could more freely accumulate through the often-essential work they provided across the French colonies. Many officials in the French Atlantic regarded the social rise of free people of African ancestry with dismay, especially in the French Caribbean. Beginning in the early eighteenth century authorities issued measures intended to obstruct their socio-economic ascent on those islands. Article LV of the *Code Noir* of the Antilles had permitted all slaveowners of legal age to manumit captives without providing any justification.[132] But this changed in 1711, when the governor and the intendant of the *Îles du Vent* of the Caribbean both decreed that from then on, no manumissions would be authorized without their approval.[133] Several years after this, a slew of regulations began to block access to multiple occupations for free people of African descent in the French Caribbean. Beginning in 1743, they were no longer allowed to make remedies or treat injuries other than snake bites, for fear of poisoning, and from 1754, they were no longer allowed to handle precious metals, for fear of theft.[134] By 1755, in Guadeloupe, a decree declared that "from now on, only whites w[ould] be allowed to work as peddlers or merchants," except in the cities of Basse-Terre, Saint-François, and Sainte-Anne.[135]

Despite this blatantly discriminatory treatment, a few free people of African descent in the French Antilles achieved remarkable economic success. Some became sought-after service providers. One of the most popular and lucrative occupations among free people of African descent in the cities of Martinique and Guadeloupe was that of cabaret owner or director. Cabarets were places where enslaved people, free Blacks, and *mulâtres*—along with white travelers, sailors, and vagabonds—smoked, ate, drank, and gambled in close proximity.[136] A Guadeloupean document written in 1711 complained that "most [manumitted slaves] [run] cabarets, even in white people's homes who are vile enough to receive them, trade with them and support their infamous and indecent business."[137] One free Black woman in Martinique, named Marie Castelet, owned one of the most successful cabarets of the French Lesser Antilles. She had come to the island from Saint-Barthelemy (a dependency of Guadeloupe) after she was manumitted by her owner in Jamaica. Her freedom was contested by the governor-general of the French Antilles, Raymond Balthazar Phélypeaux, after a man in Saint-Domingue claimed to own her. But Castelet was allowed to remain free because she had friends in high places. One of those friends was Mrs. Le Bègue, a white woman married to a French lieutenant who was a close acquaintance of Nicolas-François Arnoul de Vaucresson, the French intendant of the American islands from 1704 to 1721. Phélypeaux criticized Mrs. Le Bègue for often visiting Castelet for drinks. Castelet had gifted Mrs. Le Bègue a sumptuous apparel made of gold fabric. She had also promised to give her a generous 500 écus for her support against the governor-general. Astonishingly, Vaucresson himself eventually became a close acquaintance of Castelet as well: officials on the island complained that "the *négresse* Marie is so successful that she and her two sisters [. . .] often visit[ed] Mr. the intendant, while the [island's] judges wait[ed] [for them] behind closed doors, for three or four hours."[138]

A few other free people of African descent in the Caribbean achieved great socioeconomic mobility as successful planters. John Garrigus writes that in Saint-Domingue, "[free] mixed-race families had been wealthy and prominent residents of the southern peninsula since French colonization began."[139] In mid-eighteenth-century Martinique, a white creole man named Henry Barthélémy Larcher and his manumitted *mulâtresse* wife, Madeleine, gathered an enormous fortune through their activities as sugarcane planters. The couple owned many captives, plantations, and houses, all of which were passed on to Madeleine and to her mixed children (categorized as *métis*) after Henry's passing, along with a vast inheritance of 760,000 livres.[140]

But in the first half of the eighteenth century, most free landowners of African descent in Martinique, Guadeloupe, and Saint-Domingue only cultivated small quantities of food crops and export products on small farms.[141] Though many in Saint-Domingue owned land and enslaved people, most cultivated food crops and coffee beans on rugged mountain land.[142] Free people of African descent in Guadeloupe, too, usually resided on the island's less fertile land, such as the Grands Fonds (hilly region of Grande-Terre, on the east side of the island) and the Leeward Coast of Basse-Terre (west side of the island).[143] Most did not own any captives, although there were a few exceptions, as illustrated by the story of *mulâtresse* Alegre, a free woman who got into trouble in 1720 because she had failed to send her captives to church, in fulfillment of their Easter Duty.[144] Some free people of color in Guadeloupe cultivated small quantities of coffee and cotton, as well as foodstuffs that must have been a very welcome addition to the island's extremely scarce food provisions.

Two free Black women in Guadeloupe, in particular, cultivated essential food at a time of crisis. War and bad weather caused severe food shortages in Guadeloupe in the 1720s.[145] Thankfully, Artas and Nanon, the two women in question, owned a productive farm in the parish of Capesterre. Their estate was included by mistake in the sale of a French widow's estate to a man named Pierre du Mouchel. In 1727, Du Mouchel seized this opportunity to petition the intendant subdelegate of Guadeloupe Sieur Michel, who ordered Artas and Nanon to leave their property. Artas and Nanon successfully petitioned the court of Guadeloupe three years later in order to keep their estate. Officials' responses to the decision show that they were well aware of the colony's need for the labor of free people of African descent. They complained that this affair "had disturbed the suppliants in their peaceful ownership of a plot of land, which they have cleared and on which they have done a remarkable work over the course of six years." They also accused Du Mouchel of deceitfulness, since he was "perfectly aware that the suppliants had been established [on said land]" before the purchase and "of the considerable land-clearing work they had done there." The court overturned Michel's ruling, allowing the two women to keep their farm.[146]

It was common for free people of African ancestry in Louisiana, as well, to become landowners and to work as farmers and shepherds, producing much-needed food for the residents of the colony. Isabelle, the Black or mixed-race housekeeper of New Orleans who was manumitted in the 1730s, introduced in Chapter 5, purchased a herd of horned cattle for the significant sum of 750 livres in 1738.[147] Her probable white lover, Chavannes, helped her take care of her business: he petitioned the Superior Council over a delay in the delivery of the cattle.[148] Isabelle also acquired a lot on Royal Street, which she sold before 1739 to a white entrepreneur named Sieur Claude du Breuil for 600 livres.[149] A map indicates that in the 1720s, several free people of African descent like Isabelle owned properties in downtown New Orleans.[150]

Other free people of African descent in Louisiana cultivated precious food crops. In 1731, on the banks of the Mississippi River near New Orleans, a "free *mulâtre*" named Simon owned a plot of land of six arpens, which he cultivated with his Black wife and one captive. A free Black named Jean-Baptiste used to own a plot of four arpens nearby, which he sold to a (presumably white) tailor named Paquet. Further north, upriver, a man named Raphael, described as a "free *nègre*," owned another plot of land of three arpens.[151] Ten years later, a free *mulâtre* named Louis formed a partnership with the king's warehouse keeper at Pointe Coupée, a man named Pierre Ricard, and his son, the lieutenant François Allain, to establish a cattle-breeding estate. Louis was to receive one-tenth of the cattle in exchange for running the business.[152] By 1763, a family of free Blacks had also purchased twelve arpens of land at Cannes Brulées (just a few miles west of New Orleans) from a man called La Vierge. One Jean La Branche petitioned the Council of Louisiana because La Vierge was apparently unaware that four arpens of this land belonged to him.[153]

Other free people of African descent in Louisiana competed with underprivileged whites for employment opportunities as domestic servants. The French engineer, historian, and planter Antoine-Simon Le Page Du Pratz advised French colonists in Louisiana to use Senegambian house servants because he considered them loyal, thoughtful, appreciative of their masters and "less robust than the others when it came to field work and handling the heat."[154] Some free domestic servants achieved quite comfortable standards of living. In 1745, in Pointe Coupée, a free Black cook named Jean-Baptiste Marty (or Marly) agreed to work for an infantry officer called Jean Jose Delfaut de Pontalba for a period of three years.[155] The same Marty had acquired as many as fourteen plots of land two decades earlier, in downtown New Orleans.[156] Years earlier, another free domestic servant named Raphael Bernard had displayed remarkable strength and resourcefulness in protecting his financial interests. He petitioned the Superior Council of Louisiana in July 1724, as Artas and Nanon had done in Guadeloupe, accusing his owner, Sieur Dumanoir, of withholding his wages and repeatedly beating him with a stick. After enduring two years of his owner's abuse, Bernard petitioned the court to oblige Dumanoir to pay his wages, return his trunk, and allow him to return to France. In the end, the Council of Louisiana sided with Raphael Bernard: Dumanoir was forced to return the trunk to him, advance him 100 francs, and let him leave his service.[157] This legal dispute was not Bernard's first successful fight for justice. A couple of months earlier, in May 1724, he had already petitioned the Superior Council of Louisiana to recover 200 livres of copper money that he had lent to a man named Sieur Paulin Cadot: Cadot had been sentenced to reimburse him the money, plus interest, and to bear the expense of the trial.[158]

Like Artas, Nanon, and Bernard, other free people of African descent in the French Americas stood up in defense of their socioeconomic interests.

In 1743, still in New Orleans, a *mulâtresse* named Marie-Charlotte, who probably worked as a house servant (like Bernard), also sued her master, Sieur Raymond Amyault d'Ausseville, for keeping her enslaved unlawfully. Marie-Charlotte's former owner and possible father, Sieur Saint-Julien, had manumitted her shortly before his passing in 1735.[159] In an effort to provide for Marie-Charlotte's upbringing, Saint-Julien secured a spot for her at the boarding school of the Ursuline nuns of New Orleans. Tragically, however, he died in 1737, leaving Marie-Charlotte unprotected and vulnerable. In his role as attorney of vacant estates, d'Ausseville took it upon himself to annotate the act of manumission as invalid on the grounds that it had not been validated by the governor or *commissaire-ordonnateur* of the colony—in accordance with article L of the Louisiana *Code Noir* of 1724, which enjoined slaveowners to seek an authorization from the Superior Council of the colony to free enslaved people. He subsequently auctioned Marie-Charlotte under the false pretense that Saint-Julien's assets could not cover his debts, purchasing her for himself for 1,500 livres. After being held captive on d'Ausseville's estate for ten years, Marie-Charlotte finally took her case to court in 1745, according to her own testimony, because it was "not just that a free woman should have been kept in slavery through a trick."[160] She petitioned the court to regain her freedom and recover the wages owed to her for her ten years of unpaid work. Marie-Charlotte's efforts paid off, since the court ruled in her favor. She was manumitted again, and d'Ausseville was required to pay her 1,500 livres in compensation for her work.[161]

Around the same period, another captive of African ancestry from New Orleans, named Louis Congo, also fought to obtain remuneration for his work. Louis was nominated by the Superior Council of Louisiana in 1725 to work as the colony's public executioner, or *executeur des hautes oeuvres.* Enslaved at this time, Louis was described as the perfect man for the job: he was "strong and robust" and had already gained some necessary skills, having previously performed an execution, or macabre "*chef d'oeuvre.*" This was a high-profile position, helping French authorities maintain law and order in the colony. However, any *executeur* was also at risk of retribution. In 1726, three Indigenous maroons attempted to murder Louis in his home.[162] Louis was again assaulted by two Black men in 1737, one of whom was also a maroon.[163] But Louis ended up manipulating those risks with admirable ingenuity: he successfully negotiated his freedom, regular food rations, and two arpens of land near the city, where he was allowed to reside with his wife, Suzanne, an enslaved Black woman of the company.[164] Authorities also agreed to give him generous remuneration for his job: he was offered forty livres for each fire or wheel punishment, thirty for each execution, ten for using the whip or branding iron, and five for placing criminals on the pillory.[165]

Other free men of African descent in Louisiana, who, like Louis Congo, had acquired rare skills, practiced less dangerous activities. Among them was Antoine Beauvais, a cooper who was described as a "free *mulâtre*" when he embarked on a company's ship in 1724. Beauvais was to receive the usual salary of fifteen livres per month for his work, despite the fact that he was visually impaired.[166] Fifteen years later, in New Orleans, a free Black man named Scipion, who used to work on one of the company's ships, offered his services to a French *voyageur* called René Petit.[167] Petit was one of the many merchants who regularly traveled from Lower Louisiana to Illinois and back to procure flour for the colonies' residents. Scipion was to help him load, unload, and sail the boat to Illinois in exchange for 250 livres of flour. Scipion's salary for this voyage was much lower than that usually paid to slaveowners leasing their captives for similar ventures, which typically averaged over 1,500 livres of flour.[168] However, Scipion was authorized to seize this opportunity to conduct his own business as a merchant. His employment contract contained a special clause specifying that he would be allowed to work for his own profit and trade flour, liquor, and clothes in Illinois after discharging the cargo, so long as he returned on time to travel back to New Orleans. Petit pledged to transport any of Scipion's own merchandise back to the South.[169]

Like Scipion, other free Blacks integrated into the commercial economy of Louisiana, operating small businesses that sold (sometimes vital) necessities. A free Black in Louisiana, aptly named Jules Cesar, cleverly navigated the notarial system of Pointe Coupée to protect his own business interests. In 1762, in the office of a French notary, he secured a very advantageous trading deal with one Sieur Valentin Joutard. To compensate for a delayed delivery, Cesar convinced Joutard to give him 450 pieces of timber instead of the 150 he had initially purchased from him a year earlier. Should Joutard fail to deliver the timber on time again, he agreed to give a very generous compensation to Cesar, comprising one enslaved Black named

Sontay and three pairs of oxen.[170] Another free Black of Lower Louisiana named Jacques DuVerger, described as "a *voyageur* to Illinois," frequently boated up north to trade his merchandise. He once purchased over 900 livres worth of clothing, wine, soap, and other items in New Orleans, which he intended to resell in the Illinois Country.[171]

Like DuVerger and Scipion, several free men of African descent in the French Americas possessed nautical skills, which sometimes allowed them to achieve astonishing professional success. In Guadeloupe, a ship captain named Serville, described as a free creole *mulâtre* from French Saint-Christopher, garnered considerable wealth through his activities as a pirate. Using his Spanish ship, *La Vierge du Bail,* he plundered merchandise and silver from multiple French and English vessels on the Caribbean Sea. He also stole an English ship named *La Marguerite,* kidnapping its British crew. Surprisingly, the crew under *mulâtre* Serville's command included many white men from France, Martinique, and the Spanish and British empires. We only know of Serville's story because he was eventually arrested in 1728 in the port city of Basse-Terre in Guadeloupe. Authorities confiscated his ships and belongings, and he was sent to the galleys.[172]

Serville was not the only free man of African ancestry in the French Atlantic to have become a prosperous ship captain. Around the same period, another free man named Larue, described as a *mulâtre,* commanded a slave ship that connected the French Americas to the kingdom of France and to West Africa, through the triangular trade route. After a stop in Saint-Domingue, he arrived in New Orleans in 1734, determined to do business with French authorities.[173] His plan was to load his ship with crops, sail back to France, and from there "go fetch *nègres* from Guinea [to] bring them [to Louisiana]"—all at his own expense.[174] *Commissaire-ordonnateur* Salmon was thrilled at the prospect of doing business with Larue, since slave imports to Louisiana had almost completely ended by 1734.[175]

Skilled work in the maritime, artisanal, and other sectors of the economy provided an important avenue for socioeconomic ascent for many free people of non-European ancestries on Isle Bourbon as well. From the 1720s, Europeans on Isle Bourbon were competing with a growing number of indentured servants (*engagés*) from India for job opportunities. Despite having often escaped poverty and famine in India, most Indian *engagés* refused to cultivate the land on plantations, probably finding the task too demeaning.[176] Among those indentured servants were a group of Muslim sailors labeled "lascars." Others, often called "Malabars" (*Malabares*), practiced several artisan trades.[177] Ninety-nine Malabars were recruited in Pondicherry in the 1720s to be sent to Isle Bourbon.[178] Other Indian indentured servants on the island, labeled "coolies," worked as gunsmiths and coast watchers, sometimes joining maroon militias.[179] In 1747, the Company of the Indies employed eleven coolies to work on Isle Bourbon, paying them almost 120 livres per year—the same amount paid to European men in the same positions.[180]

Indian indentured servants played a key role in the maritime sector of the French Indian Ocean. The lascars worked with white sailors on both short-haul and long-haul vessels traveling between the Mascarenes and South Asia. The French governor, Bertrand-François Mahé de la Bourdonnais, petitioned authorities to hire more Indian lascars in the 1730s, finding European sailors too expensive.[181] At least 224 lascars were employed by the French Company of the Indies over the course of the eighteenth century.[182] The Company of the Indies also hired an Indian steerer named Tendréa in 1744, who was in charge of shuttling people among the parishes of Saint-Denis, Sainte-Suzanne, and Saint-Benoît for a respectable salary of 200 livres per year.[183]

Many Indian indentured servants on Isle Bourbon secured other respected positions as masons, joiners, and smiths—roles that were essential to the construction and maintenance of the French colony. By 1747, the Company of the Indies on the island employed thirteen masons, two brickmakers, seven blacksmiths, and two rattan makers.[184] Other Indian indentured servants, notably a joiner named Tendréa Malabar, worked for individual colonists. In 1740, Tendréa was hired by a man named Gabriel Dejean for a period of four years at a salary of 18 livres per month plus food rations. His contract was renewed for two more years in 1744, with the promise of a generous salary of 330 livres per year.[185] Another Malabar, who worked as a locksmith, performed a job for a former Isle Bourbon councilor in 1747.[186]

Many officials held these Indian indentured servants in higher esteem than they did white artisans. In 1731, authorities portrayed French artisans on Isle Bourbon as drunken fools, recommending that they be replaced with Indian indentured servants able to train enslaved people as apprentices.[187] The company approved this proposal in 1736, advising members of the Superior Council of Isle Bourbon to procure more indentured servants from India, but only "if [they] really [could not] succeed with workers from Europe."[188] Later, the directors of the company refused to recruit assayers from France to work on Isle Bourbon, describing Indian assayers as "more suitable" than the French.[189] They also complained that none of the female residents on Isle Bourbon could weave cotton and resolved to bring six female weavers from Bengal to the island, so they could serve as an example for local women.[190]

Some Indian indentured servants on Isle Bourbon amassed considerable wealth by engaging in skilled occupations traditionally practiced by whites. A slaveowner named Virapa, described as a "Malabar goldsmith," established himself in the parish of Saint-Denis and became one of the wealthiest residents of the island.[191] Virapa acquired multiple plots of land and purchased many luxury goods, worth 11,819 livres, that previously belonged to a former French councilor at the Parlement of Paris and at the Superior Council of Isle Bourbon.[192] Another man from India, also named Virapa, also did very well for himself. Established in the parish of Saint-Denis, he was described as a Malabar mason from the city of Madras. In 1754, he sold several buildings worth 100 piastres to a company employee named Bignot, as well as one cabin worth 40 piastres to another company employee named Julien Bilzie. Seven years later, he purchased a coffee plantation once owned by a French councilor, for the enormous sum of 5,500 piastres. By 1765, the former mason owned forty-four enslaved people, eighty-three arpens of land, and a few heads of livestock.[193] It was not uncommon for indentured servants from India to acquire land and captives during or after their indenture.[194]

But by the eighteenth century, Eurasians and Creole people of Malagasy and South Asian ancestries formed the largest and most successful class of landowners and slaveholders of non-European descent on Isle Bourbon. For example, in the parish of Saint-Pierre, a French-Malagasy *mulâtre* named Pierre Nativel Jr. owned a plantation with 114 enslaved people.[195] Back in Saint-Paul, in 1732, Pierre Benoît Dumas and his Eurasian wife, Marie-Gertrude Wanzyll Dumas, owned two coffee plantations, as well as 21 house servants and 140 enslaved plantation workers. Remember, also, *mulâtresse* Luce Payet and her French husband, Henry de Justamond: by 1732, the couple had amassed a considerable fortune in the parish of

Saint-Denis, including three coffee plantations, 92 captives, and dozens of heads of livestock.[196]

The Politicization of the Bourbon Island Creoles

By the early eighteenth century, many of the members of the creole planter elite of non-European descent of Isle Bourbon had garnered considerable status and influence.[197] Keeping up with the older seventeenth-century practice, many women of non-European descent on the island had formed alliances with important French officials.[198] Although Henry de Justamond was only the island's tax collector when he married the *mulâtresse* Luce Payet in 1712, he ascended to the rank of governor in 1715.[199] Pierre Benoît Dumas, the French husband of the affluent Eurasian coffee planter Marie-Gertrude Wanzyll, was one of his successors in this role.[200] Jacques Bouyer, the former French pirate from La Rochelle who married an Eurasian woman named Jeanne Wilmann in 1709, also had his mixed-race wife by his side during his political ascent. Praised for his "wisdom, integrity and devotion" to the Company of the Indies, Bouyer joined the Council of Isle Bourbon in 1715, where he stayed in office for more than ten years.[201] Joseph Choppy Desgranges, the Frenchman from Limousin who married *mulâtresse* Marianne Payet in 1728, occupied many prestigious offices on the island. Working as a notary, the colony's general-attorney, and a bookkeeper, he also became the commandant of the parishes of Saint-Pierre and Saint-Louis (in the island's Southwest) in 1732.[202]

Even more astonishingly, beginning in the early eighteenth century, local officials officially allowed creole men of non-European descent to join the Superior Council of Isle Bourbon. Not only did the office of councilor give access to jurisdictional and legal power and prestige, but it also came with generous compensation, amounting to up to 2,000 livres per year.[203] This may explain why, in 1705, Antoine Boucher reported that "the *mulâtres*' [creole fathers on Isle Bourbon] support[ed] [their sons] and demand[ed] [their] access to offices and ceremonies in public assemblies," as well as to the island's highest positions of power.[204] Those creole fathers believed that experienced mixed married men were more deserving of holding leadership roles in public assemblies than white creoles. However, their attempts to place their sons in those positions of authority faced a lot of opposition. According to Boucher, other white men on the island regarded the *mulâtres* "almost as they would the *nègres*," deeming them unworthy of holding political office.[205] Their view on the subject caused constant quarrels, which fostered a climate of political stagnation on the island.[206] Despite having a mixed-race child of his own, Boucher considered mixed-race Bourbon Island Creole men unfit for any position of authority. He addressed this offensive note to them:

> Dear creole *mulâtres*, you aspire to become white men's equals by holding the same offices as them, with no distinction between you and them [. . .]. In doing so, you aim to elevate yourselves above your origin, which still bears something of the *nègre*. Your skin color makes you despicable to others, and your actions are vile. You want to be considered white, but you live a life worthy of the *nègres*.[207]

Despite fierce opposition, the mixed-race Bourbon Island Creoles were determined to access political offices, invoking their Frenchification to convince authorities to grant them that right. Their principal argument was that they "*[took] from their fathers who [were] French* and must therefore acquire the same privileges." They added that "their color [could not] deprive them of enjoying the rights given to other colonists."[208] Amazingly, for a few years at least, their battle was successful: on November 18, 1718, the Superior Council of Isle Bourbon officially declared any mixed-race creole man (or *mulâtre*) on the island eligible to hold the office of councilor.[209]

Only three days later, a man named François Grondin became the first *mulâtre* to be made councilor at the Superior Council of Isle Bourbon.[210] Boucher unambiguously portrayed François Grondin as a "*mulâtre*," "the son of a Frenchman and a *négresse*, with a dark skin color."[211] Born in Madagascar in 1670, François Grondin was none other than the oncle of Marianne Payet—the successful *mulâtresse* whom we encountered in the opening of this book. His mother was also Louise Siaram, a Malagasy woman, and his father was Louise's first husband, a soldier from Burgundy named Étienne Grondin. The first years of François's life did not bode very well for his future. A 1690 census described him as a landless eternal bachelor (*grand garçon*) living with his stepfather, Antoine Payet, in Saint-Paul.[212] But François's life was long, and he eventually married twice. His first marriage, in 1694, was to a widowed *mulâtresse* named Jeanne Arnould, the daughter of a Black woman from Madagascar named Marie Mahon.[213] Together, François and Jeanne acquired three parcels of land in the parishes of Saint-Denis and Sainte-Suzanne, along with eight enslaved people.[214] By 1710, François was described as a hard-working and literate man who was very comfortable financially.[215] This wealth probably facilitated his political ascent: six years later, officials on the island granted him the title of councilor in a formal ceremony.[216] After Jeanne's passing in 1729, François married a *mulâtresse* named Antoinette Nativel, the sister of the *mulâtresse* Louise Nativel.[217] By 1732, the Grondins had become wealthy plantation owners.[218]

Political offices only remained officially accessible to mixed-race Bourbon Island Creoles for a decade. In 1728, the French Company of the Indies decided to reverse the declaration of 1718, issuing another one that stated that "no creole [meaning *mulâtre*] can ever be introduced into the administrative council [of the island]." This declaration must have been ineffective, since it was reiterated in 1729.[219] Ultimately, none of the measures taken by French officials ended the Bourbon Island Creoles' fierce struggle for political influence: this was just the beginning of the long battle for political equality that culminated in the Age of Revolutions.[220]

* * *

Many people of non-European descent in the French colonies managed to climb the socioeconomic ladder, shaping the empire in the process through their activities in all sectors of the economy—and, in a few cases, even as active participants in imperial politics. Unskilled captives of African and Malagasy ancestries had the lowest status across slave societies, partly because of ideas spread by Europeans and Indigenous people seeking to shield themselves from the most degrading labor in the French Americas. However, from Louisiana to Isle Bourbon, both unskilled and skilled captives could still compete with whites for work opportunities. And it was *free* people of non-European descent who by far posed the greatest threat to white socioeconomic supremacy. This is especially evident when considering eighteenth-century Isle Bourbon, which was home to a large population of economically and socially successful free people of Malagasy and South Asian descent. It was also on Isle Bourbon that an elite of non-European descent launched one of the very first Black movements for political rights in the French empire, many decades before the French and Haitian Revolutions. In fact, many of the political, legal, economic, social, and cultural developments that happened after the Seven Years' War were already underway in the seventeenth century and the first half of the eighteenth. The period of reconfiguration and ruptures that followed the Seven Years' War era should be envisioned from a *longue-durée* perspective, taking into account the ways in which the first 150-plus years of overseas colonization shaped France's future colonial projects.

Conclusion

Pierre Félix Barthélemy David was born in Marseille, France, in 1710. After joining the Company of the Indies in 1729, he became the director of the Company of Senegal in 1738. In recognition of his leadership experience, he was subsequently appointed governor-general of Isle Bourbon and Isle of France, a position he held from 1746 to 1753.[1] After this, David was chosen to take an active role in a policy of reform initiated by Marine Secretary Étienne-François, Duke of Choiseul, in the aftermath of the Seven Years' War (1756–1763). In 1767, David proposed to establish a new colony in French Guiana, where the free African and Eurafrican families he had met in Gorée would establish plantations operated by their enslaved Africans.[2] Several free Africans and Eurafricans from Gorée were subsequently sent to Cayenne, Guiana, along with enslaved Africans.[3] Echoing the "whitening" rhetoric that can be traced back to the seventeenth-century French Indian Ocean world, David insisted that the Goreans' skin color showed "no trace of their ancestors' color," to the point that they were "more white than inhabitants of the Islands usually are"—without explaining whether he was referring to the Mascarenes, where he had lived, or to the Caribbean.[4] Alexandre Ferdinand de Bessner, the incoming governor of Guiana and a friend of David, took this project one step further by endorsing intermarriage between the Goreans and poor white people in Guiana as a colonization strategy.[5] Bessner believed that the Gorean families should be encouraged to intermarry with whites so that their skin would gradually acquire "the color that should be that of slave masters in America."[6] In other words, he envisioned creating a "white" master class in Guiana that would be drawn from the mixed descendants of David's Gorean families, thereby replicating the precedent set by creole people on Isle Bourbon.

As the history of the Gorean–Guiana project demonstrates, the period following the Seven Years' War was one of resurgence, reconfiguration, and expansion of the French colonial strategies developed since the seventeenth century, even as it was a time of rupture.[7] Shortly after giving up New France and Louisiana under the terms of the Treaties of Paris and Fontainebleau in 1762 and 1763, respectively, French authorities had the ambition to create new colonies in Guiana and Madagascar in the name of the king. Now fully aware of the possibilities mixed Catholic unions could open up for populating imperial margins with scarce white colonists, French officials decided to turn to intermarriage once again in order to advance their colonial aspirations. They also revived the old "civilization" program devised decades earlier for seventeenth-century New France and Madagascar, revealing a lasting commitment to a vision dating back to the era of Roman Gaul.

At the same time, the rise of slave plantation agriculture in the Mascarene and Caribbean islands, coupled with the growing diffusion of the egalitarian ethos advanced by the French Revolution, further radicalized the set of racial policies forged since the late seventeenth century for France's slave societies.[8] In an effort to offset major losses caused by years of war, French authorities endeavored to promote sugarcane slave plantation agriculture in both the Caribbean and the Mascarene islands.[9] Beginning in the 1760s, this led the French botanist and intendant of Isle of France and Isle Bourbon, Pierre Poivre, to launch a major economic reconfiguration project in the southwest Indian Ocean. By the time of the revolutionary era, this project had generated a massive expansion in sugarcane plantation agriculture on Isle Bourbon and Isle of France, bringing a considerable surge in the captive populations of both islands.[10] The radicalization of racial policies was most pronounced in the Caribbean and the Mascarenes, where the stakes of maintaining slave plantation systems were especially high. Its transoceanic scope is often overlooked because of the compartmentalization of the field of eighteenth-century French colonial history into local and regional studies.

This book has demonstrated that much is to be gained from a transoceanic approach to French colonial history. For one, the full landscape of early French colonial policymaking cannot be fully understood without a pan-imperial outlook on France's colonial world. This is also true of the later period: strategies employed in the Indian Ocean continued to shape Atlantic policies and vice versa, as suggested by David's own previous experience as governor-general of Isle Bourbon and Isle of France. Moreover, a transoceanic perspective on France's post–Seven Years' War era strategies further illuminates two important repertoires of global French colonialism over the *longue durée*: assimilation—especially through evangelization, the "civilizing" project and intermarriage—and racial policing. French officials pursued assimilation and racial policing on a far broader scale than often recognized. From the Americas to Asia, they never really abandoned their evangelization project until the twentieth century. Well into the twentieth century, they also pursued various forms of "civilizing" missions, with very limited means and consistency over time and space.[11] From the seventeenth to the late eighteenth centuries, they (intermittently) promoted intermarriage with female Christian converts as well, in order to populate the imperial margins. Racialism, for its part, remained a constant element in French colonial policing from the late seventeenth to the twentieth centuries.[12]

But perhaps the most important pattern revealed by the transoceanic approach in this book concerns the reactions of the populations of African, Malagasy, and South Asian ancestries to the rigidification of race. A transoceanic perspective reveals that despite their distinct experiences, these racialized populations shared a common determination to fight for their interests and seek justice and protection for themselves and for their loved ones, often amid profound adversity. This pattern persisted well into the Seven Years' War and revolutionary eras, when thousands of peoples of African, Malagasy, and South Asian descent across the French Atlantic and Indian Ocean worlds began to engage in an intensified common struggle for justice and political rights.

Continuities and Reconfigurations on the Margins

In addition to echoing the strategy formulated for the French colonies of New France and Madagascar in the seventeenth century, the new assimilation projects of the 1760s were also influenced by earlier developments that happened on the ground. By that time, dozens of underprivileged Frenchmen had already improved their conditions by forming lucrative alliances with successful women of African and other non-European ancestries, possibly influencing Alexandre Ferdinand de Bessner's decision to encourage intermarriage between the Gorean women and *poor* white men in Guiana. In fact, just as Bessner was promoting his Guiana project in the 1760s, intermarriages between comfortable creole women and poor French artisans, sailors, and soldiers surged in the cities of Isle Bourbon. This development has been attributed to white men's quest for profitable property—especially enslaved people and livestock—on the island.[13]

The project of colonization formulated for Madagascar from the 1760s, for its part, echoed France's older seventeenth-century New France and Anosy "civilization" strategy.[14] One of its main proponents was the former governor of the outpost of Karikal in India, Louis-Laurent de Féderbe, Count of Modave.[15] He ambitioned to extract Madagascar's resources and use the island as a military base to protect the French Indian outposts from British incursions. Drawing his inspiration from physiocratic beliefs, he thought that the best way to advance French domination was by "civiliz[ing]" the so-called "savage" or "barbarous" populations overseas.[16] The Ministry of the Marine received about ninety memoranda advocating for the project of colonization through assimilation in Madagascar between 1770 and 1816. Supporters of the program produced multiple philosophical writings emphasizing Madagascar's alleged great potential for "civilization."[17] Commissioned by Marine Secretary Choiseul, the third edition of Abbé Raynal's *Histoire des Deux Indes* (1780), in particular, defended a so-called "soft" project of colonization (*colonisation douce*) in Madagascar—one that relied on assimilation rather than physical violence.[18]

There is little doubt that when formulating this project, French intellectuals and officials drew inspiration from the seventeenth-century grand strategy of colonization. As with the earlier plan devised for Anosy and New France in the seventeenth century, Modave's "civilization" project entailed teaching Malagasies French customs, the French language, and the Catholic faith. As before, the project also aimed to transform Malagasies into peasants and artisans trained in French arts and crafts.[19] This proposal was echoed in the writings of the physiocrats, who urged French authorities to polish the manners of overseas populations, promote trade among them, and teach them the arts and sciences.[20] A similar form of Enlightened colonialism was promoted by several Enlightenment philosophers.[21] Here is what Raynal wrote in his 1780 appeal for the colonization of Madagascar: "How glorious it would be for France to rescue a people from the horrors of barbarism; to instill in them virtuous manners, a suitable political system, wise laws, a benevolent religion, and useful and enjoyable arts; elevating them to the ranks of educated and civilized nations!"[22]

Once again, France's renewed colonial enterprise in late eighteenth-century Madagascar proved ill fated. After his appointment as governor of Fort-Dauphin, Modave arrived on the Tolagñare peninsula in 1768 with instructions from Marine Secretary Choiseul to establish a colony and put the civilizing project into practice.[23] Once again, the French faced starvation and died en masse from tropical diseases. They also became embroiled in another brutal conflict with the king of Anosy, which made it difficult for them to venture outside the French fort. Desperate, Modave rapidly abandoned his project of "civilization," planning instead to turn to violence to advance the French colonial project in Madagascar. His plan never came to fruition, and he was forced to evacuate the much-desired island in 1771, leaving Fort-Dauphin almost completely abandoned once again.[24] After this, an ambitious nobleman from Upper Hungary (today's Slovakia), named Móric Beňovský, took over Modave's master plan of colonization through assimilation, planning to establish another French foothold, this time in northern Madagascar.[25] But once again, diseases, starvation, and conflicts with several local leaders forced the French to abandon their colonial project.[26]

The Radicalization of Racial Policing in Slave Societies

Meanwhile, French colonial policies were taking a different turn in France's old island slave societies. French authorities devised an increasing number of racial laws for the Caribbean and Isle Bourbon that discriminated against "free people of color" (gens de couleur libres)—the new label given to free populations of African (as well as Malagasy or South Asian) descent in official documents. French authorities intensified their Caribbean racial policing strategy to secure the loyalty of white subjects during a period of European conflict. They were especially mindful of the poor white populations of the

French Caribbean (*les petits Blancs*), who competed with free people of color for wealth and job opportunities. This is why some of their policies began to block access to additional professions for free populations of non-European descent.[27] Their policy of exclusion culminated in 1771 in Cap-Français, Saint-Domingue, when a high-ranking man named Pierre Chapuiset de Guériné famously lost his desirable position as an army officer for being of "mixed blood."[28] French authorities also sought to protect their white subjects from the purported "stain" associated with people of African descent. In line with past attempts to prevent priests in the French Atlantic world from listing the names of mixed children's white fathers in parish registers, further legislation issued in 1763 prohibited *mulâtres* in the French Caribbean from claiming the names of their white progenitors.[29] Ten years later, officials in Guadeloupe, Martinique, and Saint-Domingue prohibited people of African descent from using white-sounding names on the grounds that such usurpation "destroy[ed] th[e] insurmountable barrier between whites and people of color, which has been established by public opinion."[30] French officials also sought to deter white people from partnering with free people of color in possible revolts against the crown. In response to those fears, Choiseul issued a new intermarriage prohibition in 1766, banning unions between white men and women of color in Saint-Domingue.[31] Public spaces in Saint-Domingue were now segregated, and officials there and in Martinique also began to abandon the old tradition of assimilation to the "white" category. All people of non-European descent were now required to state their true origins in official documents, even if they had previously been able to pass as "whites."[32]

The French Revolution ushered in what historian Laurent Dubois calls the era of "Republican racism."[33] After a long Black battle for freedom that unfolded across the Caribbean between 1789 and 1794, which culminated in one of the greatest slave revolts in history on the island of Saint-Domingue, slavery was (temporarily) abolished by the French National Convention on February 4, 1794, and full rights were granted to formerly enslaved people.[34] Free people of color had already secured a declaration of equal rights on April 4, 1792, in recognition of their efforts to quell the slave revolt of Saint-Domingue.[35] Faced with the prospect of thousands of former enslaved people becoming both free and full citizens, Caribbean planters began to seek new ways to protect their economic interests.

They pursued a policy of racial exclusion, stressing Black and mixed-race people's alleged intellectual incapacity to act as proper citizens, and seeking to maintain a rough racial labor system.[36] In accordance with the Proclamation to the Black Citizen issued in Guadeloupe on June 10, 1794, formerly enslaved people were expected to pay "the price of liberty" by serving the nation as soldiers or *cultivateurs*.[37] Five months later, local authorities in Guadeloupe mandated all formerly enslaved people to return to their former plantation, compelling them to work for little or no pay under threat of being convicted of counterrevolution and treason.[38] The French constitution of 1795 further disenfranchised Blacks and mixed-race people by making rights of citizenship suspendable for those engaged in "domestic service for wages" and by declaring property ownership a pre-condition for voting rights.[39] The dismantlement of the project of emancipation culminated in May 1802, when Napoleon decided to re-establish slavery.[40]

By the close of the eighteenth century, fearing that rights might be extended to Black and mixed-race people, the French political and intellectual elites in the Caribbean became increasingly obsessed with race and ancestry. They described intermarriage with Blacks as an "indelible stain" ("*une tâche ineffaçable*") on white families, clinging to them through the generations.[41] The anti-abolitionist Martinican creole lawyer, writer, and official historiographer of the French Ministry of the Marine, Médéric Louis Élie Moreau de Saint-Méry, insisted on the necessity of maintaining a distinction that would deny people of African descent access to economic and social opportunities.[42] Though he fathered a mixed-race daughter, Moreau de Saint-Méry emerged as one of the foremost "ideologue[s] of white superiority," to use the words of Sara E. Johnson.[43] He summarized his view in the 1790s, as follows: "the common belief, which rejects the possibility of fully erasing the mixing [. . .] is that an infinite line will always separate the white descendance from the other."[44] Moreau De Saint-Méry's infamous inventory enumerated a total of 128 racial combinations separating whites from Blacks. Among them were the categories "*mulâtres*," "*métis*," "*quarterons*," as well as "*mamelouques*" (mixed white-*quarteron*) and "*sang-mêlés*" (mixed-blood)."[45] French Caribbean creoles prided themselves in being able to detect the faintest trace of African ancestry, even when successive generations had made someone completely white.[46]

As brilliantly demonstrated by historian Nathan Marvin, the radicalization of racial policies targeting Isle Bourbon was a slower process than in the Caribbean. Until the French Revolution, French authorities continued to allow Bourbon Island Creole people to keep their "white" legal status, despite their Malagasy and South Asian origins. According to one estimate, as much as three-quarters of all "whites" on Isle Bourbon on the eve of the French Revolution had non-European ancestries.[47] Laws restricting access to certain professions only applied to manumitted people at first, and to those with recent enslaved ancestors.[48]

However, the rise of slave-based sugarcane plantation agriculture on Isle Bourbon, as well as the threat posed by the egalitarian ethos of the French Revolution, forced a rupture with this "color blind logic" during the revolutionary era.[49] This shift was spearheaded by *les gros Blancs*—a group of powerful white families—and also by a small cluster of "whitened" Bourbon Island Creoles well determined to keep their (now distant) "true" Malagasy and South Asian origins concealed.[50] Those people took measures to block access to additional careers for other populations of non-European ancestries on the island (the "libres" or "gens de couleur").[51] For example, free people of color were not allowed to serve with white men in local militias and companies of the Garde Nationale—military forces established during the French Revolution—nor could they act as their own company's highest commander.[52] They were no longer allowed to use the distinguished titles of "madame" and "monsieur" either.[53] Echoing the point of view of Moreau de Saint-Méry, a municipal agent from the parish of Saint-Paul, Isle Bourbon demanded more racial laws "to show the immense divide which existed between Blacks and whites, in a [more] conspicuous manner."[54]

Racial policing sparked a little-known episode in the history of Isle Bourbon. In 1792, in the French puppet theater room of the city of Saint-Denis (*la salle du spectacle des fantoccinis français*), a faction of free Black women married to white men organized a sit-in protest, calling for the end of segregation rules.[55] These women's white husbands joined forces with a cluster of free men of color on the island to write a lively petition for the island's assembly—which replaced royal officials after the end of the Ancien Régime—demanding an end to "the ridiculous and unfounded disdain for [them] and [their] wives."[56]

A Common Struggle for Justice and Political Rights

The shared battle for justice and political rights led by people of non-European descent across the Atlantic and Indian Oceans peaked during the Age of Revolutions. Following the foundation of the National Assembly and National Constituent Assembly (1789–1790) in the early years of the French Revolution, free property owners of color in the Caribbean petitioned French authorities for the right to representation, invoking the French republican ethos of universal rights.[57] In May 1791, the National Assembly extended equal citizenship to all freeborn men of color throughout the French colonial empire.[58] Then, in March 1792, seeking new allies during the slave revolution of Saint-Domingue, the National Assembly declared all "men of color and free *nègres*" in the colonies (who were able to pay the necessary taxes) able to "enjoy the equality of political rights," along with eligibility for all positions.[59] Free people of color from Saint-Domingue sent a delegation to France to be granted the right to representation in the National Convention (1792–1795)—the legislative and executive body established after the fall of the French monarchy. In a stunning turn of events, several representatives of color from the Northern Province of Saint-Domingue were eventually admitted to the Convention.[60]

This revolutionary battle for equal rights was not restricted to the French Atlantic. Free people of color on the Mascarene Islands, too, demanded the right to be represented in the governmental institutions of the new republic. Nathan Marvin and Sabrine Noël have uncovered an astonishing petition sent to the National Assembly by a Bourbon Island faction of twenty-nine mixed-race men and white men in April 1791 that claimed, "In this colony, some whites who married freed Black women [*affranchies*] have always enjoyed, along with their posterity, all the rights exercised by other citizens. We beg the National Assembly to confirm this disposition [as] conforming to the principles of equality that it professes." Should the National Assembly be unable to grant these rights to those free people of non-European descent, the creoles requested "a particular exception for the Island of Bourbon."[61] The Assembly of Isle Bourbon rejected the decree issued by the National Assembly in May 1791 that had extended equal citizenship to all freeborn men of color across France's colonial empire.[62] Well determined to keep fighting for their interests, however, a group of Bourbon

Island Creoles submitted another petition for political freedom and finally obtained their voting rights in 1793.[63] Of course, this was not at all the Bourbon Island Creoles' first attempt to improve their condition and obtain justice for themselves.

The story of the self-liberation of the people of non-European ancestries of the French empire becomes all the more compelling when approached from a transoceanic and *longue-durée* perspective. Many decades before free people of color were granted representation in the governmental institutions of the new French Republic, in 1718, the Bourbon Island Creoles of Malagasy and South Asian ancestries had already secured access to political offices after a heated battle against resistant whites. Throughout this book, we have also encountered dozens of people of African, Malagasy and South Asian ancestries who stood up to protect and advance their interests beyond the struggle for political rights. Remember Artas and Nanon, the two free Black women of Capesterre who successfully petitioned the court of Guadeloupe in 1730 to keep their farms after an unjust attempt to strip them of their property. Remember, too, Jules Cesar, the free Black man of Pointe Coupée, Louisiana who struck a very advantageous commercial deal in 1762 after one Sieur Valentin Joutard had failed to deliver the timber he had purchased from him a year earlier. Several years later, the *mulâtresse* Charlotte was finally able to purchase her own freedom, and that of her son, using the money she had earned working in the city of New Orleans. Grit and resourcefulness were only some of the many important qualities that tied all these distinct populations together. Much groundbreaking work is yet to be done to determine what else these different people from all corners of the colonial Atlantic and Indian Ocean worlds had in common, as well as where and how their stories deviated from one another. This book will hopefully pave the way for such studies.

Appendix

Appendix: Clusters of French Policies Targeting People of Non-European Ancestry, 1603–1758

CLUSTER NAME	POLICY NAME	EXCERPT	AUTHOR	DATE	LOCATION	OCEAN
BAPTIZING THE ENSLAVED	*Code Noir* of the Caribbean, 1685	*"All slaves shall be baptized and instructed in the Roman, Catholic, and Apostolic religion."*	The king	1685	Caribbean	Atlantic
	Letters Patent of Isle Bourbon and Isle of France, 1723	*"All slaves shall be baptized and instructed in the Roman, Catholic, and Apostolic Faith."*	The king	1723	Isle Bourbon and Isle of France	Indian Ocean
	Code Noir of Louisiana, 1724	*"All slaves shall be baptized and instructed in the Roman, Catholic, and Apostolic Faith."*	The king	1724	Louisiana	Atlantic
	Deliberation of the Superior Council of Pondicherry, 1747	*"The council . . . commands all people keeping slaves to have them instructed in the Catholic, Apostolic and Roman religion and to have them baptized . . . under the penalties of the edict of the king of March, Seventeen Hundred and Twenty Four."*	Colonial council	1747	India	Indian Ocean
SENDING PRIESTS TO THE COLONIES	Declaration of the King for the Establishment of the Company of the East Indies, 1664	*"Said company will establish clergymen on said islands of Madagascar & other territories it will conquer to instruct the people in the Catholic, Apostolic & Roman Religion."*	The king	1664	Isle Bourbon and Isle of France	Indian Ocean
	Declaration of the King for the Establishment of the Company of the East Indies, 1664	*"Said company will establish clergymen on said islands of Madagascar & other territories it will conquer to instruct the people in the Catholic, Apostolic & Roman Religion."*	The king	1664	India	Indian Ocean
	Declaration of the King for the Establishment of the Company of the East Indies, 1664	*"Said company will establish clergymen on said islands of Madagascar & other territories it will conquer to instruct the people in the Catholic, Apostolic & Roman Religion."*	The king	1664	Madagascar	Indian Ocean

	Act for the Establishment of the Company of One Hundred Associates, 1627	*"In each habitation . . . to convert the sauvages and assist the French of New France, there will be at least three clergymen."*	Richelieu	1627	New France	Atlantic
	Act of Association of the Lords of the Company of the American Islands, 1626	*"To convert [the sauvages] to the Catholic, Apostolic & Roman religion and . . . to maintain at least two or three ecclesiastics in order to administer the words of God and Catholic sacraments to Catholic people, & to instruct the sauvages."*	Richelieu	1626	Caribbean	Atlantic
	Letters Patent for the Establishment of Mainland America, 1651	*"The king . . . would not have conceded . . . the American mainland if it were not under the condition of sending clergymen, as it was done in New France, & on the Islands of Saint Christopher, Guadeloupe, Martinique and others where . . . the Catholic, Apostolic, and Roman faith which was unknown before is now well established."*	The king	1651	Guiana	Atlantic
CONVERTING LOCAL PEOPLE	Act for the Establishment of the Company of One Hundred Associates, 1627	*"To populate said land with French Catholic subjects so that, through their example, those nations would be inclined to embrace the Christian religion."*	Richelieu	1627	New France	Atlantic
	Edict for the Establishment of the Company of the West Indies, 1664	*"We consider that the primary goal of these said colonies is the glory of God by procuring salvation to Indians and sauvages."*	The king	1664	Senegal	Atlantic
	Act of Association of the Lords of the Company of the American Islands, 1626	*"To teach the inhabitants of said [islands] about the Catholic, Apostolic, and Roman religion."*	Richelieu	1626	Caribbean	Atlantic

(*continued*)

Appendix: Clusters of French Policies Targeting People of Non-European Ancestry, 1603–1758 (*Continued*)

CLUSTER NAME	POLICY NAME	EXCERPT	AUTHOR	DATE	LOCATION	OCEAN
	Edict for the Establishment of the Company of the West Indies, 1664	*"We consider that the primary goal of these said colonies is the glory of God by procuring salvation to Indians and sauvages."*	The king	1664	Guiana	Atlantic
	Declaration by the Directors of the Royal Company of Senegal of 1688	*"We order the directors & commandants to impose the practice of the Roman, Catholic, and Apostolic religion."*	Trading company	1688	Senegal	Atlantic
	Duke of Mazarin [. . .] 1663, Madagascar	*"To establish [in Madagascar] a great establishment of priests and devout people to convert and baptize most of the inhabitants of said island."*	Unknown	1663	Madagascar	Indian Ocean
	Concerning the Catholic faith in the colonies of India	*"The syndics and directors of the Company of the Indies [. . .] will propose [. . .] the erection of two parishes [in Chandernagore], one for the French [. . .] the other for the Indians of Bengal only."*	Trading company	1733	India	Indian Ocean
PROHIBITING THE PRACTICE OF RELIGIONS OTHER THAN CATHOLICISM	Edict for the Formation of the Company of the American Islands, 1642	*"The associates will not suffer . . . the practice of another religion than the Catholic, Apostolic, and Roman."*	Richelieu	1642	Caribbean	Atlantic
	Declaration by the Directors of the Royal Company of Senegal, 1688	*"To our directors & commandants to promote the practice of the [Catholic faith] in all our concessions, without allowing the practice of any other."*	Trading company	1688	Senegal	Atlantic
	Journal of François Martin, 1701	*"It is appropriate during the fifteen days of Easter to prevent the Moors, and the Gentiles to organize any ceremonies in their religions, to which we then added all Sundays."*	Governor	1701	India	Indian Ocean

CIVILIZING LOCAL PEOPLE	Directives of the Company of the East Indies, 1664	*"It must aim to make [Madagascar] entirely French, in terms of customs & language."*	Trading company	1664	Madagascar	Indian Ocean
	Statement of Intent for the Settlement of Acadia, 1603	*"Charles de Montmorency . . . driven by a singular desire and devotion that he has always had for the king . . .has concluded that he could not give him a more certain proof than by . . . bringing [Native Americans] to the civilization of their manners [and] regulation of their lives."*	Charles de Montmorancy	1603	New France	Atlantic
NATURALIZING BAPTIZED LOCAL PEOPLE	Contract for the Reestablishment of the Company of the American Islands, 1635	*"His Majesty will allow that . . . the sauvages who will convert to the faith and will practice it will be considered and known as natural-born French."*	Richelieu	1635	Caribbean	Atlantic
	Act for the Establishment of the Company of One Hundred Associates, 1627	*"The sauvages who will be brought to the knowledge of the faith and will practice it will be considered and known as natural-born French."*	Richelieu	1627	New France	Atlantic
NATURALIZING CHILDREN BORN TO BAPTIZED LOCAL PEOPLE	Regulation of the Company of the East Indies, 1664	*"Those born Catholic will be considered and known as French-born."*	Trading company	1664	Madagascar	Indian Ocean
	Regulation of the Company of the East Indies, 1664	*"Those born Catholic will be considered and known as French-born."*	Trading company	1664	India	Indian Ocean
	Edict for the Establishment of the Company of the West Indies, 1664	*"We wish that . . . those born to . . . sauvages converted to the Catholic, Apostolic, and Roman faith be considered and known as natural-born French."*	The king	1664	Caribbean	Atlantic

(*continued*)

Appendix: Clusters of French Policies Targeting People of Non-European Ancestry, 1603–1758 (*Continued*)

CLUSTER NAME	POLICY NAME	EXCERPT	AUTHOR	DATE	LOCATION	OCEAN
	Regulation of the Company of the East Indies, 1664	*"Those born Catholic will be considered and known as French-born."*	Trading company	1664	Isle Bourbon and Isle of France	Indian Ocean
ENCOURAGING INTERMARRIAGE BETWEEN THE FRENCH AND LOCAL WOMEN	King's Declaration, 1699	*"To allow the French who will settle in this country to marry with the daughters of the [sauvages]."*	The king	1699	Louisiana	Atlantic
	Champlain's Policy, 1603	*"Our young men will marry your daughters, and we shall be one people."*	Governor	1603	New France	Atlantic
	Instruction of the King to La Haye	*"To find women there, in order [for Frenchmen] to start families."*	The king	1669	India	Indian Ocean
	Letters Patent for the Establishment of the Company of the East Indies, 1642	*"A Frenchman married to a girl or woman from the island, shall not leave or abandon his wife, under any circumstances."*	The king	1642	Madagascar	Indian Ocean
LIMITING MIXED RELATIONSHIPS	Declaration by the Directors of the Royal Company of Senegal of 1688	*"Prohibition to support any négresses, go to their cabins, or let them enter their own, under any circumstances."*	Trading company	1688	Senegal	Atlantic
	Rules of the Company, 1664	*"You must prevent [Frenchmen] from giving themselves away to women of the country, who are easy, incredibly lustful and carry a venereal disease that is usually incurable."*	Trading company	1664	Madagascar	Indian Ocean

PROHIBITING INTERMARRIAGE BETWEEN BLACK AND WHITE PEOPLE	La Haye Ordinance, 1674	*"We forbid Frenchmen from marrying négresses . . . and we forbid Black men from marrying white women."*	Viceroy of the East Indies	1674	Isle Bourbon and Isle of France	Indian Ocean
	Proposal of Nadau and Marin	*"It is necessary to always keep manumitted slaves in an inferior position and to prevent them from forming alliances with whites; His Majesty [. . .] prevented the inhabitants of Louisiana of both sexes from marrying Blacks."*	Colonial lawyers	1758	Caribbean	Atlantic
	Code Noir of Louisiana, 1724	*"We forbid our white subjects, of both sexes, to marry Blacks under penalty of punishment and arbitrary fine and to all clerics, priests, or secular or regular missionaries and even chaplains of the vessels of the Marine, to marry them."*	The king	1724	Louisiana	Atlantic
	Edict Concerning Saint Domingue, 1731	*"It seems very important that we manage to prevent unions of white men with négresses and mulâtresses."*	The king	1731	Caribbean	Atlantic
	Letters Patent of Isle Bourbon and Isle of France, 1723	*"We forbid our white subjects, of both sexes, to marry Blacks under penalty of punishment and arbitrary fine and to all clerics, priests, or secular or regular missionaries and even to chaplains of the vessels of the Marine, to marry them."*	The king	1723	Isle Bourbon and Isle of France	Indian Ocean
NATURALIZING MANUMITTED PEOPLE	Letters Patent of Isle Bourbon and Isle of France, 1723	*"We declare that manumitted slaves do not need our naturalization papers to enjoy the advantages of our natural subjects in our kingdom."*	The king	1723	Isle Bourbon and Isle of France	Indian Ocean

(*continued*)

Appendix: Clusters of French Policies Targeting People of Non-European Ancestry, 1603–1758 (*Continued*)

CLUSTER NAME	POLICY NAME	EXCERPT	AUTHOR	DATE	LOCATION	OCEAN
	Code Noir of the Caribbean, 1685	*"We declare that manumitted slaves do not need our naturalization papers to enjoy the advantages of our natural subjects in our kingdom."*	The king	1685	Caribbean	Atlantic
	Code Noir of Louisiana, 1724	*"We declare that manumitted slaves do not need our naturalization papers to enjoy the advantages of our natural subjects in our kingdom."*	The king	1724	Louisiana	Atlantic
LIMITING INTERMARRIAGES WITH LOCAL WOMEN	Letter of Pilavoine, 1693	*"I will not consent to letting any of your employees commit to marriage unless he agrees to leave your service."*	Trading company	1693	India	Indian Ocean
	Proposal of La Galissonière, 1749	*"On the question of marriages of Frenchmen to native women . . . it would be easy to obtain a prohibition from the Court similar to the one it issued for the Government of Louisiana."*	Governor	1749	New France	Atlantic
	Edict of Louisiana, 1728	*"We forbid all Frenchmen and any other white subjects of the king to marry sauvagesses."*	Colonial council	1728	Louisiana	Atlantic
	Order of the Council of Isle Bourbon	*"Prohibits . . . from admitting to the council any employee who should marry a creole woman."*	Trading company	1734	Isle Bourbon and Isle of France	Indian Ocean
	Council of the Marine's Order, 1716	*"The intention of His Majesty is . . . to prevent these sorts of marriages to the full extent of their power."*	Council of the Marine	1716	Louisiana	Atlantic

	Order of the Council of Pondicherry	*Employees of the French Company in Bengal were encouraged "to marry the daughters of Frenchmen."*	Colonial council	1730	India	Indian Ocean
	Vaudreuil's Order, 1709	*Prohibition "to let the French get married with the sauvages."*	Governor	1709	New France	Atlantic
	Regulation of the Company of the Indies, 1743	*"No employee of the company, of any kind, in the Indies, on the Islands of the East, is allowed to marry without the consent of the company or the councilors and without the agreement of the governors under sentence of being expelled from the company."*	Trading company	1743	India	Indian Ocean
	Deliberation of the Council of Isle Bourbon	*"The employee cannot marry without the consent of the governor, nor marry a creole woman."*	Colonial council	1736	Isle Bourbon and Isle of France	Indian Ocean
FORBIDDING DONATIONS FROM WHITE TO BLACK PEOPLE	*Code Noir* of Louisiana, 1724	*"We forbid . . . manumitted slaves as well as free nègres from receiving any donation from whites, neither inter vivos, nor after death or for any other reason."*	The king	1724	Louisiana	Atlantic
	Royal Decree, 1726	*"In conformity with article LII of our edict of March 1724, all manumitted slaves as well as free nègres will be forbidden from receiving any donations from whites in the future, neither inter vivos, nor after death or for any other reason."*	The king	1726	Caribbean	Atlantic
	Royal Decree, 1726	*"In conformity with article LII of our edict of March 1724, all manumitted slaves as well as free nègres will be forbidden from receiving any donations from whites in the future, neither inter vivos, nor after death or for any other reason."*	The king	1726	Guiana	Atlantic

(*continued*)

Appendix: Clusters of French Policies Targeting People of Non-European Ancestry, 1603–1758 (*Continued*)

CLUSTER NAME	POLICY NAME	EXCERPT	AUTHOR	DATE	LOCATION	OCEAN
	Letters Patent of Isle Bourbon and Isle of France, 1723	*"We forbid . . . manumitted slaves as well as free nègres from receiving any donation from whites, neither inter vivos, nor after death or for any other reason."*	The king	1723	Isle Bourbon and Isle of France	Indian Ocean
CAREER PENALTIES FOR FRENCHMEN WHO MARRY LOCAL WOMEN	Strategy of the Company of the Indies, 1726	*"Texier . . . just married the bastard daughter of Sieur de Mandeville, the daughter of an enslaved sauvagesse, which prevents you from granting him his promotion."*	Trading company	1726	Louisiana	Atlantic
	Regulation of the Company of the Indies, 1748	*"Every employee [in the East Indies] who should marry a woman of Indian blood . . . will only be able to reach the rank of under-merchant."*	Trading company	1748	India	Indian Ocean
	Decision of the Company of the Indies, 1738	*"The company had approved the dismissal in 1742 and 1738 of some employees and officers . . . because they had married without the permission of the council . . . and had allowed others [in the same situation] to keep their positions, but without the prospect of ever getting promoted."*	Trading company	1738	Isle Bourbon and Isle of France	Indian Ocean
FORBIDDING LOCAL WOMEN FROM INHERITING FROM FRENCHMEN	Pilavoine's Decision, 1702	*"Regarding the matter of the succession of your company in Surat . . . , which you have instructed us to resolve in accordance with the custom of Paris . . . we are unable to complete this business for two reasons."*	Trading company	1702	India	Indian Ocean

	Decree of the Superior Council of Louisiana, 1728	*"The council . . . declares the sauvages excluded from the successions of the French."*	Colonial council	1728	Louisiana	Atlantic
ENSLAVING FREE BLACK PEOPLE CAUGHT SHELTERING MAROONS	Ordinance of the King, 1705	*"Free nègres offering asylum to maroon slaves or keeping their stolen goods, or sharing them with them, will lose their freedom."*	The king	1705	Caribbean	Atlantic
	Regulation of the Superior Council of Louisiana, 1751	*"All nègres and négresses having obtained their freedom [. . .] who will receive slaves in their home, to seduce them and incite them to steal from their masters, and lead a scandalous life, will lose their freedom."*	Colonial council	1751	Louisiana	Atlantic
ENSLAVING FREE BLACK PEOPLE CAUGHT SHELTERING MAROONS SHOULD THEY FAIL TO PAY FINE	Royal Decree, 1726	*"In accordance with the edict of March 1724 which acts as law for slaves in our province of Louisiana, should manumitted nègres or freemen who have sheltered fugitive slaves be unable to pay the fine of 300 livres of sugar due for each day of shelter, they shall be reduced to slavery."*	The king	1726	Guiana	Atlantic
	Royal Decree, 1726	*"In accordance with the edict of March 1724 which acts as law for slaves in our province of Louisiana, should manumitted nègres or freemen who have sheltered fugitive slaves be unable to pay the fine of 300 livres of sugar due for each day of shelter, they shall be reduced to slavery."*	The king	1726	Caribbean	Atlantic

(*continued*)

Appendix: Clusters of French Policies Targeting People of Non-European Ancestry, 1603–1758 (*Continued*)

CLUSTER NAME	POLICY NAME	EXCERPT	AUTHOR	DATE	LOCATION	OCEAN
	Letters Patent of Isle Bourbon and Isle of France, 1723	*"Manumitted and free nègres who will give asylum in their houses to fugitive slaves will be sentenced . . . to pay a fine of ten piastres for each day of retention . . . and if said manumitted or free nègres fail to pay the fine, they will be reduced to slavery."*	The king	1723	Isle Bourbon and Isle of France	Indian Ocean
	Code Noir of Louisiana, 1724	*"Manumitted and free nègres who will give asylum in their houses to fugitive slaves will be sentenced . . . to pay a fine of thirty livres for each day of retention . . . if said manumitted or free nègres fail to pay the fine, they will be reduced to slavery."*	The king	1724	Louisiana	Atlantic

Abbreviations

ABR	Catholic Life Center, Diocese of Baton Rouge
ADR	Archives Départementales de la Réunion
ANO	Office of Archives and Records, Archdiocese of New Orleans
ANOM	Archives Nationales d'Outre-Mer
BNF	Bibliothèque Nationale de France
CARAN	Centre d'Accueil et de Recherche des Archives Nationales
HL	Huntington Library
HNOC	Williams Research Center, Historic New Orleans Collection
HTML	Louisiana Research Collection, Howard Tilton Memorial Library, Tulane University
LOC	Library of Congress, Manuscript Division
LSA	Louisiana State Archives, Division of the Louisiana Secretary of State's Office
LSM RSCL	Louisiana Historical Center, Louisiana State Museum, Records of the Superior Council of Louisiana
LSU Hill Library	Hill Memorial Library, Louisiana State University
NOPL	New Orleans Public Library
RSC *LHQ*	Records of the Superior Council, *Louisiana Historical Quarterly*
SCD, Dupré Library, UL Lafayette	Special Collections Department, Edith Garland Dupré Library, University of Louisiana at Lafayette

Notes

All translations are my own unless otherwise noted.

Introduction

1. Camille Ricquebourg, *Dictionnaire généalogique des familles de l'Île Bourbon (La Réunion), 1665–1810*, 3 vols (Rosny-sur-Seine: C. Ricquebourg, 1976), 3:2125.

2. On the marriage of Marianne Payet, see Ricquebourg, *Dictionnaire généalogique des familles de l'Île Bourbon*, 1:483–484. For the intermarriage ban of 1723, see ADR C°940 "Lettres Patentes en forme d'Edit concernant les Esclaves Negres des Isle de Bourbon et de france 1723," n.p.

3. By 1734, Desgranges was the commandant of the parishes of Saint-Pierre and Saint-Louis (in the southwest of the island). See ADR C° 1013 "A Monsieur Dumas gouverneur pour le Roy de L'isle de Bourbon [. . .] Mr choppy des granges Capitaine des quartiers St pierre et St Loüis."

4. ADR C° 768 "1732. Recensement general."

5. Ricquebourg, *Dictionnaire généalogique des familles de l'Île Bourbon*, 1:484.

6. Ricquebourg, *Dictionnaire généalogique des familles de l'Île Bourbon*, 1:175.

7. LSM RSCL File 1745-02-23-01 "1745. Fev[rier] 23. Boyer," p. 1. See also "Pierre Boyer, will, February 23, 1745," RSC, *LHQ* vol. 13. no. 4 (Oct. 1930): 677.

8. "Agreement in Tar Trade, Oct. 9, 1739," RSC, *LHQ* vol. 7, no. 3 (1924): 494; Blaise C. D'Antoni, *Chahta-Ima and St. Tammany's Choctaws* (Mandeville: St. Tammany Historical Society, 1986), 10; Cécile Vidal, *Caribbean New Orleans: Empire, Race, and the Making of a Slave Society* (Kindle version, Chapel Hill: University of North Carolina Press, 2019), 276, 284, https://lire.amazon.fr/?asin=B07H51V6VJ&_encoding=UTF8&ref=dbs_p_ebk_r00_pbcb_rnvc00.

9. LSM RSCL File 1745-02-23-01 "1745. Fev[rier] 23. Boyer," pp. 1–2.

10. LSM RSCL File 1745-02-23-01 "1745. Fev[rier] 23. Boyer," p. 1; Jennifer Spear, *Race, Sex, and Social Order in Early New Orleans* (EBook, Baltimore: Johns Hopkins University Press, 2009), 86, https://ebookcentral.proquest.com/lib/duke/detail.action?docID=3318576.

11. LSM RSCL RSC File 1747-08-16-01 "1747. 16 Aoust. Vignon La Combe," and "Nuncupative will of Vignon, called LaCombe. 1747. August 16," RSC, *LHQ* vol. 3, no. 4 (1920): 567–569; LSM RSCL RSC File 1745-02-23-01 "1745. Fev[rier] 23. Boyer," pp. 1–2.

12. LSM RSCL File 1769-09-20-01, "La Compagnie des mulatres et negres libres de cette colonie de la Loüisianne." See also Spear, *Race, Sex, and Social Order*, 86; and Vidal, *Caribbean New Orleans*, 432.

13. ANOM A 23 "Édit du roi, ou Code noir, qui concerne entièrement les esclaves de la Louisiane, Mars 1724," article VI, f. 50.

14. For more information about this topic, see Chapter 3.

15. By the 1760s, Joseph La Combe had become a militiaman. See LSM RSCL File 1769-09-20-01 "La Compagnie des mulatres et negres libres de cette colonie de la Loüisianne."

16. Jane Burbank and Frederick Cooper, *Empires in World History: Power and Politics of Difference* (EBook, Princeton, NJ and Oxford: Princeton University Press, 2010), 2, https://www-fulcrum-org.proxy.lib.duke.edu/concern/monographs/0v838115.

17. Physical violence was not confined to sexual abuse. The French used several brutal empire-building strategies that from the seventeenth century ranged from bloody warfare to assimilation—in part through a program of acculturation and intermarriage.

18. Much of this historiography focuses on the history of slavery and capitalism. For more information, see the Introduction to Chapter 6.

19. In West Africa, the French also established short-lived trading stations at Allada and Ouidah (Dahomey) in 1670 and 1671. They stayed at Fort Arguin (Mauritania) intermittently from 1678. They also traded in the Gambia and, by the eighteenth century, at the Bight of Biafra and the coasts of Congo and Angola. See Frédéric Régent, *La France et ses esclaves. De la colonisation aux abolitions (1620–1848)* (Paris: Grasset, 2007), 45–47.

20. For an overview of some of this vast North American historiography, see Christopher Hodson and Brett Rushforth, "Absolutely Atlantic: Colonialism and the Early Modern French State in Recent Historiography," *History Compass* 8, no. 1 (2009): 101–117. For studies of empire-building centering on French administrators recently published by French scholars, see Marie Houllemare, "Procedures, Jurisdictions and Records: Building the French Empire in the Early Eighteenth Century," *Journal of Colonialism and Colonial History* 21, no. 2 (2020): n.p., and "Seeing the Empire Through Lists and Charts: French Colonial Records in the Eighteenth Century," *Journal of Early Modern History* 22 (2018): 371–391; Sylviane Llinares and Jörg Ülbert, eds., *La Liasse et la plume: Les bureau du secretariat d'Etat de la Marine (1669–1792)* (Rennes, France: Presses Universitaires de Rennes, 2017); Bernard Lutun, *La Marine de Colbert: Études d'organisation* (Paris: Economica, 2003). For some groundbreaking top-down North American approaches to France's early modern colonial history, see Kenneth Banks, *Chasing Empire across the Sea: Communications and the State in the French Atlantic, 1713–1763* (Montreal, Canada and Kingston: McGill-Queen's University Press, 2002); Alexandre Dubé, "S'approprier l'Atlantique: Quelques réflexions autour de Chasing Empire across the Sea, de Kenneth Banks," *French Colonial History* 6, no. 1 (2005): 33–44, and "Making a Career out of the Atlantic: Louisiana's Plume," in *Louisiana: Crossroads of the Atlantic World*, ed. Cécile Vidal (Philadelphia: University of Pennsylvania Press, 2013), 44–67; Laurie Wood, *Archipelago of Justice: Law in France's Early Modern Empire* (New Haven, CT: Yale University Press, 2020).

21. Marlene Daut, *Awakening the Ashes: An Intellectual History of the Haitian Revolution* (Chapel Hill: The University of North Carolina Press, 2023), 22 ("way below"); Vincent Brown, *Tacky's Revolt: The Story of an Atlantic Slave War* (EBook, Cambridge and London: Harvard University Press, 2020), 9 ("European Empires"), https://play.google.com/books/reader?id=1urODwAAQBAJ&pg=GBS.PP1.

22. Karen Marrero, *Detroit's Hidden Channels: The Power of French-Indigenous Families in the Eighteenth Century* (East Lansing: Michigan State University Press, 2020), xiii–xiv (quotation).

Similarly, Marrero notes the double erasure faced by Native American women in the Detroit area, even though they played a key role in advancing French-Indigenous commerce and diplomacy and were the first mothers of many generations of French-Indigenous families. Scholars who have worked on the experiences of enslaved women in other European colonies include Hilary Beckles, Barbara Bush, Jennifer Morgan, Marisa Fuentes, and Sasha Turner, to name just a few. On the need for more studies on women and gender in French colonial histories, see Michaela Y. Kleber, "Gendered Societies, Sexual Empires: French Colonization among the Illinois" (PhD diss., College of William and Mary, 2020), 10.

23. For a few groundbreaking studies centering on women in the seventeenth- and eighteenth-century French Atlantic world, see, for example, Arlette Gautier, *Les Soeurs de Solitude: Femmes et esclavage aux Antilles du XVIIe au XIXe siècle* (Rennes: Presses Universitaires de Rennes, 2010); Jessica Marie Johnson, *Wicked Flesh: Black Women, Intimacy, and Freedom in the Atlantic World* (EBook, Philadelphia: University of Pennsylvania Press, 2020), https://play.google.com/books/reader?id=Me7zDwAAQBAJ&pg=GBS.PP1.; and Bernard Moitt, *Women and Slavery in the French Antilles, 1635–1848* (Bloomington: Indiana University Press, 2001).

24. Quoted from Nathan E. Marvin, "Bourbon Island Creoles: Race and Revolution in the French Indian Ocean Colony of Réunion, 1767–1803" (PhD diss., Johns Hopkins University, 2018), 26. There are a few recent exceptions. For example, see Mélanie Lamotte, "Color Prejudice in the Early Modern French Empire, c. 1635–1767" (PhD diss., University of Cambridge, 2016); Marvin, "Bourbon Island Creoles," 26; Sue Peabody, *Madeleine's Children: Family, Freedom, Secrets, and Lies in France's Indian Ocean Colonies* (Oxford: Oxford University Press, 2017). In the French scholarship, see Myriam Paris, "La page blanche: Genre, esclavage et métissage dans la construction de la trame coloniale (La Réunion, XVIIIe–XIXe siècle), Réarticulation des rapports sociaux de sexe, classe et 'race,'" *Les Cahiers du Centre d'Enseignement, de Documentation et de Recherches des Études Féministes* 14 (2006): 31–51; Claude Wanquet, "La gente féminine libre à la Réunion au début du XVIIIe siècle," in *Visages de la féminité*, ed. Jean-Michel Racault and Antoine Bullier (Saint-Denis, Réunion: Université de la Réunion, 1984), 113–135.

25. This underrepresentation does not occur as much with many free and enslaved Native American populations in North America, who are centered in decades of groundbreaking historical and anthropological research. For some powerful recent publications in the field of Indigenous Studies in the United States, see Ned Blackhawk, *Violence over the Land: Indians and Empires in the Early American West* (Cambridge, MA: Harvard University Press, 2006); Roger M. Carpenter, *The Renewed, the Destroyed, and the Remade: The Three Thought Worlds of the Iroquois and the Huron, 1609–1650* (Ann Arbor: Michigan State University Press, 2004); Elizabeth Ellis, *The Great Power of Small Nations: Indigenous Diplomacy in the Gulf South* (Philadelphia: University of Pennsylvania Press, 2023); Michael Witgen, *An Infinity of Nations: How the Native New World Shaped Early North America* (Philadelphia: University of Pennsylvania Press, 2012). Many of the writings on Native Americans in French North America specifically have been produced by Canada-based scholars (by Quebec-based scholars in particular). This Canadian historiography was pioneered by scholars like Olive Patricia Dickason, Arthur J. Ray, and Sylvia Van Kirk. For a recent overview, see Allan Downey, "To Know the Indigenous Other: A Century of Indians in Canadian History," *Journal of the Canadian Historical Association* 33, no. 1 (2023):163–182. For examples of recent publications within the historiography of Canada, see the works of scholars like Robert Englebert, Allan Greer, Kathryn Magee Labelle, Nicole St-Onge, and Guillaume Teasdale. Scholars have used methods like oral history and Indigenous sources to reconstruct these histories. About these methods, see Linda Tuhiwai Smith, *Decolonizing Methodologies: Research and Indigenous Peoples* (Dunedin, New Zealand: University of

Otago Press, 1999), and Lianne C. Leddy, "Historical Sources and the Beothuk: Questioning Settler Interpretations," in *Tracing Ochre: Changing Perspectives on the Beothuk,* ed. Fiona Polack (Toronto: University of Toronto Press, 2018), 199–219.

26. About those structures and their impact, see, for example: Saidiya Hartman, "Venus in Two Acts," *Small Axe* 12, no. 2 (2008): 1–14, and Jennifer Shaw, "In the Name of the Mother: The Story of Susannah Mingo, a Woman of Color in the Early English Atlantic," *William and Mary Quarterly* (*WMQ*) 77, no. 2 (2020): 177–210, here 182.

27. Marisa Fuentes, *Dispossessed Lives: Enslaved Women, Violence and the Archives* (Philadelphia: University of Pennsylvania Press, 2016), 5. On this topic, see also Jennifer L. Morgan, *Reckoning with Slavery: Gender, Kinship, and Capitalism in the Early Black Atlantic* (EBook, Durham, NC: Duke University Press, 2021), https://read-dukeupress-edu.proxy.lib.duke.edu/books/book/2895/Reckoning-with-SlaveryGender-Kinship-and.

28. This method has been mastered by scholars of the British Americas such as Marisa Fuentes, Jennifer Morgan, and Sasha Turner.

29. Fuentes, *Dispossessed Lives,* 78, 182n45.

30. Johnson, *Wicked Flesh,* 10, 172–175 ("Black femme freedom"). For a similar perspective, see Hilary Beckles, *Centering Women: Gender Discourses in Caribbean Slave Society* (EBook, Oxford: James Currey Publishers, 1999), 38–57, https://research-ebsco-com.proxy.lib.duke.edu/c/fh2aff/search/details/il3556rhen?db=nlebk. For a critic of some publications in which enslaved women were mostly ascribed power through sex, which has informed this book's determination to also discuss the agency carved by these women beyond the sexual, see Marisa J. Fuentes, "Power and Historical Figuring: Rachael Pringle Polgreen's Troubled Archive," *Gender & History* 22, no. 3 (2010): 564–584, here 577–578.

31. Doris Garraway, *The Libertine Colony: Creolization in the Early French Caribbean* (Durham, NC: Duke University Press, 2005), 24.

32. Here, I share Walter Johnson's opinion that agency was widely confined by enslavement. See Walter Johnson, *River of Dark Dreams: Slavery and Empire in the Cotton Kingdom* (Cambridge, MA: Belknap Press of Harvard University Press, 2013), 9, and "On Agency," *Journal of Social History* 37, no. 1 (2003): 113–124. See also Saidiya Hartman, *Scenes of Subjection: Terror, Slavery, and Self-Making in Nineteenth-Century America* (New York: Oxford UP, 1997), esp. 88, 90–92, 102–104. Jennifer Shaw and others have raised concerns about interpretations that cast enslaved women "as agents and negotiators of desire" in order to redistribute agency, contending that such approaches risk minimizing the violence of slavery "by turning the trauma and coercion enforced by enslavers into narratives of power wielded by the enslaved." Quoted from Shaw, "In the Name of the Mother," 187. For a response to this critique, see the introduction to Chapter 3.

33. For some French Atlantic histories, see Guillaume Aubert, "'The Blood of France': Race and Purity of Blood in the French Atlantic World," *WMQ* 61, no. 3 (2004): 439–478; Banks, *Chasing Empire across the Sea*; Laurent Dubois, "An Enslaved Enlightenment: Rethinking the Intellectual History of the French Atlantic," *Social History* 31, no. 1 (2006): 1–14; Johnson, *Wicked Flesh*; Bill Marshall, *The French Atlantic: Travels in Culture and History* (Liverpool, UK: Liverpool University Press, 2009); Christopher Miller, *The French Atlantic Triangle: Literature and Culture of the Slave Trade* (Durham, NC: Duke University Press, 2008); Jennifer Palmer, *Intimate Bonds: Family and Slavery in the French Atlantic* (Philadelphia: University of Pennsylvania Press, 2016); Brett Rushforth, *Bonds of Alliance: Indigenous and Atlantic Slaveries in New France* (Chapel Hill: University of North Carolina Press, for the Omohundro Institute of Early American History and Culture, 2012); Trevor Burnard and John Garrigus, *The Plantation*

Machine: Atlantic Capitalism in French Saint-Domingue and British Jamaica (Philadelphia: University of Pennsylvania Press, 2016); Lorelle Semley, *To be Free and French: Citizenship in France's Atlantic Empire* (Cambridge: Cambridge University Press, 2017); Vidal, *Caribbean New Orleans*.

34. For this US historiography, see Danna Agmon, *A Colonial Affair: Commerce, Conversion, and Scandal in French India* (Ithaca, NY: Cornell University Press, 2017); Kelly Brignac, "African Indentured Labor in Senegal and Ste. Marie, Madagascar, 1817–1830," *Slavery & Abolition* 43, no. 4 (2022): 779–797; Elizabeth Cross, *Company Politics: Commerce, Scandal, and French Visions of Indian Empire in the Revolutionary Era* (New York: Oxford University Press, 2023); Marvin, "Bourbon Island Creoles"; Sue Peabody, *Madeleine's Children: Family, Freedom, Secrets, and Lies in France's Indian Ocean Colonies* (Oxford: Oxford University Press, 2017); Sophie White, "Les esclaves et le droit en Louisiane sous le régime français, carrefour entre la Nouvelle-France, les Antilles, et l'océan Indien," in *Adapter le droit et rendre la justice aux colonies: Thémis outre-mer (XVIe–XIXe siècles)*, ed. Éric Wenzel and Éric de Mari (Dijon, France: Éditions universitaires de Dijon, 2015), 57–66; Laurie M. Wood, *Archipelago of Justice: Law in France's Early Modern Empire* (New Haven, CN: Yale University Press, 2020). For this European historiography, see François-Joseph Ruggiu, "India and the Reshaping of the French Colonial Policy (1759–1789)," *Itinerario* 35, no. 2 (2011): 25–43, and Elisabeth Heijmans, *The Agency of Empire: Connections and Strategies in French Overseas Expansion (1686–1746)* (EBook, Leiden, Netherlands: Brill, 2020), https://ebookcentral.proquest.com/lib/duke/detail.action?docID=5973869#. Another US historiography by Indian Oceanists has shown how European slave traders connected the Atlantic and Indian Oceans through the commercial exchanges of captives and Indian textiles. See Robert Louis Stein, *The French Slave Trade in the Eighteenth Century: An Old Regime Business* (Madison: The University of Wisconsin Press, 1979); Richard B. Allen, "The Constant Demand of the French: The Mascarene Slave Trade and the Worlds of the Indian Ocean and Atlantic during the Eighteenth and Nineteenth Centuries," *Journal of African History* 49, no. 1 (2008): 43–72; and Richard B. Allen, *European Slave Trading in the Indian Ocean, 1500–1850* (Athens: Ohio University Press, 2014).

35. On this topic, see Cécile Vidal, "The Reluctance of French Historians to Address Atlantic History," in "Imagining the Atlantic World," special issue, *Southern Quarterly* 43, (2006): 153–189, here 156.

36. Faculty focus groups in history departments across the United States and Britain are now usually organized by time periods and geographic regions (such as North America, Asia, the Atlantic, or the Indian Ocean). Historical associations, history journals, and history conferences often embrace similar chronological and geographical structures (i.e., the Organization of American Historians, the journal *South Asian History and Culture*, or the African History Conference). Outside the discipline, histories of early modern European empires are addressed in the context of area studies (i.e., American studies, Caribbean studies, or South Asian studies), which are too often separated from each other and from history departments themselves.

37. Vidal, "The Reluctance of French Historians," 157–158.

38. Here, I am paraphrasing Vidal's well-known article on the topic. See Vidal, "The Reluctance of French Historians." Atlantic history came of age in the postwar era, largely because of the shared interests that had allied the United States and Britain through this long period of conflict and as a result of the formation of a North Atlantic alliance during the Cold War. On this topic, see Bernard Bailyn, *Atlantic History: Concept and Contours* (Cambridge, MA: Harvard University Press, 2005), 1–56; William O'Reilly, "Genealogies of Atlantic History," *Atlantic Studies* 1 (2004): 66–84.

39. Those challenges were further exacerbated by particularly violent wars of independence in Indochina and Algeria and by colonial history's loss of financial and political support after the former French colonies gained their independence. Colonial history was also disparaged for its apologism and its political and military approaches, in stark contrast to the social history of the Annales school. See Vidal, "The Reluctance of French Historians," 155.

40. Cécile Vidal paved the way for this development with a series of publications. See Vidal, "The Reluctance of French Historians," "Introduction: Le(s) monde(s) atlantique(s), l'Atlantique français, l'empire atlantique français," in "L'Atlantique Français," special issue, *Outre-mers. Revue d'histoire* 96, nos. 362–363 (2009): 7–37, "For a Comprehensive History of the Atlantic World or Histories Connected in and beyond the Atlantic World?," trans. Michèle R. Greer, *Annales. Histoire, Sciences Sociales* 67, no. 2 (2012): 279–300, and "Pour une histoire globale du monde atlantique ou des histoires connectées dans et au-delà du monde atlantique?," *Annales Histoire, Sciences Sociales* 67, no. 2 (2012): 391–413.

41. For some examples, see Introduction, n. 33.

42. See Bernard Bailyn, "Introduction: Reflections on Some Major Themes," in *Soundings in Atlantic History*, ed. Bernard Bailyn and Patricia L. Denault (Cambridge, MA: Harvard University Press, 2009), 1–43, here 3; Peter A. Coclanis, "Drang Nach Osten: Bernard Bailyn, the World-Island, and the Idea of Atlantic History," *Journal of World History*, no. 13 (2002): 169–182, and "Atlantic World or Atlantic/World?," *WMQ*, 3rd ser., 63, no. 4 (2006): 725–742; Alison Games, "Beyond the Atlantic: English Globetrotters and Transoceanic Connections," *WMQ*, 3rd ser., 63, no. 4 (2006): 675–692; Paul W. Mapp, "Atlantic History from Imperial, Continental, and Pacific Perspectives," *WMQ*, 3rd ser., 63, no. 4 (2006): 713–724. More generally, see "Forum: Beyond the Atlantic," *WMQ* 63, no. 4 (2006): 675–742. Others have described the concept as an Eurocentric projection of spatial mastery, rightfully noting that much of America (much like Africa) remained "tangibly 'Indigenous' territory well into the eighteenth century"—we will see in the following how a colonial history centering on the experiences of people of non-European ancestries can help us avoid such projection. See Paul Cohen, "Was There an Amerindian Atlantic? Reflections on the Limits of a Historiographical Concept," *History of European Ideas* 34, no 4 (2008): 388–410; Caroline Dodds Pennock, "Aztecs Abroad? Uncovering the Early Indigenous Atlantic," *American Historical Review* 125, no. 3 (2020): 787–814; Amy Turner Bushnell, "Indigenous America and the Limits of the Atlantic World, 1493–1825," in *Atlantic History: A Critical Appraisal*, ed. Jack P. Greene and Philip D. Morgan (New York: Oxford University Press, 2008), 191–221.

43. For some combined histories of the British Atlantic and Indian Oceans, see Kenneth Andrews, *Trade, Plunder and Settlement: Maritime Enterprise and the Genesis of the British Empire, 1480–1630* (Cambridge: Cambridge University Press, 1984); H. V. Bowen, "British Conceptions of Global Empire, 1756–83," *Journal of Imperial and Commonwealth History* 26, no. 3 (1998): 1–27; Coclanis, "Atlantic World or Atlantic/World"; Linda Colley, *Captives: Britain, Empire, and the World, 1600–1850* (London: Pimlico, 2002); Jonathan Eacott, *Selling Empire: India in the Making of Britain and America, 1600–1830* (Chapel Hill: University of North Carolina Press, 2016); P. J. Marshall, *The Making and Unmaking of Empires—Britain, India and America, c. 1750–1783* (New York: Oxford University Press, 2005); Philip J. Stern, *Empire, Incorporated: The Corporations That Built British Colonialism* (Cambridge, MA: Belknap Press of Harvard University Press, 2023), and Anna Winterbottom, *Hybrid Knowledge in the Early East India Company World* (New York: Palgrave Macmillan, 2016). For combined histories of the Iberian Atlantic and Indian Oceans, see Dauril Alden, *The Making of an Enterprise: The Society of Jesus in Portugal, Its Empire, and Beyond, 1540–1750* (Stanford, CA: Stanford University

Press, 1996); Francisco Bethencourt, *The Inquisition: A Global History, 1487–1834* (Cambridge: Cambridge University Press, 2009); A. R. Disney, *History of Portugal and the Portuguese Empire*, vol. 2, *The Portuguese Empire* (Cambridge: Cambridge University Press, 2009); M. D. Newitt, *A History of Portuguese Overseas Expansion* (New York: Routledge, 2004); Gabriel Paquette, *Imperial Portugal in the Age of Atlantic Revolutions: The Luso-Brazilian World, c. 1770–1850* (Cambridge: Cambridge University Press, 2013); J. R. Russell-Wood, *A World on the Move: The Portuguese in Africa, Asia, and America, 1415–1808*, 2nd ed. (Baltimore: Johns Hopkins University Press, 1998). For transnational perspectives using this approach, see C. A. Bayly, *The Birth of the Modern World, 1780–1914: Global Connections and Comparisons* (Malden, MA: Blackwell Publishing, 2004); and Jorge Canizares-Esguerra and Erik R. Seeman eds., *The Atlantic in Global History, 1500–2000* (Upper Saddle River, NJ: Pearson Prentice Hall, 2007). See also Kevin P. McDonald, *Pirates, Merchants, Settlers, and Slaves: Colonial America and the Indo-Atlantic World* (Berkeley: University of California Press, 2015).

44. Citation from Ruggiu, "Des nouvelles France aux colonies," 3–4. About this historiography in Europe, see Trevor Burnard and Cécile Vidal, "Location and the Conceptualization of Historical Frameworks: Early American History and Its Multiple Reconfigurations in the United States and in Europe," *Historians across Borders: Writing American History in a Global Age*, ed. Nicolas Barreyre, Michael Heale, Stephen Tuck, and Cécile Vidal (Berkeley: University of California Press, 2014), 141–162; Durba Ghosh, "Another Set of Imperial Turns?," *American Historical Review* 117, no. 3 (2012): 772–793; Paul Kramer, "Power and Connection: Imperial Histories of the United States in the World," *American Historical Review* 116 (2011): 1348–1391.

45. Of course, there is an older French imperial historiography produced during the colonial era, especially in the early twentieth century. However, in addition to being biased with procolonial stances, this historiography embraced a top-down approach. It extensively focused on French political and military achievements and centered on the metropole rather than telling the history of the colonies themselves and that of ordinary people of European and non-European descent. For example, see Henri Blet, *Histoire de la colonisation française: Naissance et déclin d'un empire. Des origines à 1789*, 3 vols. (Paris: Arthaud, 1946); Gabriel Hanotaux and Alfred Martineau, *Histoire des colonies et de l'expansion de la France dans le monde*, 6 vols. (Paris: Plon, 1929–1933); Jean Saintoyant, *Histoire de la colonisation française*, 2 vols. (Paris: La Renaissance du Livre, 1929). The eurocentric approach in these books is in some ways still echoed in more recent French overviews, such as Bernard Gainot's *L'Empire colonial français* (Paris: Armand Colin, 2015) and Pierre Pluchon, *Histoire de la colonisation française, t. 1: Le premier empire colonial. Des origines à la Restauration* (Paris: Fayard, 1991).

46. Ruggiu, "Des nouvelles France aux colonies," 3.

47. Trevor Burnard, "Empire Matters? The Historiography of Imperialism in Early America, 1492–1830," *History of European Ideas* 33, no. 1 (2007): 87–107, here 96.

48. Hodson and Rushforth, "Absolutely Atlantic," 103.

49. See Saliha Belmessous, *Assimilation and Empire: Uniformity in French and British Colonies, 1541–1954* (EBook, New York: Oxford University Press, 2013), https://play.google.com/books/reader?id=ElpoAgAAQBAJ&pg=GBS.PP1.

50. The east bank of the Mississippi River was subsequently integrated into the British Empire, and the western part was offered to Spain. In 1800, the French took possession of Louisiana again, and Napoleon Bonaparte eventually sold the territory to the United States in 1803.

51. Like Elizabeth Ellis and Brian DeLay, I use the notion of borderlands to designate regions over which multiple authorities attempted to apply their power, places that were home to "plural

sovereignt[ies]." See Ellis, *The Great Power of Small Nations*, 6, and Brian DeLay, ed., *North American Borderlands* (New York: Routledge, 2013), 9 (quotation).

52. This book does not present new archival research on the history of New France because this colony has already been the focus of vast national (especially Quebecois) and US historiographies on empire building, French-Indigenous contact, and slavery. Although Anglophone scholars have given relatively little attention to French Guiana, it has received considerable attention in the Francophone scholarship, from scholars like Réginald Auger, Jean-Pierre Bacot, Nathalie Cazelles, Lydie Choucoutou, Yannick Le Roux, Jean Moomou, Marie Polderman, Céline Ronsseray, Régis Verwimp, and Jacqueline Zonzon. For one powerful history of French Guiana in the Anglophone scholarship, see Miranda Spieler, *Empire and Underworld: Captivity in French Guiana* (Cambridge, MA: Harvard University Press, 2012).

53. For examples of publications about New France produced in the United States, see Christopher M. Parsons, *A Not-So-New World: Empire and Environment in French Colonial North America* (Philadelphia: University of Pennsylvania Press, 2018), and Rushforth, *Bonds of Alliance*. For a publication produced in France, see Gilles Havard, *Empire et métissages: Indiens et Français dans le Pays d'en Haut, 1660–1715*, 2nd ed. (Quebec: Septentrion, 2017). For publications by Quebec-based scholars, see Robert Englebert and Guillaume Teasdale, eds., *French and Indians in the Heart of North America, 1630–1815* (East Lansing: Michigan State University Press and University of Manitoba Press, 2013), and "Colonial Encounters and the Changing Contours of Ethnicity: Pierre-Louis de Lorimier and Métissage at the Edges of Empire," *Ohio Valley History* 18, no. 1 (2018): 45–69; Allan Greer, *Property and Dispossession: Natives, Empires and Land in Early Modern North America* (New York: Cambridge University Press, 2018); Guillaume Teasdale, "Old Friends and New Foes: French Settlers and Indians in the Detroit River Border Region," *Michigan Historical Review* 38, no. 2 (2012): 35–62.

54. For a couple of groundbreaking studies considering empire building in Lower French Louisiana that have paved the way for this book, see Ellis, *The Great Power of Small Nations*, and Shannon Lee Dawdy, *Building the Devil's Empire: French Colonial New Orleans* (Chicago: Chicago University Press, 2008).

55. For examples of works about the Illinois Country, see Winstanley Briggs, "The Forgotten Colony: Le Pays des Illinois" (PhD diss., University of Chicago, 1985); Carl J. Ekberg, *French Roots in the Illinois Country: The Mississippi Frontier in Colonial Times* (Urbana: University of Illinois Press, 1998); Kleber, "Gendered Societies"; Tracy Leavelle, *The Catholic Calumet: Colonial Conversions in French and Indian North America* (EBook, Philadelphia: University of Pennsylvania Press, 2012), https://play.google.com/books/reader?id=EAK8mbtoXwUC&pg=GBS.PP1; M. J. Morgan, *Land of Big Rivers: French and Indian Illinois, 1699–1778* (Carbondale: Southern Illinois University Press, 2010); Robert Michael Morrissey, *Empire by Collaboration: Indians, Colonists, and Governments in Colonial Illinois Country* (Philadelphia: University of Pennsylvania Press, 2015); Cécile Vidal, "Les implantations françaises au pays des Illinois au XVIIIe siècle 1699–1765" (PhD diss., EHESS, 1995); Sophie White, *Wild Frenchmen and Frenchified Indians: Material Culture and Race in Colonial Louisiana* (EBook, Philadelphia: University of Pennsylvania Press, 2012), https://play.google.com/books/reader?id=2v-TMgaC-NUC&pg=GBS.PP1.

56. For some publications by US scholars, see Charles Gayarré, *Histoire de la Louisiane*, 2 vols. (New Orleans: Magne & Weisse, 1846–1847); Gwendolyn Hall, *Africans in Colonial Louisiana: The Development of Afro-Creole Culture in the Eighteenth Century* (Baton Rouge: Louisiana State University Press, 1992); Johnson, *Wicked Flesh*; Daniel Usner, *Indians, Settlers, and Slaves in a Frontier Exchange Economy: The Lower Mississippi Valley before 1783* (EBook, Chapel Hill: University of North Carolina Press, 1992), https://play.google.com/books/reader?id=

dvTGDwAAQBAJ&pg=GBS.PP1, and *American Indians in Early New Orleans: From Calumet to Raquette* (Baton Rouge: Louisiana State University Press, 2018); Sophie White, *Voices of the Enslaved: Love, Labor, and Longing in French Louisiana* (Chapel Hill: University of North Carolina Press, 2019). For publications by French scholars, see Arnaud Balvay, *La Révolte des Natchez* (Paris: Le Félin-Kiron, 2008), and *L'épée et la plume: Amérindiens et soldats des troupes de la marine en Louisiane et au Pays d'en Haut (1683–1763)* (Quebec: Les Presses de l'Université Laval, 2006); Vidal, *Caribbean New Orleans,* and Vidal, *Louisiana: Crossroads of the Atlantic World* (Philadelphia: University of Pennsylvania Press, 2014).

57. Scholars of French Louisiana have especially connected the colony to the Caribbean and, to a lesser extent, to Senegambia. For recent publications doing this, see, for example, Johnson, *Wicked Flesh*; Emily Clark, Ibrahima Thioub, and Cécile Vidal, eds., *New Orleans, Louisiana, and Saint-Louis, Senegal: Mirror Cities in the Atlantic World, 1659–2000s* (Baton Rouge: Louisiana State University Press, 2019); Vidal, *Louisiana,* and Vidal, *Caribbean New Orleans.*

58. For example, see Ellis, *The Great Power of Small Nations*; Morrissey, *Empire by Collaboration*; Kleber, "Gendered Societies." The Small Nations included the Chitimachas, Chakchiumas, Mobilians, Tunicas, and many others. Robert M. Morrissey has focused on the ways the Illinois and French colonists "accommodated their differences" to engage in a conscious "functional and pragmatic collaboration" with imperial deputies in order to advance their own interests in the territory that came to be known as Upper Louisiana (the Illinois Country). Quoted from Morrissey, *Empire by Collaboration*, 7.

59. Research on Guadeloupe in the Anglophone world has instead focused on the late eighteenth and the nineteenth centuries. For some examples, see publications by Myriam Arcangeli, Laurent Dubois, William S. Cormack, and Lawrence C. Jennings. Recent work has instead focused on Martinique, which had a more intensive slave plantation regime than Guadeloupe and became the center of French governance for all French Caribbean islands (Chef-lieu du Gouvernement Général des Antilles) in 1668. Though other Caribbean councils continued to manage trials and register regulations, the Council of Martinique took over court cases and registered an important number of laws for other islands. The Council of Martinique continued to manage matters for Saint-Domingue until 1714 and for Guiana and Guadeloupe until 1762. Anglophone scholars who have focused on Martinique include Brett Rushforth, John Savage, Rebecca Hartkopf Schloss, Dale Tomish, and Laurie Wood. With regard to the seventeenth and early eighteenth centuries, Martinique has also received more attention than Guadeloupe in French academia. Francophone scholars who have worked on Martinique in recent years include Vincent Cousseau, Léo Elisabeth, Abel Louis, and Jessica Pierre-Louis. For one excellent recent French publication considering the early history of Guadeloupe, which focuses on slaveowners, see Fréderic Régent, *Les Maîtres de la Guadeloupe. Propriétaires d'esclaves, 1635–1848* (Paris: Taillandier 2019).

60. This especially applied to Guadeloupe, Martinique, and their dependencies. As recently demonstrated by Tessa Murphy, before the Seven Years' War, the French colony of Grenada had a lot in common with other islands in the so-called "Creole Archipelago" (in the Eastern Caribbean). People on those islands capitalized on a difficult topography, and on the presence of enemy European regimes to carve out varying degrees of autonomy. They also used versatile watercrafts to develop sea-routes that were very difficult to control. See Tessa Murphy, *The Creole Archipelago: Race and Borders in the Colonial Caribbean* (Philadelphia: University of Pennsylvania Press, 2021).

61. Saint-Domingue was also inhabited by more enslaved people than any other Caribbean island except Jamaica. See "Trans-Atlantic Slave Trade—Database," SlaveVoyages,

https://www.slavevoyages.org/voyage/database#tables, accessed July 2024. The history of Saint-Domingue has received considerable attention from Haitian scholars and US historians—many of whom have focused on tracing the revolution that culminated in the establishment of the first independent Black republic of Haiti in 1804. Scholars who have worked on Saint-Domingue include Pierre Buteau and Jean Casimir in Haiti; Marlene Daut, Laurent Dubois, Malick Gachem, David Geggus, Julia Gaffield, John Garrigus, Stewart R. King, Jeremy Popkin, Alyssa Sepinwall, Lorelle Semley, and Rob Taber in the United States; Dominique Rogers in France; Carolyn Fick and Jean-Pierre Le Glaunec in Canada; and Hank Gonzalez in the UK, to name just a few.

62. Francophone scholars who have worked on Isle Bourbon in the seventeenth and the eighteenth centuries include Georges Azéma, Jean Barassin, Robert Bousquet, Jérémy Boutier, Audrey Carotenuto, Sonia Chane-Kune, Jean-Pierre Coevoet, Yvan Combeau, Jean-Marie Desport, Prosper Ève, Jean-Claude Félix (no hyphen between Claude and Félix) Fontaine, Sudel Fuma, Hubert Gerbeau, Albert Jauze, Albert Lougnon, Rose-May Nicole, Sabrine Noël, Ho Haï Quang, Marie-Ange Payet, Jean-Valentin Payet, Myriam Paris, Claude Prud'homme, Marc Thieffry, and Serge Ycard.

63. Moreover, Isle of France did not have the impact that Isle Bourbon came to have on wider French imperial policies because it was colonized much later by the French, starting in 1715. Isle of France has received more attention from both Mauritian scholars and US- and Europe-based historians, perhaps because it came under British control in the nineteenth century. For examples of publications on Mauritius in this period, see Richard B. Allen, *Slaves, Freedmen and Indentured Laborers in Colonial Mauritius* (Cambridge: Cambridge University Press, 1999); Dorit Brixius, *Creolised Science: Knowledge in the Eighteenth-Century Indo-Pacific* (Cambridge: Cambridge University Press, 2024); Marina Carter, "Indian Slaves in Mauritius, 1729–1834," *Indian Historical Review* 15, nos. 1–2 (1989): 233–247; Joseph La Hausse de Lalouviere, "The Colonial Enlightenment and Slavery in Eighteenth-Century Mauritius," *French Historical Studies* 48, no. 1 (2025): 1–35; Vijaya Teelock, *Bitter Sugar: Sugar and Slavery in 19th Century Mauritius* (Moka, Mauritius: Mahatma Gandhi Institute, 1998), and "The Influence of Slavery in the Formation of Creole Identity," *Comparative Studies of South Asia, Africa and the Middle East* 19, no. 2 (1999): 3–8; Vijaya Teelock and Edward A. Alpers, *History, Memory and Identity* (Mauritius: Nelson Mandela Centre for African Culture and the University of Mauritius, 2001); Megan Vaughan, *Creating the Creole Island: Slavery in Eighteenth-Century Mauritius* (Durham, NC: Duke University Press, 2005); Laurie Wood, *Archipelago of Justice: Law in France's Early Modern Empire* (EBook, New Haven & London: Yale University Press: 2020), https://play.google.com/books/reader?id=mVHaDwAAQBAJ&pg=GBS.PP1. For overviews of some of the works on Mauritius, see Marina Carter, "Slavery and Unfree Labour in the Indian Ocean," *History Compass* 4, no. 5 (2006): 800–813, and Vijaya Teelock, "Breaking the Wall of Silence: Slavery in Mauritian Historiography," *Radical History Review* 91 (2005): 104–109.

64. Pier Larson's 2007 claim that "Madagascar receives scant mention in recent histories of France's ancien régime empire" is still valid today. See Pier Larson, "Colonies Lost: God, Hunger, and Conflict in Anosy (Madagascar) to 1674," *Comparative Studies of South Asia, Africa and the Middle East* 27 (2007): 345–366, here 347–348.

65. There have been a few publications on the religious missions. See Philippe Chan-Mouie, "La première évangélisation des Lazaristes: 1648–1674. Peut-on parler d'un échec?," in *Le Christianisme dans le Sud de Madagascar: Mélanges à l'occasion du centenaire de la reprise de l'évangélisation du Sud de Madagascar par la Congrégation de la Mission, 1896–1996* (Fianarantsoa, Madagascar: Baingan' Ambonzontany, 1996); Henri Froidevaux, *Les Lazaristes à*

Madagascar au XVIIe siècle (Paris: Poussielgue, 1903); Nivoelisoa Galibert, À *l'angle de la Grande Maison. Les Lazaristes de Madagascar: Correspondance avec Vincent de Paul, 1648–1661* (Paris: Presses de l'Université Paris-Sorbonne, 2007); Marc Thieffry, *Saint Vincent de Paul et la mission lazariste de Madagascar au XVIIe siècle* (Paris: L'Harmattan 2018). For the most part, other publications on the French presence in Madagascar have focused on a later period. For example, see Pier M. Larson, *Ocean of Letters: Language and Creolization in an Indian Ocean Diaspora* (New York: Cambridge University Press, 2009); Gwyn R. Campbell, "Slavery and Forced Labor in Madagascar," Oxford Research Encyclopedia of African History (2023), https://oxfordre.com/africanhistory/view/10.1093/acrefore/9780190277734.001.0001/acrefore-9780190277734-e-872; Denis Regnier and Dominique Somda, "Slavery and Post-Slavery in Madagascar: An Overview," in *African Islands: Leading Edges of Empire and Globalization*, ed. Toyin Falola, R. Joseph Parrott, and Danielle Porter Sanchez (Rochester, NY: University of Rochester Press, 2019), 345–369; Dominique Somda, "Et le réel serait passé: Le secret de l'esclavage et l'imagination de la société (Anosy, sud de Madagascar)" (PhD diss., Paris X Paris Ouest Nanterre La Défense University, 2009); Denis Regnier, *Slavery and Essentialism in Highland Madagascar: Ethnography, History, Cognition* (Abingdon, UK: Routledge, 2021); Damien Tricoire, "Une histoire franco-malgache des établissements français à Madagascar aux XVIIe et XVIIIe siècles: Identités flottantes, métissages et collaborations," *Outre-Mers. Revue d'histoire* 392–393, no. 2 (2016): 237–259; "Les Lumières, l'idéologie coloniale et Madagascar: Aux origines de la mission civilisatrice," in *Les Lumières, l'esclavage et l'idéologie coloniale, XVIII–XXe siècles*, ed. Pascale Pellerin (Paris: Classiques Garnier, 2020), 85–98; and "Enlightened Colonialism? French Assimilationism, Silencing, and Colonial Fantasy on Madagascar," in *Enlightened Colonialism: Civilization Narratives and Imperial Politics in the Age of Reason*, ed. Damien Tricoire (Basingstoke, UK: Palgrave MacMillan, 2017), 47–70. Only a few writings have focused on the earlier period of French presence on this island. See Larson, "Colonies Lost," 345–366, and "Play and Possession: Sex, Marriage and Household at Fort Dauphin (Madagascar), c. 1660s," *Journal of Southern African Studies* 48, no. 4 (2022): 685–707; Carl Henry Sobocinski, "Some God, Little Glory, No Gold: The French on Madagascar in the Seventeenth Century" (PhD diss., University of Toledo, 2001); Jean-Aimé Rakotoarisoa and Henry T. Wright, "The Context of the Flacourt Settlement: The Archaeological Evidence of Anosy Region," *Études Océan Indien* 23–24 (1998): 231–236. Many of the writings on the seventeenth-century era of French presence in Madagascar are outdated. For example, see Arthur Malotet, *Étienne de Flacourt ou les origines de la colonisation française à Madagascar, 1648–1661* (Paris: Ernest Leroux, 1898), and M. I. Guët, *Les Origines de l'île Bourbon et de la colonisation française à Madagascar* (Paris: Charles Bayle, 1888).

66. Most of the work on Saint-Louis and Gorée, by scholars in the United States, France, and Senegal, focuses on the later period of French rule, for which sources are more plentiful. Scholars are also eager to study the remarkable group of local Africans and Eurafricans who, by the late eighteenth century, formed an important merchant and political elite. For publications considering Saint-Louis and Gorée in the later period, see, for example, George E. Brooks Jr., *Eurafricans in Western Africa: Commerce, Social Status, Gender, and Religious Observance from the Sixteenth to the Eighteenth Century* (Athens: Ohio University Press, 2003); William B. Cohen, *The French Encounter with Africans: White Response to Blacks, 1530–1880* (EBook, Bloomington: Indiana University Press, 1980), https://play.google.com/books/reader?id=Swn-9NVay98C&pg=GBS.PP1; Michael Crowder, *Senegal: A Study in French Assimilation Policy* (London: Oxford University Press, 1962); Hilary Jones, *The Métis of Senegal: Urban Life and Politics in French West Africa* (Bloomington: Indiana University Press, 2013); Aissata Kane Lo, *De la Signare à la*

Diriyanké sénégalaise: Trajectoires féminines et visions partagées (EBook, Dakar, Senegal: L'Harmattan, 2014), https://play.google.com/books/reader?id=agfqAwAAQBAJ&pg=GBS.PP1; Guillaume Vial, *Femmes d'influence: Les signares de Saint-Louis du Sénégal et de Gorée, XVIIIe–XIXe siècle: Étude critique d'une identité métisse* (Paris: Maisonneuve & Larose/hémisphères éditions, 2018). There are a few exceptions, but most are rather dated: see Marie-Hélène Knight-Baylac, "La vie à Gorée de 1677 à 1789," *Revue Française d'Histoire d'Outre-Mer* 57 (1970): 377–420; Nathalie Reyss, "Saint-Louis du Sénégal à l'époque pré-coloniale: L'émergence d'une société métisse originale, 1658–1804" (PhD diss., Université de Paris I, 1983); Karen Sackur, "The Development of Creole Society and Culture in Saint-Louis and Gorée, 1719–1817" (PhD diss., School of Oriental and African Studies, University of London, 1999); Samuel Zilombo, "The Economy and Society of Saint-Louis du Sénégal with Special Reference to the Emergence of Eurafrican Influence, 1659–1809" (PhD diss., University of Birmingham, 1985). There are only a few recent publications on Saint-Louis and Gorée in the earlier period. See Guillaume Aubert's "'Nègres ou mulâtres nous sommes tous Français': Race, genre et nation à Gorée et à Saint-Louis du Sénégal, fin XVIIe–fin XVIIIe siècle," in *Français? La nation en débat entre colonies et métropole, XVIe–XIXe siècle*, ed. Cécile Vidal (Paris: Éditions EHESS, 2014), 125–147; Clark, Thioub and Vidal, eds., *New Orleans, Louisiana & Saint-Louis*; and Johnson, *Wicked Flesh*.

67. Kathleen DuVal, *The Native Ground: Indians and Colonists in the Heart of the Continent* (Philadelphia: University of Pennsylvania Press, 2006), 8. In North America, they claimed sovereignty by using their own notion of right of discovery and conquest as discussed in Michael Witgen's book on the western interior. See Witgen, *An Infinity of Nations*, 17–18.

68. In this book, I use the expression "local people" instead of "Indigenous people" to designate the populations who resided in Madagascar, Africa, and India since before the arrival of the Europeans. I do so because, in the early modern period, most of these populations did not fit the current definition often applied to "Indigenous people," as men and women who "share experiences as peoples who have been subjected to the [. . .] denial of their sovereignty, by a colonizing society that has come to dominate and determine the shape and quality of their lives." Quoted from Linda Tuhiwai Smith, *Decolonizing Methodologies: Research and Indigenous Peoples*, 3rd ed. (London: Bloomsbury Publishing, 2021), 7. I only use the word "Indigenous" in the context of American History. Historians have applied the expression "Indigenous people" to the American context since Native American people themselves embraced it beginning in the 1970s, in the context of their struggle for political justice. For examples of studies of North American borderlands showing how Native American peoples fully retained their sovereignty in the early modern period , see Juliana Barr, *Peace Came in the Form of a Woman: Indians and Spaniards in the Texas Borderlands* (Chapel Hill: University of North Carolina Press, 2007) and "Geographies of Power: Mapping Indian Borders in the 'Borderlands' of the Early Southwest," *WMQ* 68: 1 (2011): 5–46; DuVal, *The Native Ground*; Michael A. McDonnell, *Masters of Empire: Great Lakes Indians and the Making of America* (New York: Hill and Wang, 2015); and Witgen, *An Infinity of Nations*.

69. Lauren Benton, *A Search for Sovereignty: Law and Geography in European Empires, 1400–1900* (Cambridge and New York: Cambridge University Press, 2010), 279.

70. Benton, *A Search for Sovereignty*, 57–58 (quotation). As Benton demonstrates, empire in the early modern period was grounded in water (e.g., river lanes, ports, and estuaries) as much as land.

71. Quotation from DuVal, *The Native Ground*, 12.

72. As demonstrated by Jean-François Lozier, this was also true in the context of the French mission settlements of the seventeenth-century Saint Lawrence valley, for example. Jean-François Lozier, *Flesh Reborn: The Saint Lawrence Valley Mission Settlements through the Seventeenth*

Century (EBook, Montreal: McGill-Queen's University Press, 2018), 13, https://play.google.com/books/reader?id=SKxuDwAAQBAJ&pg=GBS.PR1. As hinted in Danna Agmon's recent work on Pondicherry, the French objectives in India were imperialist and colonialist indeed, in addition to being commercial. This is illustrated by the brutal evangelization campaign initiated by the French Company of the East Indies and driven by the Jesuits in Pondicherry. See Agmon, *A Colonial Affair*.

73. Greer, *Property and Dispossession*, 2. Greer's observations align with Ellis's claim that sovereignty in North American Native American terms did not mean "asserting exclusive control over a territory." Instead, according to her, Native Americans saw the sharing of territory as a source of power for each group through "their webs of interdependent relationships with others." See Ellis, *The Great Power of Small Nations*, 6.

74. Here too, I am using the language applied by DuVal to the Arkansas River valley. See DuVal, *The Native Ground*, 10.

75. DuVal, *The Native Ground*, 7; McDonnell, *Masters of Empire*, 15.

76. Eager to form new military alliances and trade tools, iron, and other goods with the Europeans, Dian Ramach, the king of Anosy, initially approached the French to tell them that "they were welcome to stay among his people," though only "on condition that they would not make a nuisance in his States." François Cauche, *Relations veritables et curieuses de l'Isle de Madagascar et du Brésil* (Paris: A. Courbé, 1651), 12. It should come as no surprise that the king of Anosy immediately approached the French upon their arrival: he was already very familiar with Europeans, since he had spent time with the Portuguese in Mozambique, and in Goa, where he had been baptized and educated in the Catholic faith. On Dian Ramach's previous experiences, see Larson, "Colonies Lost," 355–356, 358.

77. Benton, *A Search for Sovereignty*, 2, xiii.

78. Quoted from Greer, *Property and Dispossession*, 6. See Michael Witgen, *An Infinity of Nations*, 18; Amy Turner Bushnell, "Indigenous America and the Limits of the Atlantic World, 1493–1825," in *Atlantic History: A Critical Appraisal*, ed. Jack Greene and Philip D. Morgan (Oxford and New York: Oxford University Press, 2009), 191–221, here 191; Bushnell usefully divides the Indigenous populations of the American continent into three categories: "incorporated peoples" who lived inside European empires, those on "the frontiers of empire[s]," and "autonomous peoples" beyond those frontiers. Witgen also claims that "the Native social formations [in the western interior] were not, in spite of European claims, the subjects of European empires or their settler colonies." See *An Infinity of Nations*, 215.

79. About the complex history of the rulers of Anosy and the Zafiraminia *roandria*, see Somda, "Et le réel serait passé," 21–26. About the societies of Anosy, see Larson, "Colonies Lost," 348–349.

80. Quoted from Burbank and Cooper, *Empires in World History*, 8, and Gilles Havard and Cécile Vidal, *Histoire de l'Amérique française*, 2nd ed. (Paris: Flammarion, Champs Histoire, 2019), 16. As beautifully demonstrated by Allan Greer, early modern "empires" were not all about land possession. He rightfully explains, "The navigators who ventured across the seas in the 'Age of Discovery' were generally more interested in controlling trade, plundering treasure, extending the reach of Christendom and enhancing the glory of their respective monarchs than they were in appropriating territory." See Greer, *Property and Dispossession*, 5. Those definitions are wider than the one that was used in the early modern period. In fact, the French in the early modern period rarely used the word "empire" to designate the colonies, and the term was rarely used altogether. For a study of the notion of "empire" in early modern France, see Ruggiu, "Des Nouvelles Frances aux colonies."

81. See Greer, *Property and Dispossession*, 6.

82. All foundation dates are listed in Laurie Wood, "Îles de France: Law and Empire in the French Atlantic and Indian Oceans, 1680–1780" (PhD diss., University of Texas at Austin, 2013), 11. About the Councils of Saint-Louis and Gorée, see Laurie Wood, "Îles de France," 108 n221. This book does not discuss North Africa and China because the French had no significant political presence (e.g., no councils) in those areas during the early modern period.

83. Quoted from Havard and Vidal, *Histoire de l'Amérique*. This was true even of the French outposts in Senegambia and India.

84. According to James Pritchard, the voice of the French crown was fragmented, and royal authorities were unable to formulate a clear imperial policy. See James Pritchard, *In Search of Empire: The French in the Americas, 1670–1739* (Cambridge: Cambridge University Press, 2004). Others have reached similar conclusions. See Banks, *Chasing Empire across the Sea*; Philip Boucher, *France and the American Tropics to 1700: Tropics of Discontent?* (Baltimore: Johns Hopkins University Press, 2008); Dale Miquelon, *New France, 1701–1744: A Supplement to Europe* (Toronto: McClelland and Stewart, 1987). They have made this claim despite the fact that the legal system in metropolitan France was also very fragmented and despite the fact that the king there was also unable to fully apply his authority. Moreover, as noted by Michaela Kleber, the fact that all French colonies and outposts were placed under the Paris Custom (*la Coutume de Paris*) gave more uniformity to the French colonial legal system than to the metropolitan one. See Kleber, "Gendered Societies," 11n11.

85. Nancy Christie, Michael Gauvreau, and Matthew Gerber, "Introduction: 'The King is Listening'—Toward a Social and Political History of Legal Pluralism in the Early Modern French Empire," in *Voices in the Legal Archives in the French Colonial World: "The King Is Listening"* (New York: Routledge, 2020), 1–60, esp. 4 ("Bourbon monarchy"). For another study stressing the importance of legal particularisms, see Rushforth, *Bonds of Alliance*. For example, while slavery was a cornerstone of the imperial strategy in many colonies, enslavement in *metropolitan* France was open to legal contestation because of the "free soil principle"—a legal maxim of obscure origins recorded in eighteenth-century judicial handbooks. See Sue Peabody, *"There Are No Slaves in France": The Political Culture of Race and Slavery in the Ancien Régime* (EBook, New York and Oxford: Oxford University Press, 1996), https://ebookcentral.proquest.com/lib/duke/reader.action?docID=241471&c=UERG&ppg=5, and "An Alternative Genealogy of the Origins of French Free Soil: Medieval Toulouse," *Slavery & Abolition* 32, no. 3 (2011): 341–362; Miranda Spieler, "L'enlèvement des esclaves à Paris," in *Colonisations: Notre Histoire*, ed. Arthur Asseraf, Guillaume Blanc, Nadia Yala Kisukidi, Mélanie Lamotte and Pierre Singaravélou (Paris: Éditions du Seuil, 2023), 670–672. A similar view existed in England by the early eighteenth century. Some believed that "as soon as a Negro comes into England, he becomes free." On this topic, see Shaw, "In the Name of the Mother," 198.

86. As recent historiography makes clear, the role of French chartered companies extended well beyond trading. See Agmon, *A Colonial Affair*, and Heijmans, *The Agency*. In 1664, King Louis XIV described the Company of the East Indies and the West India Company (la Compagnie des Indes Occidentales) as "sovereign" entities in a declaration. See *Déclarations du Roy: L'une, portant établissement d'une compagnie pour le commerce des Indes Orientales; l'autre [du 27 août 1664]* [. . .] (Paris: les imprimeurs ordinaires du Roy, 1664), articles XVI and XXXVI, 17–18. On the close relationship between the crown and the trading companies, see the introductions to Chapters 1 and 2.

87. Quoted from Ann Stoler, *Haunted by Empire: Geographies of Intimacy in North American History* (Durham, NC: Duke University Press, 2006), 4. See also Stoler's *Carnal Knowledge and*

Imperial Power: Race and the Intimate in Colonial Rule (Berkeley: University of California Press, 2002), 42, 47; Julie Hardwick, Sarah M. S. Pearsall, and Karin Wulf, "Introduction: Centering Families in Atlantic Histories," *WMQ*, 3rd ser., 70, no. 2 (2013): 205–224.

88. Quoted from Dawdy, *Building the Devil's Empire*, 18, and Hodson and Rushforth, "Absolutely Atlantic," 109. On this topic, see also Allan Greer, "Comparisons: New France," in *A Companion to Colonial America*, ed. Daniel Vickers (Malden, MA: Blackwell, 2003), 469–488. The vision of state power as a negotiated process in this book aligns with recent research in the history of absolutism in the kingdom of France, which centers royal attempts to secure cooperation from distant French subjects. For example, see William Beik, "The Absolutism of Louis XIV as Social Collaboration," *Past & Present* 188, no. 1 (2005): 195–224; James B. Collins, *The State in Early Modern France*, 2nd ed. (Cambridge: Cambridge University Press, 2009); Sharon Kettering, *Patrons, Brokers, and Clients in Seventeenth-Century France* (New York: Oxford University Press, 1986). For a long time, scholars have, however, considered the history of the early modern French empire a story of failure. This vision can be traced back to the work of historian Francis Parkman in the nineteenth century.

89. In short, this book is an answer to this call by historian Robert M. Morrissey: "Moving beyond the question of success and failure, a better question is: what was the nature of colonialism?" See *Empire by Collaboration*, 5.

90. As Morrissey puts it in his study of Upper Louisiana, "So much of the nature of imperialism was so unintentional, so accidental." See Morrissey, *Empire by Collaboration*, 5.

91. For some examples, see Lauren Benton, *Law and Colonial Cultures: Legal Regimes in World History 1400–1900* (Cambridge: Cambridge University Press, 2002); Brian P. Owensby and Richard J. Ross, eds., *Justice in a New World: Negotiating Legal Intelligibility in British, Iberian, and Indigenous America* (New York: New York University Press, 2018); Julia Stephens, *Empires of Complaint: Mughal Law and the Making of British India, 1765–1793* (Cambridge: Cambridge University Press, 2022).

92. It has so far received in-depth treatment especially in the context of North America, as well as eighteenth- and nineteenth-century India. Julie Marquet explains that "in Pondicherry, like in most colonies, law and justice were the product of multiple accommodations." See Julie Marquet, "Accommoder le droit en situation coloniale: Le rôle du comité consultatif de jurisprudence indienne de Pondichéry au XIXe siècle," *Revue d'histoire du XIXe siècle* 60, no. 1 (2020): 257–273, here 273. See also Danna Agmon, "Historical Gaps and Non-existent Sources: The Case of the Chaudrie Court in French India," *Comparative Studies in Society and History* 63, no. 4 (2021): 979–1006; Marie Houllemare, "La justice française à Pondichéry au xviiie siècle, une justice en zone de contact," in *Adapter le droit aux colonies: Thémis outre-mer (xvie–xixe siècle)*, ed. Éric Wenzel and Éric de Mari. (Dijon: Éditions Universitaires de Dijon, 2015), 147–157; Gauri Parasher, "The Religion of the Tribunal: Legal Transculturality in Eighteenth-Century Pondicherry," (PhD diss., Université de Heidelberg, in progress). For a study considering legal accommodation to local practices in the Illinois Country, see Morrissey, *Empire by Collaboration*.

93. For example, see DuVal, *The Native Ground*; McDonnell, *Masters of Empire*. This practice was not restricted to the French world. For two excellent studies of other worlds where Europeans were "indigenized," "Indianized," or strategically adapted to local customs, see Barr, *Peace Came in the Form of a Woman*; and Guido van Meersbergen, *Ethnography and Encounter: The Dutch and English East India Companies in Seventeenth-Century South Asia* (Leiden, Netherlands: Brill, 2021). Cultural exchanges in Senegambia and Anosy were mutual. On this topic in French North America, see Havard, *Empire et métissages*; Lozier, *Flesh Reborn*; Leavelle, *The Catholic Calumet*; Laurier Turgeon, *Une histoire de la Nouvelle-France: Français et*

Amérindiens au XVIe siècle (Paris: Belin, 2019); Richard White, *The Middle Ground: Indians, Empires, and Republics in the Great Lakes Region, 1650–1815* (Cambridge and New York: Cambridge University Press, 1991); White, *Wild Frenchmen*. The French practice of cultural adaptation had deep roots going as far back as the sixteenth century. On this topic, see Olive Patricia Dickason, "Dyewood to Furs: The Brazilian Origins of French–Amerindian Trade," *Yearbook (Conference of Latin Americanist Geographers)* 10 (1984): 19–34.

94. In the 1990s, Raymond DeMallie made a call to historians to recognize the importance of kinship in Native American societies. See Raymond J. DeMallie, "Kinship: The Foundation for Native American Society," in *Studying Native America: Problems and Prospects*, ed. Russell Thornton (Madison: University of Wisconsin Press, 1998), 306–356. Kinship also played an important role in the political culture of the kingdom of France. On this topic, see Peter Cook, "Vivre comme frères: Le rôle du registre fraternel dans les premières alliances franco-amérindiennes au Canada (vers 1580–1650)," *Recherches amérindiennes au Québec* 31, no. 2 (2001): 55–65, here 57.

95. For an overview of some of this historiography, see Ann L. Stoler, "Tense and Tender Ties: The Politics of Comparison in North American History and (Post) Colonial Studies," *Journal of American History* 88, no. 3 (2001): 829–865. See also Stoler's *Carnal Knowledge and Imperial Power* and *Haunted by Empire*, 4.

96. Cécile Vidal defines *métissage* as "what people in the eighteenth century conceived of as interracial sexuality." See Cécile Vidal, "Caribbean Louisiana: Church, Métissage, and the Language of Race in the Mississippi Colony during the French Period," in Cécile Vidal ed., *Louisiana: Crossroads of the Atlantic World* (Philadelphia: University of Pennsylvania Press, 2014), 125–146, here 126.

97. This history has long been erased from popular memory as a result of past attempts, on Réunion Island, to destroy the documents attesting to the importance of interracial relationships in the first decades of colonization. As explained by Nathan Marvin and Myriam Paris, "The very reality of the 'Black first mothers' of Bourbon Island was [then] systematically erased from history books and popular memory, leaving behind only a 'blank page.'" Marvin, "Bourbon Island Creoles," 26 (quotation); Paris, "La page blanche."

98. See Marie Houllemare, "The Constitution of the Colonial Archives and the Emergence of Imperial Awareness," *Revue d'histoire moderne et contemporaine* 61, no. 2 (2014): 7–31, and "Procedures, Jurisdictions and Records."

99. See Ira Berlin, *Many Thousands Gone: The First Two Centuries of Slavery in North America* (Cambridge, MA: Harvard University Press, 1998), 8–9.

100. Dawdy, *Building the Devil's Empire*, 18. See also Hodson and Rushforth, "Absolutely Atlantic," 109.

101. Relatively few publications have considered institutionalized forms of Black politicization in French context before the Haitian Revolution. For a publication with French content considering Black politicization in the Atlantic before the era of the Haitian Revolution in a few passages, see Laurent Dubois and Julius S. Scott, *Origins of the Black Atlantic* (New York: Routledge, 2010). This argument only applies to institutionalized forms of politicization: marronage, slave revolts, and other forms of resistance occurred as well, of course, and they have received substantial attention, though especially for the later period here as well. For some powerful recent examples, see Catherine Benoît, "Les jardins: Espaces de contestation," in *Colonisations*, ed. Singaravélou *et al.*, 673–674; Prosper Ève, *Les esclaves de Bourbon, la mer et la montagne* (Paris: Karthala, 2003); John Garrigus, *A Secret among the Blacks: Slave Resistance before the Haitian Revolution* (Cambridge, MA: Harvard University Press, 2023); Tayzhaun Glover,

"Freedom on the Horizon: Transmarine Marronage and the Abolition of Slavery in Dominica, Martinique, and St. Lucia, 1824–1848" (PhD diss., Duke University, 2024); Aline Helg, *Plus jamais esclaves! De l'insoumission à la révolte, le grand récit d'une émancipation (1492–1838)* (Paris: La Découverte, 2016); Dominique Cyrille, "Musique, danse et résistance en Guadeloupe et en Martinique," *Africultures* 98, no 2 (2014): 116–125. For an overview of some other works on slave resistance, see Jean-Pierre Le Glaunec, "Résister à l'esclavage dans l'Atlantique français: Aperçu historiographique, hypothèses et pistes de recherche," *Revue d'histoire de l'Amérique française* 71, no. 1–2 (2017): 13–33.

102. See Chapter 4.

103. For a groundbreaking work tracing the diffusion of Black rebellions through the circulation of news in a later period, see Julius S. Scott, *The Common Wind: Afro-American Currents in the Age of the Haitian Revolution* (New York and London: Verso, 2020).

104. On the circulation of people, see, for example, Dubé, "S'approprier l'Atlantique;" Palmer, *Intimate Bonds*; Scott, "The Common Wind;" Rebecca J. Scott and Jean M. Hébrard, *Freedom Papers: An Atlantic Odyssey in the Age of Emancipation* (Cambridge, MA: Harvard University Press, 2012). On the circulation of people and ideas, Guillaume Aubert and Cécile Vidal, for example, have studied patterns in the circulation of racial discourse in official documents and church records across the North Atlantic. See Aubert, "'The Blood of France'" and "'To Establish One Law and Definite Rules': Race, Religion, and the Transatlantic Origins of the Louisiana Code Noir," in Vidal, *Louisiana*, 21–43; Vidal, "Caribbean Louisiana" and *Caribbean New Orleans*.

105. For some examples, see Agmon, *A Colonial Affair*; Erin Greenwald, *Marc-Antoine Caillot and the Company of the Indies in Louisiana: Trade in the French Atlantic World* (Baton Rouge: Louisiana State University Press, 2016); Erin Greenwald, ed., *A Company Man: The Remarkable French-Atlantic Voyage of a Clerk for the Company of the Indies* (New Orleans: Historic New Orleans Collection, 2013); Mélanie Lamotte, "Beyond the Atlantic: Unifying Racial Policies across the Early French Empire," *WMQ*, 3rd ser., 81, no. 1 (2024): 3–36; Peabody, *Madeleine's Children*; Miranda Spieler, *Slaves in Paris: Hidden Lives and Fugitive Histories* (Cambridge, MA: and London, Harvard University Press, 2025); Wood, *Archipelago of Justice*.

106. Houllemare, "Procedures, Jurisdictions and Records"; "La fabrique des archives coloniales et la naissance d'une conscience impériale (France, XVIIIe siècle)," *Revue d'histoire moderne et contemporaine* 2, no. 61-2 (2014): 7–31; "Vers la centralisation des archives coloniales françaises au XVIIIe siècle: Destruction et conservation des papiers judiciaires," in *Pratiques d'archives à l'époque moderne: Europe, mondes coloniaux*, ed. Maria-Pia Donato and Anne Saada (Paris: Classiques Garnier, 2018): 349–367, and "Seeing the Empire through Lists and Charts: French Colonial Records in the Eighteenth Century," *Journal of Early Modern History* 22 (2018): 371–391.

107. Map I.1 was developed using a Python script to query the database Mémoire des Hommes, section "Compagnies des Indes," subsection "Armements des Navires." I then verified the content of the dataset in the original CSV tables on which the database is based. We performed a word frequency analysis on the notices describing each ship's destination and ports of call to identify groups of commonly occurring keywords suggesting the departure and arrival of a ship at a particular port or colony. We then defined a mapping from port name to colony: for example, the words "Guadeloupe," "Martinique," or "Port-au-Prince" all suggest a presence in the Caribbean, while the words "Nouvelle-Orléans" and "Louisiane" suggest a presence in Louisiana. Because the focus of this book is on pan-imperial mobility within the French Atlantic and Indian Oceans, all ports that were not located within French colonies or outposts were

subsequently removed from the dataset. Territories that fell into the hands of other nations for brief periods of time, such as Guadeloupe and Pondicherry, are included for the entire period between 1713 and 1763. The dataset was then displayed in a network visualization library. Mémoire des Hommes database, section "Compagnies des Indes," subsection "Armements des Navires," Ministère des Armées, accessed November 9, 2021, https://www.memoiredeshommes.sga.defense.gouv.fr/fr/arkotheque/client/mdh/compagnie_des_indes/armement_navires.php. I thank Jean-Michel André for sharing precious information about this database with me.

108. Although the bulk (48 percent, or 1,118) of the journeys recorded in this database for the period between 1713 and 1791 were made by the vessels of the French Company of the Indies, 34 percent (795) were by private merchants, 4 percent (89) by the royal navy, and 2 percent (53) by other French trading companies, including the Company of Senegal (54 percent), the West India Company (34 percent), the Companies of the Indies Malouines (7 percent), and the Company of Isle Saint-Jean (3 percent). The proportion of voyages performed by ships belonging to private merchants in the dataset grew after 1767, when the company relinquished its monopoly over the Indian Ocean. I am very grateful to Daniel Ohayon for making the analysis of this data possible.

109. See Banks, *Chasing Empire across the Sea*; Pritchard, *In Search of Empire*.

110. Pritchard, *In Search of Empire*, 403.

111. For an overview of the ways this development unfolded in the British context, see Stern, *Empire, Incorporated*.

112. For an illustration of this, see Cross, *Company Politics*. These commercial connections were with local populations across the Americas, Africa, and Asia and also with other European nations. On the latter kind of connections, see John Shovlin, *Trading with the Enemy: Britain, France, and the 18th-Century Quest for a Peaceful World Order* (New Haven, CT: Yale University Press, 2021).

113. The data presented here was extracted from the Mémoire des Hommes database, section "Compagnies des Indes," subsection "Équipages et passagers," using a text mining algorithm. Created by the association Les Amis du Service Historique de la Défense à Lorient, this database provides information about the ages, origins, professions, and itineraries of thousands of people, most of whom traveled aboard ships whose trajectories are featured on Map I.1. The members of the association Les Amis du Service Historique de la Défense à Lorient who have contributed to the making of the "Équipages et passagers" subsection are Jean-Michel André, Yves Bannalec, Annie Blayo, René Estienne, Jean-Paul Even, Jean-Yves Le Lan, Louis Le Ruyet, Henri Maurel, Chantal Plevert, Rémy Richet, Alain Terras, and Joël Vaillant. Mémoire des Hommes database, section "Compagnies des Indes," subsection "Équipages et passagers," Ministère des Armées, accessed November 9, 2021, https://www.memoiredeshommes.sga.defense.gouv.fr/fr/arkotheque/client/mdh/compagnie_des_indes/equipages_et_passagers.php. I am grateful to Jean-Michel André, René Estienne, Chantal Plévert, and the members of the Association des Amis du Service historique de la Défense in Lorient for sharing precious information about this other database with me. I also thank Daniel Ohayon for making the analysis of this data possible.

114. Banks, *Chasing Empire*, 155–156, 173.

115. Banks, *Chasing Empire*, 5.

116. Philippe Haudrère, *La Compagnie française des Indes au XVIIIe siècle*, 2nd ed., 2 vols. (Paris: Les Indes Savantes, 2005), 1:339. By 1746, the French company's 250,000-ton capacity by far surpassed that of its British counterpart (90,000). Haudrère, *La Compagnie*, 1:338. By 1752–1753, the French company's sales equalled those of the British East India Company. See Haudrère, *La Compagnie*, 1:333.

117. The number of such voyages increased throughout the eighteenth century.

118. For example, the first Guadeloupean man ever recorded in the censuses of Isle Bourbon was a white surgeon named Louis César Bertrand Moreau, who arrived on Isle Bourbon in 1726 and became a successful coffee planter. See ADR C°770 "Recensement general, 1735," ff. 177v–178v; Ricquebourg, *Dictionnaire généalogique des familles de l'Île Bourbon,* 2:1965.

119. For examples of travelers on their way to the Indian Ocean who stopped in Cape Verde, see these narratives: François Cauche, *Relations véritables et curieuses de l'Isle de Madagascar et du Brésil* (Paris: Augustin Courbe, 1651); Charles Dellon, *Relation d'un voyage des Indes orientales dédié à Monseigneur l'evêque de Meaux,* 2 vols. (Paris, 1685); Du Bois, *Les voyages faits par le sieur D.B aux isles Dauphine ou Madagascar, et Bourbon ou Mascarenne, és années 1669, 70, 71 et 72* (Paris: Claude Barbin, 1674); François Leguat, *Voyages et aventures de François Leguat et de ses compagnons en deux îles désertes des Indes orientales,* 2 vols. (Amsterdam: Jean Louis de Lorme, 1708).

120. Those exchanges gave birth to others, including a slave trade between Madagascar and the Antilles and between Senegambia and Isle Bourbon. For more information on those slave trades, see Allen, "The Constant Demand of the French," 62, 70, and *European Slave Trading*; Banks, *Chasing Empire,* 437; Haudrère, *La Compagnie,* 1:437, 444–445; Wood, *Archipelago of Justice,* 136–137, 155.

121. The Company of the Indies transported a total of 2,000–3,500 enslaved people from West Africa to the Mascarenes from the 1700s to 1767. See Allen, "The Constant Demand of the French," 70; Marvin, "Bourbon Island Creoles," 101n114. They also started another (smaller) slave trade from Madagascar to the French Caribbean: see Wood, *Archipelago of Justice,* 136–137, 155.

122. See Erin Greenwald, "Abandoning Louisiana, Embracing India: The French Company of the Indies in the 1720s and 30s," paper presented at the 2014 Annual Meeting of the Society for French Historical Studies, Montreal, Canada, April 2014, 9, and *Marc-Antoine Caillot*; Haudrère, *La Compagnie,* 1:333.

123. On Isle Bourbon's role as an *escale,* see Sonia Chane-Kune, *Aux origines de l'identité réunionnaise* (Paris: L'Harmattan, 1993), 20–21; Jean-Michel Filliot, *La traite des esclaves vers les Mascareignes au XVIIIe siècle* (Paris: ORSTOM, 1974), 132–133; Albert Lougnon, *Sous le signe de la tortue: Voyages anciens à l'Île Bourbon, 1611–1725* (Sainte-Clotilde, Réunion: Orphie, 2005), 35. On Madagascar's initial intended function as a settler colony, see Larson, "Colonies Lost," 358.

124. Wood, *Archipelago of Justice,* 136–137, 155.

125. Paul Kaeppelin, *Les escales françaises sur la route de l'Inde* (Paris: Augustin Challamel, 1908).

126. This definition has been employed by many historians of the early modern period. See Mélanie Lamotte and Emily Marker, "Race," in *The Cambridge Companion to the French Empire,* ed. Alice Conklin and Owen White (Cambridge: Cambridge University Press, forthcoming). I also draw on the definition provided in the Oxford English Dictionary. See s.v "Race," accessed April 11, 2025, https://www.oed.com/dictionary/race_n6?tab=meaning_and_use.

127. Angela Barreto Xavier, "Purity of Blood and Caste: Identity Narratives among Modern Goan Elites," in *Race and Blood in the Iberian World,* ed. Max Hering Torres, Maria Elena Martinez, and David Nirenberg (Zurich: Lit Verlag GmbH, 2012), 125–150; Maria Elena Martinez, *Genealogical Fictions: Limpieza de Sangre, Religion, and Gender in Colonial Mexico* (Stanford, CA: Stanford University Press, 2008); Jean-Paul Zuñiga, *Espagnols d'Outre-Mer: Émigration, métissage, et reproduction sociale à Santiago de Chili au 17e siècle* (Paris: Édition de l'École des Hautes Études en Sciences Sociales, 2002).

128. Noémie Ndiaye, *Scripts of Blackness: Early Modern Performance Culture and the Making of Race* (Philadelphia: University of Pennsylvania Press, 2022), 10.

129. From 1778, legislation also required Black residents to carry identity cards. Pierre Boulle, *Race et esclavage dans la France de l'Ancien Régime* (Paris: Perrin, 2007), 26, 76; Peabody, "*There Are No Slaves in France*," 68, 73–74, 128–131. They have attributed this emerging policing of race within the metropole to the "free soil principle the legal notion that all enslaved people who set foot on French soil became free, stemming from an interpretation of an ordinance issued by Louis X in 1315. Boulle, *Race et esclavage*, 29; Peabody, *"There Are No Slaves in France,"* 4–5, 68–69.

130. Spieler, *Slaves in Paris*, 98 (quotation), 50.

131. See Anne Lafont, "How Skin Color Became a Racial Marker: Art Historical Perspectives on Race," *Eighteenth-century Studies* 51, no. 1 (2002): 89–113; Ndiaye, *Scripts of Blackness*. See also the papers presented at the roundtable "Race in Early Modern France II / Le concept de race dans la France de la première modernité II," The Society for Interdisciplinary French Seventeenth-Century Studies, Virtual (Zoom) Conference, 2020.

132. Boulle, *Race et esclavage*, 26, 76; Erick Noël, *Être Noir en France au XVIIIe siècle* (Paris: Tallandier, 2006), 32; Peabody, *"There Are No Slaves in France,"* 68, 74.

133. *Dictionnaire de l'Académie française* (Paris: Jean-Baptiste Coignard, 1694).

134. On uses of the word "race" in this period, see Pierre Boulle, "La construction du concept de race dans la France d'ancien régime," *Outre-mers. Revue d'Histoire* 89 (2002): 155–175.

135. Leonard Hodges has demonstrated that the people labeled *Portugais/es* by the French in India were in most cases of Luso-Indian descent. See Leonard Hodges, "Configuring Colonial Families in Chandernagore (1719–1769)" (unpublished essay, King's College London, 2016), n.p.

136. For example, see ANOM C3 1 "Memoires du Pere Bernardin, 1687–1688," f. 63.

137. See, for example, ANOM F3 205 "Reglement 8 Janvier 1730," p. 108; Robert Challe, *Journal d'un voyage fait aux Indes orientales, par une escadre de six vaisseaux commandez par Mr. Du Quesne, depuis le 24 Février 1690, jusqu'au 20 Août 1691*, 3 vols. (Rouen, France: Jean Batiste Machuel le Jeune, 1721), 2:176–178; Dellon, *Relation d'un voyage des Indes orientales*, 1:96–97, 200, 204, 238, 249.

138. *Dictionnaire de l'Académie française*; Challe, *Journal d'un voyage fait aux Indes orientales*, 2:176; Dellon, *Relation d'un voyage des Indes orientales*, 1:96.

139. See Van Meersbergen, *Ethnography and Encounter*.

140. Furtière's *Universal Dictionary* of 1690 specified that "almost all of America turned out to be populated with *sauvages*" and added, "most *sauvages* are cannibals, who wander naked and are covered with hairs." For more information on the concept of *l'homme sauvage* in this time period, see Olive Patricia Dickason, "The Concept of *l'homme sauvage* and early French colonialism in the Americas," *Revue française d'histoire d'outre-mer* 234 (1977): 5–32.

141. Guillaume Aubert, "'Français, Nègres et Sauvages': Constructing Race in Colonial Louisiana" (PhD diss. Tulane University, 2002), 122; Jean Baptiste Du Tertre, *Histoire générale des Antilles habitées par les François*, 3 vols. (Paris: Thomas Jolly, 1667–1671), 2:512 (quotation).

142. Régent, *La France et ses esclaves*, 10.

143. María Elena Martínez, *Genealogical Fictions*, 164.

144. Research in genetics has demonstrated that there is no biological basis to racial categories, since most genetic diversity occurs within the alleged "races" and very little is found between them. In fact, only 6 percent of genetic variation is between populations traditionally

defined as "races." On this topic, see Marcus Feldman Richard Lewontin, and Mary-Claire King, "Race: A Genetic Melting-Pot," *Nature* 424 (2003): 374.

145. On this subject, see Cécile Vidal, "Francité et situation coloniale: Nation, empire et race en Louisiane française (1699–1769)," in *Annales, Histoire, Sciences Sociales* 64 (2009): 1019–1050, here 1031, 1036, 1045.

146. Martinez, *Genealogical Fictions,* 135 (quotation)–137.

147. For example, see Galibert, *À l'angle de la Grande Maison,* 110; Letter n°XVI, Toussaint Bourdaise to Vincent de Paul, January 10, 1656, in *À l'angle de la Grande Maison,* ed. Galibert, 322, 326; Letter n°XIX, Toussaint Bourdaise to Vincent de Paul, February 19, 1657, in *À l'angle de la Grande Maison,* ed. Galibert, 343.

148. For some examples from Guadeloupe, see ANOM F3 221 "7 Avril 1664. Arrest du conseil d'Etat du Roy," 355; ANOM G1 469 "Recensement 1664 [. . .] Role des habitans dans les quartiers qui estoient de la colonie de Mr d'Herblay"; Père André Chevillard, *Les desseins de son Eminence de Richelieu pour l'Amérique, reproduction de l'édition de 1659* (Basse-Terre, Guadeloupe: Société d'histoire de la Guadeloupe, 1973), 270. For some examples from Louisiana, see ANOM G1 464 "Recensement des habitans du fort Louis de la Mobile et ses villages Circonvoisins [. . .] ce 28 Juin 1721," 12; ANOM A 23 "Arrêt qui fait cesser l'envoi de vagabonds et de criminels en Louisiane (n° 21) (9 mai 1720)," f. 29v; ANOM A 22 "Lettres patentes en faveur d'Antoine Crozat, conseiller et secrétaire des finances, pour le monopole, pendant quinze années, de la création de tout établissement de commerce et d'industrie en Louisiane, [. . .] 14 septembre 1712," f. 4. For some examples from Isle Bourbon, see ANOM C3 1 "20 May 1692. Interrogatoire du nommé Valleau de l'Isle de Rhé," f. 185v; ANOM C3 1 "Memoires du Pere Bernardin 1687–1688," ff. 63–63v; ANOM G1 477 "Liste des habitans de Lisle de bourbon du mois de Septembre 1690."

149. For instances of uses of the word *mulâtre* on Isle Bourbon, see ANOM C3 1 "Memoire sur l'Isle de Bourbon Brest 1687 [. . .]," f. 63v; Antoine Boucher, "Le mémoire pour servir à la connaissance particulière de chacun des habitans de l'isle Bourbon, (1679–1725)," in Jean Barassin, "La vie quotidienne des colons au début du XVIIIe siècle" (PhD diss., Aix-en-Provence, 1976). For examples of uses of the word *métis* in India, see Challe, *Journal d'un voyage fait aux Indes orientales,* 2:171; ANOM C3 5 "Recensemens de Chandernagor 1751–1768," f. 1; ANOM C6 116–117 "Remarques sur Pondichery," n.p.

150. Van Meersbergen, *Ethnography and Encounter.*

151. Officials in the French stations of India sometimes used the word *Noirs* to designate free Asian people as well.

152. Van Meersbergen, *Ethnography and Encounter,* 63, 221 n4.

153. Alfred Rosset, *Les premiers colons de l'île Bourbon* (Paris: Éditions du Cerf-volant, 1967). See his chapter "Blanc de Bourbon," 147–159.

154. Simone Delesalle and Lucette Valensi, "Le mot 'nègre' dans les dictionnaires français d'ancien régime: Histoire et lexicographie," *Langue Française* 15 (1972): 79–104.

155. François Pomey, *Dictionnaire royal augmenté,* 2nd ed. (Lyon: Antoine Molin, 1671).

156. As opposed to scholars of the Anglophone, Hispanophone, and Lusophone worlds, French colonial history specialists do not have firsthand slave narratives at their disposal. For a publication discussing this problem and how it can be addressed, see White, *Voices of the Enslaved,* 1–26.

157. Enslaved people in the French empire were only allowed to testify under limited circumstances. But their court testimonies still give us a wealth of information about their daily lives. Although court reports were usually written by white clerks, French law demanded a complete

and accurate transcription of court testimonies, and their recording was thoroughly regulated. White, *Voices of the Enslaved*, 7. See also Frédéric Régent, Gilda Gonfier, and Bruno Maillard, eds., *Libres et sans fers, Paroles d'esclaves français* (Paris: Fayard, 2015); Dominique Rogers, ed., *Voix d'esclaves, Antilles, Guyane et Louisiane françaises XVIIIe–XIXe siècle* (Paris: Karthala, 2015); Sophie White and Trevor Burnard ed., *Hearing Enslaved Voices: African and Indian Slave Testimony in British and French America, 1700–1848* (New York: Routledge, 2020). See also Sophie White's digital project in the OI Reader, "Voices of the Enslaved: A Digital Humanities Approach to Encountering the Archive," accessed April 14, 2025, https://oireader.wm.edu/open_oi/voices-of-the-enslaved/.

158. Quoted from Morgan, *Reckoning with Slavery*, 13 n28.

159. See Morgan, *Reckoning with Slavery.*

160. For instances of directives being given to agents in charge of making the censuses, see HL "Vaudreuil Papers," LO 325 "Ordre de commandement pour Mr de Macarty major du païs des Illinois Du 8 mars 1751"; ANOM F3 205 "Ordonnance du Conseil du 5 mai 1753," p. 405; ANOM C3 5 "Memoire de l'Isle de Bourbon," article 3, f. 8; ANOM F3 221 "30 Decembre 1670, Le Sieur de Baas Gouverneur et Lieutenant general pour le Roy dans les Isles françoises de l'Amerique," p. 447; ANOM C3 2 "20 decembre 1703, Memoire Sur L'Isle de Bourbon," f. 11.

161. "Actual occupancy," accomplished through settlement, was one of the major tenets of the European "Doctrine of Discovery" that developed from the time of the Crusades and was codified much later, in the late nineteenth century. On this topic, see Robert Miller and Olivia Stitz, "The International Law of Colonialism in East Africa: Germany, England, and the Doctrine of Discovery," *Duke Journal of Comparative & International Law* (2021): 1–59.

162. Saidiya Hartman, *Lose Your Mother: A Journey along the Atlantic Slave Route* (New York: Farrar, Straus and Giroux, 2007), 6.

163. Like Jennifer Morgan, I believe that reconstructing Black life in this period requires "inhabit[ing] multiple spaces." Quoted from Morgan, *Reckoning with Slavery*, 23.

164. Gabriel Debien, *Les esclaves aux Antilles Françaises (XVIIe–XVIIIe siècles)* (Basse-Terre and Fort-de-France: Société d'histoire de la Guadeloupe and Société d'histoire de la Martinique, 1974), 439 n. 1; Sudipta Das, "Myths and Realities of French imperialism in India, 1763–1783" (PhD dissertation, Tulane University, 1989), v.

165. Leonard Robin Hodges, "Sovereign Spaces: The Compagnie des Indes and the Imperial State, 1699–1761" (PhD diss., King's College London, 2019), 10.

166. ANOM C13 A8 "Du 20 May 1724. Sur la Representation faite par Le nommé Antoine Beauvais mulatre Libre, pour Servir La Compagnie des Indes en qualité de matelot," f. 104v.

167. ANOM F3 206 "1736. Etat General de la Depense a faire au comptoir de L'Isle de Bourbon," f. 183.

168. ANOM F3 206 "1736. Etat General de la Depense a faire au comptoir de L'Isle de Bourbon," f. 181.

1. "We Shall Be One People"

1. "Relation de ce qui s'est passé en La Nouvelle France, en l'année 1633. Paul le Jeune," in Reuben Gold Thwaites, The Jesuit Relations and Allied Documents: Travels and Explorations of the Jesuit Missionaries in New France, 1610-1791. The Original French, Latin, and Italian Texts, with English Translations and Notes, 73 vols. (Burrows Brothers, Cleveland, 1896–1901) (henceforth Thwaites, JR) (1632–1633), 5: 210.

2. The "one people" rhetoric was especially (though not exclusively) used by the Haudenosaunee (Iroquois). See Alain Beaulieu, "'Ne faire qu'un seul peuple?' Iroquois et Français à l''âge héroïque' de la Nouvelle France (1600–1660)" (PhD diss., Université Laval, 1992). Peter Cook observes a similar rhetoric among the Algonquians. See Cook, "Vivre comme frères, 61. On the importance of kinship in the American Northeast, see Heidi Bohaker, "Nindoodemag: The Significance of Algonquian Kinship Networks in the Eastern Great Lakes Region, 1600–1701," *WMQ*, 3rd ser., 63, no. 1 (2006): 23–52.

3. See Peter Cook, "Onontio Gives Birth: How the French in Canada Became Fathers to Their Indigenous Allies, 1645–73," *Canadian Historical Review* 96, no. 2 (2015): 165–193, and "Vivre comme frères"; Marrero, *Detroit's Hidden Channels*, 10.

4. "Relation de ce qui s'est passé en la Nouvelle France, és années 1640. et 1641. Paul le Jeune," in JR (1641–1642), 21: 44. For other examples, see Beaulieu, "'Ne faire qu'un seul peuple?'" Of course, we will never know for sure if those quotations are faithful transcriptions: early modern European observers often distorted Indigenous people's speech to suit their own agendas and satisfy their readers' appetite for sensationalism. Yet, as several scholars of New France have noted, European observers paid particular attention to Native Americans' use of kinship metaphors because they were a key element of Native American diplomacy in the American Northeast and beyond. On this topic, see Cook, "Onontio Gives Birth," 169.

5. François Charpentier, *Relation de l'établissement de la compagnie Françoise, pour le commerce des Indes Orientales* (Paris: Sebastien Mabre-Cramoisy, 1665), 102.

6. "Lettre du ministre Colbert à Talon (5 avril 1667)" in Rapport de l'Archiviste de la Province de Québec pour 1930–1931 (Quebec: Rédempti Paradis, 1931), 72.

7. Charpentier, *Relation de l'établissement*, 100.

8. For a definition of the word "assimilation" in this historical context, see Sara Melzer, "L'Histoire oubliée de la colonisation française: Universaliser la 'Francité,'" *Dalhousie French Studies* 65 (2003): 36–44, here 37.

9. For example, see Aubert, "'The Blood of France,'" 450, 453; Belmessous, *Assimilation and Empire*; Cornelius Jaenen, *Friend and Foe: Aspects of French-Amerindian Cultural Contact in the Sixteenth and Seventeenth Centuries* (New York: Columbia University Press, 1976), 153.

10. Saliha Belmessous, "Assimilation and Racialism in Seventeenth and Eighteenth-Century French Colonial Policy," *The American Historical Review* 110, no. 2 (April 2005): 322–349, here 327 ("distinctive"); White, *Wild Frenchmen*, 7 ("reserved").

11. Alice Bairoch de Sainte-Marie, "Les colonies françaises et le droit: Une approche globale, 1600–1750," *Études canadiennes / Canadian Studies* 82 (2017): 87–119, here 111.

12. For example, see Charpentier, *Relation de l'établissement*, 100; Jules Sottas, *Histoire de la Compagnie Royale des Indes Orientales, 1664–1719* (Paris: Librairie Plon, 1905), 20, 37, 60–61; Éric Roulet, *La Compagnie des îles de l'Amérique* (Rennes: Presses universitaires de Rennes, 2017), 158–162, 168–170.

13. For a fresh perspective on those mission settlements, see Lozier, *Flesh Reborn*, espy. 6–9.

14. For work that considers the ways local actors shaped French laws in the eighteenth and nineteenth centuries, see Marquet, "Accommoder le droit"; Agmon, "Historical Gaps and Nonexistent Sources"; Houllemare, "La justice française à Pondichéry"; Parasher, "The Religion of the Tribunal"; Morrissey, *Empire by Collaboration*; Jérémy Boutier, *La question de l'assimilation politico-juridique de l'île de La Réunion à la métropole (1815–1906)* (PhD diss., Aix-Marseille University, 2015).

15. On this topic, see Belmessous, *Assimilation and Empire*, 5.

16. Saliha Belmessous, "Être français en Nouvelle-France: Identité française et identité coloniale aux dix-septième et dix-huitième siècles," *French Historical Studies* 27, no. 3 (2004): 507–540, here 512–513; Gilles Havard, "'Les forcer à devenir Cytoyens': État, Sauvages et citoyenneté en Nouvelle-France (XVIIe–XVIIIe siècle)," *Annales. Histoire, Sciences Sociales* 64, no. 5 (2009): 985–1018, here 990.

17. See Belmessous, *Assimilation and Empire*, 4–5.

18. On Christianization in the Spanish and Portuguese empires, see Herman Bennett, *Africans in Colonial Mexico: Absolutism, Christianity, and Afro-Creole Consciousness, 1570–1640* (Bloomington: Indiana University Press, 2005); Larissa Brewer-García, *Beyond Babel: Translations of Blackness in Colonial Peru and New Granada* (Cambridge: Cambridge University Press, 2020); Mariana Candido, *An African Slaving Port and the Atlantic World: Benguela and its Hinterland* (Cambridge: Cambridge University Press, 2013); Inga Clendinnen, *Ambivalent Conquests: Maya and Spaniard in Yucatán, 1517–1570* (Cambridge: Cambridge University Press, 1987); Roquinaldo Ferreira, *Cross-Cultural Exchange in the Atlantic World: Angola and Brazil during the Era of the Slave Trade* (Cambridge: Cambridge University Press, 2012); Sabine MacCormack, *Religion in the Andes: Vision and Imagination in Early Colonial Peru* (Princeton, NJ: Princeton University Press, 1991); Nancy van Deusen, *Embodying the Sacred: Women Mystics in Seventeenth-Century Lima* (Durham, NC: Duke University Press, 2017). In the British context, most seventeenth-century colonial charters made no mention of evangelization. However, the Charter of Virginia (1606) described the colonial project as "so noble a Work, which may [. . .] tend to the Glory of his Divine Majesty, in propagating of Christian Religion to such People, as yet live in Darkness and miserable Ignorance of the true knowledge and Worship of God." See Kenneth Mills and Allan Greer, "A Catholic Atlantic," in *The Atlantic in Global History*, ed. Jorge Canizares-Esguerra and Erik R. Seeman (Upper Saddle River, NJ: Pearson Prentice Hall, 2007), 3–19, here 7. On the British approach to evangelization, see also Patricia Seed, "Taking Possession and Reading Texts: Establishing the Authority of Overseas Empires," *WMQ* 49, no. 2 (1992): 183–209.

19. Felix Hinz, "The Process of Hispanization in Early New Spain: Transformation of Collective Identities during and after the Conquest of Mexico," *Revista de Indias* 68, no. 243 (2008): 9–35, here 21–22, and 22 n29.

20. See Boucher, *France and the American Tropics*, 23; Cohen, *The French Encounter with Africans*, 291. Translations include, for example, Joseph D'Acosta, *Histoire naturelle et moralle des Indes, tant Orientalles qu'Occidentalles* (Paris: Robert Regnault, 1598, 1600, 1606, and 1619); François Coreal, *Voyages aux Indes Occidentales, contenant ce qu'il y a vu de plus considérable, pendant son séjour de 1666 à 1697*, 2 vols. (Paris: A. Cailleau, 1722); Thomas Gage, *Nouvelle Relation contenant les Voyages de Thomas Gage, dans la Nouvelle-Espagne*, 2 vols. (Paris: Paul Marret, 1676).

21. Jean Baptiste Du Tertre, *Histoire générale des Antilles*, vol. 1, *Réedition exécutée d'après l'édition de 1667–1671* (Fort-de-France, Martinique: C.E.P., 1958), 458; Robert Dellon, *Relation d'un voyage des Indes Orientales. Dédié à Monseigneur l'Evêque de Meaux* (Paris: Claude Barbin, 1685), 1:93.

22. Sara Melzer, *Colonizer and Colonized: The Hidden Colonial Stories of Early Modern French Culture* (EBook, Philadelphia: University of Pennsylvania Press, 2012), 113–115, https://ebookcentral.proquest.com/lib/duke/detail.action?docID=3441950#.

23. Belmessous, *Assimilation and Empire*, 27; Melzer, "L'Histoire oubliée," 37.

24. Frances Gardiner Davenport, ed., *European Treaties Bearing on the History of the United States and Its Dependencies to 1648*, 4 vols. (Washington, DC: Carnegie Institution of Washington,

1917), 1:72–78. See also Belmessous, *Assimilation and Empire,* 6; John H. Elliott, *Empires of the Atlantic World: Britain and Spain in America, 1492–1830* (New Haven, CT: Yale University Press, 2007), 11, 67; Patricia Seed, "'Are These Not Also Men?': The Indians' Humanity and Capacity for Spanish Civilisation," *Journal of Latin American Studies* 25, no. 3 (1993), 629–652, here 635, 649; Tyler M. Schwaller, "The Use of Slaves in Early Christianity: Slaves as Subjects of Life and Thought" (PhD diss., Harvard University, 2017), 112.

25. See ANOM B1 "Provisions de gouverneur & Lieuteunant general en l'Isle Dauphine & autres Isles pour M de Mondevergue," f. 37v. One year later, the French writer François Charpentier declared that France had to conquer Indian Ocean territories in order to develop trade, promote Christianity, and because "barbarians need[ed] to experience [. . .] the kindness of [French] dominion, and be policed by its example." See Charpentier, *Relation de l'établissement,* 1 (quotation).

26. Elliott, *Empires of the Atlantic World,* 69, 186, 269; Seed, "'Are These Not Also Men?,'" 634–635, 644.

27. Andrea Daher, "L'impératif théologique de la colonisation française de Maragnan," in Daher, *Les singularités de la France équinoxiale,* 95–145.

28. Melzer, *Colonizer and Colonized,* 92.

29. Claude d'Abbeville, *Histoire de la mission des pères capucins en l'isle de Maragnan* [. . .] (Paris: François Huby, 1614), 369. Also cited in Melzer, *Colonizer and Colonized,* 92.

30. Melzer, *Colonizer and Colonized,* 91–92; Andrea Daher, "Les expériences coloniales françaises au Brésil," in *Colonisations,* ed. Singaravélou *et al.*, 576–577, here 576.

31. "Commission de M. le cardinal de Richelieu aux Sieur d'Enambuc et du Rossey," in Réal Ouellet, ed., *La colonisation des Antilles: Textes français du XVIIe siècle,* 2 vols. (Paris: Hermann, 2014), 1:106.

32. "Acte pour l'établissement de la Compagnie des Cent Associés pour le commerce du Canada [. . .] le 29 avril 1627," in *Édits Ordonnances Royaux, Déclatations et Arrêts du Conseil d'Etat du Roi Concernant le Canada,* 2 vols. (Quebec: E. R. Fréchette, 1854), 1:1–11, here 5.

33. "Acte pour l'établissement de la Compagnie des Cent Associés," 3.

34. ANOM C14 1 "Lettres-patentes du roi en forme de concession accordées aux sieurs de L'Isle-Marivault, de Royville et leurs associés, pour l'établissement des colonies dans la Terre ferme de l'Amérique. Copie (septembre 1651)," f. 19. Cited in Martijn Van Den Bel and Gérard Collomb, *La colonisation de la Guyane (1626–1696). Volume 1: 1626–1652* (Paris: Hermann Éditeurs, 2021), 216–219, here 217.

35. Data for Madagascar: Nivoelisoa Galibert, *À l'angle de la Grande Maison: Les Lazaristes de Madagascar: correspondance avec Vincent de Paul (1648–1661)* (Paris: Presses de l'Université Paris-Sorbonne, 2007), 98, 124, 163n55, 173, 239n12; Letter n°I, Vincent de Paul to Charles Nacquart, March 22, 1648, in *À l'angle de la Grande Maison,* ed. Galibert, 173; Letter n°VII, Charles Nacquart to Vincent de Paul, February 9, 1650, in *À l'angle de la Grande Maison,* ed. Galibert, 239 n12. Modeste Rakotondrabe counts forty-five missionaries, including forty-one Lazarists and four secular priests, in "Les premiers catéchismes en langue malgache: 1657, 1785, et 1841," *Recherches et documents* 918 (1990), 8. According to Philippe Chan-Mouie, from 1648 to 1674, twenty-five missionaries and twelve secular priests worked in Madagascar. See Chan-Mouie, "Première évangélisation des Lazaristes," 14. Data for New France: Leavelle, *The Catholic Calumet,* 32.

36. Letter n°VIII, Charles Nacquart to Vincent de Paul, February 16, 1650, in *À l'angle de la Grande Maison,* ed. Galibert, 253.

37. George F. G. Stanley, "'The Policy of 'Francisation' as Applied to the Indians during the Ancien Regime," *Revue d'histoire de l'Amérique française* 3, no. 3 (1949): 333–348, here 335–336.

38. Letter n°VII, Charles Nacquart to Vincent de Paul, February 9, 1650, in *À l'angle de la Grande Maison,* ed. Galibert, 236–237.

39. On the Ursulines in French North America, see the works of Emily Clark, Natalie Zemon Davis, Mary Dunn, and Anya Mali.

40. Letter n°XIX, Toussaint Bourdaise to Vincent de Paul, February 19, 1657, in *À l'angle de la Grande Maison,* ed. Galibert, 382.

41. Letter n°VI, Charles Nacquart to Vincent de Paul, February 5, 1650, in *À l'angle de la Grande Maison,* ed. Galibert, 222, 225; Letter n°XII, Jean-François Mousnier to Vincent de Paul, February 6, 1655, in *À l'angle de la Grande Maison,* ed. Galibert, 274.

42. For example, see Letter n°VI, Charles Nacquart to Vincent de Paul, February 5, 1650, in *À l'angle de la Grande Maison,* ed. Galibert, 222, 227–228; Letter n°XIX, Toussaint Bourdaise to Vincent de Paul, February 19, 1657, in *À l'angle de la Grande Maison,* ed. Galibert, 366; Letter n°XXI, Vincent de Paul to Nicolas Étienne, November 22, 1659, in *À l'angle de la Grande Maison,* ed. Galibert, 387. Most of these trips to the countryside lasted less than a week because the missionaries were needed in Fort-Dauphin for Sunday service and Christian holidays. Nacquart's correspondence contains multiple accounts of his evangelical expeditions to the closest mountains, plains, and valleys of Fanjahira (Fanshere), Ambolo (Amboule), and the wider Anosy region, southeast of Madagascar. See Galibert, *À l'angle de la Grande Maison.*

43. Letter n°VI, Charles Nacquart to Vincent de Paul, February 5, 1650, in *À l'angle de la Grande Maison,* ed. Galibert, 224.

44. Letter n°XII, Jean-François Mousnier to Vincent de Paul, February 6, 1655, in *À l'angle de la Grande Maison,* ed. Galibert, 271; see also Letter n°VI, Charles Nacquart to Vincent de Paul, February 5, 1650, in *À l'angle de la Grande Maison,* ed. Galibert, 218, and Letter n°XII, Jean-François Mousnier to Vincent de Paul, February 6, 1655, in *À l'angle de la Grande Maison,* ed. Galibert, 272.

45. "Clerc pour escrire," in *Dictionnaire de la langue de Madagascar,* by Étienne Flacourt (Paris: G. Josse, 1658), 32.

46. Letter n°XIII, Toussaint Bourdaise to Vincent de Paul, February 6, 1655, in *À l'angle de la Grande Maison,* ed. Galibert, 277–278; Letter n°XVI, Toussaint Bourdaise to Vincent de Paul, January 10, 1656, in *À l'angle de la Grande Maison,* ed. Galibert, 331; Letter n°XIX, Toussaint Bourdaise to Vincent de Paul, February 19, 1657, in *À l'angle de la Grande Maison,* ed. Galibert, 377. About the *oly,* see Étienne Flacourt, *Histoire de la grande isle de Madagascar* (Paris: Pierre Bien-Fait, 1661), 189–193.

47. Letter n°XIII, Toussaint Bourdaise to Vincent de Paul, February 6, 1655, in *À l'angle de la Grande Maison,* ed. Galibert, 278.

48. Letter n°XVI, Toussaint Bourdaise to Vincent de Paul, January 10, 1656, in *À l'angle de la Grande Maison,* ed. Galibert, 331.

49. Letter n°XVI, Toussaint Bourdaise to Vincent de Paul, January 10, 1656, in *À l'angle de la Grande Maison,* ed. Galibert, 329.

50. Letter n°XIX, Toussaint Bourdaise to Vincent de Paul, February 19, 1657, in *À l'angle de la Grande Maison,* ed. Galibert, 345.

51. Letter n°VII, Charles Nacquart to Vincent de Paul, February 9, 1650, in *À l'angle de la Grande Maison,* ed. Galibert, 235; Letter n°VIII, Charles Nacquart to Vincent de Paul, February 16, 1650, in *À l'angle de la Grande Maison,* ed. Galibert, 249.

52. Letter n°XII, Jean-François Mousnier to Vincent de Paul, February 6, 1655, in *À l'angle de la Grande Maison,* ed. Galibert, 272; Letter n°XIX, Toussaint Bourdaise to Vincent de Paul, February 19, 1657, in *À l'angle de la Grande Maison,* ed. Galibert, 382–383, 346.

53. Sue Peabody, "'A Nation Born to Slavery': Missionaries and Racial Discourse in Seventeenth-Century French Antilles," *Journal of Social History* 38, no. 1 (2004): 113–126, here 117–118.

54. Samuel de Champlain, *Voyages et découvertes faites en la nouvelle France, depuis l'année 1615 jusques à la fin de l'année 1618* (Paris: Claude Collet, 1619), "Epistre au roy."

55. Demanet spent time in Senegambia in the 1760s. See Abbé Demanet, *Nouvelle Histoire de l'Afrique Françoise,* 2 vols. (Paris: Veuve Duchesne, 1767), 2:194.

56. Queen Isabel made this decision in 1501, and it was inscribed in legislation in 1542. See Seed, "'Are These Not Also Men?,'" 649 (quotation), 651.

57. Bradley Folsom, "Spanish La Junta de los Rios: The Institutional Hispanicization of an Indian Community along New Spain's Northern Frontier, 1535–1821" (MA thesis, University of North Texas, 2008), 2; David J. Weber, *The Spanish Frontier in North America* (EBook, New Haven, CT: Yale University Press, 2009), 81, https://ebookcentral.proquest.com/lib/duke/reader.action?docID=3420585&c=UERG&ppg=1.

58. Belmessous, "Assimilation and Racialism," 331.

59. See Philip Boucher, *France and the American Tropics*, 132; Jean-Pierre Sainton, *Couleur et société en contexte post-esclavagiste: La Guadeloupe à la fin du XIXe siècle* (Pointe-à-Pitre, Guadeloupe: Jasor, 2009), 246.

60. "Acte pour l'établissement de la Compagnie des Cent Associés," 10.

61. "Contrat du rétablissement de la Compagnie des îles de l'Amérique, avec les articles accordés par Sa Majesté aux seigneurs associés," in *La colonisation des Antilles,* Ouellet ed., 1:121–122.

62. "Édit du Roi en faveur de la compagnie des îles de l'Amérique," in Ouellet ed., *La colonisation des Antilles,* Ouellet ed., 1:203.

63. Melzer, *Colonizer and Colonized,* 107.

64. Havard, "'Les forcer à devenir Cytoyen,'" 989.

65. See Perry Anderson, *Lineages of the Absolutist State* (London: New Left Books, 1975).

66. For publications considering the French policy of "civilization" (or "Frenchification") in North America, see Belmessous, "Assimilation and Racialism" and "Être français en Nouvelle-France"; Havard, "'Les forcer à devenir Cytoyens'"; Cornelius Jaenen, "The Frenchification and Evangelization of the Amerindians in Seventeenth-Century New France," *Canadian Catholic Historical Association, Study Sessions* 35 (1968): 57–71, and *Friend and Foe*; Sara Melzer, "The Underside of France's Civilizing Mission: Assimilationist Politics in 'New France,'" *Biblio* 17 (2001): 151–164, and "L'Histoire oubliée"; White, *Wild Frenchmen.*

67. For example, see "Civiliser," in *Dictionnaire de l'Académie française* (Paris: Jean Baptiste Coignard, 1694).

68. "Civil," in *Dictionnaire de l'Académie française* and *Dictionnaire de l'Académie française,* 5th ed. (Paris: J. J. Smits, 1798). On the "civilizing process" in Europe itself, see Norbert Elias, *The Civilizing Process: The History of Manners* (New York: Urizen Books, 1978), first published in German in 1939.

69. White, *Wild Frenchmen,* 6. The Company of the East Indies harbored the same linguistic ambitions in the Indian Ocean. On October 26, 1664, it declared its intention "to make [Madagascar] entirely French, in terms of customs & *language*." Charpentier, *Relation de l'établissement*, 102.

70. For a detailed study of this episode, see Beatriz Perrone-Moisés, "Performed Alliances and Performative Identities: Tupinamba in the Kingdom of France," in *Performing Indigeneity: Global Histories and Contemporary Experiences*, ed. Laura R. Graham and H. Glenn Penny (Lincoln: University of Nebraska Press, 2014), 110–135.

71. "Spain: October 1550," in *Calendar of State Papers, Spain, 1550–1552*, vol. 10, ed. Royall Tyler (London: His Majesty's Stationery Office, 1914), 182. Also cited in Melzer, *Colonizer and Colonized*, 200.

72. Melzer, *Colonizer and Colonized*, 92.

73. See Belmessous, *Assimilation and Empire*, 38; Gilles Havard, "Francité et citoyenneté en contexte colonial, La politique d'assimilation des Amérindiens en Nouvelle France," in *Français? La nation en débat entre colonies et métropole (XVIe–XIXe siècle)*, ed. Cécile Vidal (Paris: éditions de l'école des Hautes études en Sciences Sociales, 2014), 105–123, here 108–110.

74. Spear, *Race, Sex, and Social Order*, 9.

75. Larson, "Colonies Lost," 363; ANOM C5 A1 "Duc de Mazarin [. . .] 1663 Madagascar," 1.

76. On the Iberian project of civilization, see Ferreira, *Cross-Cultural Exchange in the Atlantic World*; Hinz, "The Process of Hispanization"; John Leddy Phelan, *The Hispanization of the Philippines: Spanish Aims and Filipino Responses, 1565–1700* (Madison: University of Wisconsin Press, 2010).

77. Hinz, "The Process of Hispanization," 18–19.

78. Cited in Belmessous, *Assimilation and Empire*, 22.

79. Letter n°VIII, Charles Nacquart to Vincent de Paul, February 16, 1650, in *À l'angle de la Grande Maison*, ed. Galibert, 249.

80. The early modern French colonial expansion incited French observers to focus on the question of what it actually meant to be French. On this subject, see Belmessous, "Assimilation and Racialism," 330, and "Être français en Nouvelle-France"; Vidal, "Francité et situation coloniale." On the gradual emergence of a French national consciousness, see David Bell, "Recent Works on Early Modern French National Identity," *Journal of Modern History* 68, no. 1 (1996): 84–113.

81. On this topic, see also White, *Wild Frenchmen*, 6.

82. Belmessous, *Assimilation and Empire*, 31–32.

83. Hinz, "The Process of Hispanization," 22; Weber, *The Spanish Frontier in North America*, 76–77.

84. *Mercure François*, 2nd ed. (Paris: Estienne Richer, 1617), 3:171. Also cited in Melzer, *Colonizer and Colonized*, 101.

85. "Relation de ce qui s'est passé dans le Pays des Hurons en l'annee 1636," Thwaites, *JR* (1636), 10:26.

86. Flacourt, *Histoire de la grande isle*, 1–2.

87. Charpentier, *Relation de l'établissement*, 76–77.

88. "Art," in *Dictionnaire de l'Académie française* (Paris: Jean-Baptiste Coignard, 1694). See also *Dictionnaire de l'Académie française*, 5th edition (Paris: J. J. Smits, 1798).

89. His hope was echoed about twenty years later in the words of the intendant of New France, Jacques de Meulles, when he expressed his anticipation that Native American girls would learn "spin[ning]," and "knit[ting]" techniques so they could "live like villagers in France." ANOM C11 A6 "DeMeulles 12th November 1682," cited in Sylvia Van Kirk, "From 'Marrying-In' to 'Marrying-Out': Changing Patterns of Aboriginal/Non-Aboriginal Marriage in Colonial Canada," *Frontiers: A Journal of Women Studies* 23, no. 3 (2002): 1–11, here 3.

90. Melzer, "L'Histoire oubliée," 39. For a study of Frenchification in North America that centers on clothing habits, see White, *Wild Frenchmen*.

91. D'Abbeville, *Histoire de la mission*, 369. Also cited in Melzer, *Colonizer and Colonized*, 92.

92. For example, see "Relation de ce qui s'est passé en la Nouvelle France, en l'année 1637," Thwaites, *JR* (1637), 12:15, 46, 62, 114; "Relation de ce qui s'est passé en la Nouvelle France, és années 1643 & 1644," Thwaites, *JR* (1642–1644), 25:230; "Relation de ce qui s'est passé en la

Nouvelle France, en l'année 1639," Thwaites, *JR* (1638–1639), 15:226. See also Melzer, "L'Histoire oubliée," 39.

93. On this topic, see Letter n°XV, Toussaint Bourdaise to Vincent de Paul, February 8, 1655, in *À l'angle de la Grande Maison,* ed. Galibert, 304.

94. ANOM C5 A1 "Extrait du Reglement Du 17e Novembre 1665," p. 51.

95. Letter n°VII, Charles Nacquart to Vincent de Paul, February 9, 1650, in *À l'angle de la Grande Maison,* ed. Galibert, 236.

96. Letter n°XVI, Toussaint Bourdaise to Vincent de Paul, January 10, 1656, in *À l'angle de la Grande Maison,* ed. Galibert, 329.

97. Letter n°XIII, Toussaint Bourdaise to Vincent de Paul, February 6, 1655, in *À l'angle de la Grande Maison,* ed. Galibert, 277–278.

98. Martinez, *Genealogical Fictions,* 256–257; Schwaller, "Defining Difference in Early New Spain," 117, 118n24.

99. Schwaller, "Defining Difference in Early New Spain," 116–117 (quotation), 118n24.

100. Chaturvedula, "Preserving Purity."

101. Ulbe Bosma and Remco Raben, *Being "Dutch" in the Indies: A History of Creolisation and Empire, 1500–1920,* trans. Wendie Shaffer (Athens: Ohio University Press, 2008), 27; Van Meersbergen, *Ethnography and Encounter,* 222, 229.

102. Van Meersbergen, *Ethnography and Encounter,* 224.

103. Melzer, *Colonizer and Colonized,* 91–102.

104. See Jennifer Heuer, "The One-Drop Rule in Reverse? Interracial Marriages in Napoleonic and Restoration France," *Law and History Review* 27, no. 3 (2009): 515–548, here 526; Nathan Marvin, "The 'Ambroise Affair': White Women, Black Men, and the Limits of Métissage in Revolution-Era Réunion," *French History* 32, no. 4 (2018): 493–510.

105. About these women, see ANOM C5 A1 "Madagascar de la Bretesche Major de l'Ile Dauphine 22 Aoust 1674," ff. 1–4, and Marie-Ange Payet, "Les femmes dans le marronnage à l'île Bourbon de 1662 à 1848" (PhD diss., City University of New York, 2009), 21–22.

106. Joan-Lluis Palos and Magdalena S. Sanchez eds., *Early Modern Dynastic Marriages and Cultural Transfer* (London and New York: Routledge, 2016). On the origins and decline of this practice in Europe, see John Watkins, "Peacemaking, Interdynastic Marriage, and the Rise of the French Novel," *Common Knowledge* 22, no. 2 (2016): 256–276.

107. For example, see Matthew Dennis, *Cultivating a Landscape of Peace: Iroquois-European Encounters in Seventeenth-Century America* (Ithaca, NY and London: Cornell University Press, 1993), 220.

108. Devrim Karahasan, "Métissage in New France: Frenchification, Mixed Marriages and Métis as Shaped by Social and Political Agents and Institutions 1508–1886" (PhD diss., European University Institute, 2006), 100–141.

109. For example, see Carpeau du Saussay, *Voyage de Madagascar, connu aussi sous le nom de l'isle de St Laurent* (Paris: Jean-Luc Nyon, 1722), 256; Galibert, *À l'angle de la Grande Maison,* 158. About *vodin'omby* (local) marriages *à la mode du pays*, see Larson, "Play and Possession," 701.

110. Flacourt, *Histoire de la grande isle,* 446.

111. Larson, "Play and Possession," 698.

112. Dennis, *Cultivating a Landscape of Peace,* 8–9, 234–235.

113. Solofo Randrianja and Stephen Ellis, *Madagascar: A Short History* (Chicago: University of Chicago Press, 2009), 5, 13, 24, 28, 36, 40, 45, 61.

114. Larson, "Play and Possession," 703; Randrianja and Ellis, *Madagascar,* 7, 68–69, 77–78, 83–84.

115. Paul Ottino, "La hiérarchie sociale et l'alliance dans le royaume de Matacassi des XVI et XVIIe siècles," *Asemi* 4, no. 4 (1973): 53–89, here 77.

116. About Dian Manor, see Tricoire, "Une histoire franco-malgache," 246n32.

117. On food shortages and Pronis's imprisonment, see Tricoire, "Une histoire franco-malgache," 247. See also Randrianja and Ellis, *Madagascar,* 86.

118. Flacourt, *Histoire de la grande isle,* 446; Letter n°XIX, Toussaint Bourdaise to Vincent de Paul, February 19, 1657, in *À l'angle de la Grande Maison,* ed. Galibert, 365, 371, 377–378; Larson, "Play and Possession," 698, 701. On traded goods, see Larson, "Colonies Lost," 360; Payet, "Les femmes dans le marronnage," 56.

119. Flacourt, *Histoire de la grande isle,* 457.

120. "De par le Roy. Status, Ordonnances et reglemens," Charpentier, *Relation de l'établissement,* article IV, pp. 78–79; Flacourt, *Histoire de la grande isle,* 85.

121. Souchu de Rennefort, *Histoire des Indes Orientales* (Paris: Arnoul Seneuze and Daniel Hortemels, 1688), 1:77; Payet, "Les femmes dans le marronnage," 21.

122. By the end of the seventeenth century, only 2,000 people lived in the four or five mission communities of the Saint Lawrence River valley studied by Jean-François Lozier. See Lozier, *Flesh Reborn,* 6. On indigenized Christianities in North America, see the works of Allan Greer, Tracy Leavelle, and Lozier. On religious conversion in the Illinois Country, see White, *Wild Frenchmen.*

123. The Jesuits of New France also resolved to abandon the "civilizing" (or "Frenchification") program as a result of ongoing warfare with the English and their Native American allies, which had a very disruptive effect on France's religious missions. They also engaged in cultural accommodation in their reductions. See Leavelle, *The Catholic Calumet,* 33–34; Lozier, *Flesh Reborn,* 6.

124. Havard, "'Les Forcer à devenir Cytoyens,'" 995; Stanley, "'The Policy of 'Francisation,'" 339–343.

125. They did so decades before the appearance of the Frenchified group of Illinois female converts studied by Sophie White who lived in French villages "composed entirely of farmers" in the Illinois Country. White, *Wild Frenchmen,* 30.

126. Letter n°VI, Charles Nacquart to Vincent de Paul, February 5, 1650, in *À l'angle de la Grande Maison,* ed. Galibert, 222; Letter n°VII, Charles Nacquart to Vincent de Paul, February 9, 1650, in *À l'angle de la Grande Maison,* ed. Galibert, 242.

127. Galibert, *À l'angle de la Grande Maison,* 113.

128. Letter n°VI, Charles Nacquart to Vincent de Paul, February 5, 1650, in À *l'angle de la Grande Maison,* ed. Galibert, 232.

129. Letter n°XIII, Toussaint Bourdaise to Vincent de Paul, February 6, 1655, in *À l'angle de la Grande Maison,* ed. Galibert, 277; Letter n°XVI, Toussaint Bourdaise to Vincent de Paul, January 10, 1656, in *À l'angle de la Grande Maison,* ed. Galibert, 322; Letter n°XIX, Toussaint Bourdaise to Vincent de Paul, February 19, 1657, in *À l'angle de la Grande Maison,* ed. Galibert, 378 (quotation).

130. Monsieur Etienne to Monsieur Almeras, January 15, 1664, in Marc Thieffry, ed., "La mission Lazariste à Madagascar, de 1648 à 1674," (2013), 386 (unpublished manuscript).

131. Agmon has already noted how French officials, especially the Jesuits, led a fierce evangelization campaign beginning in the early eighteenth century and launched multiple assaults against Hindu practices in Pondicherry. See Agmon, *A Colonial Affair.* A possible reason for this brutal approach to evangelization might have been the limited success of the religious missions in Madagascar and New France.

132. Glenn Joseph Ames, "Colbert's Indian Ocean Strategy of 1664–1674: A Reappraisal," *French Historical Studies* 16, no. 3 (1990): 536–559, here 540.

133. Of the 5.4 million livres invested in the Company of the East Indies by 1667, 2 million came from the French crown, and the rest came from private investors. See Ames, "Colbert's Indian Ocean Strategy," 540.

134. ANOM C5 A1 "Duc de Mazarin [. . .] 1663 Madagascar," f. 1.

135. "Déclarations du Roy portant établissement d'une compagnie pour le commerce des Indes Orientales [. . .] premier Septembre 1664," article XXX, in Élie Dernis, *Recueil ou collection des titres, édits, déclarations, arrêts, règlements et autres pièces concernant la Compagnie des Indes orientales établie au mois d'août 1664*, 4 vols. (Paris: Antoine Boudet, 1755), 1:61. See also ANOM C2 3 "Articles et conditions sur lesquelles les Marchands Negotians du Royaume Supplient tres-humblement le Roy de leur accorder sa Declaration [. . .] pour l'établissement d'une Compagnie pour le commerce des Indes Orientales, à Paris [. . .] 26 Mai 1664," article XXX, f. 30.

136. Charpentier, *Relation de l'établissement*, "Epitre," (quotation). In 1733, a regulation for the Company of the Indies ordered the establishment of two parishes and a church in Chandernagore for French and Indian residents. See ANOM C2 290 bis "11 février 1733. Concernant le culte catholique dans Les Colonies de l'Inde," articles 2 and 4, pp. 16–18.

137. On the history of the Christianization of Isle Bourbon, see Barassin, *Naissance d'une chrétienté*.

138. Hodges, "Sovereign Spaces"; Agmon, *A Colonial Affair*.

139. "Édit du Roi pour l'établissement de la Compagnie des Indes occidentales," in Ouellet ed., *La colonisation des Antilles*, 357–358.

140. ANOM C6 1 "17 Janvier 1688, De Par le Roy Et Messieurs de la Companie Royale du Senegal," article 2, n.p.; ANOM C6 6 "Du 14 e Mars 1721. Reglements de La Compagnie Royalle [*sic*] du Senegal Et Coste d'affrique [*sic*]," article 3, p. 2.

141. "Édit du Roi pour l'établissement de la Compagnie des Indes occidentales," in *La Colonisation des Antilles*, ed. Ouellet, 1:366. Later, in 1728, the Superior Council of Louisiana went back on that decision by stating that Catholic marriage "takes the place of the nationality" for Native American women. Cited in Kleber, "Gendered Societies," 216.

142. "Déclarations du Roy portant établissement d'une compagnie pour le commerce des Indes Orientales [. . .] premier Septembre 1664," article XXXVIII, in Dernis, *Recueil ou collection des titres, édits, déclarations, arrêts, règlements*, 1: 63. See also ANOM C2 3 "Articles et conditions sur lesquelles les Marchands Négociants du Royaume Supplient tres-humblement le Roy de leur accorder sa Declaration, pour l'établissement d'une Compagnie pour le commerce des Indes Orientales, à Paris, 26 Mai 1664," article XXXVIII, f. 31v.

143. *Code Noir*, article II, in *Recueil d'Edits, Declarations et Arrests De Sa Majesté, Concernant l'Administration de la Justice & de la Police des Colonies Françaises de l'Amérique, & les Engagés*, 2 vols. (Paris: Libraires Associez, 1744–1745), 2:82–83. This provision was reiterated in 1724 in the *Code Noir* of Louisiana. See *Recueil d'Edits*, 2:137.

144. *Code Noir*, article LVII, in *Recueil d'Edits*, 2:99.

145. Charpentier, *Relation de l'établissement*, 102.

146. ANOM C2 3 "Ordonnances et règlements que la Compagnie établie pour le commerce des Indes Orientales," article IV, f. 71v.

147. ANOM C6 A1 "Extrait du Règlement de la Compagnie en France pour le Commerce de l'Isle St Laurent dite Madagascar du 27 Octobre 1664," pp. 18–19 (quotations).

148. ANOM C6 A1 "3 Mars 1670 Madagascar Etat de Lisle Dauphine lors du départ du navire le St Denis," f. 11v.

149. ANOM C2 3 "Ordonnances et règlements que la Compagnie établie pour le commerce des Indes Orientales," article IV, ff. 71–71v.

150. ANOM B1 "Instruction que le roi a donnée au sieur de La Haye, lieutenant général des armées, partant commander les troupes dans l'isle Dauphine et aux Indes orientales, avec une escadre de six vaisseaux (5 décembre 1669)," ff. 178v (quotation)–179.

151. Hodges, "Configuring Colonial Families in Chandernagore."

152. Adrian Carton, *Mixed-Race and Modernity in Colonial India: Changing Concepts of Hybridity Across Empires* (EBook, London and New York: Routledge, 2012), 71–72, https://play.google.com/books/reader?id=qbK8OJJc3ioC&pg=GBS.PP1.

153. The presence of these women in India dated back to the Portuguese occupation from the fifteenth century. On this topic, see Carton, *Mixed-Race and Modernity*, 26–27, 81–82, 90; Hodges, "Configuring Colonial Families."

154. In Brazilian cities, and in late eighteenth-century Portuguese Luanda, Luso-African women were often classified as "whites" in censuses. See Joseph Calder Miller, *Way of Death: Merchant Capitalism and the Angolan Slave Trade, 1730–1830* (EBook, Madison: University of Wisconsin Press, 1988), 292, https://www-fulcrum-org.proxy.lib.duke.edu/epubs/p2676z18p?locale=en#page=1; Mariana P. Candido, "Strategies for Social Mobility: Liaisons between Foreign Men and Slave Women in Benguela, ca. 1770–1850," in *Sex, Power and Slavery*, ed. Gwyn Campbell and Elizabeth Elbourne (EBook, Athens: Ohio University Press, 2014), 272–288, here 274, https://ebookcentral.proquest.com/lib/duke/detail.action?docID=1869112#.

155. See G. V. Scammell, "Indigenous Assistance in the Establishment of Portuguese Power in the Indian Ocean," in *Indo-Portuguese History: Sources and Problems*, ed. John Correia-Afonso (Bombay: Oxford University Press, 1981), 74–78.

156. Cited in Honorius Provost, "Mariages entre Canadiens et sauvages," *Bulletin de Recherches historiques* 54 (1948): 46–57, here 49. On revived attempts to promote intermarriage in New France, see also Aubert, "'The Blood of France,'" 452–460; Havard, *Empire et métissages*, 647.

157. He explicitly stressed the need to seed Christianity in the colony. Cited in Spear, *Race, Sex, and Social Order*, 36.

158. Cited in Spear, *Race, Sex, and Social Order*, 36.

2. *Shifting Strategies*

1. Souchu de Rennefort, *Relation du premier voyage de la Compagnie des Indes Orientales en l'Isle de Madagascar ou Dauphine* (Paris: Pierre Aubüin, 1668), 112 (quotation), 109; Carpeau du Saussay, *Voyage de Madagascar, connu aussi sous le nom de l'isle de St Laurent* (Paris: Jean-Luc Nyon, 1722), 223.

2. See Souchu de Rennefort, *Relation du premier voyage*, 102–131, and *Mémoire pour servir à l'histoire des Indes orientales* (Paris: Arnoul Seneuze and Daniel Horthemels, 1688), 61–70; M. R. De La Blanchère, *Un épisode d'histoire coloniale, le Vacher de la Case à Madagascar: discours prononcé dans la séance solennelle de rentrée des écoles d'enseignement supérieur de l'Académie d'Alger* (Alger, Algeria: Adolphe Jourdan, Libraire-Éditeur, 1884), 4–8, 10–14. For more stories regarding La Case, see also M. de Richemond, "Vacher de La Case, prince d'Amboule," *Bulletin de la Société de Géographie de Rochefort* 22 (1900): 137–144; E. -F. Gautier and H. Froidevaux, *Un manuscrit arabico-malgache sur les campagnes de la Case dans l'Imoro de 1659 à 1663* (Paris: Imprimerie Nationale, 1907).

3. Burbank and Cooper, *Empires in World History*, 16.

4. For example, according to Vidal and Havard, the French in North America embraced a flexible mode of colonization grounded in the formation of alliances with Native American populations. See Havard and Vidal, *Histoire de l'Amérique française*. See also Morrissey, *Empire by Collaboration*. For more information about this historiography, see White, *Wild Frenchmen*, 27–28. As already demonstrated by Andrea Daher and Olive Patricia Dickason, this pattern of alliance formation can even be traced back to French-Tupi relationships in sixteenth-century Brazil, which were rooted in the trade of brazilwood (pau-brazil) and other exotic goods. See Daher, "L'impératif théologique," 128, 132, 136; Olive Patricia Dickason, "The Brazilian Connection. A Look at the Origin of French Techniques for Trading with Amerindians," *Outre-Mers. Revue d'histoire* 264–265 (1984): 129–146.

5. About French cultural adaptation to local practices in North America, see Havard, *Empire et métissages*; Leavelle, *The Catholic Calumet*; Lozier, *Flesh Reborn*; McDonnell, *Masters of Empire*; White, *The Middle Ground*; White, *Wild Frenchmen*.

6. About the *fahensa* and its origins, see Étienne de Flacourt, *Histoire de la grande isle Madagascar* (Paris: Nicolas Oudot, 1661), 315. 332. This tribute is only mentioned in passing in a footnote to an article by the late Pier Larson. See Larson, "Colonies Lost," 362n79.

7. White, *The Middle Ground*. For example, see DuVal, *The Native Ground*; Ellis, *The Great Power of Small Nations*; McDonnell, *Masters of Empire*; Morrissey, *Empire by Collaboration*; Witgen, *An Infinity of Nations*.

8. White's framework has been applied to other European positions in places as far away as the Indian Ocean. For a publication applying the notion of Middle Ground to South Asia, see Carton, *Mixed-Race and Modernity*, 12.

9. DuVal, *The Native Ground*, 5.

10. For example, see Guillaume Aubert, "'Nègres ou mulâtres nous sommes tous français'"; Clark, Vidal, and Thioub, *New Orleans, Louisiana, and Saint-Louis*, "Part 1: Negotiating Slavery and Freedom," 33–188; Johnson, *Wicked Flesh*.

11. Quoted from Tricoire, "Une histoire franco-malgache," 238 ("players"), 258 ("non-colonial"), and Sobocinski, "Some God, Little Glory, No Gold," iii ("failed").

12. Quoted from Larson, "Play and Possession," 688, and "Colonies Lost," 359.

13. Larson, "Colonies Lost," 360.

14. Dellon, *Relation d'un voyage des Indes orientales*, 1:33; Du Bois, *Les voyages*, 109; Larson, "Colonies Lost," 360–361.

15. Larson, "Colonies Lost," 360n67.

16. François Cauche, *Relations véritables et curieuses de l'Isle de Madagascar et du Bréesil* (Paris: Augustin Courbe, 1651), 24–25.

17. Cauche, *Relations véritables et curieuses*, 25–26.

18. Cauche, *Relations véritables et curieuses*, 62–63.

19. Cauche, *Relations véritables et curieuses*, 26, 28; Tricoire, "Une histoire franco-malgache," 245–246.

20. Flacourt, *Histoire de la grande isle* (2007), 266; Tricoire, "Une histoire franco-malgache," 243.

21. Flacourt, *Histoire de la grande isle* (2007), 311, 320–321.

22. Flacourt, *Histoire de la grande isle* (2007), 311.

23. Flacourt, *Histoire de la grande isle* (2007), 311.

24. Garnier was Dian Tallach's own son-in-law. See Flacourt, *Histoire de la grande isle* (2007), 320–321.

25. Flacourt, *Histoire de la grande isle*, 329.

26. Flacourt, *Histoire de la grande isle*, 365.

27. Flacourt, *Histoire de la grande isle*, 372.

28. Larson, "Play and Possession," 692.

29. Pierre Coste ed., *Saint Vincent de Paul, Correspondance, entretiens, documents, I. Correspondance, tome III (août 1646–mars 1650)* (Paris: J. Gabalda éditeur, 1921), 583.

30. Larson, "Play and Possession," 698.

31. For more information about those unions, see Chapter 3.

32. Cauche, *Relations véritables et curieuses*, 90.

33. Larson, "Colonies Lost," 362.

34. Du Bois, *Les voyages*, 85.

35. Du Bois, *Les voyages*, 120.

36. Du Bois, *Les voyages*, 86–87.

37. Du Bois, *Les voyages*, 119; Larson, "Colonies Lost," 353–354, 356n47.

38. Randrianja and Ellis, *Madagascar*, 86; Tricoire, "Une histoire franco-malgache," 252.

39. Carpeau du Saussay, *Voyage de Madagascar*, 258–264; Flacourt, *Histoire de la grande isle*, 54.

40. Carpeau du Saussay, *Voyage de Madagascar*, 258–263; Flacourt, *Histoire de la grande isle* (2007), 128.

41. Flacourt, *Histoire de la grande isle* (2007), 59, 84–85.

42. Cauche, *Relations véritables et curieuses*, 69–73.

43. Tricoire, "Une histoire franco-malgache," 246.

44. For example, see Du Bois, *Les voyages*; Flacourt, *Histoire de la grande isle* (2007); Carpeau du Saussay, *Voyage de Madagascar*; Souchu de Rennefort, *Relation du premier voyage*.

45. Tricoire stresses this problem. See "Une histoire franco-malgache," 248n44.

46. See Larson, "Colonies Lost," 348, 359. For evidence of local people's responses to European weapons, see Flacourt, *Histoire de la grande isle* (2007), 325.

47. Larson, "Play and Possession," 686, 688–689.

48. Flacourt, *Histoire de la grande isle* (2007), 278.

49. Flacourt, *Histoire de la grande isle* (2007), 266–267, 278–279; Tricoire, "Une histoire franco-malgache," 248.

50. Flacourt, *Histoire de la grande isle* (2007), 325, 337–348.

51. Flacourt, *Histoire de la grande isle* (2007), 327; Larson, "Colonies Lost," 359.

52. About the *Lohavohits*, see Somda, "Et le réel serait passé," 25.

53. Flacourt, *Histoire de la grande isle* (2007), 337 (quotation)–338.

54. Flacourt, *Histoire de la grande isle* (2007), 337; Souchu de Rennefort, *Histoire des Indes Orientales*, ed. Dominique Huet (Sainte-Clotilde, France: ARS Terres Créoles, 1988), 126.

55. Flacourt, *Histoire de la grande isle*, 340.

56. Flacourt, *Histoire de la grande isle*, 342.

57. Flacourt, *Histoire de la grande isle* (2007), 339 (quotation); Souchu de Rennefort, *Relation du premier voyage*, 83, 109. On the origins of Dian Manangue, see Tricoire, "Une histoire franco-malgache," 248n42.

58. Souchu de Rennefort, *Relation du premier voyage*, 110.

59. Tricoire, "Une histoire franco-malgache," 250.

60. Souchu de Rennefort, *Histoire des Indes Orientales*, 49–50.

61. One of those Greats was Dian Ramael—Dian Rassisate's own enemy. Souchu de Rennefort, *Relation du premier voyage*, 78–79, 104–105.

62. Quoted from Souchu de Rennefort, *Histoire des Indes Orientales* (1688), 51.

63. Carpeau du Saussay, *Voyage de Madagascar*, 64–66; Souchu de Rennefort, *Relation du premier voyage*, 235–237.

64. Du Bois, *Les voyages,* 142–146.

65. Carpeau du Saussay, *Voyage de Madagascar,* 64–65; Du Bois, *Les voyages*, 145.

66. Larson, "Play and Possession," 701.

67. Carpeau du Saussay, *Voyage de Madagascar,* 65–66; Larson, "Play and Possession," 691.

68. Carpeau du Saussay, *Voyage de Madagascar,* 73.

69. Larson, "Play and Possession," 691.

70. Du Bois, *Les voyages*, 141–142

71. Du Bois, *Les voyages,* 139, 155; Flacourt, *Histoire de la grande isle,* 111–113 (quotation).

72. Du Bois, *Les voyages,* 154; Flacourt, *Histoire de la grande isle,* 111.

73. Souchu de Rennefort, *Relation du premier voyage,* 81, 83.

74. Souchu de Rennefort, *Relation du premier voyage,* 109.

75. Souchu de Rennefort, *Relation du premier voyage,* 82, 109, 117, 120; Tricoire, "Une histoire franco-malgache," 249.

76. Souchu de Rennefort, *Relation du premier voyage,* 84.

77. Souchu de Rennefort, *Relation du premier voyage,* 88–89.

78. Carpeau du Saussay, *Voyage de Madagascar,* 191.

79. Carpeau du Saussay, *Voyage de Madagascar,* 193–194.

80. Carpeau du Saussay, *Voyage de Madagascar,* 237.

81. Souchu de Rennefort, *Histoire des Indes Orientales* (Paris: Arnoul Seneuze and Daniel Hortemels, 1688), 389.

82. Souchu de Rennefort, *Histoire des Indes Orientales,* 58; Tricoire, "Une histoire franco-malgache," 251.

83. Larson, "Colonies Lost," 363.

84. On the anti-colonial revolt led by Dian Manangue, see Jean Barassin, *Naissance d'une Chrétienté. Bourbon des origines jusqu'en 1714* (Saint-Denis and Paris: Cazal and Maison Provinciale, 1953), 115–116 and "L'esclavage à Bourbon avant l'application du Code Noir de 1723," *Recueil de documents et travaux inédits pour servir l'histoire de la Réunion* 2 (1957):, 11–57, here 12; Jean-Claude Félix Fontaine, *Deux siècles et demi de l'histoire d'une famille réunionnaise, 1665–1915,* vol. 1, *Jacques et Gilles Fontaine: Les aventuriers, 1664–1729* (Paris: L'Harmattan, 2001), 107; Lougnon, *Sous le signe de la tortue*, 214.

85. Larson, "Colonies Lost," 347, 362–363. Larson deconstructs the assumption by historian Isidore Guët that the massacre of Fort-Dauphin was initiated by a group of jealous Malagasy women who sought revenge after their French partners had decided to break their alliance with them to marry the French women who had arrived at Fort-Dauphin. M. I. Guët, *Les origines de l'île Bourbon* (Paris: Librairie Militaire de L. Baudon et Ce, 1885), 107, 113–117.

86. Michel Jajolet de La Courbe, *Premier voyage du Sieur de la Courbe fait à la coste d'Afrique en 1685*, ed. P. Cultru (Paris, Édouard Champion and Émile Larose, 1913), 25.

87. Quoted from Randy Sparks, *Where the Negroes Are Masters: An African Port in the Era of the Slave Trade* (EBook, Cambridge, MA: Harvard University Press, 2014), 4, https://ebookcentral.proquest.com/lib/duke/detail.action?docID=3301371. See also, for example, Mariana Candido, *An African Slaving Port and the Atlantic World: Benguela and its Hinterland* (New York: Cambridge University Press, 2013); Robin Law, *The Oyo Empire, c. 1600–c. 1836: A West African Imperialism in the Era of the Atlantic Slave Trade* (Oxford: Clarendon Press, 1977); Patrick Manning, *Slavery, Colonialism and Economic Growth in Dahomey, 1640–1960* (Cambridge: Cambridge University Press, 1982); Rebecca Shumway, *The Fante and the Transatlantic Slave Trade* (Rochester, NY: University of Rochester Press, 2011); John Thornton, *Africa and Africans in the Making of the Atlantic World, 1400–1800* (2nd Edition, New York: Cambridge University Press, 1998).

88. Cohen, *The French Encounter with Africans*, 120; Eugene Richard Henry Tesdahl, "Bonds of Money, Bonds of Matrimony?: French and Native Intermarriage in 17th and 18th Century Nouvelle France and Senegal" (MA thesis, Miami University, 2003), 7, 24–25.

89. Dickason, "The Brazilian Connection," 131.

90. See Havard, *Empire et métissages*, 294–295, 534. According to Gilles Havard, by the eighteenth century, presents (including rifles, bullets, powder, and blankets) amounted to 5 to 10 percent of French officials' annual expenses in the Pays d'en Haut. Gilles Havard, "L'empire du milieu," in *Colonisations*, ed. Singaravélou *et al.*, 609–610, here 610.

91. Havard, *Empire et métissages*, 313.

92. Jean-Baptiste Labat, *Nouvelle Relation de l'Afrique Occidentale*, 5 vols. (Paris: Guillaume Cavelier, 1728), 4:378. See also Heijmans, *The Agency of Empire*, 131–132.

93. Heijmans, *The Agency of Empire*, 107, 110–111, 124.

94. Hanes Walton Jr., "Toward a Theory of Black African Civilizations: The Problem of Authenticity," *Journal of Black Studies* 1, no. 4 (1971): 477–487, 479.

95. David Northrup, *Africa's Discovery of Europe, 1450–1850* (Third Edition, EBook, Oxford: Oxford University Press, 2014), 58, https://hdl.handle.net/2027/heb31093.0001.001; J. O. Ijoma, "Portuguese Activities in West Africa before 1600," *Transafrican Journal of History* 11 (1982): 136–146, 145.

96. "Brak" (or "Braque") was the title given to the king of Waalo before the nineteenth century. See Boubacar Barry, *The Kingdom of Waalo: Senegal before the Conquest* (New York: Diasporic Africa Press, 2017).

97. La Courbe, *Premier voyage*, 73–74.

98. In Anosy, beads were often gifted by the French to members of allied factions, precisely because beads made of glass, coral, pearls, grains, gold, and crystal formed a central part of women and men's jewelry (*firavach* or *miranacque*) on the island. Du Bois, *Les voyages*, 109; Carpeau du Saussay, *Voyage de Madagascar*, 248–249; Flacourt, *Histoire de la grande isle*, 81–82.

99. Havard, "L'empire du milieu," 609, and *Empire et métissages*, 140, 364.

100. La Courbe, *Premier voyage*, 36 (quotation), 71–72.

101. La Courbe, *Premier voyage*, 36 (quotation), 72.

102. La Courbe, *Premier voyage*, 36. About the convoys, see Martin Klein, "The Role of Slavery in the Economic and Social History of Saint-Louis, Senegal," in Clark, Vidal, and Thioub, *New Orleans, Louisiana, and Saint-Louis, Senegal*, 37n6, 37–38.

103. La Courbe, *Premier voyage*, 71–2.

104. La Courbe, *Premier voyage*, 115.

105. For examples of publications stressing the role of the *folgars* as a site for the formation of commercial and affectionate relationships between African women and white men, see, for example, Brooks, *Eurafricans in Western Africa*, 216–217; Johnson, *Wicked Flesh*, 30; and Kane Lo *De la Signare*, 190.

106. Kane Lo, *De la Signare*, 190.

107. Kane Lo, *De la Signare*, 190.

108. Michel Adanson, *Histoire Naturelle du Sénégal. Avec la Relation abrégée d'un Voyage fait en ce pays, pendant les années 1749, 50, 51, 52 & 53* (Paris: Claude-Jean Baptiste Pauche, 1757), 61–62; Antoine Edme Pruneau de Pommegorge, *Description de la nigritie* (Paris: Chez Maradan, 1789), 6 (quotation). See also Kane Lo, *De la Signare*, 190–191.

109. For example, see Brooks, *Eurafricans in Western Africa*, 216–217; Johnson, *Wicked Flesh*, 30; and Kane Lo, *De la Signare*, 190.

110. Kane Lo, *De la Signare*, 191.

111. La Courbe, *Premier voyage*, 114, 117.

112. La Courbe, *Premier voyage*, 114.

113. La Courbe, *Premier voyage*, 115–116.

114. La Courbe, *Premier voyage*, 116. This was a possible reference to Blockula, a legendary island where the devil was said to hold his earthly court during the witches' sabbath.

115. La Courbe, *Premier voyage*, 117.

116. La Courbe, *Premier voyage*, 118. For more information about the *laptots*, see La Courbe, *Premier voyage*, 17–18, 35, 37. At least some of the *laptots* might have been enslaved. See Johnson, *Wicked Flesh*, 39.

117. Klein, "The Role of Slavery in the Economic and Social History of Saint-Louis Senegal," 37.

118. On this topic, see Karen Amanda Sackur, "The Development of Creole Society and Culture in Saint-Louis and Gorée, 1719–1817" (PhD diss., University of London, 1999), 61; and Johnson, *Wicked Flesh*, 24.

119. La Courbe, *Premier voyage*, 32.

120. Klein, "The Role of Slavery in the Economic and Social History of Saint-Louis, Senegal," 35–36.

121. La Courbe, *Premier voyage*, 35.

122. La Courbe, *Premier voyage*, 35.

123. La Courbe, *Premier voyage*, 35.

124. La Courbe, *Premier voyage*, 118–119.

125. La Courbe, *Premier voyage*, 119.

126. La Courbe, *Premier voyage*, 101, 104, 107–108. On sexual violence in Senegambia, see Johnson, *Wicked Flesh*.

127. Jennifer Morgan, *Laboring Women: Reproduction and Gender in New World Slavery* (EBook, Philadelphia: University of Pennsylvania Press, 2004), 62, https://ebookcentral.proquest.com/lib/duke/reader.action?docID=3442010&ppg=1&c=UERG.

128. Johnson, *Wicked Flesh*, 21.

129. Johnson, *Wicked Flesh*, 24. On the lack of skills among Europeans in Saint-Louis, see La Courbe, *Premier voyage*, 39.

130. Johnson, *Wicked Flesh*, 29; James Searing, *West African Slavery and Atlantic Commerce: The Senegal River Valley, 1700–1860* (Cambridge: Cambridge University Press, 1993), 96–100.

131. La Courbe, *Premier voyage*, 28.

132. Johnson, *Wicked Flesh*, 24.

133. Johnson, *Wicked Flesh*, 18.

134. Klein, "The Role of Slavery in the Economic and Social History of Saint-Louis, Senegal," 38.

135. See Brooks, *Eurafricans in Western Africa*; Pernille Ipsen, *Daughters of the Trade: Atlantic Slavers and Interracial Marriage on the Gold Coast (The Early Modern Americas) (Philadelphia: University of Pennsylvania Press, 2015)*, 9; Peter Mark, "The Evolution of 'Portuguese' Identity: Luso-Africans on the Upper Guinea Coast from the Sixteenth to the Early Nineteenth Century," *Journal of African History* 40 (1999): 173–191, and *'Portuguese' Style and Luso-African Identity: Precolonial Senegambia, Sixteenth–Nineteenth Centuries* (Bloomington: Indiana University Press, 2002).

136. Johnson, *Wicked Flesh*, 23.

137. Johnson, *Wicked Flesh*, 33.

138. ANOM C6 15 "Memoire sur Gorée par Mr Adanson 1763," f. 5.

139. George Brooks Jr., "The Signares of Saint-Louis and Gorée: Women Entrepreneurs in Eighteenth-Century Senegal," in *Women in Africa. Studies in Social and Economic Change*, ed. Nancy Hafkin and Edna Bay (EBook, Stanford, CA: Stanford University Press, 1976), 19–44, here 22, https://hdl-handle-net.proxy.lib.duke.edu/2027/heb02070.0001.001; Tesdahl, "Bonds of Money, Bonds of Matrimony?," 37–38, 42–43.

140. La Courbe, *Premier voyage*, 198; Labat, *Nouvelle Relation*, 4:377–378.

141. Sparks notes another example of such a maneuver in Annamaboe, on the Gold Coast. Sparks, *Where the Negroes Are Masters*, 4.

142. Labat, *Nouvelle Relation*, 4:377–378.

143. Labat, *Nouvelle Relation*, 4:378.

144. La Courbe, *Premier voyage*, 39.

145. La Courbe, *Premier voyage*, 39.

146. ANOM C6 11 "A Gorée ce 6 Juillet 1737."

147. ANOM C14 35 "1767. M. David Mémoire," f. 313; ANOM C6 15 "Memoire sur Gorée par Mr Adanson 1763," f. 5.

148. Klein, "The Role of Slavery in the Economic and Social History of Saint-Louis, Senegal," 35–36.

149. For more information about the *Jaam*, see Mamadou Diouf, *Le Kajoor au XIXe siècle. Pouvoir ceddo et conquête coloniale* (Paris: Karthala, 2014); Johnson, *Wicked Flesh*, 37–38; Klein, "The Role of Slavery in the Economic and Social History of Saint-Louis, Senegal," 37.

150. In 1763, the former governor of Senegal, Pierre Félix Barthélemy David, explained that free Black families in the region purchased enslaved people who worked as "sea or river sailors [. . .] forming the crews of [the company's] trade boats." See ANOM C14 35 "David. Mémoire daté de 1767," f. 313.

151. Many other communities of Africans and Eurafricans on the Atlantic coast also enjoyed wealth and influence. For another example, see Ipsen, *Daughters of the Trade*, 9.

152. Johnson, *Wicked Flesh*, 29–30. For more information about the *indiennes*, see Krystel Gualdé, "L'engouement pour les indiennes," in *Colonisations*, ed. Singaravélou *et al.*, 644–646.

153. Historian Pernille Ipsen has observed a similar pattern among Eurafrican women in Osu (a small town on the Gold Coast). See Ipsen, *Daughters of the Trade*, 10. On this topic, see also Thornton, *Africa and Africans*, 8.

154. La Courbe, *Premier voyage*, 196–197; Labat, *Nouvelle Relation*, 4:378–380.

155. La Courbe, *Premier voyage*, 71–72.

156. La Courbe, *Premier voyage*, 71–72, 74.

157. La Courbe, *Premier voyage*, 138.

158. La Courbe, *Premier voyage*, 71–72, 75.

159. La Courbe, *Premier voyage*, 100–101.

160. La Courbe, *Premier voyage*, 101.

161. La Courbe, *Premier voyage*, 104, 107–108.

162. La Courbe, *Premier voyage*, 109, 112.

163. Étienne-Félix Berlioux, *André Brue ou l'origine de la colonie française du Sénégal* (Paris: Guillemion et Compagnie, 1874), 49–50.

164. La Courbe, *Premier voyage*, 113.

165. La Courbe, *Premier voyage*, 119–120.

166. La Courbe, *Premier voyage*, 140 (quotation), 138–141.

167. Marvin, "Bourbon Island Creoles," 27; Daniel Vaxelaire, *Le grand livre de l'histoire de La Réunion: Des origines à 1848*, 2 vols. (Sainte-Clotilde, Réunion: Orphie, 1999), 1:92.

168. This story can be compared to the peopling of Isle of France, which nevertheless did not develop such a large free creole population of non-European ancestry. On this subject, see Vaughan, *Creating the Creole Island.*

169. Souchu de Rennefort, *Relation du premier voyage,* 162.

170. Marvin, "Bourbon Island Creoles," 21.

171. Article XII, "De Par Le Roy. Status, Ordonnances et Reglemens," in Charpentier, *Relation de l'établissement,* 91.

172. Marvin, "Bourbon Island Creoles," 22–23.

173. Barassin, *Naissance d'une chrétienté,* 118; Jean Defos Du Rau, "L'Île de la Réunion: Étude de géographie humaine" (PhD diss., Institut de géographie, Faculté des Lettres Bordeaux, 1960), 133; Fontaine, *Deux siècles et demi de l'histoire d'une famille réunionnaise,* 1:218.

174. For more information on this topic, see Chapter 3.

175. ANOM C6 A1 "Extrait du Règlement de la Compagnie en France pour le Commerce de l'Isle St Laurent dite Madagascar du 27 [Octo]bre 1664," pp. 18–19 ("women of the country"). For the data, see Jean Barassin, *La vie quotidienne des colons de l'île Bourbon à la fin du règne de Louis XIV, 1700–1715* (Saint Denis : Cercle Généalogique de Bourbon, 2005), 104; ANOM G1 477 "Liste des habitans de Lisle Bourbon, Enfans et Negres Ceci doit estre du mois de Septembre 1690"; ANOM C3 1 "A Monsieur Le Marquis de Seigneulay, 1686," f. 55 ("miserable men").

176. Marvin, "Bourbon Island Creoles," 28.

177. ANOM G1 477 "Liste des habitans de Lisle Bourbon, Enfans et Negres Ceci doit estre du mois de Septembre 1690."

178. ANOM G1 477, "Recensement de L'isle de Bourbon en general, fait en Mars 1709"; ANOM G1 477 "Reçenssement [*sic*] general Du quartier St Paul de l'année 1719."

179. ANOM G1 477 "Recensement de L'isle de Bourbon en general, fait en Mars 1709."

180. See Marvin, "Bourbon Island Creoles," 30–31.

181. ANOM C3 3 "Memoire Dobservation Sur Celuy de Lisle de Bourbon, adressé à Monsieur De Foucherolle," f. 23v.

182. ANOM C3 3 "Memoire Dobservation," f. 23v.

183. ANOM C3 3 "Memoire Dobservation," f. 23v.

184. ANOM C3 3 "Memoire Dobservation," f. 24v; ANOM DPPC 62 Antoine Desforges-Boucher, "Le mémoire pour servir a la connoissance particulière de chacun des habitans de L'Isle de Bourbon," p. 151.

185. ANOM 5 DPPC 62 Boucher, "Le mémoire pour servir," p. 151, 154; ADR C°767 "Recensement général de l'Isle de bourbon année, 1708," f. 36.

186. ANOM 5 DPPC 62 Boucher, "Le mémoire pour servir," p. 154.

187. ANOM C3 3 "Memoire Dobservation," f. 24.

188. ANOM C3 3 "Memoire Dobservation," ff. 24–24v (quotations).

189. ANOM G1 477 "1704 et avril 1705 Resencement [*sic*] General de tous les Habitans." They did so decades before French observers in the Illinois Country noted the formation of villages, by Frenchmen and their Frenchified Illinois wives, that were likewise "composed entirely of farmers who live[d] there very comfortably." White, *Wild Frenchmen,* 30.

190. ANOM G1 477 "Liste des habitans de Lisle Bourbon, Enfans et Negres Ceci doit estre du mois de Septembre 1690"; ADR C°767 "Recensement Général Du nombre Des habitans qui sont Sur Lisle de Bourbon hommes femmes Enfans Esclaves, année 1708," f. 19v, 21; ANOM 5 DPPC 62 Boucher, "Le mémoire pour servir," p. 64 (quotations).

191. Fontaine, *Deux siècles et demi de l'histoire,* 1:187, 193, 224, 256, 246–248.

192. ADR C°767 "Recensement général de l'Isle de bourbon année 1708," f. 29v.

193. ANOM G1 477 "Reçenssement general Du quartier St Paul de l'année 1719," p. 9; Fontaine, *Deux siècles et demi de l'histoire*, 1: 247–248, 256.

194. Marvin, "Bourbon Island Creoles," 29; Barassin, "L'esclavage à Bourbon," 11; Serge Gélabert ed., *La Réunion: Histoire d'une île déserte* (Paris: Gélabert; 1997), 10. Marvin, "Bourbon Island Creoles," 29.

195. ANOM G1 477 "1704 et avril 1705, Resencement General de tous les Habitans"; Yvan Combeau, Prosper Ève, Sudel Fuma, and Edmond Maestri, eds., *Histoire de La Réunion: De la colonie à la région* (Paris: Nathan-VUEF, 2002), 26.

196. Barassin, *Naissance d'une chrétienté*, 200; Sonia Chane-Kune, *Aux origines de l'identité réunionnaise* (Paris, 1993), 27. According to Richard Allen, "Slavery was a de facto reality on the island by 1687." See Allen, "The Constant Demand of the French," 49.

197. Chane-Kune, *Aux origines de l'identité réunionnaise*, 27.

198. ADR C°2793 "Lezin Rouillard Concessions," p. 41.

199. ANOM G1 477 "Liste des habitans de Lisle Bourbon, Enfans et Negres Ceci doit estre du mois de Septembre 1690"; ANOM G1 477 "Recensement des habitans de L'Isle de Bourbon en 1711."

200. ANOM 5 DPPC 62 Boucher, "Le mémoire pour servir," p. 34.

201. ANOM 5 DPPC 62 Boucher, "Le mémoire pour servir," p. 34. On the hypersexualizing trope, see Chapter 5.

202. ANOM 5 DPPC 62 Boucher, "Le mémoire pour servir," pp. 60–61 (quotation).

203. For additional examples, see ANOM F3 208 "Isle de Bourbon Ordonnance du Gouverneur pour l'Education de la jeunesse 27 Mars 1690," pp. 33–34.

204. ANOM C3 3 "Memoire Dobservation," f. 23.

205. ANOM C3 3 "Memoire Dobservation," f. 24.

206. ANOM C3 3 "Memoire Dobservation," f. 23 ("Please tell me"), f. 24v (Messrs. white men).

207. ANOM G1 477 "Liste des habitans de Lisle Bourbon, Enfans et Negres Ceci doit estre du mois de Septembre 1690"; ANOM G1 477 "1704 et avril 1705, Resencement General de tous les Habitans."

208. ANOM G1 477 "Reçenssement [*sic*] general Du quartier St Paul de l'année 1719." Creole, Creole–Creole, and French–Creole households are not included in the data given here for the years 1704 and 1719, because the origins of Creole people were not recorded in local censuses.

209. Vauboulon became unpopular because of his policies on taxation, concession ownership (for which he began to require payment), and hunting rights (which he restricted considerably). He was imprisoned in Saint-Paul and died in 1692, possibly from poisoning. Barquissau, Foucque, and de Cordemoy, *L'Île de La Réunion*, 49; Fontaine, *Deux siècles et demi de l'histoire*, 1:157. The Council of the Six Seniors encountered difficulties having its authority recognized across several areas of the island. On this topic, see Barassin, *Naissance d'une chrétienté*, 215–216; Fontaine, *Deux siècles et demi de l'histoire*, 1:157.

210. Raphaël Barquissau, Hippolyte Foucque, and Hubert Jacob de Cordemoy, eds., *L'Île de La Réunion, ancienne Île Bourbon* (Paris, 1925), 49; Fontaine, *Deux siècles et demi de l'histoire*, 1:154, 157; Enis Omar Rockel, *Histoires Extraordinaires de l'Isle Bourbon (Île de la Réunion)* (Sainte-Marie, Réunion: Orphie: 2004), 120.

211. Ricquebourg, *Dictionnaire généalogique des familles de l'Île Bourbon*, 3:2125; ADR C°2793 "Antoine Payet Concession," pp. 94–95.

212. ANOM DPPC G1 477 "Recensement de L'isle de Bourbon en general, fait en Mars 1709"; Barassin, "L'esclavage à Bourbon," p. 36.

213. Ricquebourg, *Dictionnaire généalogique des familles de l'Île Bourbon*, 2:1114; ANOM DPPC G1 477 "Liste des habitans de Lisle de bourbon du mois de Septembre 1690"; ADR C°767 "Recensement général de l'Isle de bourbon année 1708," f. 35v. For more information about Monique after Louis's passing, see ANOM G1 477 "Reçenssement general Du quartier St Paul de l'année 1719," p. 18.

214. Ricquebourg, *Dictionnaire généalogique des familles de l'Île Bourbon*, 3:2772. ANOM 5 DPPC 62 Boucher, "Le mémoire pour servir," pp. 67–68 (quotation); see also ANOM 5 DPPC 31 and "Recensement general de tous les Habitans chefs de familles, femmes, enfans et esclaves qui sont dans l'isle de bourbon [. . .]," Quartier de St Paul, 1705 et avril 1705, f. 2 and "Recensement de l'Isle de Bourbon en général, fait en Mars 1709. On one occasion, Elisabeth was mistakenly categorized as an Indian woman. ANOM 5 DPPC 31 "Liste des habitans de Lisle Bourbon, enfans et negres," Quartier St Paul.

215. ANOM 5 DPPC 62 Boucher, "Le mémoire pour servir," p. 67.

216. ANOM 5 DPPC 62 Boucher, "Le mémoire pour servir," p. 68. For more information about Elisabeth after Athanase's passing, see ANOM G1 477 "Reçenssement general Du quartier St Paul de l'année 1719," p. 5.

217. ANOM G1 477 "1704 et avril 1705 Resencement General de tous les Habitans," f. 2; ANOM G1 477 "Recensement de L'isle de Bourbon en general, fait en Mars 1709."

218. ANOM 5 DPPC 62 Boucher, "Le mémoire pour servir," p. 68.

219. See Sabine Noël, *Amours et familles interdites. Blancs et Noirs à l'île Bourbon (La Réunion) au temps de l'esclavage (1665–1848)* (Paris, Les Indes Savantes, 2022), 193. Antoine was baptized in 1709. He initially took the name of his white father, "Antoine Desforges." Boucher denied the allegation that Antoine was his son, and even petitioned the Superior Council of the island to prevent the boy from using his name.

3. *Empire of* Métissage

1. Louise Siaram bore many mixed children, including both Louise and her younger brother Laurent—who later fathered Marianne Payet, the comfortable coffee planter introduced in "A Tale of Two Mariannes." Ricquebourg, *Dictionnaire généalogique des familles de l'Île Bourbon*, 3: 2125–2126.

2. ADR C°2793 "Contract de mariage de Jacques Maçé Et Louise payet Veuve Cauzan," f. 29.

3. ANOM 5 DPPC 62 Boucher, "Le mémoire pour servir," p. 93.

4. On laundry washing as a signal of adhesion to European notions of cleanliness, see White, *Wild Frenchmen*, 19. ANOM 5 DPPC 62 Boucher, "Le mémoire pour servir," p. 93.

5. ANOM 5 DPPC 62 Boucher, "Le mémoire pour servir, p. 94.

6. ADR C°767 "Recensement général de l'Isle de bourbon année 1708," f. 27v.

7. Silk and shirts from France: ADR C°2793 "Vente publique faite des Effets apartenant a Deffun Pierre Folio." Wheat: ADR C°767 "Recensement général de l'Isle de bourbon année 1708," f. 27v; Wine grapes: ANOM 5 DPPC 62 Boucher, "Le mémoire pour servir," pp. 93–94.

8. ANOM 5 DPPC 62 Boucher, "Le mémoire pour servir," p. 94.

9. Ricquebourg, *Dictionnaire généalogique des familles de l'Île Bourbon*, 1:429.

10. Ricquebourg, *Dictionnaire généalogique des familles de l'Île Bourbon*, 2:1762.

11. On France's patriarchal culture and inheritance customs, see Marvin, "Bourbon Island Creoles," 6–7.

12. ADR C°2793 "27 mars 1714," ff. 5–5v. Earlier, in 1707, Louise and François had already given a generous loan of 1,500 livres to Henry. See ADR C°2793 "22 aoust 1715," f. 16v. Louise also gifted an enslaved Malagasy woman to her niece Agatte Hoareau. See ADR C°2793 "18 nov[embre] 1715," f. 26.

13. ADR C°2793 "Lan mil Sept Cens quatorze, et Le Vingt quatre Decembre [. . .]," f. 9.

14. ADR C°2793 "16 Sept[embre] 1715," f. 17v.

15. ADR 3E03 "Succession Louise Payet. Inventaire après décès de Louise Payet épouse Jacques Macé St Paul, 21 Mars 1730."

16. For a convincing explanation of why the term "assimilation" is appropriate in this context, see Jessica Pierre-Louis, "Les Libres de couleur face au préjugé: Franchir la barrière à la Martinique aux XVIIe–XVIIIe siècles" (PhD diss., Université des Antilles-Guyane, 2015), 231–236.

17. For recent publications in this field, see C. Cowling, M. H. Pereira Toledo Machado, D. Paton, and E. West, "Mothering Slaves: Comparative Perspectives on Motherhood, Childlessness, and the Care of Children in Atlantic Slave Societies," *Slavery & Abolition* 38, no. 2 (2017): 223–231; Sasha Turner, "Home-Grown Slaves: Women, Reproduction, and the Abolition of the Slave Trade, Jamaica 1788–1807," *Journal of Women's History* 23, no. 3 (2011): 39–62, and *Contested Bodies: Pregnancy, Childrearing and Slavery in Jamaica* (EBook, Philadelphia: University of Pennsylvania Press, 2017), https://ebookcentral.proquest.com/lib/duke/detail.action?docID=4854373. Scholars have been eager to study slave reproduction in this later period because of the major slave trade blockages caused by the Seven Years' War and by the rise of the British abolitionist movement from the 1780s. For an important exception, see Morgan, *Laboring Women.*

18. See especially Arlette Gautier, *Les Soeurs de Solitude: Femmes et esclavage aux Antilles du XVIIe au XIXe siècle* (Rennes, France: Presses Universitaires de Rennes, 2010).

19. There are only a few publications considering assimilation in the historiography on the early modern French colonies. On the French Caribbean, see Pierre-Louis, "Les Libres de couleur face au préjugé," 25–28; Frédéric Régent, "Les Blancs métissés en Guadeloupe au XVIIIe siècle," *Ultramarines* 24 (2004): 25–28, "La fabrication des Blancs dans les colonies françaises," in *De quelle couleur sont les Blancs ? Des 'petits Blancs' des colonies au 'racisme anti-Blancs'*, ed. Sylvie Laurent (Paris: La Découverte, 2013), 67–75, and "Blancs, demi-Blancs, libres de couleur et esclaves dans les colonies françaises avant 1848," *La traite négrière, l'esclavage et leurs abolitions: Mémoire et histoire. Séminaire national organisé le 10 mai 2006. Paris* (Versailles: CRDP de l'académie de Versailles, 2007), 31–40. For some examples from Saint-Domingue, see Laurent Dubois, *Avengers of the New World: The Story of the Haitian Revolution* (Cambridge: Belknap Press of Harvard University Press, 2004), 61; Stewart R. King, *Blue Coat or Powdered Wig: Free People of Color in Pre-Revolutionary Saint Domingue* (Athens: University of Georgia Press, 2001), 158–179; John Garrigus, *Before Haiti: Race and Citizenship in French Saint-Domingue* (New York: Palgrave Macmillan, 2006), 45–49. On the Illinois Country, see White, *Wild Frenchmen.*

20. See White, *Wild Frenchmen,* 30; Kleber, "Gendered Societies," 3, 223.

21. Quoted from Kleber, "Gendered Societies," 10. Sophie White also refers to a "unique pattern of conversion and sacramental intermarriages" in her study of the Illinois Country. See White, *Wild Frenchmen,* 13.

22. Pier Larson treats these relations peripherally in "Play and Possession," and much of the work considering this topic for Senegambia focuses on the later period. For example, see Brooks, *Eurafricans in Western Africa*; Jones, *The Métis of Senegal*; Ken Lo, *De La Signare*; Vial, *Femmes d'influence.*

23. For example, see Johnson, *Wicked Flesh*; Beckles, *Centering Women*, 38–57.

24. Quoted from Shaw, "In the Name of the Mother," 187. See also Fuentes, "Power and Historical Figuring: Rachael Pringle Polgreen's Troubled Archive," *Gender & History* 22, no. 3 (2010): 564–584, 578. Saidiya Hartman goes even deeper by presenting seduction as a pattern upholding the enslaved people's "perfect submission" because it could convince slaveowners to make the lives of their captives more livable and in the process extinguish rebellious stances that could have ended the institution of slavery. According to Hartman, however, at the same time as it upheld the enslaved people's "perfect submission," seduction could also very well "assert the agency of the dominated." See Hartman, *Scenes of Subjection*, 88.

25. Johnson, *River of Dark Dreams*, 9.

26. Fuentes, "Power and Historical Figuring," 566.

27. I pay less attention to abuses perpetrated by white women against enslaved men and to same-sex sexual abuses, since they are less visible in the archives. For an explanation of why this was the case, see the section in Chapter 5 titled "Sexual Violence: A Large-Scale Weapon of Domination in Slave Societies."

28. On this topic, see Beckles, *Centering Women*, 22–37, esp. 23.

29. *Oxford English Dictionary*, s.v. "consent," accessed December 1, 2024, https://www.oed.com/dictionary/consent_n?tab=meaning_and_use#8580221. See Hartman, *Scenes of Subjection*, 80; Tiya Miles, *Ties That Bind: The Story of an Afro-Cherokee Family in Slavery and Freedom* (Berkeley, University of California Press., 2005), esp. chap. 3; Shaw, "In the Name of the Mother," 185–186.

30. Sharon Block, *Rape and Sexual Power in Early America* (EBook, Williamsburg: University of North Carolina Press, 2006), 3, https://heinonline-org.proxy.lib.duke.edu/HOL/P?h=hein.beal/rasxpweam0001&i=1; *Oxford English Dictionary*, s.v. "rape," accessed December 1, 2024, https://www.oed.com/dictionary/rape_n3?tab=meaning_and_use#27092043.

31. According to Joan Dayan, Doris Garraway, and Saidiya Hartman, affection and desire existed, but only to further complicate power relations between slaveowners and enslaved people. See Joan Dayan, *Haiti, History, and the Gods* (EBook, Berkeley: University of California Press, 1995), 56, https://hdl-handle-net.proxy.lib.duke.edu/2027/heb04571.0001.001; Garraway, *The Libertine Colony*, 22; Hartman, *Scenes of Subjection*.

32. Hartman, *Scenes of Subjection*, 5.

33. LSM RSCL File 1752-06-13-01 "Proces Verbal de declaration des Negresses 13 Juin 1752," p. 5.

34. On Isle Bourbon, in 1729, the Superior Council merely declared, "We will make sure that no soldier will entice or abduct a *négresse* [. . .] We must prevent married and unmarried men from abusing their *négresses*." ANOM F3 205 "26 Mars 1729," pp. 158–159 (quotations). Likewise, rapes of enslaved women were not criminalized in the antebellum South. See Hartman, *Scenes of Subjection*, 79.

35. Garraway, *The Libertine Colony*, 341n21.

36. Article XLIV of the *Code Noir* of 1685 defined "slaves" as *meubles* ("movables"). See *Recueils de reglemens, édits, déclarations, et arrêts, concernant le commerce, l'administration de la Justice, et la police des colonies françaises de l'Amérique, & les engagés. Avec le code noir et l'addition audit code*, 2 vols. (Paris: Libraires Associez, 1745), 2:95.

37. *Recueils de reglemens*, 2:85.

38. *Recueils de reglemens*, article XXX, 2:92; ANOM A 23 "Édit du roi, ou Code noir, qui concerne entièrement les esclaves de la Louisiane, Mars 1724," p. 54; ADR C° 940, "Lettres Patentes en forme d'Edit concernant les Esclaves Negres des Isle de Bourbon et de france, 1723."

39. Here, I agree with Spear. Spear, *Race, Sex and Social Order*, 72–73.

40. Johnson, *Wicked Flesh*, 80–81; Stephanie E. Smallwood, *Saltwater Slavery: A Middle Passage from Africa to American Diaspora* (EBook, Cambridge, MA: Harvard University Press, 2007), 158–166, https://research-ebsco-com.proxy.lib.duke.edu/c/fh2aff/search/details/r22z6cvthj?db=nlebk.

41. Quoted from Johnson, *Wicked Flesh*, 83.

42. Johnson, *Wicked Flesh*, 84.

43. Du Tertre, *Histoire générale des Antilles*, 2:512.

44. Du Tertre, *Histoire générale des Antilles*, 2:512.

45. Jean-Baptiste Labat, *Nouveau voyage aux isles de l'Amerique*, 8 vols. (Paris: Guillaume Cavelier Père, 1742), 2:185.

46. Labat, *Nouveau voyage (1742)*, 2:185–186.

47. ANOM F3 221 "Du 3 octobre 1672," p. 478.

48. Du Tertre, *Histoire générale des Antilles*, 2:432.

49. Jean-Baptiste Labat, *Nouveau voyage aux isles de l'Amerique*, 2 vols. (The Hague: Husson *et al.* 1724), 1:330.

50. Labat, *Nouveau voyage* (1724), 1:330.

51. Du Tertre, *Histoire générale des Antilles*, 2:512–513.

52. Labat, *Nouveau voyage* (1742), 2:191.

53. ANOM F3 248 "Extrait des avis de Mr de Blenac et Patouet sur divers object d'administration, 1681," f. 687. Blenac's position echoed that of late eighteenth-century British abolitionists who wished to use slave reproduction in Jamaica to create "metropolitan whites: Christian, married, industrious, independent, and responsible." See Turner, *Contested Bodies*, 9.

54. Labat, *Nouveau voyage* (1742), 2:192 (quotation), 191–193.

55. Aubert, "'To Establish One Law,'" 35–36.

56. Camillia Cowling, *Conceiving Freedom: Women of Color, Gender, and the Abolition of Slavery in Havana and Rio de Janeiro* (Chapel Hill: University of North Carolina Press, 2013), 54.

57. On this topic, see Jennifer L. Morgan, "*Partus sequitur ventrem*: Law, Race, and Reproduction in Colonial Slavery," *Small Axe* 22, no. 1 (March 2018): 1–17.

58. See Cowling, *Conceiving Freedom*, 53–54; Cowling et al., "Mothering Slaves," 224; Morgan, *Laboring Women* and *Reckoning with Slavery*; Turner, *Contested Bodies*, 11, and "Slavery, Freedom, and Women's Bodies," *Journal of Women's History* 29, no. 1 (2017): 177–187, here 177–178.

59. Such was the case despite the fact that the intendant of the French Antilles, Jean-Baptiste Patoulet, justified the French king's decision to enslave the *mulâtres* by invoking their alleged "bad dispositions" and "libertinage." ANOM F3 248, "Extrait des avis de Mr de Blenac et Patoulet sur divers objects d'administration, 1681," f. 687. Patoulet's rhetoric was partly intended to erect boundaries between Blacks and whites and thereby protect the slave system.

60. Gautier, *Les Soeurs de Solitude*, 69, 87; Turner, *Contested Bodies*, 11.

61. Gautier, *Les Soeurs de Solitude*, 69.

62. Morgan, *Laboring Women*, 9. Of course, those measures were not as extensive as those taken in the wake of the Seven Years' War and the abolitionist eras, which included balancing sex ratios, improving maternity care, or shielding pregnant women from exhausting work. For examples of measures taken in the British context in this later era, see Turner, *Contested Bodies*, 6–9.

63. Du Tertre, *Histoire générale des Antilles*, 2:504.

64. Cited in Gautier, *Les Soeurs de Solitude*, 57.

65. Gautier, *Les Soeurs de Solitude*, 57–58.

66. Cited in Gautier, *Les Soeurs de Solitude*, 65.

67. Cited in Barassin, "L'esclavage à Bourbon," 40.

68. Guadeloupe: ANOM G1 468 "1671, Desnombrement general des hommes, femmes, garçons, filles, serviteurs, servans, neigres, neigresses, neigrillons, Mulastres, Sauvages"; ANOM G1 469 "1696. Recensement general des Isles Guadeloupe Grande Terre, & les Saintes." Martinique: Léo Elisabeth, *La société martiniquaise aux XVIIe et XVIIIe siècles 1664–1789* (EBook, Paris: Karthala, 2003), 28, https://play.google.com/books/reader?id=A9vPu82grIcC&pg=GBS.PP1.

69. Régent, *La France et ses esclaves*, 111. For more information about enslaved craftsmen and domestic servants in the Caribbean, see Labat, *Nouveau voyage* (La Hague, 1724), 1:328–330.

70. The expression was coined by Orlando Patterson. See Patterson, *Slavery and Social Death: a Comparative Study* (EBook, Cambridge, MA: Harvard University Press, 1982), 133, https://hdl-handle-net.proxy.lib.duke.edu/2027/heb03237.0001.001. For examples from different areas, see Jayne Boisvert, "Colonial Hell and Female Slave Resistance in Saint-Domingue," *Journal of Haitian Studies* 7, no. 1 (2001): 61–76; Marcela Echeverri, "'Enraged to the Limit of Despair': Infanticide and Slave Judicial Strategies in Barbacoas, 1788–98," *Slavery & Abolition* 30, no. 3 (2009): 403–426; Mary Frederickson and Delores Walters, eds., *Gendered Resistance: Women, Slavery, and the Legacy of Margaret Garner* (Urbana: University of Illinois Press, 2013). On this topic, see also Morgan, *Laboring Women*; Sasha Turner, "The Nameless and the Forgotten: Maternal Grief, Sacred Protection, and the Archive of Slavery," *Slavery & Abolition* 38, no. 2 (2017): 232–250, 233.

71. Labat, *Nouveau voyage* (1742), 2:188.

72. Labat, *Nouveau voyage* (1742), 2:184, 187.

73. Quoted from Morgan, *Reckoning with Slavery*, 4–5i; Cowling et al., "Mothering Slaves," 224, 226; Turner, "The Nameless and the Forgotten"; Rhaisa Kameela Williams, "Toward a Theory of Black Maternal Grief," *Journal of the Association of Black Anthropologists* 24, no. 1 (2016): 17–30.

74. Du Tertre, *Histoire générale des Antilles*, 2:510.

75. On these tropes in the British Atlantic context, see Jennifer L. Morgan, "'Some Could Suckle over Their Shoulder': Male Travelers, Female Bodies, and the Gendering of Racial Ideology, 1500–1770," *WMQ* 54, no. 1 (1997): 167–192, and *Laboring Women*, chap. 1.

76. Du Tertre, *Histoire générale des Antilles*, 2:505–506.

77. Carpeau du Saussay, *Voyage de Madagascar*, 253–254.

78. *Recueils de reglemens*, 2:85.

79. Many European fathers in Dutch Batavia legitimized their mixed children and manumitted them, thereby granting them Dutch status. See Bosma and Raben, *Being "Dutch" in the Indies*.

80. Pierre-Louis, "Les libres de couleur face au préjugé," 155.

81. Cited in Marvin, "Bourbon Island Creoles," 7n8. By the 1770s, Spanish authorities even granted "white" status to wealthy *pardos* (mixed European, Native American, and/or African people) in exchange for a payment. See Ann Twinam, *Purchasing Whiteness: Pardos, Mulattos, and the Quest for Social Mobility in the Spanish Indies* (Stanford, CA: Stanford University Press, 2015).

82. Pierre-Louis, "Les libres de couleur face au préjugé," 155–156.

83. Pierre-Louis, "Les libres de couleur face au préjugé," 240; Régent, *La France et ses esclaves*, 64. They stopped turning a blind eye to this practice in the second half of the eighteenth century (see Conclusion).

84. Victor Schöelcher, *Des colonies françaises: abolition immédiate de l'esclavage* (Paris: Pagnerre, 1842), 182.

85. ANOM G1 469 Vol. 2 "Extrait du Recenssement [*sic*] genera(l) de L'Isle Guadeloupe L'année 1686."

86. Jean-Pierre Sainton, *Histoire et civilisation de la Caraïbe (Guadeloupe, Martinique, petites Antilles): La construction des sociétés antillaises des origines au temps présent, structures et dynamiques* (Paris: Editions Maisonneuve et Larose, 2004), 1:225.

87. ANOM G1 468 "1671, Desnombrement general."

88. ANOM 85MIOM182 "Capesterre 1639–1791."

89. Du Tertre, *Histoire générale des Antilles,* 2:513.

90. ANOM G1 469 "Recensement 1664."

91. For more information on the way relationships between white women and men of non-European descent were perceived, and why, see Chapter 5.

92. ANOM C7 A1 "Du Lion Commandant à la Guadeloupe. A St germain en Laye, le 16e aoust 1669," f. 58.

93. Bernard Moitt, *Women and Slavery in the French Antilles, 1635–1848* (Bloomington: Indiana University Press, 2001), 14–15.

94. ANOM G1 468 "1671, Desnombrement general."

95. Labat, *Nouveau voyage* (1724), 1:35.

96. Labat, *Nouveau voyage* (1724), 1:35.

97. ANOM 85MIOM276 "Pointe Noire, 1673–1759."

98. ANOM F3 133 "Appel comme d'abus mariage jugé, 5 Décembre 1667," f. 36.

99. ANOM F3 133 "Appel comme d'abus mariage jugé, 5 Décembre 1667," f. 36.

100. Régent, *La France et ses esclaves,* 335–336.

101. Lucien-René Abénon, *Petite histoire de la Guadeloupe* (Paris: L'Harmattan, 1992), 60; Nick Nesbitt, *Voicing Memory: History and the Subjectivity in French Caribbean Literature* (Charlottesville: University of Virginia Press, 2003), 7.

102. Pierre-Louis, "Les libres de couleur face au préjugé," 364.

103. Frédéric Régent, "Le métissage des premières générations de colons en Guadeloupe et à l'Île Bourbon (Réunion)," in *Mariage et métissage dans les sociétés coloniales: Amériques, Afrique et Iles de l'Océan Indien (XVIe–XXe siècles)*, ed. Guy Brunet (Bern: Peter Lang, 2015), 111–32, here 113–144, and "Les Blancs métissés," 25.

104. See Régent, "Le métissage des premières générations," 112–117.

105. Larson, "Play and Possession," 701–703.

106. Larson, "Play and Possession," 691.

107. Quoted from Larson, "Play and Possession," 691.

108. Quoted from Charpentier, *Relation de l'établissement,* 88.

109. Charpentier, *Relation de l'établissement,* 91.

110. Larson, "Play and Possession," 693.

111. Galibert, *À l'angle de la Grande Maison,* 163.

112. Letter n°XVI, Toussaint Bourdaise to Vincent de Paul, January 10, 1656, in *À l'angle de la Grande Maison,* ed. Galibert, 321.

113. Du Bois, *Les voyages faits par le sieur D.B,* 70.

114. Lougnon, *Sous le signe de la tortue,* 214.

115. Lougnon, *Sous le signe de la tortue,* 215.

116. ANOM G1 477, "Liste des habitans de Lisle Bourbon, Enfans et Negres Ceci doit estre du mois de Septembre 1690." See also ANOM C3 1 "Memoires du Pere Bernardin 1687–1688," ff. 61–63v.

117. For a history of the Christianization of Isle Bourbon, see Barassin, *Naissance d'une chrétienté*.

118. Larson, "Play and Possession," 687.

119. Sieur L'Huillier, *Voyage du Sieur Luillier aux grandes Indes* (Paris: Claude Cellier, 1705), 150.

120. Marvin, "Bourbon Island Creoles," 28.

121. Barassin, *La vie quotidienne des colons de l'Île Bourbon*, 265; Jean-François Samlong, *Les engagés malgaches à la Réunion: Documents et recherches* (Saint-Denis, Réunion: les Cahiers de notre histoire, 1995), 21.

122. ANOM F3 208 "Isle de Bourbon Ordonnance de M de La Haye [. . .] 1er Decembre 1674," 19.

123. On the racial labels used on Isle Bourbon, see Nathan Marvin, "Incertaines catégories raciales," in *Colonisations*, ed. Singaravélou *et al.*, 702–703.

124. Barassin, *La vie quotidienne des colons de l'Île Bourbon*, 155.

125. Especially those practicing Hinduism. On the origins of Portuguese opposition to intermarriage in Goa, see Nandini Chaturvedula, "Preserving Purity: Cultural Exchange and Contamination in Late Seventeenth-Century Portuguese India," in "Goa: 1510–2010," *Ler Historia* 50 (2010): 99–112.

126. Ordre et Instruction, January 8, 1701, quoted in Barassin, *La vie quotidienne des colons de l'Île Bourbon*, 155.

127. ANOM F3 208 "Isle de Bourbon Ordonnance de M de La Haye," p. 19.

128. Serge Gélabert ed., *La Réunion: histoire d'une île déserte* (Paris: Gélabert; 1997), 10.

129. Filliot, *La traite des esclaves*, 31.

130. ANOM DPPC G1 477 "1704 avril 1705 Resencement General de tous les Habitans."

131. ANOM G1 477 "1704 et avril 1705, Resencement General de tous les Habitans chefs de familles, femmes, Enfans Et Esclaves."

132. ADR GG1 "Bl, Libres, Escl. 1667–1718" "Saint-Paul," "Fontaine Jacques baptisé 26 Mai 1674" (quotation); Ricquebourg, *Dictionnaire généalogique des familles de l'Île Bourbon*, 1:904.

133. ANOM 5 DPPC 62 Boucher, "Le mémoire pour servir à la connaissance," p. 134.

134. Ricquebourg, *Dictionnaire généalogique des familles de l'Île Bourbon*, 2:1528.

135. Ricquebourg, *Dictionnaire généalogique des familles de l'Île Bourbon*, 1:904, 1:925, 2:1528, 2:1727; ADR GG1 "Saint-Paul." See also Fontaine, *Deux siècles et demi de l'histoire*, 1:90, 98, 102, 104, 109–110, 158–161.

136. About their role in the plantation economy, see Chapter 6.

137. Marvin, "Bourbon Island Creoles," 30.

138. ANOM DPPC G1 477 "Recensements Île Bourbon 1678–1719."

139. ANOM DPPC G1 477 "1704 avril 1705 Resencement General de tous les Habitans"; ANOM DPPC G1 477 "Recensement de L'isle de Bourbon en general, fait en Mars 1709"; ANOM DPPC G1 477 "Recensement des quartiers de St Paul et St Denis en L'Isle de Bourbon 1711."

140. It also categorized all enslaved people as "Blacks and *négresses*" (*Noirs et négresses*). See ANOM DPPC G1 477 "Recensement de lile de Bourbon en 1713."

141. Carton, *Mixed-Race and Modernity*, 63–64; Philippe Haudrère, *La Compagnie Française des Indes au XVIIIe siècle*, 2 vols. (Paris: Les Indes Savantes, 2005), 2:594–595; Hodges, "Configuring Colonial Families."

142. Hodges, "Configuring Colonial Families."

143. About the *topas*, see Adrian Carton, "Shades of Fraternity: Creolization and the Making of Citzenship in French India, 1790–1792," *French Historical Studies* 31, no. 4 (2008): 581–607, here 581.

144. ANOM C2 66 "Coppie [*sic*] de la Lettre Ecritte [*sic*] à la compagnie par M. Pilavoine et les marchands du comptoir de Suratte [*sic*]. A Surate 6e février 1702," pp. 280–281.

145. Hodges, "Sovereign Spaces," 44. Their husband's salary and commercial activities could allow them to enhance their condition. See ANOM C2 64 "Coppie de la lettre Ecrite a la Compagnie des Indes Orientalles par Mr Pilavoine Directeur du Comptoir de Suratte [. . .] A Surate Le 20 Janvier 1693," f. 55.

146. Robert Challe, *Journal d'un voyage fait aux Indes orientales [. . .] depuis le 24 février 1690, jusqu'au 20 août 1691* (Rouen: Jean Batiste [*sic*] Machuel, 1721), 2:171.

147. ANOM C2 64 "Coppie de la lettre Ecrite a la Compagnie des Indes Orientalles par Mr Pilavoine Directeur du Comptoir de Suratte [. . .] A Surate Le 20 Janvier 1693," f. 55.

148. Here I agree with Leonard Hodges, "Configuring Colonial Families."

149. ANOM C6 116–117 "Memoire Concernant Les Colonies des françois dans Les Indes Orientales, Pondichéry," f. 17.

150. Cited in Hodges, "Configuring Colonial Families."

151. ANOM 1DPPC4496 "Double du Registre des Mariages de la chapelle et de L'Eglise de St Lasare Et de Notre Dame des Anges des RP Capucins de Pondichery depuis Lan 1687 Jusqu'en 1719."

152. Three unions likely involved two Luso-Indian spouses, and four involved a spouse whose possible origins could not be determined.

153. Carton, *Mixed-Race and Modernity*, 63–65, ead in Bengal, 72.

154. Carton, *Mixed-Race and Modernity*, 64–65, 67; Hodges, "Configuring Colonial Families."

155. For example, see those records of public sales and estate inventory involving the Bourbon Island Creoles Gilles Fontaine, Daniel Payet and Marianne Fontaine: ADR C°2793 "Vente publique faite des Effets apartenant a Deffun Pierre Folio;" ADR C° 3E03 "Succession Marianne Fontaine Inventaire Fontaine épouse [. . .] St Paul 1730."

156. Marvin, "Bourbon Island Creoles," 5; Pierre-Louis, "Les libres de couleur face au préjugé," 240–241, 244, 246, 250, 268–315; Régent, *La France et ses esclaves*, 182, and "La fabrication des Blancs dans les colonies françaises," 70.

157. Régent, "La fabrication des Blancs dans les colonies françaises," 73.

158. Frédéric Régent, *Esclavage, métissage, liberté: La Révolution française en Guadeloupe 1789–1802* (Paris: Grasset, 2004), 206.

159. Pierre-Louis, "Les libres de couleur face au préjugé," 241.

160. Challe, *Journal d'un voyage* (Rouen, 1721), 2:171.

161. Guy Le Gentil de La Barbinais, *Nouveau voyage autour du monde* (Paris: Flahault, 1727), 3: 125.

162. Challe, *Journal d'un voyage* (Rouen, 1721), 171.

163. Labat, *Nouveau voyage* (1742), 2:190.

164. For more information about La Vente, see Chapter 4.

165. Cited in Spear, *Race, Sex, and Social Order*, 33.

166. Guy Le Gentil de La Barbinais, *Nouveau voyage autour du monde* (Paris: Flahault, 1727), 3:125–126.

167. Kleber, "Gendered Societies," 187–188, 194–196.

168. Kleber, "Gendered Societies," 177–197, 227, and Spear, *Race, Sex and Social Order*, 49, 244n154.

169. The accounts of missionaries must be taken with reservations, since their authors were likely to inflate the impact of their own work to gain support from metropolitan authorities.

Letter n°XII, Jean-François Mousnier to Vincent de Paul, February 6, 1655, in *À l'angle de la Grande Maison,* ed. Galibert, 273; Galibert, *À l'angle de la Grande Maison,* 156, quotation at 163.

170. Letter n°XVI, Toussaint Bourdaise to Vincent de Paul, January 10, 1656, in *À l'angle de la Grande Maison,* ed. Galibert, 318.

171. Letter n°XVI, Toussaint Bourdaise to Vincent de Paul, January 10, 1656, in *À l'angle de la Grande Maison,* ed. Galibert, 318.

172. Letter n°XIX, Toussaint Bourdaise to Vincent de Paul, February 19, 1657, in *À l'angle de la Grande Maison,* ed. Galibert, 378.

173. Letter n°XIX, Toussaint Bourdaise to Vincent de Paul, February 19, 1657, in *À l'angle de la Grande Maison,* ed. Galibert, 347–348.

174. Kleber, "Gendered Societies," 221, 229.

175. "Letter by Father Jacques Gravier in the form of a Journal of the Mission of l'Immaculée Conception de Notre Dame in the Illinois country," 13 Feb., 1694, Thwaites, JR (1694), 64:212–213; Kleber, "Gendered Societies," 177, 179; Spear, *Race, Sex and Social Order,* 49, 244n154.

176. Letter n°XIX, Toussain Bourdaise to Vincent de Paul, February 19, 1657, in *À l'angle de la Grande Maison,* ed. Galibert, 349.

177. Flacourt, *Histoire de la grande isle,* 85.

178. Larson, "Play and Possession," 701–705.

179. On this topic in North America, see, for example, Olive Patricia Dickason, "From 'One Nation' in the Northeast to 'New Nation' in the Northwest: A Look at the Emergence of the Métis," *American Indian Culture and Research Journal* 6, no. 2 (1982): 1–21, here 7–8; Daniel A. Scalberg, "The French-Amerindian Religious Encounter in Seventeenth and Early Eighteenth-Century New France," *French Colonial History* 1 (2002): 101–112, here 106.

180. Letter n°XVI, Toussaint Bourdaise to Vincent de Paul, January 10, 1656, in *À l'angle de la Grande Maison,* ed. Galibert. However, the handful of French women in Madagascar were not setting the best example. They reportedly threatened to get married *à la mode des Noirs* ("in accordance with Black customs") or else run away if local officials persisted in keeping them unmarried until their planned departure for Bourbon. ANOM C5 A1 "Madagascar de la Bretesche Major de l'Ile Dauphine 22 Aoust 1674," f. 3v.

181. Larson, "Play and Possession," 701.

182. Larson, "Play and Possession," 701.

183. Flacourt, *Histoire de la grande isle,* 82.

184. Larson, "Play and Possession," 703.

185. Larson, "Play and Possession," 701.

186. Quoted from Cauche, *Relations véritables et curieuses,* 111. Pronis waited another three years to marry the woman in the Catholic Church, and together, the couple had a daughter who was baptized by the missionary Nacquart. Galibert, *À l'angle de la Grande Maison,* 157–158; Letter n°XVI, Toussaint Bourdaise to Vincent de Paul, January 10, 1656, in *À l'angle de la Grande Maison,* ed. Galibert, 325.

187. Tricoire, "Une histoire franco-malgache," 247.

188. Payet, "Les femmes dans le marronnage," 68.

189. In 1734, after presenting a title of succession, the Frenchmen who had married Native American women in the Illinois Country were granted the plots of land that had been abandoned by the Kaskaskias. On this subject, see Kleber, "Gendered Societies," 232–233.

190. Du Bois, *Les voyages,* 153. See also Tricoire, "Une Histoire Franco-Malgache," 252.

191. Cauche, *Relations véritables et curieuses,* 32; Flacourt, *Histoire de la grande isle,* 82.

192. Flacourt, *Histoire de la grande isle,* 446.

193. Some Indigenous women in the Pays d'en Haut also took that role. See Marrero, *Detroit's Hidden Channel*, 17.

194. La Blanchère, *Un Episode d'Histoire Coloniale*, 10.

195. See ANOM C6 A1 "1671. Memoire de l'estat ou est presentement L'isle dauphine et des difficultés qui se trouvent a lexecution des ordre laissés par Monsieur de la haye a son depart pour les indes," ff. 1–iv.

196. Larson, "Play and Possession," 698.

197. Payet, "Les femmes dans le marronnage," 68–69.

198. Flacourt, *Histoire de la grande isle* (2007), 278–279.

199. Similarly, the French fur traders and soldiers of the Pays d'en Haut and the Illinois Country who married Indigenous women integrated kinship networks. For example, see Kleber, "Gendered Societies," 177.

200. Pier Larson has already noted how "interracial relationships, whether or not sealed by an indigenous and/or a Catholic marriage, emerged as important affective foci for trade" in seventeenth-century Anosy. See Larson, "Play and Possession," 703; Tricoire, "Une histoire franco-malgache," 256.

201. Tricoire, "Une histoire franco-malgache," 256.

202. ANOM C5 A1 "Lestat de L'Ile Dauphine lors du depart du Navire le sainct Denis troisiesme mars mil six centz septante," f. 8v. Cited in Larson, "Play and Possession," 703. European traders on the east coast of Madagascar continued to marry Malagasy women in the eighteenth century, which helped them acquire and sell merchandise. See Tricoire, "Une histoire franco-malgache," 256.

203. ANOM C6 15 "Memoire sur Gorée par Mr Adanson 1763," f. 5.

204. La Courbe, *Premier voyage*, 28.

205. He also prohibited Frenchmen from going to these women's cabins outside the fort, under penalty of paying a fine, and ordered the construction of a kitchen so that Frenchmen would no longer need their services. La Courbe, *Premier voyage*, 36–39.

206. BNF Mss. fr. 21690, "Rel. du sieur Mathelot, 1687," 216v in La Courbe, *Premier voyage*, 26n1.

207. La Courbe, *Premier voyage*, 196.

208. Many French contemporaries commented on how common divorce was in North America. In Louisiana, the *commissaire-ordonnateur* Jean-Baptiste Duclos thought that Native American women were unable to stay with their husbands "for the rest of their lives." ANOM C13 A3 "La Louisianne. Le S. du Clos, 25 Decembre 1715," p. 820. Metropolitan authorities repeated what they heard from the colonies, stating in 1716 that "these *sauvagesses* are used to a libertine way of life and leave their husbands to take others whenever they want." ANOM C13 A4 "1716, Projet ou Mémoire du Roy au Srs de l'Espinay gouverneur et Hubert commissaire ordonnateur a la Loüisiane," p. 977.

209. Carpeau du Saussay, *Voyage de Madagascar*, 252.

210. Du Bois, *Les voyages faits par le sieur D.B*, 114.

211. Carpeau du Saussay, *Voyage de Madagascar*, 252.

212. Dellon, *Relation d'un voyage des Indes orientales*, 1:47.

213. Du Bois, *Les voyages faits par le sieur D.B*, 115. Flacourt claimed about Malagasy women that "if their husband upsets them, they leave him easily, and go spend time with whomever they want." Flacourt, *Histoire de la grande isle*, 85.

214. ANOM C2 3 "Articles et conditions [. . .] pour l'établissement d'une Compagnie pour le commerce des Indes Orientales, à Paris 26 Mai 1664," article V, f. 71v (quotation); Charpentier, *Relation de l'etablissement de la compagnie Françoise*, 89.

215. Letter n°XIII, Toussaint Bourdaise to Vincent de Paul, February 6, 1655, in *À l'angle de la Grande Maison*, ed. Galibert, 279

216. Thieffry, *La mission lazariste à Madagascar*, 385.

217. Jean-Pierre Biondi, *Saint-Louis du Sénégal: Mémoires d'un métissage* (Paris: Denoël, 1987), 47–56; Brooks, "The Signares of Saint-Louis and Gorée," 34–38; Cohen, *The French Encounter with Africans*, 125; Knight-Baylac, "La vie à Gorée de 1677 à 1789," 399; Amanda Sackur, "The French Revolution and Race Relations in Senegal, 1780–1810," in *People and Empires in African History: Essays in Memory of Michael Crowder*, ed. J. F. Ade Ajayi and J. D. Y. Peel (London: Longman, 1992), 69–87, here 69–70.

218. Ipsen has identified a similar practice on the Danish Gold Coast. See Ipsen, *Daughters of the Trade*, 1, 9.

219. Cited in Tesdahl, "Bonds of Money, Bonds of Matrimony?," 35.

220. René Claude Geoffroy de Villeneuve, *L'Afrique, ou histoire, moeurs, usages, et coutumes des Africains, Le Sénégal, Vol. 1* (Paris: Nepveu, 1814), 68.

221. Johnson, *Wicked Flesh*, 31, 64; Tesdahl, "Bonds of Money, Bonds of Matrimony?," 28.

222. BNF Mss. fr. 21690 "Rel. du sieur Mathelot, 1687," 216v in La Courbe, *Premier voyage*, 26 n. 1.

223. ANOM C6 1 "17 Janvier 1688. De Par le Roy Et Messieurs de la Companie Royale du Senegal et coste d'Affrique [*sic*]," article III and IV, n.p.

224. ANOM C6 1 "17 Janvier 1688."

225. Belmessous, "Assimilation and Racialism," 346–348; Karahasan, "Métissage in New France," 123.

4. *Unifying Racial Policies*

1. Jay Higginbotham, *Old Mobile: Fort Louis de la Louisiane: 1702–1711*, 2nd ed. (Tuscaloosa: University of Alabama Press, 1991), 139.

2. ANOM G1 477 "Liste des habitans de Lisle Bourbon [. . .] 1690."

3. For more about La Vente's story, see Higginbotham, *Old Mobile*, 139–140.

4. ANOM, C13 A1 "Extrait des lettres de la Louisianne de l'Année 1706," p. 536.

5. ANOM C13 A2 "Memoire [. . .] 21 Juin 1710," p. 565.

6. For a study of the evangelization of Isle Bourbon, see Barassin, *Naissance d'une chrétienté*.

7. ANOM G1 477 "Liste des habitans de Lisle Bourbon [. . .] 1690."

8. ANOM C13 A2 "D'Artaguiette to Minister, June 20, 1710," pp. 544–545; ANOM C13 A3 "La Louisiane. Le S. du Clos, 25 Decembre 1715," pp. 819–824; ANOM C13 A4 "1716, Projet ou Mémoire du Roy au Srs de l'Espinay," pp. 977–978.

9. ANOM, C13 A4 "1716, Projet ou Mémoire," pp. 977–978.

10. Cornelius J. Jaenen, "Miscegenation in Eighteenth Century New France," in *New Dimensions in Ethnohistory: Papers of the Second Laurier Conference on Ethnohistory and Ethnology*, ed. Barry Gough and Laird Christie (Hull, Quebec: Canadian Museum of Civilization, 1991), 79–115, esp. 97.

11. Philippe Haudrère, "L'origine du personnel de direction générale de la Compagnie française des Indes, 1719–1794," *Revue française d'histoire d'outre-mer* 67, nos. 248–249 (1980): 339–371, esp. 340; Pritchard, *In Search of Empire*, 246.

12. For more information about this company, see Philippe Haudrère, *La Compagnie française des Indes au XVIIIe siècle. 1719–1795*, 4 vols. (Paris: Librairie de L'Inde, 1989).

13. ANOM 2866 "1726, Etat des Eclaircissemens que la Compagnie demande," f. 121–122.

14. ANOM F3 205 "Des Mariages, de leur convenance, et de la Discipline qui S'y doit observer," pp. 40–41; Alfred Martineau, *Correspondance du Conseil supérieur de Pondichéry avec le Conseil de Chandernagor. 1728–1757. Vol 1.* (Pondicherry: Société de l'histoire de l'Inde, 1915), 178.

15. For recent publications considering the transoceanic body of racial policies, see Lamotte, "Beyond the Atlantic," and "Clusters of French Policies Targeting People of Non-European Ancestry, 1603–1757," OI Reader—Omohundro Institute, January 2024.

16. There are a few exceptions. In the Anglo-American scholarship, see Lamotte, "Colour Prejudice"; Marvin, "Bourbon Island Creoles." In the French scholarship, see Paris, "La page blanche"; Sabine Noël, *Amours et familles interdites: Blancs et Noirs à l'île Bourbon (la Réunion) au temps de l'esclavage (1665–1848)* (Paris: Les Indes Savantes, 2022).

17. In particular, see Aubert, "'The Blood of France'" and "'To Establish One Law'"; Vidal, "Caribbean Louisiana" and *Caribbean New Orleans*.

18. Houllemare, "Procedures, Jurisdictions and Records," n.p. ("unified"); Christie, Gauvreau, and Gerber, "Introduction," 4 ("uniform legislation"). Ironically, the example given in Christie, Gauvreau, and Gerber's "Introduction," 7, to illustrate the claim that the Bourbon monarchy was not interested in establishing uniform legislation is article VI of the 1724 *Code Noir* of Louisiana, which contained identical terms to Letters Patent issued for Isle Bourbon and Isle of France in 1723.

19. Aubert, "'The Blood of France.'"

20. For publications attributing the emergence of race to the expansion of plantation slavery in the Americas, see Gwendolyn Hall, *Social Control in Slave Plantation Societies: A Comparison of St. Domingue and Cuba* (1971; repr., Baton Rouge: Louisiana State University Press, 1996), 153; Usner, *Indians, Settlers, and Slaves*, 210; Boulle, *Race et esclavage*, 26, 71. For research stressing the role that failed assimilation policies played in New France, see Masarah Van Eyck, "'We Shall Be One People': Early Modern French Perceptions of the Amerindian Body" (PhD diss., McGill University, 2001); Aubert, "'The Blood of France,'" 442; Belmessous, "Assimilation and Racialism," 322–349.

21. Julie Hardwick, Sarah M. S. Pearsall, and Karin Wulf, "Introduction: Centering Families in Atlantic Histories," *WMQ*, 3rd ser., 70, no. 2 (2013): 205–224; Stoler, *Haunted by Empire*, 4, *Carnal Knowledge and Imperial Power*, 42.

22. Several scholars have already made this link between marriage and inheritance. See, for example, Kleber, "Gendered Societies," 266. Inheritance had already been one of the "central stakes" in an attempt by French officials to redefine legitimate marriage in more restrictive terms in the kingdom of France beginning in the sixteenth century. See Matthew Gerber, *Bastards: Politics, Family, and Law in Early Modern France* (New York: Oxford University Press, 2012), 38–41, quotation 41. See also Aubert, "'The Blood of France,'" esp. 446–448.

23. Sarah Hanley, "Engendering the State: Family Formation and State Building in Early Modern France," *French Historical Studies* 16 (1989): 1–27, here 10.

24. Carl Brasseaux, *France's Forgotten Legion: Service Records of French Military and Administrative Personnel Stationed in the Mississippi Valley Gulf Coast Region, 1699–1760* (Baton Rouge: Louisiana State University Press: 2000), 43–44; Vaxelaire, *Le grand livre de l'histoire de la Réunion*, 1:119.

25. The number of Europeans who moved to the island was large enough to prompt officials to add the category "Europeans" (*Européens*) to their censuses by 1744. See ADR C°771 "Recensement Général en date du 19 Mai 1744."

26. Brasseaux, *France's Forgotten Legion*, 43–44.

27. Brasseaux, *France's Forgotten Legion*, 43–44; Haudrère, *La Compagnie française des Indes*, 1:110. The growth of Louisiana's settler population contributed to the foundation of New Orleans in 1718, Yazoo in 1719, Fort de Chartres (Illinois) in 1720, the Arkansas settlement in 1721, and La Balize in 1723.

28. ANOM 5 DPPC 053 "Recensement general fait dans l'Isle de la Martinique pendant les mois de Septembre et Octobre 1719"; ANOM G1 469 Vol. 1 "La Guadeloupe. Recensement Année 1724."

29. ANOM G1 464 "Recensement des habitans du fort Louis de la Mobile [. . .] 28 Juin 1721" and "Recensement General de La Ville de la Nouvelle Orleans [. . .] de Janvier 1732."

30. ANOM C3 5 "Année 1731 Extrait de la recapitulation du recensement general des habitans de L'un et Lautre Sexe," f. 164. After he spent time on Isle Bourbon in the 1720s, Jesuit missionary to China Antoine Gaubil specified that "part [of these women] are *mulâtres*." See Lougnon, *Sous le signe de la tortue*, 243.

31. The notion of "racial capitalism" was coined by Cedric J. Robinson in *Black Marxism: The Making of the Black Radical Tradition* (London: Zed Books, 1983).

32. Louisiana was placed under the control of the Company of the Indies until 1731. That year, lacking capital and facing financial bankruptcy, the Compagnie des Indes ceded Louisiana to the crown. LSM RSCL File 1731-01-24-03 "Black books," year 1731, "Retrocession of Louisiana to the king by the company of the west."

33. Malick W. Ghachem, "The Mississippi Bubble in Saint-Domingue (Haiti)," in *Boom, Bust, and Beyond: New Perspectives on the 1720 Stock Market Bubble*, ed. Stefano Condorelli and Daniel Menning (Berlin: De Gruyter, 2019), 95–116, esp. 102–103.

34. André Scherer, *Histoire de la Réunion* (Paris: Presses Universitaires de France, 1974), 15–16; Philippe Haudrère, *L'empire des rois, 1500–1789* (Paris: Denoel, 1997), 165.

35. ANOM G1 477 "Recensement de lile de Bourbon en 1713"; ANOM C3 5 "Année 1731, Extrait de la recapitulation du recensement general des habitants de L'un et Lautre Sexe," f. 164. About Isle Bourbon's central role as a coffee producer, see Haudrère, *L'empire des rois*, 165; Scherer, *Histoire de la Réunion*, 16.

36. About this process of centralization, see Houllemare, "The Constitution of the Colonial Archives," esp. III–IV, IX. Documents from both the royal colonies and the first trading companies were collected in the archives. See Houllemare, "The Constitution of the Colonial Archives," VI. See also Houllemare, "Procedures, Jurisdictions and Records," n.p.

37. Haudrère, "L'origine du personnel," 340.

38. For example, Vidal has argued, "The early legal interdiction of interracial marriage and concubinage in the Mississippi colony was not the result of local developments but of the transfer of a *Code Noir* from the Antilles, which had been modified in reaction to what had happened in the islands." Vidal, *Caribbean New Orleans*, 509. Aubert seems to embrace the same argument in "'To Establish One Law,'" 41. For work acknowledging the issuance of intermarriage bans in the Indian Ocean, see Lamotte, "Colour Prejudice," 227–228, 322–323; Marvin, "Bourbon Island Creoles," 44, 131n20; Peabody, *Madeleine's Children*, 55.

39. ANOM C6 A1 "Extrait du Règlement de la Compagnie [. . .] du 27 Octobre 1664," p. 19.

40. ANOM F3 133 "Appel comme d'abus mariage jugé, 5 Décembre 1667," f. 36.

41. Van Meersbergen, *Ethnography and Encounter*, 222.

42. ANOM F3 208 "Isle de Bourbon Ordonnance de M de La Haye [. . .] 1er Decembre 1674," 19.

43. "Ordre et Instruction que Messieurs les Directeurs generaux de la Compagnie des Indes Orientales desirent être executez en l'Isle de Bourbon par le sieur de Villers. . . . ," *Bulletin of the New York Public Library* 13, no. 1 (1909): 7–12, esp. 7–10 (quotation, 10).

44. Quoted in Barassin, *La vie quotidienne des colons de l'Île Bourbon*, 155.

45. *Recueils de reglemens*, 2:85.

46. On the role of Colbert in shaping the *Code Noir* of 1685, see Vernon Palmer, "Essai sur les origines et les auteurs du Code Noir," *Revue internationale de droit comparé* 50, no. 1 (1998): 111–140.

47. John Rule, "Jean-Frédéric Phélypeaux comte de Pontchartrain et Maurepas: Reflections on His Life and His Papers," *Journal of the Louisiana Historical Association* 6 (1965): 365–377.

48. Houllemare, "The Constitution of the Colonial Archives."

49. When he took over the office of Marine secretary, Maurepas took further steps to complete the general collection of all laws previously issued for the French Atlantic and Indian Ocean colonies. Houllemare, "Procedures, Jurisdictions and Records," n.p.

50. Elisabeth, *La société martiniquaise*, chap. 7. Maurepas explicitly stated his opposition to intermarriage in the Caribbean multiple times. In 1731, he described mixed unions as "a stain on white people." Elisabeth, *La société martiniquaise*, 294.

51. ADR C° 940 "Lettres Patentes en forme d'Edit concernant les Esclaves Negres des Isle de Bourbon et de france 1723," n.p.; ANOM A 23 "Édit du roi, ou Code noir, qui concerne entièrement les esclaves de la Louisiane, Mars 1724," f. 50.

52. ADR C° 940 "Lettres Patentes"; ANOM A 23 "Édit du roi," f. 51.

53. Spear, *Race, Sex, and Social Order*, 54.

54. ANOM 5 DPPC 16 "Année 1706. Denombrement des familles et habitans qui Sont a La Louisiane."

55. Gwendolyn Hall, "The Formation of Afro-Creole Culture," in *Creole New Orleans: Race and Americanization*, ed. Arnold R. Hirsch and Joseph Logsdon (Baton Rouge and London: Louisiana State University Press, 1992), 58–87, here 67; Daniel Usner, "Frontier Exchange in the Lower Mississippi Valley: Race Relations and Economic Life in Colonial Louisiana, 1699–1783" (PhD diss., Duke University, 1981), 5.

56. Régent, *La France et ses esclaves*, 335.

57. ANO SR/56 "St. Louis Cathedral, New Orleans, Marriage Index, 1720–1730."

58. ANOM A 23 "Édit du roi, ou Code noir, qui concerne entièrement les esclaves de la Louisiane, Mars 1724," f. 51.

59. For example, see Vidal, *Caribbean New Orleans*, 509, and Aubert "'To Establish One Law,'" 41.

60. In the past, some scholars have mentioned an intermarriage ban that was allegedly issued in Guadeloupe in 1711 (no archival reference was given for it). After a thorough study of the documents deposited in the French Overseas Archives, I was unable to verify the existence of this ban. For example, see Cohen, *The French Encounter with Africans*, 50. Today, scholars agree that no intermarriage ban was issued in the Caribbean. For example, Vidal argues, "Marriage between whites and blacks was almost immediately outlawed in Louisiana. [. . .] By contrast, no prohibition against interracial sexuality was ever laid out in the French Caribbean." See her *Caribbean New Orleans*, 509. Vincent Cousseau agrees that "marriages between white men and women of color were never formally prohibited" in the French Caribbean. See Vincent Cousseau, "La famille invisible: Illégitimité des naissances et construction des liens familiaux en Martinique (XVIIe siècle–début du XIXème siècle)," *Annales de Démographie Historique* 2, no. 122 (2011): 41–67, here 47.

61. Aubert, "'To Establish One Law,'" 41.

62. However, in 1741, Maurepas did allow French colonial officials in Cayenne to prohibit marriages between white men and Black women. Elisabeth, *La société martiniquaise*, 316. For more details on intermarriage in Saint-Domingue, see Chapter 6.

63. The island was home to up to five times as many white men as white women by 1760. I thank Robert D. Taber for sharing this data with me. Robert D. Taber, "Family Formation, Race, and Honor in Colonial Haiti's Free Communities, 1670–1789," in *French Connections: Cultural Mobility in North America and the Atlantic World, 1600–1875*, ed. Robert Englebert and Andrew Wegmann (Baton Rouge: Louisiana State University Press, 2020), 146–169, here 158. For more data on intermarriage in Saint-Domingue, see Taber, "Family Formation," 146–169.

64. See Garraway, *The Libertine Colony*, 235.

65. The only law dealing with intermarriage in early eighteenth-century Saint-Domingue was a metropolitan edict issued in 1731 by Marine Secretary Maurepas, intended to *discourage* (not prohibit) mixed relationships. See Elisabeth, *La société martinique*, 294.

66. In Guadeloupe, a first marriage authorization was granted by the governor in 1722. See Elisabeth, *La société martiniquaise*, chapter 3.

67. Jean-Baptiste Du Tertre, *Histoire générale des Antilles habitées par les François*, 3 vols. (Paris: Thomas Jolly, 1667–1671) 2:443.

68. Elisabeth, *La société martiniquaise*, 152; Pierre François Régis Dessalles, *Annales du Conseil Souverain de la Martinique*, 1 (1): 8–9.

69. Elisabeth, *La société martiniquaise*, 170.

70. ANOM 5 DPPC 22 "Denombrement General de l'isle Guadeloupe et dependances de L'année 1699"; ANOM G1 497 "Recencement [*sic*] Géneral du Gouvernement de l'Isle Guadeloupe et Dépendances [. . .] Année Mil Sept cens cinquante trois."

71. Régent, *La France et ses esclaves*, 335–336. The proportion of enslaved African-descended peope in Saint-Domingue grew considerably as well, from 37 percent of the population in 1697 (24,156 people) to 90 percent (172,548) by 1754. See Régent, *La France et ses esclaves*, 337.

72. ANOM F3 224 "Du Jeudy Sixieme Du mois de mars mil Sept Cent Vingt Sept . . . ," p. 217.

73. ANOM F3 224 "Du Jeudy Sixieme Du mois de mars mil Sept Cent Vingt Sept . . . ," p. 221.

74. ANOM F3 224 "Du Jeudy Sixieme Du mois de mars mil Sept Cent Vingt Sept . . . ," pp. 215, 223.

75. ANOM F3 224 "Du Jeudy Sixieme Du mois de mars mil Sept Cent Vingt Sept . . . ," pp. 223–224.

76. ANOM F3 224 "Du Jeudy Sixieme Du mois de mars mil Sept Cent Vingt Sept . . . ," pp. 213–239; ANOM F3 224 "12 Mars 1727, Extrait d'une lettre Escrite par Mr Dorillac Procureur general du Conseil Superieur de la Guadeloupe a M. Blondel Intendant," pp. 241–244.

77. ANOM F3 90 "Isles du Vent 1758, Proposition de Mrs Nadau et Marin Pour la Reforme de quelques articles du code et autres ordonnances à l'occasion des Esclaves," f. 88.

78. For example, see Jaenen, "Miscegenation in Eighteenth-Century New France," or Karahasan, "Métissage in New France."

79. ANOM C2 64 "Coppie de la lettre Ecrite a la Compagnie des Indes Orientalles par Mr Pilavoine [. . .] A Surate Le 20 Janvier 1693," ff. 55–56v.

80. ANOM C2 64 "Coppie de la lettre Ecrite a la Compagnie des Indes Orientalles par Mr Pilavoine [. . .] A Surate Le 20 Janvier 1693," f. 56v.

81. ANOM C2 64 "Coppie de la lettre Ecrite a la Compagnie des Indes Orientalles par Mr Pilavoine [. . .] A Surate Le 20 Janvier 1693," f. 55v.

82. Pilavoine himself mentioned several company employees "with families in Surat." ANOM C2 64 "Coppie de la lettre Ecrite a la Compagnie des Indes Orientalles par Mr Pilavoine [. . .] A Surate Le 20 Janvier 1693," f. 55v.

83. There were complaints that Frenchmen who married Native American women, especially in the Illinois Country, did not stay in the French settlements and "raised [their mixed children] like the *sauvages*." Cited in Étienne Rivard, "Colonial Cartography of Canadian Margins: Cultural Encounters and the Idea of Métissage," *Cartographica: The International Journal for Geographic Information Geovisualization* 43, no. 1 (2008): 45–66, here 52.

84. Karahasan, "Métissage in New France," 123.

85. Quoted in Jaenen, "Miscegenation in Eighteenth-Century New France," 97.

86. Jaenen, "Miscegenation in Eighteenth Century New France," 98.

87. ANOM C13 A2 "Le S Dartaguiette, 20 Juin 1710," p. 545; ANOM C13 A3 "La Louisianne. Le S. du Clos, 25 Decembre 1715," p. 823.

88. ANOM C11 A30 "14 novembre 1709," f. 81, quoted in Havard, "'Les forcer à devenir Cytoyens,'" 1003.

89. ANOM C13 A4 "1716, Projet ou Mémoire du Roy au Srs de l'Espinay gouverneur et Hubert," pp. 977–978.

90. ANOM C13 A4 "1716, Projet ou Mémoire du Roy au Srs de l'Espinay gouverneur et Hubert," p. 977.

91. ANOM C13 A4 "1716, Projet ou Mémoire du Roy au Srs de l'Espinay gouverneur et Hubert," 977.

92. ANOM C13 A4 "1716, Projet ou Mémoire du Roy au Srs de l'Espinay gouverneur et Hubert," 978.

93. ANOM C11 A43 "Résumé d'une lettre de Vaudreuil datée du 6 octobre 1721 et délibération du Conseil de Marine, 23 Décembre 1721," ff. 320–331v; Karahasan, "Métissage in New France," 131.

94. Haudrère, "L'origine du personnel," 340.

95. ANOM 2866 "1726, Etat des Eclaircissemens que la Compagnie demande," f. 121.

96. ANOM 2866 "1726, Etat des Eclaircissemens que la Compagnie demande," f. 122.

97. ANOM F3 205 "Des Mariages, de leur convenance, et de la Discipline qui S'y doit observer," p. 41.

98. ANOM F3 205 "11 Decembre 1734," p. 87.

99. ANOM F3 205 "Des Devoirs de L'Employé," p. 26 ("creole women"); ANOM F3 205 "25 mars 1754," f. 44 ("*sang mêlés*"); ANOM F3 205 "Des motifs Sur lesquels on peut Exclure du Service [. . .] L'Employé," f. 46. Since this is a copy, the language used in the original documents might have been different.

100. ANOM F3 205 "25 mars 1754," p. 44.

101. ANOM C7 11 "2 janvier 1755," f. 14v.

102. Cited in Carton, *Mixed-Race and Modernity*, 69–70.

103. Cited in Hodges, "Configuring Colonial Families," n.p.

104. Haudrère, *La Compagnie française des Indes*, 2:594n352.

105. ANOM C2 34 "1748. Arrangemens," f. 172v.

106. ANOM C2 34 "1748. Arrangemens," f. 172v.

107. See Spear, *Race, Sex and Social Order*, 31–32; Barbara B. Diefendorf, "Widowhood and Remarriage in Sixteenth-Century Paris," *Journal of Family History* 7 (1982): 379–395.

108. ANOM C2 66 "Copie de la Lettre écrite à la compagnie par M. Pilavoine," p. 280.

109. ANOM C2 66 "Copie de la Lettre écrite à la compagnie par M. Pilavoine," p. 281.

110. ANOM C2 66 "Copie de la Lettre écrite à la compagnie par M. Pilavoine," p. 281.

111. Michel Vergé-Franceschi, "Les officiers de vaisseaux issus de la Compagnie des Indes: l'exemple des frères Périer," in *Les flottes des Compagnies des Indes, 1600–1857*, ed. Philippe

Haudrère (Vincennes, France: Service historique de la Marine, 1996), 87–98, esp. 87–88, 91–93.

112. ANOM A 23, "Arrest du Conseil Superieur de la Louisianne du 18 Decembre 1728," f. 103.

113. ANOM A 23 "Arrest du Conseil Superieur de la Louisianne [*sic*] du 18 Decembre 1728," f. 103; Spear, *Race, Sex, and Social Order*, 32; White, *Wild Frenchmen*, 132; Kleber, "Gendered Societies," 334–335.

114. Jacques de La Chaise to Company of the Indies, February 15, 1729, in Charles Gayarré, *Histoire de la Louisiane* (New Orleans: Magne & Weisse, 1846), 1:239, quoted (in translation) in Spear, *Race, Sex, and Social Order*, 32.

115. LSM RSCL File 1746-07-22-1, "A Nos seigneurs Du Conseil Superieur de la Loüisianne."

116. In practice, most Native American wives in the Illinois Country were not affected by this legislation. See White, *Wild Frenchmen*, 133–134.

117. ADR C° 940 "Lettres Patentes en forme d'Edit," article LI; ANOM A 23 "Édit du roi, ou Code noir," article LII, fol. 56.

118. According to Spear, there might have been 585 free people of color in New Orleans by 1763, amounting to 2 to 14 percent of the colonial population there. Spear, *Race, Sex, and Social Order*, 96.

119. Some became landowners and worked as farmers and shepherds, but few owned enslaved people. Some worked as domestic servants, while others secured opportunities in skilled sectors of the economy. See Chapter 6.

120. It has been argued that a decision made in 1703 by the Superior Council of Martinique to refuse to register the titles of nobility of two Frenchmen "because they had led a contemptible life and married 2 *mulâtresses*" set a legal precedent for the issuance of article LII of the *Code Noir* of Louisiana of 1724. It is true that the governor-general of the French American islands, Charles-François de Machault, blamed those two Frenchmen for having formed "shameful alliances [*alliances honteuses*] that would give access to nobility titles to negroes [*nègres*]." However, the Superior Council of Martinique did not prohibit donations from whites to Blacks. See Aubert, "'To Establish One Law,'" 40.

121. *Recueils de reglemens*, 2:99.

122. Many examples can be found in ANOM C3 3 "Antoine Desforges-Boucher. Memoire Dobservation Sur Celuy de L'isle de Bourbon, adressé a Monsieur De foucherolle."

123. ANOM F3 236 "Déclaration du Roi En interprétation des articles 39, 56, 57 et 59 de l'Edit du mois de mars 1685," pp. 676–677; ANOM A 25 "Déclaration du roi interprétant l'édit de mars 1685 sur les esclaves Negres des Isles du Vent. A Versailles 5 février 1726," f. 59.

124. Régent, *La France et ses esclaves*, 336–337.

125. Garrigus, *Before Haiti*; Régent, *La France et ses esclaves*, 207–208.

126. For such claims, see Aubert, "'Nègres ou mulâtres nous sommes tous Français,'" 127, 132, 134.

127. Aubert, "'Nègres ou mulâtres nous sommes tous Français,'" 130.

128. ANOM C6 6 "Du 14 e Mars 1721. Reglements de La Compagnie Royalle du Senegal Et Coste d'affrique," p. 6 (article XVI), p. 3 (article IV).

129. ANOM C6 6 "Du 14 e Mars 1721. Reglements de La Compagnie Royalle du Senegal Et Coste d'affrique," p. 3 (article IV).

130. ANOM C6 6 "Du 14 e Mars 1721. Reglements de La Compagnie Royalle du Senegal Et Coste d'affrique," pp. 3–4.

131. ANOM C6 15 "Mémoire sur le Sénégal Postérieur à 1758," ff. 5 (quotation)–f6v.

132. ANOM C6 6 "Du 14 e Mars 1721. Reglements de La Compagnie Royalle du Senegal Et Coste d'affrique," p. 2.

133. ANOM C6 6 "Du 14 e Mars 1721. Reglements de La Compagnie Royalle du Senegal Et Coste d'affrique," p. 10.

134. ANOM C6 6 "Du 14 e Mars 1721. Reglements de La Compagnie Royalle du Senegal Et Coste d'affrique," p. 10.

135. ANOM C6 6 "Du 14 e Mars 1721. Reglements de La Compagnie Royalle du Senegal Et Coste d'affrique," p. 10; *Dictionnaire de l'Académie française*, 4th ed. (Paris: Veuve Bernard Brunet, 1762).

136. ANOM C6 8 "Par la Flutte l'Elephant le Sr Pichon allant à Nantes. Du Senegal le 25 May 1724. M Du Bellay," ff. 5 (quotation)–5v.

137. ANOM C6 11 "Au Senegal Le 2 Aoust 1737," n.p.

138. ANOM C6 1 "17 Janvier 1688. De Par le Roy Et Messieurs de la Companie Royale du Senegal et coste d'Affrique [*sic*]."

139. ANOM C6 11 "Au Senegal Le 2 Aoust 1737," n.p.

140. ANOM C6 11 "Au Senegal Le 2 Aoust 1737," n.p.

141. For more information on the *capitation* in the French colonies, see "Capitation et société," in Elisabeth, *La société martiniquaise*, 297–312.

142. ANOM F3 90 "Isles du Vent 1758, Proposition de Mrs Nadau et Marin Pour la Reforme de quelques articles du code et autres ordonnances à l'occasion des Esclaves," f. 88.

143. See Auguste Lebeau, *De la condition des gens de couleur libres sous l'ancien régime: D'après des documents des Archives coloniales* (Paris: Guillaumin & Cie., 1903), 57. I thank Nathan Marvin for sharing this reference with me. Saint-Domingue only became a French colony in the late seventeenth century, while Isle Bourbon was under the authority of the Company of the East Indies when the tax was first established.

144. Louis XIV also levied the *capitation* in the kingdom of France to finance his wars. François Bluche and Jean-François Solnon, *La véritable hiérarchie sociale de l'ancienne France: Le tarif de la première capitation* (1695) (Genève: Droz, 1983).

145. Twinam, *Purchasing Whiteness*, 103.

146. ANOM C7 A1 "Reglement fait par M.de Tracy pour le gouvernent et police de la Guadeloupe, Avril 1665," article 10, f. 40v ("gentlemen," "white girls and women"); ANOM F3 221 "Reglement Faict par Nous Alexandre de Prouville Chevalier Seigneur de Tracy Conseiller du Roy en ses Conseils," articles 3 and 10, pp. 373 ("white children")–375.

147. ANOM G1 469 "Recensement 1664."

148. Louis-Elie Moreau de Saint-Méry, *Loix et constitutions des colonies françoises de l'Amérique Sous le Vent*, 6 vols. (Paris: Quillau and Mequignon, 1784–1790), 1:214.

149. Elisabeth, *La société martiniquaise*, 247; Moreau de Saint-Méry, *Loix et constitutions*, 1:214–215.

150. Elisabeth, *La société martiniquaise*, 247.

151. ANOM 5 DPPC 23 "Desnombrement General de Lisle de la martinique de l'année 1694."

152. Elisabeth, *La société martiniquaise*, 249.

153. Elisabeth, *La société martiniquaise*, 250.

154. Elisabeth, *La société martiniquaise*, 250.

155. Elisabeth, *La société martiniquaise*, 251.

156. Elisabeth, *La société martiniquaise*, 247.

157. ANOM F3 225 "Extrait de la Lettre du Ministre a Mrs. De Champigny et de la Croix Du 11 Mars 1738," p. 339.

158. ANOM F3 225 "Extrait de la Lettre du Ministre a Mrs. De Champigny et de la Croix Du 11 Mars 1738," p. 339.

159. ANOM F3 248 "Extrait des arrets et ordonnances Rendus pour la Police des nègres au Conseil Souverain de l'Isle Martinique, 1678," f. 101.

160. ANOM F3 236 "Edit du Roi Concernant la discipline, l'Etat et la qualité des negres esclaves aux Isles de l'amerique. Du mois de mars 1685," p. 672.

161. ANOM F3 236 "Ordonnance du Roi portant que les negres libres qui retireront chès eux les nègres marrons, ou receleront les vols qu'ils feront, ou les partageront avec eux, seront déchus de leur liberté. Du 10 juin 1705," p. 166.

162. ANOM F3 236 "Ordonnance du Roi [. . .] Du 10 juin 1705," p. 166.

163. Henri Bangou, *La Guadeloupe. Histoire de la colonisation de l'île, 1492–1848*, 2 vols. (Paris: L'Harmattan, 1987), 1:101.

164. For example, see Du Tertre, *Histoire générale des Antilles*, 1:500–502; ANOM F 133 "Nègres Révolte. 1 aout 1657, Arret qui Ordonne Information Sur declaration," pp. 33–34; Cohen, *The French Encounter with Africans*, 47; Hall, *Social Control in Slave Plantation Societies*, 62.

165. ADR C° 940 "Lettres Patentes en forme d'Edit concernant les Esclaves Negres des Isle de Bourbon et de france, 1723."

166. ANOM F3 236 "Edit du Roi Concernant la discipline, l'Etat et la qualité des negres esclaves aux Isles de l'amerique Du mois de mars 1685," p. 672.

167. André Scherer, *Histoire de la Réunion* (Paris: Presses Universitaires de France, 1974), 15–16; Philippe Haudrère, *L'empire des rois, 1500–1789* (Paris: Denoel, 1997), 165.

168. ANOM F3 205 "De la Police qui S'Exerce au Sujet des Noirs," pp. 75–76; ANOM F3 208 "De la commune des habitants, et des regles Etablis pour ce qui La Regarde," p. 385.

169. ADR C°2430 "Motifs des habitans de L'isle de Bourbon dans leur deputation En france," (quotation).

170. See, for example, ADR C°2516 "Arrest[s] du Conseil, 1715–1724"; C° 2794 "Registre des Actes Publics du quartier de St Paul passés pour moy Desforges, 1718"; ADR C°2517 "Plainte portée par le Sr Gabriel Dumas," pp. 103–105; ADR C°1013 "A Monsieur Dumas gouverneur pour le Roy de L'isle de Bourbon."

171. ANOM A 23 "Édit du roi, ou Code noir, qui concerne entièrement les esclaves de la Louisiane, Mars 1724," f. 54.

172. On plantation agriculture: HL "Vaudreuil Papers," LO 191 "28 Août 1749"; HTML "Louisiana Research Collection, French Colonial Period, 1655–1731," Box 1, "1724/12/20, Description of the Bayagoulas concession"; Hall, *Africans in Colonial Louisiana*, 148–160. Tobacco was initially cultivated in the region of Natchez, and following the destruction of Fort Rosalie by the Natchez Indians in 1729, smaller tobacco plantations appeared around Pointe Coupée. Indigo was mainly cultivated on plantations within a twenty-five-mile radius of New Orleans. Rice and corn were produced to feed the colony and for export to the Caribbean. See Spear, *Race, Sex, and Social Order*, 56–59.

173. ANOM F3 236 "Ordonnance du Roi . . . Du 10 juin 1705," p. 166.

174. ANOM C13 A35 "Reglement Donné à la Nouvelle Orleans, 17 fevrier 1751," article 10, f. 44.

175. ANOM F3 236 "Ordonnance du Roi . . . Du 10 juin 1705," p. 166.

176. ANOM F3 236 "Déclaration du Roi En interprétation des articles 39, 56, 57 et 59 de l'Edit du mois de mars 1685," p. 676; ANOM A 25 "Déclaration du roi interprétant l'édit de mars 1685 sur les esclaves Negres des Isles du Vent A Versailles 5 février 1726," f. 59.

5. Sex and Racial Power

1. About this Roman Law Principle, see Chapter 3.

2. ANOM F3 226 "Motifs du Jugement rendû le 8 fevrier 1738," p. 294.

3. ANOM F3 225 "Extrait de la lettre du ministre [. . .] 26 aoust 1738," p. 349. For the ordinance of 1713, see ANOM F3 236 "Ordonnance du Roi Concernant l'affranchissement des esclaves Du 24 [Octo]bre 1713," p. 681.

4. ANOM F3 226 "Motifs du Jugement rendû le 8 fevrier 1738," p. 300.

5. ANOM F3 226 "Motifs du Jugement rendû le 8 fevrier 1738," p. 301. Slavery was in theory prohibited in the French kingdom because of the famous so-called free soil principle. This principle derived from a legal maxim that probably went back to the medieval era, according to which "there are no slaves in France." On this topic, see Peabody, *"There Are No Slaves in France"* and "An Alternative Genealogy of the Origins of French Free Soil: Medieval Toulouse," *Slavery & Abolition* 32, no. 3 (2011): 341–362.

6. ANOM F3 226 "Motifs du Jugement rendû le 8 fevrier 1738," p. 302.

7. ANOM F3 226 "Motifs du Jugement rendû le 8 fevrier 1738," p. 296.

8. ANOM F3 226 "Motifs du Jugement rendû le 8 fevrier 1738," p. 303.

9. ANOM F3 225 "Extrait de la lettre du ministre [. . .] Du 26 aoust 1738," pp. 349–351.

10. ANOM F3 226 "Motifs du Jugement rendû le 8 fevrier 1738," pp. 291–332; ANOM F3 225 "Extrait de la lettre du ministre [. . .] 26 aoust 1738," pp. 349–351.

11. For studies underestimating the scope of mixed relationships in Louisiana, see Aubert, "'The Blood of France,'" 475 ("small number"); William H. Baker, "Louisiana," in *Encyclopedia of the North American Colonies*, ed. Jacob Ernest Cooke (EBook, New York: C. Scribner's Sons, 1993), 2: 175 ("largely distinct"), https://www.google.com/books/edition/Encyclopedia_of_the_North_American_Colon/ZPgpAQAAMAAJ?hl=en; Thomas Ingersoll, *Mammon and Manon in Early New Orleans: The First Slave Society in the Deep South, 1718–1819* (Knoxville: University of Tennessee Press, 1999), 140. For studies underplaying the scope of mixed relationships on Isle Bourbon, see Raphaël Barquissau, Hippolyte Foucque, and Hubert Jacob de Cordemoy, *L'Ile de La Réunion (Ancienne Ile Bourbon)* (2nd edition, Paris: Émile Larose, 1925), 21; Albert Corre, *Nos Créoles* (Paris: P.-V Stock, Éditeur, 1902), 23; Isidore Guët, *Les Origines de l'île Bourbon et de la colonisation française à Madagascar* (Paris: Charles Bayle, 1888), 76–77. However, it is true that not all parishes in Lower Louisiana were home to widespread mixed relationships between white men and Black women. In fact, no *mulâtres* were recorded in the parish registers of Mobile from 1724 to 1763 and only five in Natchitoches between 1729 and 1763. See Jacqueline Vidrine, trans. and ed., *Love's Legacy: The Mobile Marriages Recorded in French, Transcribed, with Annotated Abstracts in English, 1726-1786* (Lafayette: Center for Louisiana Studies, University of Southwestern Louisiana, 1985); SCD, Dupré Library, UL Lafayette, "Natchitoches Parish Registers, 1729–1792." This observation adds nuance to Vidal's recent claim that "many illicit relationships took place while their protagonists lived in distant outposts such as La Balise or Mobile." See Vidal, *Caribbean New Orleans*, 280. Two factors may explain these low *métissage* rates in Mobile and Natchitoches. First, by the 1720s, white men and white women had already reached demographic parity in those two parishes: indeed, ratios of free men to free women were 1:1 in Mobile, Dauphin Island, and Natchitoches by 1721 and 1722. Second, few settlers in Natchitoches owned enslaved people: there were only eight slave-owning households in this parish in 1722. See ANOM 5 DPPC "Recencement [*sic*] des habitans du fort Louis de la Mobile et ses villages Circonvoisins," June 28, 1732; ANOM 5 DPPC "Les Natchitoches Recensement Des habitans du fort St Jean Baptiste de Natchitoches," May 22, 1722.

12. Vidal has recently noted this pattern in the historiography. Citation from Vidal, *Caribbean New Orleans*, 248. Nathan Marvin, too, has criticized scholars' tendency to consider *métissage* as a sign of "racia[l] harmon[y]." See his "Bourbon Island Creoles," 246.

13. Gwendolyn Hall, *Africans in Colonial Louisiana: The Development of Afro-Creole Culture in the Eighteenth Century* (EBook, Baton Rouge, LA.: Louisiana State University Press, 1995), 270 ("openness"), 271, 12, 374, https://play.google.com/books/reader?id=bom100wjmvgC&pg=GBS.PA1; Gary B. Nash, *Red, White, and Black: The Peoples of Early North America*, 3rd ed. (Hoboken, NJ: Prentice-Hall, 1992), 106 ("no embarrassment"). For more examples, see Nash, *Red, White, and Black*, 107.

14. For publications considering the power dynamics in sexual relations in the context of colonialism, see Ann M. Little, "Gender and Sexuality in the North American Borderlands, 1492–1848," *History Compass* 7, no. 6 (2009): 1606–1615; Gary Nash, "The Hidden History of Mestizo America," *Journal of American History* 82, no. 3 (1995): 941–964; Ann L. Stoler, "Carnal Knowledge and Imperial Power: Gender, Race, and Morality in Colonial Asia," in *Gender at the Crossroads of Knowledge: Feminist Anthropology in the Postmodern Era*, ed. Micaela di Leonardo (Berkeley: University of California Press, 1991), 51–101, and *Carnal Knowledge and Imperial Power*; Richard Trexler, *Sex and Conquest: Gendered Violence, Political Order and the European Conquest of the Americas* (Ithaca, NY: Cornell University Press, 1995).

15. Citations from Trévor Burnard, *Mastery, Tyranny, and Desire: Thomas Thistlewood and His Slaves in the Anglo-Jamaican World* (EBook, Chapel Hill: University of North Carolina Press, 2004), 175 ("institutional dominance"), https://play.google.com/books/reader?id=JsVIcJiGOVMC&pg=GBS.PP1; Spear, *Race, Sex, and Social Order*, 7 ("racial orders"). On the use of sexual violence in slave societies, see also Block, *Rape and Sexual Power*; Kathleen M. Brown, *Good Wives, Nasty Wenches, and Anxious Patriarchs: Gender, Race, and Power in Colonial Virginia* (EBook, Chapel Hill: University of North Carolina Press, 1996), 355–356, https://heinonline-org.proxy.lib.duke.edu/HOL/P?h=hein.beal/gowvnstaxp0001&i=339. My thinking here owes much to Ann Laura Stoler's work. See, for example, her *Race and the Education of Desire: Foucault's History of Sexuality and the Colonial Order of Things* (Durham, NC: Duke University Press, 1995), *Carnal Knowledge and Imperial Power*, and "Tense and Tender Ties."

16. It then dropped to 4,598 in 1763 due to the cessation of slave imports. ANOM 5 DPPC 16 "[1721] Recensement des habitans Et Concessionaires de la Nouvelle Orleans et lieux circonvoisins"; Hall, *Africans in Colonial Louisiana*, 9.

17. There is one important exception for Isle Bourbon: see Paris, "La page blanche."

18. Vincent Brown, "Social Death and Political Life in the Study of Slavery," *The American Historical Review*, 114, no. 5 (2009): 1231–1249. About the practice of patriarchy in early modern France, see Julie Hardwick, *The Practice of Patriarchy: Gender and the Politics of Household Authority in Early Modern France* (University Park: Pennsylvania State University Press, 1998).

19. Angela Davis, "Reflections on the Black Woman's Role in the Community of Slaves," in "Woman: An Issue," special issue, *Massachusetts Review* 13, no. 1/2 (1972): 81–100.

20. For one powerful example, see [Harriet Jacobs], Linda Brent [pseudonym], and Lydia Maria Child [editor], *Incidents in the Life of a Slave Girl, written by herself* (Boston: Thayer & Eldridge 1861).

21. For an overview of the vast historiography dealing with sodomy cases in Latin America, see Zeb Tortorici, "Against Nature: Sodomy and Homosexuality in Colonial Latin America," *History Compass* 10, no. 2 (2012): 161–178.

22. See Laura Gowing, *Common Bodies: Women, Touch and Power in Seventeenth-Century England* (New Haven, CT: Yale University Press, 2003), 30, 59, 204, 208; Peter Stallybrass,

"Patriarchal Territories: The Body Enclosed," in *Rewriting the Renaissance: The Discourses of Sexual Difference in Early Modern Europe,* ed. Margaret W. Ferguson, Maureen Quilligan, and Nancy Vickers (Chicago: University of Chicago Press, 1986), 123–142, here 128.

23. ANOM 5 DPPC 62 Boucher, "Le mémoire pour servir à la connaissance," pp. 95–97.

24. ADR C°2519 "6 Septembre 1733, Arret qui condamne le nommé Janets dit Rochefort a être Blamé et en trente livres d'amande," ff. 26–26v.

25. ADR C 4 "Du vingt trois aoust 1742, Envoy de plusieurs ouvriers a l'Isle De france pour Cause de libertinage," ff. 157v (quotation)–158.

26. ANOM F3 226 "La Guadeloupe Conseil de May 1744," p. 161.

27. ANOM F3 226 "La Guadeloupe Conseil de May 1744," pp. 161–162.

28. LSM RSC File 1752-06-13-01 "Proces Verbal de declaration des Negresses 13 Juin 1752."

29. LSM RSCL File 1752-06-12-02 Black Books "June 12 1752. Examination of Pochenet" (quotation); LSM RSCL File 1752-06-12-02 "12 Juin 1752." This might not have been Pochenet's first sexual assault. The court of Louisiana accused the French soldier of hiding the truth on the grounds that "he had [already] knifed a woman in France in the town of Metz." Quoted from White, *Voices of the Enslaved*, 71.

30. LSM RSCL File 1752-06-12-02 "12 Juin 1752"; LSM RSCL File 1752-06-13-01 "Proces-verbal de declaration des Negresses"; LSM RSCL File 1752-06-12-02 Black Books "June 12, 1752 Examination of Pochenet"; "Criminal Trial for Assassination, June 8, 1752"; "Report of Surgeon Gueydon on wound of Babet"; "Complaint of Membrede and petition of the Procureur General against Antoine Dochenet [*sic*], June 12, 1752"; "Interrogation of Dochenet [*sic*], June 12, 1752"; "Interrogation of Dochenet [*sic*], June 12, 1752"; "Proces verbal of declaration of the two wounded negresses, June 13, 1752"; "Arrest and Imprisonment of Dochenet [*sic*], June 17, 1752"; "Second interrogation of the accused, June 19, 1752"; "Conclusions of the Procureur General in the criminal suit against Dochenet [*sic*], June 26, 1752"; "Procureur Général v. Pierre Antoine Pochenet," June 12–28, 1752," RSC, *LHQ* 21 no. 2, (1938): 567–573.

31. LSM RSCL 1730-09-05-02 "1730. A Messieurs du Conseil superieur an la Province de la Loüisiane" ("crushed"/ "blow"); LSM RSCL 1730-04-29-01 "Du 25 avril 1730" ("complains").

32. LSM RSCL 1730-09-05-02 "1730. A Messieurs du Conseil superieur an la Province de la Loüisiane"; LSM RSCL 1730-04-29-01 "Du 25 avril 1730"; "Jan. 17, 1730, Examination of a Delinquent Steward," "April 29, 1730, "'To Sieur Roy,'" RSC, *LHQ* 4, no. 4 (1921), 510, 521; "Aug. 28, 1730, Decisions in Sundry Suits"; "Sept. 4, 1730, Decisions in Sundry Suits"; "Sept. 5, 1730, Petition to Prosecute Scoundrel Overseer"; "Sept. 5, 1730, D'Auseville vs. Charpentier (Le Roy)"; "Sept. 5 1730, D'Auseville vs. Charpentier alias Le Roy"; "Sept. 7, 1730, Petition to Reinforce Prosecution"; "Nov. 22 1730, Petition in Recovery [. . .] Jacques Roy], formerly steward for Mr. D'Auseville"; "Dec. 1, 1730, Remonstrance. Councillor D'Auseville reviews [the demands of his tenant Roy]," "Court Summons. Sheriff Dargaway notifies Jacques Charpentier alias Le Roy [. . .]," RSC, *LHQ* 5, no. 1 (1922), 87, 89, 91, 92, 94, 102, 103–104, 107. See also White, *Voices of the Enslaved*, 127–129.

33. Cited in Elisabeth, *La société martiniquaise*, 221.

34. ANOM F3 206 "Lettre de la Compagnie des Indes à Mrs du Conseil Superieur de Bourbon Sur plusieurs objets et notamment Sur le Café Paris 24 Septembre 1729," ff. 62v–63.

35. ADR C°301 "Au Port Louis, Isle de France [. . .]," undated document.

36. ANOM F3 205 "26 Mars 1729," pp. 158–159 (quotation).

37. ADR 2MI 19 C°3 "Renvoy en france du nommé jean Nicole et joseph pascal Commandeur," f. 42v. Pascal continued to visit that same enslaved woman to have sex with her even after he was dismissed from his position.

38. ADR 2MI 19 C°3 "Renvoy en france du nommé jean Nicole et joseph pascal Commandeur," f. 43.

39. ADR 2MI 19 C°3 "Renvoy en france du nommé jean Nicole et joseph pascal Commandeur," f. 42v. The third Frenchman who was expelled from Isle Bourbon was a cadet in the garrison of the town of Saint-Denis named Sieur de Langle de la Potinerie. He was sent away in 1737 on the grounds that he was a drunk and a thief who led a "libertine life [. . .] going to people's cabins to corrupt the *négresses.*" ADR 2 MI 19 C°3 "Du 11 mars 1737 pour renvoyer le Sr de Langle a L'isle de France," f. 91.

40. Quoted from Vidal, *Caribbean New Orleans*, 274–275. On the *ménagères* of the Antilles, Dominique Rogers, "Les libres de couleur dans les capitales de Saint-Domingue: fortunes, mentalités et intégration à la fin de l'Ancien Régime (1776–1789) (PhD diss., Université Bordeaux III, 1999), chap. 10, sec. 2. For a definition of "ménagère," see Nathalie Dessens, "Les 'ménagères' de Saint-Domingue et de Louisiane," in *Colonisations,* ed. Singaravélou *et al.*, 717–718.

41. Unfortunately, the incidence of this practice cannot be assessed for the 1740s and 1750s because of the lack of censuses for those periods.

42. ANOM 5 DPPC 16 "Louisiane Recensement 1721 [. . .] Recensement des habitans Et Concessionaires de la Nouvelle Orleans et lieux circonvoisins."

43. All three were single. ANOM 5 DPPC 16 "Louisiane Recensement 1721 [. . .] Recensement des habitans Et Concessionaires de la Nouvelle Orleans et lieux circonvoisins."

44. We do not know how many of them were single. ANOM 5 DPPC 16 "Louisianne Recensement 1731 [. . .] Recensement des habitations le long du fleuve."

45. ANOM G1 464 "Recensement General de La Ville de la Nouvelle Orleans [. . .] fait au mois de Janvier 1732"; ANO SR/1 "Saint-Louis Cathedral, New Orleans, baptisms, burials, marriages, 1731–1733," ff. 27, 40v.

46. ANO SR/2 "Saint-Louis Cathedral, New Orleans, baptisms, 1744–1753"; ANO SR/3 "St. Louis Cathedral, New Orleans, Baptism, 1753-1759." This data (184 *mulâtres*) includes all baptized children, as well as their relatives and godparents. ANOM C13 C4 "Récapitulatif du recensement général de la Louisiane en 1737," f. 197. Vidal, *Caribbean New Orleans*, 118–121.

47. ANO SR/2 "Saint-Louis Cathedral, New Orleans, baptisms, 1744–1753."

48. ANO SR/4 "Saint-Louis Cathedral, New Orleans, baptisms, marriages, 1759–1762."

49. Vidal, *Caribbean New Orleans,* 121.

50. ANO "Saint Louis Cathedral. Baptisms, Vol II. January 1 1744 to May 15 1753," p. 276.

51. See Hall, *Africans in Colonial Louisiana*, 268.

52. Hall, *Africans in Colonial Louisiana*, 278.

53. Gwendolyn Hall has emphasized the role of isolation, and of "closeness and intimacy," in bringing "extensive [. . .] race mixture" at Pointe Coupée. Hall, *Africans in Colonial Louisiana*, 278, 294 ("race mixture").

54. HL "Vaudreuil Papers," LO 54 "1745 Dec. 20 Pointe Coupée Louisiana Recencement [*sic*] General des habitans de la paroisse de la Pointe Coupée"; ABR "St Francis of Pointe Coupee New Roads L.A, Baptisms, Marriages, Burials, 1756–1769."

55. HL "Vaudreuil Papers," LO 54 "1745 Dec. 20 Pointe Coupée Louisiana Recencement General des habitans de la paroisse de la Pointe Coupée."

56. Garrigus, *Before Haiti*, 154–155.

57. ANOM C8 B8 "Lettre du père Mane, 30 septembre 1722," f. 124. Cited in Cousseau, "La famille invisible," 47–48.

58. ANOM C8 B8 "Lettre du père Mane, 30 septembre 1722," f. 124. Cited in Cousseau, "La famille invisible," 51 ("masters"), 63n51 ("seduction").

59. Cited in Elisabeth, *La société martiniquaise*, 197. Other enslaved mixed children were also recorded in Guadeloupe, including fifteen *mulâtres* and *quarterons* who were listed in the well-preserved parish registers of Le Gosier between the 1720s and 1750s, born to enslaved women and unidentified white men, some of whom might have been their owners. See ANOM 85MIOM197 "Le Gozier, 1688–1772." Most of those *mulâtres* spent their entire lives in slavery, being listed alongside *nègres* in several Martinican censuses. Adrien Dessalles, *Histoire générale des Antilles* (Paris: Libraire-éditeur quai Malaquais, 1847), 4:574.

60. Rose-May Nicole, *Noirs, cafres et créoles: Étude de la representation du non blanc réunionnais* (Paris: L'Harmattan, 1996), 80.

61. Bernardin de Saint-Pierre, *Voyage à L'isle de France, à l'isle de Bourbon, au Cap de Bonne-Espérance etc., avec des observations nouvelles sur la nature et les hommes*, 2 vols. (Amsterdam: Chez Merlin, 1773), 1:184.

62. Saint-Pierre, *Voyage à l'isle de Bourbon*, 1:185–186.

63. Challe, *Journal d'un Voyage*, 2:191 (filles de mauvaise vie), 192 (same price as valets).

64. Marisa J. Fuentes, "Power and Historical Figuring: Rachael Pringle Polgreen's Troubled Archive," *Gender & History* 22, no. 3 (2010): 564–584, here 576 ("function"/"performative") –577 ("degrading"/"owner"/"mutuality"), 571.

65. Challe, *Journal d'un Voyage*, 2:191.

66. Challe, *Journal d'un Voyage*, 2:192–193 (quotation).

67. Challe, *Journal d'un Voyage*, 2:191.

68. Challe, *Journal d'un Voyage*, 2:192.

69. ANOM F3 222 "Reglement concernant Les affranchissements des Esclaves Du 15 août 1711," p. 189.

70. ANOM F3 226 "Motifs du Jugement rendû le 8 fevrier 1738," p. 318.

71. For Hartman's interpretation of the notion of Black seduction in the context of slavery, see Hartman, *Scenes of Subjection*, 102–105. See also Cowling et al., "Mothering Slaves," 228–229; Garraway, *The Libertine Colony*, 232. For another example from the French historiography, see Elsa Dorlin, *La matrice de la race: Généalogie sexuelle et coloniale de la Nation française* (Paris: La Découverte, 2006), 220.

72. ANOM F3 252 "25 Octobre 1722 [. . .] Desny Duvanel Curé," p. 528. When, five years later, a relative attempted to exclude the Black widow of a diseased white man named Gilles Petit from family inheritance in Guadeloupe, the French attorney-general described Petit as an honest man who had been "seduced by the tricks of th[is] *négresse*." ANOM F3 224 "Du Jeudy Sixieme Du mois de mars mil Sept Cent Vingt Sept," p. 216. For more information about this case, see Chapter 4.

73. Article IX of the *Code Noir* of 1685 prescribed the systematic manumission of enslaved women who married freemen and of their mixed children. See *Recueils de reglemens*, 2:85.

74. See Spear, *Race, Sex and Social Order*, 31–32; Vaughan Baker, Amos Simpson, and Mathé Allain, "Le Mari Est Seigneur: Marital Laws Governing Women in French Louisiana," in *Louisiana's Legal Heritage*, ed. Edward F. Haas (Pensacola, FL: Perdido Bay Press, 1983), 7–17; Barbara B. Diefendorf, "Widowhood and Remarriage in Sixteenth-Century Paris," *Journal of Family History* 7, no. 4 (1982): 379–395.

75. Elisabeth, *La société martiniquaise*, 222.

76. Elisabeth, *La société martiniquaise*, 290.

77. For example, in 1733 and 1734, they authorized two Frenchmen to marry *mulâtresses* in Fort-Royal. See Elisabeth, *La société martiniquaise*, 315. In 1749, intendant of the *Îles du Vent* Jean Louis Albert de Ranché authorized the wedding of a Frenchman from Bordeaux with a free

Black woman in Fort-Royal. His successor as intendant, Charles-Martin Hurson, authorized only one intermarriage during his time in office from 1749 to 1755, presumably because the couple already had one child out of wedlock. Elisabeth, *La société martiniquaise,* 316.

78. Elisabeth, *La société martiniquaise,* 228–229.

79. ANOM 85MIOM197 "Le Gozier, 1688–1772."

80. ANOM 85MIOM197 "Le Gozier, 1688–1772."

81. ANOM 85MIOM197 "Le Gozier, 1688–1772." Prior to having a relationship with Nicolas Delbourg, in 1747, the *mulâtresse* Marie Rose Taouïra had another child out of wedlock with a white man named Louis de Revenes.

82. Vidrine, *Love's Legacy*; SCD, Dupré Library, UL Lafayette, "Natchitoches Parish Registers, 1729–1792."

83. ABR "St Francis of Pointe Coupee New Roads L.A, Baptisms, Marriages, Burials, 1756–1769"; ANO SR/56, "St. Louis Cathedral, New Orleans, Marriage Index, 1720–1730."

84. ANO SR/56, "St. Louis Cathedral, New Orleans, Marriage Index, 1720–1730," pp. 89–90. See also Spear, *Race, Sex, and Social Order,* 79–80.

85. ANO SR/2, "Saint-Louis Cathedral, New Orleans, baptisms, 1744–1753," p. 114.

86. ANO SR/2, "Saint-Louis Cathedral, New Orleans, baptisms, 1744–1753," p. 114.

87. ANO SR/210, "Saint-Charles Borromeo, Destrehan, Combination book, 1739–1755," p. 95; ANO SR/3, "Saint-Louis Cathedral, New Orleans, baptisms, 1753–1759," p. 23. The other case is mentioned in Vidal, "Caribbean Louisiana," 128.

88. Matthew Gerber, *Bastard: Politics, Family, and Law in Early Modern France* (EBook, Oxford: Oxford University Press, 2012), 27–34, https://play.google.com/books/reader?id=pXLRCwAAQBAJ&pg=GBS.PR1.

89. Vidal, *Caribbean New Orleans*, 286.

90. By contrast, the parish registers of Isle Bourbon contain only a few mentions of "unknown father[s]." For some examples, see ADR GG44 "ST Denis 2 MIEC773"; ADR 1 GG1 "Bl, Libres, Escl 1667–1718"; ADR 2MIEC 780 "St Pierre."

91. Pierre François Régis Dessalles, *Les Annales du Conseil Souverain de la Martinique ou Tableau historique du gouvernement de cette colonie*, 2 vols. (Bergerac: J.B. Puynesge, 1786), 1 (1): 104.

92. Cousseau, "La famille invisible," 52–53.

93. Cousseau, "La famille invisible," 51–53.

94. Elisabeth, *La société martiniquaise*, 317.

95. Cousseau, "La famille invisible," 53.

96. Cousseau, "La famille invisible," 49.

97. ANO SR/2 "Saint-Louis Cathedral, New Orleans, baptisms, 1744–1753."

98. ANO SR/4 "Saint-Louis Cathedral, New Orleans, baptisms, marriages, 1759–1762"; LSM RSCL File 1769-09-20-01 "La Compagnie des mulatres et nêgres libres de cette colonie de la Loüisianne."

99. "Feb. 14 [1745] Procuration granted by Jacques Forcade [. . .] to Anne Galbreon," RSC, *LHQ* 13, no. 4 (1930): 671.

100. As Cécile Vidal puts it, "Most slaveholding societies throughout world history authorized manumission, for the hope of freedom constituted an instrument of social control that masters could use as leverage over those they held in bondage." Vidal, *Caribbean New Orleans*, 508.

101. LSM RSCL File 1737-06-29-01 "Pierre Garzou dit Leveillé Declaration [. . .]"; "Aug. 23, 1736, Power of Attorney. Cannes Brulees," RSC, *LHQ* 5, no. 3 (1922): 384; "June 29. 1737 Declaration in Registry of Superior Council by Pierre Garçon called l'Eveillé," RSC, *LHQ* 9 no. 2 (1926): 299.

102. LSM RSCL File 1762-02-08-02 "1762 8 fevrier. Chenet Liberté accordée a hypolite negresse Et a Izidore Son fils."

103. On manumissions in Louisiana, see Chapter 4.

104. Vidal, *Caribbean New Orleans*, 277–281.

105. LSM RSCL File 1735-10-09-01 "Je soussigné Sr Pierre de St Julien [. . .]," n. p. (quotation); "Oct. 9 [1735] Manumission of Marie Charlotte and Louise [. . .] by their master, St. Pierre de St. Julien," RSC, *LHQ* 8, no. 1 (1925): 143–144. A note declared this act of manumission invalid, on the grounds that St. Julien owed three times the amount of the value of his estate.

106. LSM RSCL File 1738-08-26-03 "L'an Mil Sept Cent trente huit. Le ving sixieme aoust avant Midy. Par devant Le notaire Royal de La Province de La Loüisianne [. . .]," n. p. For information about Diron d'Artaguiette's position concerning French–Native American intermarriage, see Chapter 4. Marianne was, by all evidence, d'Artaguiette's concubine. D'Artaguiette fathered several mixed children with her. Although this document refers to her as a *mulâtresse*, she was likely of Native American descent. Françoise is explicitly described as d'Artaguiette's daughter in this document: LSM RSCL File 1747-07-01-03 "Je Mathias Berthelot." D'Artaguiette had another mixed-race son named Jean-Baptiste. LSM RSCL File 1747-07-01-01 "A Nos Seigneurs du Conseil Supérieur de la Province de la Louisiane"; LSM RSCL File 1747-07-01-02 "Je Mathias Berthelot." For more information about D'Artaguiette, Marianne and two of their children, see Vidal, *Caribbean New Orleans*, 279–280.

107. "Nov. 14 [1745] Report on legal freedom. Vincent Le Porche files a statement," RSC, *LHQ* 14, no. 4 (1931): 598.

108. Régent, *La France et ses esclaves*, 337; Garraway, *The Libertine Colony*, 211.

109. About manumissions in Santo Domingo, see Richard Turits, "Par-delà les plantations. Question raciale et identités collectives à Santo Domingo," *Genèses* 66 (2007): 51–68, here 51. I thank Richard Turits for sharing this article with me.

110. ANOM, G1 497 "Recencement [*sic*] de l'Isle de la Guadeloupe Et Dependances Pour l'année 1731"; Elisabeth, *La société martiniquaise*, 314 (Martinique); Régent, *La France et ses esclaves*, 337 (Saint-Domingue).

111. On this topic, see: Debien, *Les esclaves aux Antilles françaises*, 376; Garraway, *The Libertine Colony*, 211, 290; Jacques Houdaille, "Le métissage dans les anciennes colonies françaises," *Population (French Edition)* 36, no. 2 (1981): 267–286, here 272; King, *Blue Coat or Powdered Wig*, 44.

112. Elisabeth, *La société martiniquaise*, 306.

113. Houdaille, "Le métissage dans les anciennes colonies françaises," 276.

114. ANOM A 23 "Édit du roi, ou Code noir, qui concerne entièrement les esclaves de la Louisiane, Mars 1724," article LII, fol. 56.

115. LSM RSCL File 1727-07-13-01 "Last will and testament of Francois Deserboy," Black Books (quotation); "July 13 1727, Will of Francois Deserboy," *LHQ* 4, no. 2 (1921): 222; "May 28, 1728, Petition for Prompt Settlement. Joseph Lazou [*sic*], executive for the late Francois Deserboy," *LHQ* 4, no. 4 (1921): 485.

116. ANOM DPPC 2866 "1727. Memoire touchant quelques particuliers qui sont a la Louisianne," f. 141.

117. This case is surprising because the donation ban in the *Code Noir* only targeted Blacks and did not mention enslaved Native Americans. LSM RSCL File 1729-10-22-01 "A Messieurs du Conseil Superieur de la province de la Louisiane. 22 Oct. 1729," (quotation); "Oct. 22, 1729, Petition for emancipation of Indian slave by Duplessis, settler at Natchitoches, according to the will of the late Francois," *LHQ* 4, no. 3 (1921): 355.

118. ANOM A 23 "Édit du roi, ou Code noir, qui concerne entièrement les esclaves de la Louisiane, Mars 1724," f. 54.

119. Though Jean-Baptiste was described as the son of a formerly enslaved man named Louis Connard, he might have been Jacques's son since they shared the same name. LSM RSCL File 1739-03-04-03 "A nos Seigneurs du Conseil Superieur de la province de La Louisianne."

120. "Aug. 24 [1743], Conclusions of Procureur General in the case of Baptiste. He demands his conviction and that he be reduced to slavery and sold," RSC *LHQ* 11, no. 4 (1928): 652–653; "Sept. 10, 1743, Interrogation of Pantalon [. . .] accused of Stealing shirts and handkerchiefs [. . .] He denies complicity with Jean Baptiste"; "Sept. 11, 1743, Confrontation of Jean Baptiste and Pantalon"; "Sept. 14 [1743], Conclusions of the Procureur General, finding Jean Baptiste guilty and recommending that he be reduced to slavery for the benefit of the hospital"; "No. 950 Sentence passed by Council. This follows the views of the Procureur," RSC, *LHQ* 12, no. 1 (1929): 145–147.

121. "April 8 [1747] Sale of a Free Negress"; "April 11. [1747]. Sale and adjudication of Jeannette, a free negress," RSC, *LHQ* 18, no. 1 (1935): 168; For more on her story, see "April 27, [1747], St. Martin de Jauregibery seeks to recover 35 piastres out of the proceeds of the sale of the free negress Jeannette condemned to slavery for theft and other misconduct," RSC, *LHQ* 18, no. 1 (1935): 189.

122. "Sale of a negress for 17,500 livres and a mulatto girl for 4,000 livres by Benoist Payen de Chavoye to André Jung," RSC, *LHQ* 24, no. 2 (1941): 582–583.

123. LSM RSCL File 1767-07-09-02 "9 Juillet 1767. Information contre Jourdan"; LSM RSCL File 1767-07-12-02 "12 Juillet 1767. Confrontation du Nègre Louis avec la négresse Catherine"; "Du 12 Juillet 1767"; "Le 22 aoust 1767"; LSM RSCL File 1767-08-08-04 "A Nos Seigneurs du Conseil Superieur de la province de la Louisiane." See also Vidal, *Caribbean New Orleans*, 274.

124. ANO SR/2 "Saint-Louis Cathedral, New Orleans, baptisms, 1744–1753," p. 223; Spear, *Race, Sex, and Social Order*, 263n84.

125. Spear, *Race, Sex, and Social Order*, 86.

126. LSM RSCL File 1738-02-15-03 "De Chavannes habitant vous Supplie tres humblement de faire homologuer la Liberté qu'il a accordé a Marie Angelique dite Isabelle Negresse [. . .] 5 [Septem]bre 1732." Isabelle was sometimes categorized as a Black woman (a "*négresse*"), sometimes as a *mulâtresse*, and in one document as a "quadroon" ("*quarteronne*"). Vidal, *Caribbean New Orleans*, 275–276.

127. LSM RSCL File 1738-02-15-03 "De Chavannes habitant vous Suplie tres humblement de faire homologuer la Liberté qu'il a accordé a Marie Angelique" (quotation); "Feb. 15 [1738], Petition of M. de Chavannes for homologation of freedom granted to Marie Angelique, a negress he bought [. . .]," RSC, *LHQ* 9, no. 4 (1926), 722.

128. For example, see "January 27 [1748], Petition to Superior Council by Mr. de St. Martin to whom Sr. de Chavannes sold a negress and her child," RSC, *LHQ* 19, no. 1 (1936), 236–237; "Politics in Louisiana in 1724"; "Testimony of Sr de Chavannes March 17, 1727"; "French testimony of Sr de Chavannes"; "Dec. 3, 1737. Petition for Secure Title," RSC, *LHQ* 5, no. 3 (1722): 303, 309, 313, 423.

129. Vidal, *Caribbean New Orleans*, 276.

130. LSM RSCL File 1752-12-02-02 "Entre La Nommée Isabelle Negresse Libre demande En Requete," p. 8.

131. LSM RSCL File 1752-12-02-02 "Entre La Nommée Isabelle Negresse Libre demande En Requete," p. 8; LSM RSCL File 1752-12-02-02 "Black Books"; "December 2, 1752, Executive session of the superior council."

132. ANO SR/2 "Saint-Louis Cathedral, New Orleans, baptisms, 1744–1753," p. 223. Rançon may have fathered another child with Marie-Jeanne a few years later, a girl described as a "free" *mulâtresse*. Vidal, *Caribbean New Orleans*, 271–272.

133. ANOM F3 236 "Ordonnance du Roi Concernant l'affranchissement des esclaves Du 15 juin 1736," pp. 681–683, 682 (quotation); Debien, *Les esclaves aux Antilles françaises*, 373.

134. Moitt, *Women and Slavery in the French Antilles*, 151.

135. Spear, *Race, Sex, and Social Order*, 83–84.

136. Charlotte and her father had a contentious relationship. See "June 15, 1751, Order to hear witnesses in case of Battard vs. Derneville"; "June 15, 1751, Proces verbal on witnesses, on request of Derneville"; "Testimony of Francois Nantais"; "Testimony of Antoine Grenet"; "Testimony of Charles Blanc"; Testimony of Pierre Viaud"; "Testimony of Jean Marie Pupil Du Sablon"; "Testimony of Pierre Michel"; "Testimony of Louis," RSC, *LHQ* 20, no. 4 (1937): 1122–1126; Spear, *Race, Sex, and Social Order*, 82–84.

137. Moitt, *Women and Slavery in the French Antilles*, 159.

138. ANOM F3 227 "La Guadeloupe 10 Septembre 1758," pp. 249–253.

139. For a biography on Chevalier de Saint-Georges, see Gabriel Banat, *The Chevalier de Saint-Georges: Virtuoso of the Sword and the Bow* (Hillsdale, NY: Pendragon Press, 2006).

140. Banat, *The Chevalier de Saint-Georges*, 43–44.

141. Banat, *The Chevalier de Saint-Georges*.

142. LSM RSCL File 1757-07-01-01 "1757 Juin 20, Decour Liberté accordée a Rozette mulatresse," p. 1.

143. On this topic, see Chapter 3.

144. Especially on Isle Bourbon and in French India.

145. Carton, *Mixed-Race and Modernity*, 71–72; Hodges, "Configuring Colonial Families."

146. Carton, *Mixed-Race and Modernity*, 71–74.

147. Catherine Manning, *Fortunes à Faire: The French in Asian Trade, 1719–48* (Aldershot, UK: Variorum, 1996), 54.

148. Manning, *Fortunes à Faire*, 66.

149. Additionally, a scholar working on the French Company of the Indies concludes that "by a conservative estimate [. . .] during the first half of the eighteenth century, at least half of colonial, married households in Chandernagore had a Luso-Indian wife." Hodges, "Configuring Colonial Families."

150. Quotation in Carton, *Mixed-Race and Modernity*, 69.

151. Haudrère, *La Compagnie française des Indes*, 2:595. As we saw in Chapter 3, the *topas* were Indians who had been Christianized and exposed to European customs during the earlier period of Portuguese presence.

152. Alfred Martineau, ed., *Mémoire de François Martin, fondateur de Pondichéry* (Paris: Société d'Edition Géographiques, Maritimes et Coloniales, 1932), 423 (quotation); Philippe Le Tréguilly and Monique Morazé eds., *L'Inde et la France. Deux siècles d'histoire commune, 17e-18e siècles. Histoire, sources, bibliographie* (Paris: C.N.R.S. Éditions, 1995), 95.

153. Alfred Martineau, *Correspondance du Conseil supérieur de Pondichéry avec le Conseil de Chandernagor*, 3 vols. (Pondicherry: Société de l'histoire de l'Inde, 1915–1927), 1: 119.

154. Hodges, "Configuring Colonial Families."

155. Manning, *Fortunes à Faire*, 54.

156. Carton, *Mixed-Race and Modernity*, 72, 74–75.

157. Some were former prisoners recruited in overcrowded prisons. Carton, *Mixed-Race and Modernity*, 71.

158. Carton, *Mixed-Race and Modernity*, 75; Hodges, "Configuring Colonial Families."

159. Carton, *Mixed-Race and Modernity*, 74–75.

160. Tréguilly and Morazé ed., *L'Inde et la France*, 91.

161. Carton, *Mixed-Race and Modernity*, 68–69.

162. Manning, *Fortunes à Faire*, 121–122, 124.

163. Hodges, "Configuring Colonial Families."

164. Martineau, *Correspondance du Conseil supérieur de Pondichéry*, 1: 178.

165. Hodges, "Configuring Colonial Families."

166. La Barbinais, *Nouveau voyage*, 3:124.

167. ANOM F3 205 "Des Mariages, de leur convenance, et de la Discipline qui S'y doit observer," p. 43.

168. Ricquebourg, *Dictionnaire généalogique des familles de l'Île Bourbon*, 1:230; ADR C°767 "Resancement [*sic*] Général Du nombre Des habitans qui sont Sur Lisle de Bourbon [. . .] en Lannée Mil Sept Cent huit," f. 5v; ANOM DPPC G1 477 "Recensement de L'isle de Bourbon en general, fait en Mars 1709." By 1732, Jeanne Royer and Henri-Guilbert Wilmann had become comfortable coffee bean planters and slaveowners. See ADR C° 768 "1732 Récensement général."

169. ADR C°2792 "2e Janvier 1715, serment des Conseillers." He might have unofficially occupied this position even before 1715. See Delabarre de Nanteuil, *Législation de l'Ile de la Réunion: Répertoire raisonné des lois, ordonnances locales, décrets coloniaux, décrets impériaux, et règlements et arrêtés*, 6 vols. (Paris: E. Donnaud, 1861), 4:546.

170. I have not been able to ascertain the date and location of the marriage between Dumas and Marie Gertrude.

171. ANOM C3 6 "Correspondance générale Ile Bourbon 1732," ff. 74–89.

172. ANOM C3 6 "Correspondance générale Ile Bourbon 1732," ff. 74, 80.

173. ANOM C3 6 "Correspondance générale Ile Bourbon 1732," f. 81.

174. ANOM C3 6 "Correspondance générale Ile Bourbon 1732," f. 80, 88v.

175. ANOM C3 6 "Correspondance générale Ile Bourbon 1732," f. 88v. Another factor may have led the controller-general to side with Marie-Gertrude: Dumas had made many enemies on Isle Bourbon by supporting a decision made by the Company of the Indies to force local planters to drop the sale price of coffee. See ADR C°2430 "Extrait de registre du greffe du Conseil Superieur de lisle de Bourbon Du 1er Juillet 1732. Motifs des habitans de L'isle de Bourbon dans leur deputation En France."

176. ADR C°768 "1732, Recensement general," f. 91. For more information on Dumas and Marie-Gertrude's fortune, see Chapter 6.

177. On the topic of women marrying young on Isle Bourbon, see: Noël, *Amours et familles interdites*, 42.

178. Kleber, "Gendered Societies," 236.

179. Marvin, "Bourbon Island Creoles," 6–7.

180. ANOM DPPC G1 477 "1704 et avril 1705 Resencement General de tous les Habitans chefs de familles, femmes, Enfans Et Esclaves Qui Sont dans L'Isle de bourbon," ff. 1–1v.

181. Ricquebourg, *Dictionnaire généalogique des familles de l'Île Bourbon*, 1:205, 3:2126.

182. ANOM 5 DPPC 62 Boucher, "Le mémoire pour servir à la connaissance," pp. 171 (quotation)–172.

183. ANOM DPPC G1 477 "Recensement de L'isle de Bourbon en general, fait en Mars 1709"; ANOM 5 DPPC 62 Boucher, "Le mémoire pour servir à la connaissance," pp. 172–173.

184. Ricquebourg, *Dictionnaire généalogique des familles de l'Île Bourbon*, 2:1441.

185. ADR C° 768 "1732 Recensement general."

186. ADR C°808 "Recensement St Denis, Ste Marie, St Paul, 1763."

187. Ricquebourg, *Dictionnaire généalogique des familles de l'Île Bourbon,* 2:1566. On Anne Launay and Jacques Aubert: ANOM G1 477 "1704 et avril 1705, Resencement General de tous les Habitans," f. 3; and ANOM 5 DPPC 62 Boucher, "Le mémoire pour servir," pp. 64, 117–118. Anne was the daughter of the wealthy Frenchman Gilles Launay and the Black Malagasy woman Anne Caze, discussed in Chapter 2. About Anne Caze and Gilles Launay: ANOM 5 DPPC 62 Boucher, "Le mémoire pour servir," p. 64; ADR C°767 "Recensement Général Du nombre Des habitans qui sont Sur Lisle de Bourbon hommes femmes Enfans Esclaves, année 1708," f. 19v, p. 21.

188. ADR C° 2794 "Registre des Actes Publics du quartier de St Paul," p. 3.

189. ANOM DPPC G1 477 "Recensement de L'isle de Bourbon en general, fait en Mars 1709."

190. ADR C°2793 "Le present Registre [. . .] Commencé Le dix huit Septembre 1713, Et finy Le Seize Novembre 1716," ff. 4v–5.

191. ANOM DPPC G1 477 "Reçenssement [*sic*] general Du quartier St Paul de l'année 1719," pp. 12–13.

6. Empire of Labor

1. Ricquebourg, *Dictionnaire généalogique des familles de l'Île Bourbon,* 3:2022. Marvin, "Bourbon Island Creoles," 23, 25.

2. Ricquebourg, *Dictionnaire généalogique des familles de l'Île Bourbon,* 1:356; ANOM DPPC G1 477 "Recensement general Du quartier St Paul de l'année 1719," p. 2.

3. Marvin, "Bourbon Island Creoles," 23.

4. ADR C° 768 "1732. Recensement géneral"; ANOM G1 477 "1704 et avril 1705. Recensement General de tous les Habitans chefs de familles, femmes, Enfans Et Esclaves Qui Sont dans L'Isle de Bourbon," f. 39; Marvin, "Bourbon Island Creoles," 23–24 (quotation). Ricquebourg, *Dictionnaire généalogique des familles de l'Île Bourbon,* 1:356, 3:2022.

5. For more information regarding the *capitation,* see Chapter 4. For information regarding the *corvée* system in the eighteenth-century French colonies, see Anne Conchon, "La corvée au XVIIIe siècle: Des formes plurielles de réquisition dans les colonies françaises," in *Travail servile et dynamiques économiques XVIe–XXe siècle,* ed. Anne Conchon, Myriam Cottias, and Alessandro Stanziani (Vincennes, France: Institut de la gestion publique et du développement économique, 2024), 77–94.

6. Some reinforced the ossification of the French colonies' socio-racial orders by acquiring large numbers of enslaved people.

7. The expression "slaves' economy" was coined by Ira Berlin and Phil Morgan. See Ira Berlin and Philip Morgan, eds., *The Slaves' Economy: Independent Production by Slaves in the Americas* (London: Frank Cass, 1991).

8. Many full-length studies have focused on the late eighteenth and the nineteenth centuries. For Caribbean examples, see: Jacques Adélaïde-Merlande, "Travail libre et travail servile (Antilles et Guyanes françaises, 1840–1848)," *Bulletin de la Société d'Histoire de la Guadeloupe,* no. 75–78 (1988): 3–16; Josette Fallope, "Les occupations d'esclaves à la Guadeloupe dans la première moitié du XIXe siècle," *Revue française d'histoire d'outre-mer* 74, no. 275 (1987), Économie et société des Caraïbes XVII-XIXe s. (Partie 1), pp. 189–205; Abel Louis, *Les Libres de couleur en Martinique,* 3 vols. (Paris: L'Harmattan, 2012), and "Les Libres de couleur en Martinique des origines à 1815: L'entre-deux d'un groupe social dans la tourmente coloniale"

(PhD diss., Université Antilles-Guyane, 2011); Jean-François Niort, "La condition des libres de couleur aux Îles du Vent (XVIIe–XIXe siècles): Ressources et limites d'un système ségrégationniste," *Bulletin de la Société d'histoire de la Guadeloupe*, no. 131 (2002) 61–112; Dominique Rogers, "Réussir dans un monde d'hommes: Les stratégies des femmes de couleur du Cap-Français," *Journal of Haitian Studies* 9, no. 1 (2003): 40–51; Julius S. Scott, *The Common Wind: Afro-American Currents in the Age of the Haitian Revolution* (London: Verso, 2018). For some Louisiana examples, see Donald E. Everett, "Free Persons of Color in Colonial Louisiana," *Louisiana History: The Journal of the Louisiana Historical Association* 7, no. 1 (1966): 21–50; Laura Foner, "The Free People of Color in Louisiana and St. Domingue: A Comparative Portrait of Two Three-Caste Slave Societies," *Journal of Social History* 3, no. 4 (1970): 406–430; Mary Gehman, *The Free People of Color of New Orleans: An Introduction*, 5th ed. (Chelsea, MI: Sheridan Books); Sybil Klein, *Creoles: The History and Legacy of Louisiana's Free People of Color* (Baton Rouge: Louisiana University Press, 2000). For a few exceptions, see: Caroline Oudin-Bastide, *Travail, Capitalisme et Société Esclavagiste: Guadeloupe, Martinique* (Paris: Éditions La Découverte, 2005); Anna Forestier, "Défendre son île: Les esclaves et les hommes de couleur dans la milice, XVIIe–XVIIIe siècles," (PhD diss., Sorbonne Université, 2018); Caroline Oudin-Bastide, "La relation au travail dans la société esclavagiste de la Guadeloupe et de la Martinique (xviie–xixe siècles)," *Travailler* 20, no. 2 (2008): 137–154.

9. Citations from Olivier Pétré-Grenouilleau, "Colonial Trade and Economic Development in France, Seventeenth to the Twentieth Centuries," in *A Deus Ex Machina Revisited: Atlantic Colonial Trade and European Economic Development*, ed. Pieter Emmer, Olivier Pétré-Grenouilleau, and Jessica Roitman (Leiden, Netherlands: Brill, 2006), 225–261, here 261 ("a long way"), and Guillaume Daudin, "How Important Was the Slavery System to Europe?," *Slavery & Abolition* 42, no. 1 (2021): 151–157, here 153 ("the existence"). For another publication in the same vein, see Guillaume Daudin, "Comment calculer les profits de la traite?," in "Traites et esclavages: Vieux problèmes, nouvelles perspectives?," ed. Olivier Pétré-Grenouilleau, special issue, *Outre-mers* 89, no. 336–337 (2002): 43–62. Pétré-Grenouilleau's and Guillaume Daudin's claims echo much older US discourse that can be traced back to the abolitionist era. On this topic, see Edward E. Baptist, *Slavery and the Making of American Capitalism* (New York: Basic Books, 2014), xviii–xix. It is already clear from many publications that colonial commodities had an enormous impact on cultural developments in France. For example, see Elizabeth Abbott, *Le sucre. Une histoire douce-amère* (Montréal: Fides, 2008); Ina Baghdiantz McCabe, *Orientalism in Early Modern France: Eurasian Trade, Exoticism, and the Ancien Régime* (Oxford: Berg, 2008); Madeleine Dobie, *Trading Places: Colonization and Slavery in Eighteenth-Century French Culture* (Ithaca, NY: Cornell University Press, 2010); Elizabeth Heath, "Sugarcoated Slavery: Colonial Commodities and the Education of the Senses in Early Modern France," *Critical Historical Studies* 5, no. 2 (2018): 169–207; Sidney W. Mintz, *Sweetness and Power: The Place of Sugar in Modern History* (New York: Penguin Books, 1986).

10. Citations from W. E. B. Du Bois, *Black Reconstruction: An Essay toward a History of the Part Which Black Folk Played in the Attempt to Reconstruct Democracy in America, 1860–1880* (New York: Harcourt, Brace, 1935), 15, 16. Marx and Eric Williams famously considered slavery in the context of European imperialisms central to the accumulation of the capital that made possible the emergence of industrialized capitalist systems in the West. Karl Marx, *Capital: A Critique of Political Economy* (New York: International Publishers, 1967), 751; Eric Williams, *Capitalism and Slavery* (Chapel Hill: University of North Carolina Press, 1944). For three powerful books emphasizing the impact of slave labor on the wealth of the West, see Sven Beckert, *Empire of Cotton: A Global History* (New York: Vintage Books, 2014); Baptist, *Slavery*

and the Making of American Capitalism; Johnson, *River of Dark Dreams*. For a nuanced discussion of slavery and capitalism that engages with Eric Williams' important work, see Paul Cheney, "Le Débat sur capitalisme et esclavage: un débat inachevé," *Travail servile et dynamiques économiques XVIe-XXIe siècle*, ed. Anne Conchon, Myriam Cottias and Alessandro Stanziani (Paris: IGPDE-Comité pour l'histoire économique et financière de la France, 2024), 97–116.

11. Heath, "Sugarcoated Slavery."

12. I leave the question of the economic impact of Black slavery on the European economy to economic historians. Several publications have paved the way for this chapter. Much of the work on slave labor in the early French context appears in passages in Francophone surveys on French slavery, sugarcane production or other related topics. For surveys on French slavery and other topics discussing slave labor, see Bousquet, *Les esclaves et leurs maîtres à Bourbon*; Debien, *Les esclaves aux Antilles françaises*; Anne Pérotin-Dumon, *La ville aux îles. La ville dans l'île. Basse-Terre et Pointe-à-Pitre* (Paris: Karthala, 2000); Prosper Ève, *Le corps des esclaves: histoire d'une reconquête* (Paris: Sorbonne Université Presses, 2013); and Régent, *La France et ses esclaves*. For examples of studies focusing on sugarcane production in the French colonies that also discuss slave labor, see Abbott, *Le sucre*; Mintz, *Sweetness and Power*; and Robert Louis Stein, *The French Sugar Business in the Eighteenth Century* (Baton Rouge-London: Louisiana State University Press, 1988).

13. Quoted from John Donoghue and Evelyn P. Jennings, *Building the Atlantic Empires: Unfree Labor and Imperial States in the Political Economy of Capitalism, ca. 1500–1914* (EBook, Leiden, The Netherlands & Boston: Brill, 2016), 2, https://ebookcentral.proquest.com/lib/duke/detail.action?docID=4007430.

14. A. Baillardel and A. Prioult, *Le Chevalier de Pradel. Vie d'un Colon Français en Louisiane au XVIIIe siècle. D'après sa correspondance et celle de sa famille* (Paris: Librairie Orientale et Américaine, 1928), 260 (quotation); LSU Hills Library "Jean Charles Pradel family papers, 1718–1954," Mss. 2866, "April 10 1755. Letter. Pradel to his brother. Montplaisir."

15. Boucher, *France and the American Tropics*, 60, 70.

16. Boucher, *France and the American Tropics*, 11–12, 69, 89, 121–122, 134, 151–152; Du Tertre, *Histoire générale des Antilles*, 2:478–480.

17. Rushforth, *Bonds of Alliance*, 362. By 1671 in Guadeloupe, only 2 percent of the enslaved population was Amerindian. See Régent, *La France et ses esclaves*, 38.

18. Jean-Baptiste Du Tertre, *Histoire générale des Isles de S. Christophe, de la Guadeloupe, de la Martinique et autres dans l'Amerique* (Paris: Jacques Langlois, 1654), 480–481.

19. Du Tertre, *Histoire générale des Antilles*, 2:489.

20. Du Tertre, *Histoire générale des Antilles*, 2:486.

21. Labat, *Nouveau voyage* (1724), 2:112.

22. Régent, *La France et ses esclaves*, 39.

23. Du Tertre, *Histoire générale des Antilles*, 2:486.

24. Labat, *Nouveau voyage* (1724), 2:75.

25. Du Tertre, *Histoire générale des Isles*, 476.

26. Marcel Chatillon ed., "L'évangélisation des esclaves au XVIIe siècle. Lettres du R. P. Jean Mongin," *Bulletin de la Société d'Histoire de la Guadeloupe*, 61–62 (1984): 3–136, here 130.

27. On this topic, see Abbott, *Le sucre*; Heath, "Sugarcoated Slavery"; Mintz, *Sweetness and Power*.

28. Régent, *La France et ses esclaves*, 97. Saint-Domingue also became a major indigo producer, while cacao, coffee, and cotton production expanded in Martinique. Silvia Marzagalli, "Commerce," in *The Oxford Handbook of the Ancien Régime*, ed. William Doyle (Oxford: Oxford University Press, 2012), 252–266, here 257.

29. "Périer to [the Abbé Raguet] [. . .]. May 12, 1728," *Mississippi Provincial Archives: 1701–1729, French Dominion*, ed. Dunbar Rowland and Albert G. Sanders (Jackson, MS: Press of the Mississippi Department of Archives and History, 1929), 2: 573 ("little service")–574 ("not suited").

30. ANOM C13 A12 "Le S. de la Salle a la Louisiane, 12 May 1709," p. 401.

31. Rushforth, *Bonds of Alliance*, 362.

32. Vidal, *Caribbean New Orleans*, 308–311.

33. ANOM A 23 "Arrêt qui fait cesser l'envoi de vagabonds et de criminels en Louisiane, 9 mai 1720," f. 29v.

34. LSM RSCL File 1724-09-02-01 "2 Septembre 1724."

35. Vidal, *Caribbean New Orleans*, 310.

36. Vidal, *Caribbean New Orleans*, 311.

37. See, for example, ANOM G1 464 "1726, 1 Janvier, Recensement general des habitations Et habitans de la Colonie"; ANOM G1 464 "Recensement General des habitans Negres Esclaves Sauvages et Bestiaux du Departement de la Nouvelle Orleans [. . .] Juillet 1727"; HL "Vaudreuil Papers," LO 130 "Touchant la Culture du tabac En Ce pays"; Hall, *Africans in Colonial Louisiana*, 148–160. Rice was also cultivated in the Lower Mississippi valley. See, for example, ANOM G1 464 "Les terres de la Nouvelle Orleans"; LOC "Louisiana Miscellany, 1724–1837," Mss. 17, 495, reel no. 1, Dumont De Montigny, "Histoire de la Louisiane: poème en quatre chants, circa 1736," p. 152.

38. ANOM F3 206 "Lettre des administrateurs de l'Ile Bourbon. La Compagnie des Indes. Du 15 [Décem]bre 1734," ff. 108–108v, 131.

39. Sieur L'Huillier, *Voyage du Sieur Luillier aux grandes Indes* (Paris: Claude Cellier, 1705), 247.

40. ANOM C3 2 "Mémoire Circonstantier De L'isle de Bourbon En Général," f. 70v.

41. ANOM C3 3 "31 Octobre 1710, Mémoire sur L'Isle de Bourbon," f. 111.

42. Jauze Albert, "Malgaches et Africains à Bourbon: La Réunion à l'époque de l'esclavage," *Hommes et Migrations* 1275 (2008): 150–157.

43. Haudrère, *L'empire des rois*, 165; Scherer, *Histoire de la Réunion*, 16.

44. ANOM C3 3 "31 Octobre 1710, Mémoire sur L'Isle de Bourbon," f. 111; ANOM F3 205 "Lettre. 11 Decembre 1734," p. 429.

45. ANOM F3 133 "Lettre des administrateurs de l'Ile Bourbon [. . .] Du 15 [Décem]bre 1734. Et Reponse de la Compagnie Du 23 Janvier 1736," f. 139v ("weak and lazy"); ANOM C2 117 "Mémoires généraux," f. 137 ("witty").

46. Vaxelaire, *Le grand livre de l'histoire*, 1:173.

47. ANOM F3 133 "Lettre des administrateurs de l'Ile Bourbon [. . .] Du 15 [Décem]bre 1734. Et Reponse de la Compagnie Du 23 Janvier 1736," f. 139v.

48. ADR C° 768 "1732, Recensement général."

49. ADR C° 669 "Instructions et ordres de la Compagnie des Indes," article 47 (quotation); ADR C°2 "Registre de transcription des décisions, ordres, instructions, lettres du Conseil Superieur [. . .] du 23 septembre 1724 au 29 avril 1733," pp. 157–158.

50. ADR C°2 "Registre de transcription des décisions," p. 158.

51. Gwendolyn Hall discussed the application of this project to Louisiana but made no reference to its application to the Indian Ocean. See Hall, *Africans in Colonial Louisiana*, 154–156.

52. Quoted from Hall, *Africans in Colonial Louisiana*, 156. ANOM F3 206 "Lettre de la Compagnie des Indes au conseil de Bourbon Sur l'administration de cette Colonie Paris ce 22 Sept[embre] 1731," f. 92.

53. ANOM F3 208 "Réglement qui fixe par un tarif les Salaires des ouvriers et le prix des principaux ouvrages 11 [Novem]bre 1734," p. 477 (quotation).

54. ANOM F3 206 "Lettre de la Compagnie des Indes au conseil de Bourbon Sur l'administration de cette Colonie. Paris ce 22 Septembre 1731," f. 92 (quotation)–92v.

55. An edict and a declaration issued in the metropole in 1716 and 1738, respectively, allowed slaveowners to take their captives to the kingdom of France to have them learn a trade useful to the colonies. In reality, a relatively small proportion of those who were supposed to learn a trade in France apprenticed. This edict was mostly used as an excuse by slaveowners to bring their captives to France despite the free soil principle. See Peabody, *"There Are No Slaves in France,"* 16–17, 81–83, and Debien, *Les esclaves aux Antilles françaises,* 378. About the free soil principle, see Introduction.

56. ANOM F3 205 "Des Ouvriers, des Traitemens qu'on leur doit faire," p. 272.

57. ANOM F3 205 "Des apprentissages 23 avril 1723," p. 1.

58. ADR C°2 "Registre de transcription des décisions, ordres, instructions, lettres du Conseil Superieur [. . .] Du 23 septembre 1724 au 29 avril 1733," p. 177.

59. ANOM F3 205 "Des apprentissages [. . .] 25 Mars 1741," p. 1.

60. Hall, *Africans in Colonial Louisiana,* 156.

61. Hall, *Africans in Colonial Louisiana*, 156.

62. LSM RSCL File "Black Books"; "August 29, 1763. Contract of Apprenticeship."

63. "Feb. 13 [1744] Sale to Sr. Brosset by Francoise Hubert. Transfer of a negro joiner, a slave in payment of a debt," RSC, *LHQ* 12, no. 4 (1929): 661 (quotation); "Jan. 9 [1745]. Contract between Sr. Germain and George Vappo, cooper," RSC, *LHQ* 13, no. 3 (1930): 494.

64. Hall, *Africans in Colonial Louisiana*, 154–158.

65. LSM RSCL File 1729-07-05-01 "Rolle des officiers Mariniers et Matelosts qui Sont au Service de la Compagnie des indes le premier janvier 1729."

66. Usner, *Indians, Settlers and Slaves,* 107, 220, 228–230, 277.

67. ADR C°2 "Registre de transcription des décisions, ordres, instructions, lettres du Conseil superieur [. . .] Du 23 septembre 1724 au 29 avril 1733," p. 158; ANOM F3 206 "Lettre des administrateurs de l'Ile Bourbon. La Compagnie des Indes. Du 15 [Décem]bre 1734 Et Reponse de la Compagnie Du 23 Janvier 1736," f. 161v.

68. ADR C°2 "Registre de transcription des décisions, ordres, instructions, lettres du Conseil superieur [. . .]. Du 23 septembre 1724 au 29 avril 1733," p. 158.

69. ADR C°2 "Registre de transcription des decisions, ordres, instructions, lettres du Conseil superieur [. . .]. Du 23 septembre 1724 au 29 avril 1733," p. 177.

70. Examples from Isle Bourbon: ADR C°2 "Registre de transcription des décisions, ordres, instructions, lettres du Conseil superieur [. . .]. Du 23 septembre 1724 au 29 avril 1733," p. 158.

71. Régent, *La France et ses esclaves,* 126.

72. Régent, *La France et ses esclaves,* 109.

73. ANOM F90 "Martinique, Le 30 Janvier 1754," f. 72.

74. This fear was not always unfounded. For a recent book demonstrating just that, see Garrigus, *A Secret among the Blacks*.

75. ANOM F3 221 "18 Juin 1674," pp. 519–520.

76. "June 9, [1748]. Slaves[of Sr. Dubreuil] held for theft"; "June 10, 1748. Interrogation of Louis, accused of theft," RSC, *LHQ* 19, no. 4 (1936):1089, 1091–1092; LSM RSCL File 1748-06-09-01 "A Nos Seigneurs Du Conseil Superieur"; Hall, *Africans in Colonial Louisiana*, 162.

77. Hall, *Africans in Colonial Louisiana*, 162.

78. LSM RSCL File 1752-06-13-01 "Proces Verbal de déclaration des negresses."

79. ANOM F3 222 "Brevés du Roy des biens de Jeanne Fary en faveur de Sr Houel. 6 Octobre 1716," p. 451.

80. ANOM F3 222 "Brevés du Roy des biens de Jeanne Fary en faveur de Sr Houel. 6 Octobre 1716," p. 452.

81. For a couple of publications considering the slaves' economies in the French context, see Jérome Jambu, "Le travail rémunéré des esclaves antillais: une porte ouverte sur la consommation et vers la liberté," in *Travail servile et dynamiques économiques,* ed. Anne Conchon, Myriam Cottias, Alessandro Stanziani (Paris, France: IGPDE, 2024) 159–180; Sophie White, "Slaves' and Poor Whites' Informal Economies in an Atlantic Context," in Vidal, *Louisiana,* 89–102. For some publications on the slaves' economy in other European empires and the United States, see Hilary Beckles, "An Economic Life of their Own: Slaves as Commodity Producers and Distributors in Barbados," *Slavery & Abolition* 12, no. 1 (1991): 31–47; Berlin and Morgan eds., *The Slaves' Economy*; Justene Hill Edwards, *Unfree Markets: The Slaves' Economy and the Rise of Capitalism in South Carolina* (New York: Columbia University Press, 2021); Roderick McDonald, *The Economy and Material Culture of Slaves: Goods and Chattels on the Sugar Plantations of Jamaica and Louisiana* (Baton Rouge: Louisiana State University Press, 1993).

82. ANOM F3 236 "Edit du Roi Concernant la discipline, l'Etat et la qualité des negres esclaves aux Isles de l'amerique. Du mois de mars 1685," p. 668; ADR C° 940 "Lettres Patentes en forme d'Edit concernant les Esclaves Negres des Isle de Bourbon et de france 1723," n.p; ANOM A 23 "Édit du roi, ou Code noir, qui concerne entièrement les esclaves de la Louisiane, Mars 1724," f. 50.

83. ANOM G1 465 "Reponses au Chefs Daccusations. Memoire Pour Repondre aux accusations formées Contre J.B Fauçon Dumanoir, 1731," n.p.

84. ANOM F3 236 "1695, Arrêt en Réglement du Conseil Souverain de la Guadeloupe qui defend d'acheter des nègres Sans billet de leurs maîtres," p. 3; ANOM F3 221 "Extrait Des Registres Du Conseil Souverain De L'Isle Guadeloupe Du 2 Janvier 1696," p. 889; ANOM F3 221 "Du 7 Octobre 1697 Extrait Des Registres Du Conseil Souverain de L'Isle Guadeloupe," p. 929.

85. ANOM F3 236 "Edit du Roi Concernant la discipline, l'Etat et la qualité des negres esclaves aux Isles de l'amerique, Du mois de mars 1685," p. 671; ADR C° 940 "Lettres Patentes en forme d'Edit concernant les Esclaves Negres des Isle de Bourbon et de france, 1723"; ANOM A 23 "Édit du roi, ou Code noir, qui concerne entièrement les esclaves de la Louisiane, mars 1724," f. 53; Jérémy Boutier, "Essai d'historiographie du 'code noir' applicable à l'île Bourbon," *Revue historique de l'océan Indien* 21 (forthcoming).

86. Du Tertre, *Histoire générales des Antilles,* 2:518–519.

87. ANOM F133 "17 Juillet 1673," p. 40.

88. ANOM F3 90 "20 mars 1682. Esclaves Memoire au Roy," f. 6; ANOM F3 90 "13 Fevrier 1683. Memoire pour le Röy Sur le religion, La police, la nourriture, et les autres matieres," f. 12; ANOM "Edit du Roi Concernant la discipline, l'Etat et la qualité des negres esclaves aux Isles de l'amerique Du mois de mars 1685," p. 670.

89. ANOM F3 221 "Du 7 Octobre 1697. Extrait Des Registres Du Conseil Souverain de L'Isle Guadeloupe," pp. 919–920.

90. ANOM F3 222 "Charles Bénard conseiller du Roy en ses conseils, Intendant de justice pour les finances et marine des Isles françoises de Lamerique," p. 643.

91. LOC "Memoranda on French colonies in America, including Canada, Louisiana, and the Caribbean, 1702–1750," "Memoire de l'etablissement des isles françoises de l'Amerique, 26 Octobre 1728," p. 88.

92. ANOM F3 226 "Arrêt Sur Remontrance concernant La police des Nègres du 9 Juillet 1746," p. 271; ANOM F3 226 "Du 2 [Septem]bre 1748," p. 414.

93. Franz Tardo-Dino, *Le Collier de servitude. La condition sanitaire des esclaves aux Antilles françaises* (Paris: Éditions caribéennes, 1985), 215.

94. See, for example, LOC "The Louisianan Collection," Mss. 17, 495, reel no. 2 of 5, "Louisiana Miscellany 1724–1837," "Fortifications. Etat des journées que le nommé Deslaurier Le Dret, et les Denommez Cy apres ont employé [*sic*] a faire les Comptoirs [. . .] depuis le 28 Septembre jusqu'au Vingt trois octobre [. . .] 1754," p. 1140, "Nouvelle Orleans, 27 Nov. 1754. Fortification. Estat Des materiaux et Des journées que François Lioteau Mason a fourny [*sic*]," p. 1144, and "Etat Des journées Des ouvriers qui ont travaillé a la Demolition Du Vieux Gouvernement Depuis Le 23eme Janvier [. . .] 1744," f. 1069; "July 12, 1739 Memorandum on Hired Slaves," RSC, *LHQ* 6, no. 4 (1923): 663.

95. About the flour industry in the Illinois Country, see Carl J. Ekberg, "The Flour Trade in French Colonial Louisiana," *Louisiana History: The Journal of the Louisiana Historical Association* 37, no. 3 (1996): 261–282. For some examples, see: "Aug. 15, 1737. Lease of Two Negroes," "Aug. 16 [1737]. Lease of A Negro," "Aug. 16. Lease of a Negro," RSC, *LHQ* 9, no. 2 (1927): 319–320; "April. 9 [1738]. Lease of a Negro" RSC, *LHQ* 10, no. 1 (1927): 97–98.

96. ANOM F3 236 "Arrêt en Reglement du Conseil Souverain Portant défenses de faire travailler les négres étrangers Sans billet de leurs maîtres Du 5 avril 1666," pp. 482–483; ANOM F3 236 "Arrêt En Reglement du Conseil Souverain Portant défense aux esclaves de louer des maisons et Boutiques, meme avec billets de leurs maîtres, et d'acheter et revendre Sans permission par Ecrit de leurs maîtres, 1749," p. 714; ANOM F3 226 "Arrêt Sur Remontrance Concernant La police des nègres, 1749," p. 485.

97. ANOM F3 226 "Arrêt Sur Remontrance Concernant La police des négres [*sic*], 1749," pp. 478 and 476 (quotations), 475–479.

98. ANOM F3 226 "Arrêt Sur Remontrance Concernant La police des négres, 1749," p. 476.

99. ANOM F3 226 "Arrêt Sur Remontrance Concernant La police des négres, 1749," p. 476; ANOM F3 222 "Reglement concernant Les affranchissements des Esclaves Du 15 août 1711," p. 189.

100. Labat, *Nouveau voyage* (1742), 4:468.

101. ANOM F3 222 "Ordonnance Sur La Plantation Des Magnocs Du 3 Mars 1714," p. 333; ANOM F3 222 "Ordonnance concernant Les Plantations de Magnocs," p. 21; ANOM F3 222 "Ordonnance touchant La Plantation des Magnocs," p. 465; ANOM A1 "Ordonnance portant que chaque habitant des îles du Vent sera tenu d'avoir, sur son habitation, cinq cent fosses de culture en manioc," f. 46; ANOM F3 226 "Du 2 [Septem]bre 1748," p. 413; ANOM F3 226 "Ordonnance des adm. Concernant les plantations & La Culture des magnocs, Bananiers du 24e Juillet 1751," p. 676.

102. ANOM F3 226 "Du 2 Septembre 1748," pp. 414, 416.

103. ANOM F3 226 "Ordonnance des adm. Concernant [l]es plantations & La Culture des magnocs, Bananiers [. . .] du 24e Juillet 1751," p. 676.

104. Brasseaux, *France's Forgotten Legion*, 27–28.

105. "Memoir of d'Artaguiette to Pontchartrain on the present condition of Louisiana, May 12, 1712," in Dunbar Rowland and A. G. Sanders, eds., *Mississippi Provincial Archives, 1701–1729: French Dominion*, 3 vols. (Jackson: Press of the Mississippi Department of Archives and History, 1919–1932), 2:60–67, quotation on 60. See also Carl A. Brasseaux, "The Image of Louisiana and the Failure of Voluntary French Emigration, 1683–1731," in *The Louisiana Purchase Bicentennial Series*, ed. Glenn Conrad (Lafayette: Center for Louisiana Studies, University of Southwestern Louisiana, 1995), 153–162, here 156.

106. LSM RSCL File 1724-12-28-02 "A Messieurs du Conseil Supérieur [. . .];" ANOM C13 A17 "M Diron 7 mars 1733," f. 210; ANOM C13 A23 "Colonies M de Bourbon 26 Fevrier 1738," f. 176v.

107. For studies on slave gardens in the Caribbean, see Catherine Benoît, "Gardens in the African Diaspora: Forging a Creole Identity in the Caribbean and the US," in *Gardens and Cultural Change: A Pan-American Perspective*, ed. Michel Conan and Jeffrey Quilter (Washington, DC: Dumbarton Oaks Research Library and Collection, 2007), 29–46; Lucien Degras, *Le Jardin créole: Repères culturels, scientifiques et techniques*, 2nd ed. (Pointe-à-Pitre, Guadeloupe: Éditions Jasor/Archipel des sciences, 2016). Regulations issued in the 1720s also allowed enslaved people on Isle Bourbon and in Louisiana to go hunting and fishing, as long as they carried an authorization. See ANOM F3 208 "Ordonnance Sur plusieurs objets non prévus par le code noir à L'égard des Esclaves, 1727," p. 314; ANOM A 23 "Arrêt du conseil supérieur de la Louisiane qui interdit aux habitants d'acheter du gibier aux sauvages, esclaves ou engagés et des habits et légumes aux esclaves sans billet du maître, 1723," ff. 43–44; ANOM A 23 "Arrêt du conseil supérieur de la Louisiane fixant les peines à infliger à ceux qui débauchent les esclaves, 1725," f. 64.

108. Catherine Benoît, "Les jardins: Espaces de contestation," in *Colonisations*, 673–674.

109. Cited in Barassin, *Naissance d'une chrétienté*, 270.

110. Saint-Pierre, *Voyage à l'Isle de Bourbon*, 259; Laurence Verran, "Premiers esclaves aux Petites Antilles d'après les chroniques et récits de voyages français (XVIIe siècle)," in *L'Esclave et les plantations: De l'établissement de la servitude à son abolition*, ed. Philippe Hrodej (Rennes, France: Presses Universitaires de Rennes, 2008), 85–102, here 97.

111. ANOM F3 225 "Arrêt du huit Novembre 1735," p. 133; ANOM F3 225 "Arrêt Sur remonstrance concernant Les Negres Colporteurs Du 8 Novembre 1735," 142. See also Labat, *Nouveaux Voyages aux Isles* (1742), 4: 461.

112. ANOM F3 236 "Mémoire de M. Patoulet Sur la Conservation, la police, le jugement, et le chastiment des esclaves, 1680," p. 555; ANOM F3 236 "Ordonnance de MM Les Général et Intendant Qui enjoint aux maîtres de Fournir des Billets à leurs esclaves pour aller vendre quelque denrée, 1747," pp. 712–714; ANOM F3 236 "Arrêt En Reglement du Conseil Souverain Portant défense aux esclaves de louer des maisons et Boutiques, 1749," pp. 713–714; ANOM F3 226 "Arrêt Sur Remontrance Concernant La police des négres du 2 [Septem]bre 1749," pp. 476–479.

113. See ANOM F3 236 "Reglement Général fait par M. de Tracy Gouverneur General des Isles et Terre ferme de l'amerique, 1664," p. 621; ANOM F3 236 "Arrêt du Conseil Souverain, 1667," p. 3; ANOM F3 236 "Mémoire de M. Patoulet Sur la Conservation, la police, le jugement, et le chastiment des esclaves, 1680," p. 555; ANOM F3 236 "Ordonnance de MM Les Général et Intendant Qui enjoint aux maîtres de Fournir des Billets à leurs esclaves pour aller vendre quelque denrée, 1747," p. 712; ANOM F3 236 "Arrêt En Reglement du Conseil Souverain Portant défense aux esclaves de louer des maisons et Boutiques," p. 713; ANOM F3 226 "Arrêt Sur Remontrance Concernant La police des négres, 1749," pp. 479, 482, 484; ANOM C3A 35 "Reglement Donné à la Nouvelle Orleans, 1751," ff. 45v–46; *Recueil d'Edits, Declarations et Arrests De Sa Majesté*, 2:88, 141.

114. ANOM F3 208 "Isle de Bourbon Réglement du Conseil Provincial Sur divers objets de la police générale, 1715," p. 102.

115. *Recueil d'Edits, Declarations et Arrests De Sa Majesté*, 2:141 (Louisiana); Jean-Baptiste-Étienne Delaleu, ed., *Code des Îles de France et de Bourbon* (2nd ed., Port-Louis, Mauritius:

Tristan Mallac, 1826), 248 (Isle Bourbon). They had to carry a permission from their master to do so.

116. ANOM F3 226 "Arrêt Sur Remontrance Concernant La police des négres, 1749," p. 477.

117. ANOM F3 226 "Arrêt Sur Remontrance Concernant La police des négres, 1749," p. 479.

118. ANOM F3 226 "Arrêt Sur Remontrance Concernant La police des négres, 1749," p. 479 ("stalls"), 475–476 ("like white people").

119. ANOM F3 236 "Arrêt En Reglement du Conseil Souverain Portant défense aux esclaves de louer des maisons et Boutiques [. . .] 1749," article 2, pp. 713–714; ANOM F3 226 "Arrêt Sur Remontrance Concernant La police des négres, 1749 [. . .] 1749," article 2, p. 484.

120. "Code Noir ou Recueil d'Edits [. . .] Mars 1685," *Recueil d'Edits, Declarations et Arrests De Sa Majesté*, article XVIII, 2: 87–88; ANOM F3 236 "Arrêt du Conseil Souverain Concernant les ventes faites par les nègres de bois, planches, Cannes à Sucre, Syrops [. . .] Du 6 [Septem]bre 1725," p. 703; ANOM F3 236 "Ordonnance de MM Les Général et Intendant Qui défend aux nègres de vendre du caffé, 1734," p. 704; ANOM F3 236 "Ordonnance de MM Les Général et Intendant Qui défend aux esclaves de vendre du Cotton. Du 15 avril 1735," pp. 704–705; ANOM F3 226 "Arrêt Sur Remontrance Concernant La police des nègres [. . .] 1749," pp. 480–481.

121. See, for example, ANOM A 23 "Ordonnance de La Motte-Cadillac, gouverneur de Louisiane, et de Duclos, commissaire-ordonnateur, qui défend aux habitants de faire du commerce avec les esclaves [. . .] 1714," f. 4v; ANOM F3 236 "Ordonnance de MM Les Général et Intendant Qui défend aux négres de vendre du caffé [. . .] 1734," p. 704.

122. ANOM F3 225 "Arrêt du huit Novembre 1735," p. 132.

123. Labat, *Nouveaux voyages* (1724), 2:59.

124. See, for example, Bill Barron, ed., *The Vaudreuil Papers: A Calendar and Index of the Personal and Private Records of Pierre de Rigaud de Vaudreuil, Royal Governor of the French Province of Louisiana, 1743–1753* (New Orleans: Polyanthos 1975), 26; HL "Vaudreuil Papers," Lo 121 "20 Mars 1748," pp. xxiv–xxv; ANOM A2 "A la Guadeloupe Le 22e Juillet 1672. Le S. du Lion," f. 87.

125. Du Tertre, *Histoire générale des Antilles*, 2:521.

126. Du Tertre, *Histoire générale des Antilles*, 2:520–521.

127. ANOM 1323 "Reglement fait par Messieurs les Général et Intendant, Concernant Les habillemens des Nègres et Mulâtres, Le quatrième du mois de Juin de l'année Mil Sept Cent Vingt."

128. Slaveholders liked to display their wealth by dressing their servants with fine fabrics, jackets, and hats. ANOM 1323 "Reglement fait par Messieurs les Général et Intendant, Concernant Les habillemens des Nègres et Mulâtres."

129. ANOM F3 226 "Arrêt Sur Remontrance Concernant La police des négres [. . .] 1749," p. 475.

130. ANOM F3 222 "Reglement concernant Les affranchissements des Esclaves Du 15 août 1711," p. 189; ANOM F3 236 "Ordonnance du Roi Concernant l'affranchissement des esclaves, 1713," p. 681 (quotation).

131. "Code Noir ou Recueil d'Edits [. . .] Mars 1685," *Recueils de reglemens, edits, declarations et arrets*, article V, 2: 153 (quotation)–154.

132. "Code Noir ou Recueil d'Edits [. . .] Mars 1685," *Recueils de reglemens, edits, declarations et arrets*, article LV, 2: 98–99.

133. Aubert, '"To Establish One Law,"' 39.

134. ANOM F3 236 "Déclaration du Roi Sur les nègres composant des Remedes Du 1er fevrier 1743," pp. 753–754; ANOM 1323 "Tarif Général fait par Messieurs les Général et intendant

Le vingt troisième Jour du Mois de Septembre de l'année Mil Sept Cent Cinquante trois; il a été Registré le sixiéme Novembre mil Sept Cents Cinquante quatre."

135. ANOM F3 227 "Arrêt du Conseil Supérieur de L'Ile G[uadelou]pe du 4 Janvier 1755," article 2, p. 2.

136. For more information about the cabarets, see Mélanie Lamotte, "Intimacy beyond Sex: A Study of Everyday Cross-Racial Interactions in the Early French Atlantic and Indian Oceans," in "Interracial Intimacies in France and the French Empire," special issue, *French Politics, Culture, and Society* (forthcoming).

137. ANOM F3 222 "Reglement concernant Les affranchissements des Esclaves Du 15 août 1711," p. 189.

138. Elisabeth, *La société martiniquaise*, 263, quotation at 264.

139. Garrigus, *Before Haiti*, 227.

140. Jessica Pierre-Louis, "Fortune et catégorisation des Libres de couleur," in "Couleur et liberté dans l'espace colonial français (début XVIIIe—début XIXe siècle)," special issue, *Cahiers des Anneaux de la mémoire* 17, 2017: 66–90, here 70–75.

141. Before the late eighteenth century, there was no wealthy elite in the free population of color in Guadeloupe. See Régent, *La France et ses esclaves*, 208.

142. Garrigus, *Before Haiti*; Régent, *La France et ses esclaves*, 207–208.

143. Such was still the case in the late eighteenth century. Régent, *La France et ses esclaves*, 206.

144. ANOM F3 222 "Charles bénard conseiller du Roy en ses conseils Intendant de justice pour les finances et marine des Isles françoises de Lamerique," p. 643.

145. A letter written by the governor of the island, Alexandre Vaultier de Moyencourt, in 1723, begged the governor-general of the *Îles du Vent* for help, to "prevent starvation from taking over [the island] entirely." ANOM C7 A9 "Copie de la lettre ecrite par Monsieur Le Comte de Moyencourt Gouverneur de la Guadeloupe." See also Lucien-René Abénon, *La Guadeloupe de 1671 à 1759. Étude politique, économique et sociale*, 2 vols. (Paris: L'Harmattan, 1987), 1:292.

146. ANOM A2 "Arrêt qui renvoie par devant les administrateurs des îles du Vent les contestations entre les nommées Artas et Nanon, négresses libres établies à la Guadeloupe [. . .] 14 janvier 1730," f. 3 ("disrupted"), f. 5 ("aware"/"land-clearing"), ff. 4–5.

147. LSM RSCL File 1740-07-29-02 "A la N[ouv]elle Orleans ce 29 Juillet 1740."

148. LSM RSCL File 1740-07-29-02 "A la N[ouv]elle Orleans ce 29 Juillet 1740."

149. LSM RSCL File 1739-03-20-01 "1739. 20 Mars Marie Angelique negresse Libre Vente a Dubreuil"; "Dec. 9 [1739] Sale by Sr. Claude Joseph Du Breuil Villars to Sieur Joseph Meunier," RSC, *LHQ* 7, no. 3 (1924): 515; "March 20, 1739 Sale of Property [. . .] Marie Angelique, called Isabelle, a free negro woman, formerly owned by Mr. de Chavannes," RSC, *LHQ* 6, no. 2 (1923): 310.

150. LOC "Louisiana Miscellany, 1724–1837," "Estat des Personnes auxquelles l'on a marqué [. . .] des Emplacements pour batir Suivant le Projet de la Ville de la Nouvelle Orleans," ff. 447–453v.

151. ANOM G1 464 "Recensement des habitations Le Long du fleuve. 1731."

152. LSM RSCL "Black books," "9 October 1762, Contract between Pierre Ricard and Francois Allain with a free mulatto named Louis"; LSM RSCL File 1762-11-08-02 "9 Octobre 1762."

153. The final outcome of this request is unknown. LSM RSCL File 1763-03-05-03 "A Nos Seigneurs du Conseil Superieur de la province de la Louisianne."

154. Antoine Le Page du Pratz, *Histoire de Louisiane, contenant la découverte de ce vaste pays*, 3 vols. (Paris: De Bure, 1758), 1:344.

155. "Nov. 9 [1745] Jean Baptiste Marly, free negro, agrees to serve Mr. Jean Jose Delfaut de Pontalba," RSC, *LHQ* 14, no. 4 (1931): 594.

156. LOC "Louisiana Miscellany, 1724–1837," "Estat des Personnes auxquelles l'on a marqué [. . .] des Emplacements pour batir Suivant le Projet de la Ville de la Nouvelle Orleans," ff. 453–453v.

157. LSM RSCL File 1724-07-27-01 "Monsieurs Du Conseil Superieur De la province De La Louisianne Le 26 Juillet 1724"; LSM RSCL File 1724-09-20-02 "20 Septembre [. . .] Le Conseil Condamne Le Sr Dumanoir;" "July 26, 1724 Petition of Recovery and Restitution," "September 20, 1724 Decisions in Three Civil Suits," RSC, *LHQ* 1, no. 3 (1918): 242, 245–246.

158. LSM RSCL File 1724-05-09-02 "Suplie tres humblement Le nomme Raphael appartenant au Sr Dumanoir [. . .] A La Nouvelle Orleans Ce neuf May 1724"; "May 9, 1724 Petition of Recovery. Raphael, a negro belonging To Mr. Dumanoir lent 200 francs (copper) to Mr. Cadot," RSC, *LHQ* 1, no. 4 (1918): 238.

159. LSM RSCL File 1735-10-09-01 "Je soussigné Pierre dit de St. Julien" (quotations). Vidal, *Caribbean New Orleans*, 278.

160. Cited in Vidal, *Caribbean New Orleans*, 279.

161. "Feb. 6 [1745]. A mulattress sues the estate of Sr. D'Ausseville, alleging that she was freed by her master in 1735," RSC, *LHQ* 13, no. 3 (1930): 517; "Nov. 23 [1743] Petition to the Governor and to the Ordonnateur of Louisiana [. . .] stating that Marie Charlotte formerly owned by Sr. de Pierre de Saint Julien," RSC, *LHQ* 12 no. 3 (1929): 486; Vidal, *Caribbean New Orleans*, 278–279.

162. ANOM C13 A9 "Du 21e Novembre 1725. Représentation de M. Fleuriau," f. 268 (quotations); LSM RSCL File 1726-08-17-03 "Louis Congo negre executeur de la haute justice"; "August 17, 1726, Attorney General on 'Desertions,' Prompted by a murderous attack on Louis Congo negro executioner by three runaway savages," *LHQ* 3, no. 3 (1922): 414.

163. LSM RSCL File 1737-01-24-04 "Francois et Louis Declaration Janvier 24 1737"; "Jan. 24, 1737 Complaint in Registry by a negro named Congo, public executioner," RSC, *LHQ* 8, no. 4 (1925): 694.

164. ANOM C13 A9 "Du 21e Novembre 1725. Représentation de M. fleuriau," ff. 267v–268v.

165. ANOM C13 A9 "Du 21e Novembre 1725. Représentation de M. fleuriau," ff. 267v–268v. For more information on Louis Congo, see Spear, *Race, Sex, and Social Order*, 87–88; Hall, *Africans in Colonial Louisiana*, 154; "Aug. 13, 1739 Report on Dead Slave," RSC, *LHQ* 6, no. 4 (1923): 663.

166. The average salary for white sailors at the service of the company also amounted to fifteen livres. ANOM C13 A8 "Du 20 May 1724. Sur le Representation faite par Le nommé Antoine Beauvais mulatre Libre, pour Servir La Compagnie des Indes en qualité de matelot," f. 104v; LSM RSCL File 1729-07-05-01 "Rolle des officier Mariniers et Matelots qui Sont au Service de la Companie des Indes le premier Janvier, 1729."

167. LSM RSCL File 1739-03-10-03 "10 mars 1739. Scipion negre Engagement avec Mr petit."

168. For example, see: "Aug. 15, 1737. Lease of Two Negroes," "Aug. 16 [1737]. Lease of A Negro," RSC, *LHQ* 9, no. 2 (1927): 319–320; "April. 9 [1738]. Lease of a Negro" RSC, *LHQ* 10, no. 1 (1927): 97–98.

169. LSM RSCL File 1739-03-10-03 "10 mars 1739 Scipion negre Engagement avec Mr petit," "March 10, 1739. Contract by a Free Negro [Scipion] to Act as Supercargo," RSC, *LHQ* 6, no. 2 (1923): 306.

170. LSM RSCL File 1762-04-03-01 "1762. 3e avril. Pardevant Le Notaire de la Pointe Coupée."

171. LSM RSCL File 1739-07-07-01 "Jacques Duverge negre. Obligation a piemont Dit Duverge Negre Libre a Cremont Pour Marchandises a luy Livré"; LSM RSCL File 1739-07-07-01 "7 Juillet 1739 fut present En Sa personne Jacques DuVerger Negre Libre voyageur des Illinois"; RSC, *LHQ* 7 (1924): 348; LSM "Black Books," "1739 July 7."

172. The Frenchmen in his crew were expelled from the colony and sent back to France. ANOM F3 224 "6 Juillet 1728. Extrait des registres Du Conseil Superieur de l'Isle Guadeloupe," pp. 429–435.

173. ANOM C13A 19 "22 Octobre 1734, Monseigneur M Salmon," ff. 88v–89.

174. ANOM C13 A19 "22 Octobre 1734, Monseigneur M Salmon," f. 88v.

175. The final outcome of this business plan is unknown. ANOM C13 A19 "22 Octobre 1734, Monseigneur M Salmon," ff. 88–89.

176. Bousquet, *Les esclaves et leurs maîtres à Bourbon,* 2:437–439, 462–463; Bernardin de Saint-Pierre, *Voyage à l'Isle de Bourbon,* 1:189.

177. Saint-Pierre, *Voyage à l'isle de Bourbon,* 1:188.

178. Bousquet, *Les esclaves et leurs maîtres à Bourbon,* 2:432.

179. Bousquet, *Les esclaves et leurs maîtres à Bourbon,* 2:432, 435.

180. ADR C°1682 "Etat des gages dus aux ouvriers indiens [. . .] 31 décembre 1747," cited in Bousquet, *Les esclaves et leurs maîtres à Bourbon,* 2: 437. See also ANOM F3 206 "30 [Octo]bre 1736 Etat General de la Depense a faire au comptoir de L'Isle de Bourbon," f. 182.

181. Bousquet, *Les esclaves et leurs maîtres à Bourbon,* 2:430–431, 444.

182. Data extracted from the database, "Compagnie des Indes," section "Équipage et passagers," of the Ministère de la Défense - Mémoire des Hommes, https://www.memoiredeshommes.sga.defense.gouv.fr/fr/arkotheque/client/mdh/compagnie_des_indes/equipages_et_passagers.php, accessed January 2025.

183. ADR C° 1624 "Etat de la dépense à faire au comptoir de Bourbon [. . .] Saint Denis, 2 avril 1744," cited in Bousquet, *Les esclaves et leurs maîtres à Bourbon,* 2:436.

184. Bousquet, *Les esclaves et leurs maîtres à Bourbon,* 2:437. See also ADR 2 Mi 47 C°808 "Recensement St Denis, Ste Marie, St Paul, 1763."

185. ADR 3E36 "Marché et convention passés par Gabriel Dejean avec Tendréa, le 17 septembre 1740"; Bousquet, *Les esclaves et leurs maîtres à Bourbon,* 2:435–436.

186. Bousquet, *Les esclaves et leurs maîtres à Bourbon,* 2:437.

187. ANOM F3 205 "Des apprentissages, 22 Septembre 1731," p. 1.

188. ANOM F3 206 "Lettre des administrateurs de l'Ile Bourbon. La Compagnie des Indes. Du 15 [Décem]bre 1734 Et Reponse de la Compagnie Du 23 Janvier 1736," ff. 92–92v.

189. ANOM C2 31 "Extrait du Registre general des deliberations de la Compagnie des Indes Du 15e Juin 1745," ff. 155v–156.

190. ANOM F3 205 "Le 23 aout 1723. L'Intention de la Compagnie," f. 10. See also Du Rau, *L'Île de la Réunion,* 144.

191. ADR C° 2521–1 "Vû par notre Conseil Superieur de l'isle de Bourbon," f. 13 (quotation); ADR C° 775 "Isle de Bourbon année 1752. Recensement General 1752."

192. Bousquet, *Les esclaves et leurs maîtres à Bourbon,* 2:495–498.

193. Bousquet, *Les esclaves et leurs maîtres à Bourbon,* 2:499.

194. Saint-Pierre, *Voyage à l'isle de Bourbon,* 1:188.

195. ADR C° 768 "1732, Recensement général"; ADR C°778 "1756, Recensement General," f. 21v.

196. ADR C° 768 "1732, Recensement général."

197. By contrast, during the first half of the eighteenth century, nearly all high-income and respected positions in the Caribbean were held by whites. Only whites held government offices in Guadeloupe. Régent, *La France et ses esclaves,* 202.

198. See Chapter 2.

199. ADR GG13 "Saint-Paul," f. 2v.

200. ADR C° 768 "1732, Recensement général."

201. ADR C°2792 "2e Janvier 1715, serment des Conseillers." The evidence suggests that he officially occupied this position even before 1715. See Delabarre de Nanteuil, *Législation de l'Ile de la Réunion,* 4:546.

202. Albert Jauze, "Notaires et notariat: Le notariat français et les hommes dans une colonie à l'Est du Cap de Bonne-Espérance, Bourbon-la Réunion: 1668–milieu du XIXe siècle" (PhD diss., Université de la Réunion, 2004), 383; ADR C° 768 "1732. Recensement general." See also ADR C° 1013 "A Monsieur Dumas gouverneur pour le Roy de L'isle de Bourbon. Mr choppy des granes Capitaine des quartiers St pierre et St Loüis."

203. ANOM F3 206 "1736. Etat General de la Depense a faire au comptoir de L'Isle de Bourbon," f. 181.

204. ANOM C3 3 "Memoire Dobservation Sur Celuy de Lisle de Bourbon," p. 9.

205. ANOM C3 3 "Memoire Dobservation Sur Celuy de Lisle de Bourbon," p. 8v.

206. ANOM C3 3 "Memoire Dobservation Sur Celuy de Lisle de Bourbon," f. 9v.

207. ANOM C3 3 "Memoire Dobservation Sur Celuy de Lisle de Bourbon," ff. 25v–26. Ricquebourg, *Dictionnaire généalogique des familles de l'Île Bourbon,* 1:230.

208. ANOM C3 3 "Memoire Dobservation Sur Celuy de Lisle de Bourbon," ff. 8v–9.

209. ANOM F3 208 "Sur Le Procureur Général, Conseillers, Administration de La justice," p. 127.

210. ANOM F3 208 "Sur Le Procureur Général, Conseillers, Administration de La justice," p. 128; ADR C°2516 "Sermant de francois grondain pour Conseiller," f. 33v; Boutier, "Essai d'historiographie."

211. ANOM 5 DPPC 62 Boucher, "Le Memoire pour Servir a la connaissance," p. 6.

212. ANOM G1 477 "Liste des habitans de Lisle Bourbon, Enfans et Negres Ceci doit estre du mois de Septembre 1690."

213. Ricquebourg, *Dictionnaire généalogique des familles de l'Île Bourbon,* 1:28. About Jeanne Arnould, see ANOM 5 DPPC 62 Boucher, "Le memoire pour servir," p. 6. About Marie Mahon, see ANOM 5 DPPC 62 Boucher, "Le Memoire pour Servir a la connaissance," p. 29.

214. ANOM G1 477 "1704 et avril 1705 Resencement General de tous les Habitans," f. 57; ADR C°767 "Recensement général de l'Isle de bourbon, année 1708," f. 4v; ANOM G1 477 Recensement de L'isle de Bourbon en general, fait en Mars 1709"; ANOM G1 477 "Recensement du quartier de St Paul Isle de Bourbon, 1711."

215. ANOM 5 DPPC 62 Boucher, "Le Memoire pour Servir a la connaissance," p. 6–7.

216. ADR C°2516 "Serment de Francois Grondain pour Conseiller," f. 33v.

217. Ricquebourg, *Dictionnaire généalogique des familles de l'Île Bourbon,* 2:1114.

218. ADR C° 768 "1732. Recensement general."

219. ANOM F3 206 "Lettre de la Compagnie des Indes à Mrs du Conseil Superieur de Bourbon Sur plusieurs objets et notamment Sur le Café, Paris 24 Septembre 1729," f. 60v. By 1791, the Bourbon Island Creoles claimed to have "always enjoyed, along with their posterity, all the rights exercised by other citizens." See ANOM C3 11 "Pétitions de la colonie de Bourbon à l'Assemblée nationale du 21 avril 1791 au 24 avril, fait à St Paul en assemblée coloniale,"

in Sabine Noël, *Amours et familles interdites. Blancs et Noirs à l'île Bourbon (La Réunion) au temps de l'esclavage (1665-1848)* (Paris: Les Indes Savantes, 2022), 573.

220. Marvin, "Bourbon Island Creoles."

Conclusion

1. ANOM E 111 "David, Pierre-Félix-Bathélemy." See especially "Extrait du Mémoire des Services de M. David," and "6 Mars 1746. Nomination des syndics Et Directeurs de la Compagnie des Indes En faveur du Sr. Pierre Felix Barthelmy [*sic*] David pour remplir la place de Gouverneur Général des Isles de France et de Bourbon."

2. ANOM C14 35 "M. David Mémoire, 313–318." I thank Barbara Traver for sharing a picture of this manuscript with me. See also Barbara Traver, "'The Benefits of Their Liberty': Race and the Eurafricans of Gorée in Eighteenth-Century French Guiana," *French Colonial History* 16 (2016): 1–26.

3. Pernille Roge, *Economistes and the Reinvention of Empire: France in the Americas and Africa, c. 1750–1802* (Cambridge: Cambridge University Press, 2019), 177.

4. Quoted in Traver, "'The Benefits of Their Liberty,'" 14. Although this episode has already garnered significant attention in the historiography, Nathan Marvin is the only one to have made the link with David's previous experience in the Mascarenes. See Marvin, "Bourbon Island Creoles," 57–58.

5. Traver, "'The Benefits of Their Liberty,'" 12.

6. Quoted from Traver, "'The Benefits of Their Liberty,'" 6.

7. French officials were extremely well positioned to undertake a policy of reform because the Ministry of the Marine took further steps to classify colonial documents and, according to Marie Houllemare, "get a full picture of colonial law." Houllemare, "Procedures, Jurisdictions and Records," n.p.

8. Marvin, "Bourbon Island Creoles, 248.

9. Marvin, "Bourbon Island Creoles," 4, 73.

10. For studies on slavery and the sugar economy on Isle Bourbon and Isle of France, see Jean-François Géraud and Xavier Le Terrier, *Faire du sucre à La Réunion: Une technologie créole d'excellence, 1783–1914* (Saint-André, Île de La Réunion: Epica Éditions, 2016); Vijaya Teelock, *Bitter Sugar: Slavery and Sugar in Nineteenth Century Mauritius* (Moka: Mahatma Gandhi Institute, 1998).

11. See Osama W. Abi-Mershed, *Apostles of Modernity: Saint-Simonians and the Civilizing Mission in Algeria* (Stanford, CA: Stanford University Press, 2010); Alice Conklin, *A Mission to Civilize: The Republican Idea of Empire in France and West Africa, 1895–1930* (Stanford, CA: Stanford University Press, 1997); Henry Laurens, *Les Origines intellectuelles de l'expédition d'Égypte: L'orientalisme islamisant en France (1698–1798)* (Istanbul: Éditions Isis, 1987); Carl Ludwig Lokke and Gabriel Debien "L'Expédition d'Égypte et les projets de cultures coloniales," *Bulletin de la Société royale de géographie d'Égypte* 20, no. 3 (1940): 337–356; Tricoire, "Les Lumières, l'idéologie coloniale et Madagascar," 97. The early modern and modern projects of "civilization" had a lot in common but also some major differences. For comparisons, see Saliha Belmessous, *Assimilation and Empire,* and Mélanie Lamotte, "Aux origines de l'empire," in *Colonisations,* ed. Singaravélou *et al.*, 557–570, here 565–566.

12. On race in the later period of French colonization, see, for example, the works of Alice Conklin, Frederick Cooper, Naomi Davidson, Silyane Larcher, Herman Lebovics, Kris Manjapra, Adrian Muckle, Emily Marker, Damiano Matasci, William Max Nelson, Carole

Reynaud-Paligot, Jennifer Pitts, Todd Shepard, Emmanuelle Saada, Emmanuelle Sibeud, Ann Stoler and Kristen Stromberg Childers.

13. Marvin, "Bourbon Island Creoles," 131, 137.

14. Tricoire, "Les Lumières, l'idéologie coloniale et Madagascar," 91.

15. Bernard Foury, "Maudave et la colonisation de Madagascar (1ère partie)," *Revue d'histoire des colonies* 42 (1955): 343–404; Tricoire, "Enlightened Colonialism?," 48–50; Tricoire, "Les Lumières, l'idéologie coloniale et Madagascar," 89.

16. Tricoire, "Les Lumières, l'idéologie coloniale et Madagascar," 90–92.

17. Tricoire, "Enlightened Colonialism?," 50. For example, see Guillaume Le Gentil de La Galaisière, *Voyage dans les mers de l'Inde, fait par ordre du roi, à l'occasion du passage de Vénus sur le disque du soleil le 6 juin 1761, et le 3 du même mois 1769*, 2 vols. (Paris: Imprimerie royale, 1779), 2:367–628; Alexis Rochon, *Voyage à Madagascar et aux Indes orientales* (Paris: Prault, 1791), 16–19; Jean-François Charpentier de Cossigny, *Observation sur le Manuel du commerce des Indes orientales et de la Chine* (Paris: Gagnard et al., 1808), 8.

18. Here is what Diderot stated in Raynal's *Histoire*: "A wise people would not allow any attack on property nor on freedom [. . .] they would wait for a while for a change in manners [. . .] it is in this way that [a people] will be naturalized." See Abbé Raynal, *Histoire philosophique et politique des établissements et du commerce des Européens dans les deux Indes*, 5 vols. (Geneva: Pellet, 1780), 1(4): 545. See also Tricoire, "Enlightened Colonialism?," 47.

19. Tricoire, "Enlightened Colonialism?," 48.

20. Tricoire, "Les Lumières, l'idéologie coloniale et Madagascar," 91.

21. Tricoire, "Les Lumières, l'idéologie coloniale et Madagascar," 85; Michèle Duchet, *Anthropologie et histoire au siècle des Lumières* (Paris: François Maspéro, 1971).

22. Raynal, *Histoire des deux Indes*, 1 (4): 418.

23. Tricoire, "Enlightened Colonialism?," 48, 50.

24. Tricoire, "Enlightened Colonialism?," 50–52, 60.

25. Tricoire, "Les Lumières, l'idéologie coloniale et Madagascar," 96, and "Beňovský on Madagascar: The Self-Fashioning, Career and Knowledge Production of a Central European Actor in the French Colonial Empire," *European Review* 26, no. 3 (2018): 471–480.

26. Tricoire, "Enlightened Colonialism?," 53.

27. Marvin, "Bourbon Island Creoles," 70–71.

28. Marvin, "Bourbon Island Creoles," 62–63. For more information regarding the Chapuiset case, see Garrigus, *Before Haiti*, 141–170.

29. Frédéric Régent, *Esclavage, métissage, liberté: La Révolution française en Guadeloupe, 1789–1802* (Paris: Grasset: 2004), 159–160.

30. Médéric Louis Elie Moreau de Saint-Méry, "Loix et constitutions des colonies françoises de l'Amerique sous le vent [. . .] depuis 1766 jusqu'en 1779 inclusivement," 6 vols. (Paris: Published by the author, 1785), 5:449.

31. Marvin, "Bourbon Island Creoles," 72; Régent, *La France et ses esclaves*, 197.

32. Marvin, "Bourbon Island Creoles," 70. Because the practice of assimilation was drawing to an end in the Caribbean, beginning in the 1760s, there was also a growth in the number of people classified as "free-colored" in Saint-Domingue. Laurent Dubois, *Avengers of the New World: The Story of the Haitian Revolution* (EBook, London: The Belknap Press of Harvard University Press, 2004), 61, https://ebookcentral.proquest.com/lib/duke/detail.action?docID=3300610; Garrigus, *Before Haiti*, 4; Marvin, "Bourbon Island Creoles," 59.

33. Quoted from Laurent Dubois, "Inscribing Race in the Revolutionary French Antilles," in *The Colors of Liberty: Histories of Race in France*, ed. Sue Peabody and Tyler Stovall (Durham,

NC: Duke University Press, 2003), 95–107, here 96. About the rise of Republican racism, see also Semley, *To Be Free and French*.

34. Dubois, "Inscribing Race in the Revolutionary French Antilles," 95, and *A Colony of Citizens: Revolution and Slave Emancipation in the French Caribbean, 1787–1804* (Chapel Hill: University of North Carolina Press, 2004), 10.

35. Laurent Dubois, "Republican Antiracism and Racism: A Caribbean Genealogy," *French Politics, Culture & Society* 18, no. 3 (2000): 5–17, here 7 and 9.

36. Laurent Dubois, "Inscribing Race in the Revolutionary French Antilles," 96, and *A Colony of Citizens*, 3–4.

37. Laurent Dubois, "'The Price of Liberty': Victor Hugues and the Administration of Freedom in Guadeloupe, 1794–1798," *WMQ* 56, no. 2 (1999): 363–392, here 382.

38. Dubois, "The Price of Liberty," 375, 383, 385.

39. See Marlene Daut, "L'héritage controversé de Napoléon," *Colonisations*, ed Singaravélou *et al.*, 748–749.

40. On the dismantlement of the project of emancipation, see Dubois, *A Colony of Citizens*, Part 3.

41. Marvin, "Bourbon Island Creoles," 65.

42. Sara E. Johnson, *Encyclopédie noire: The Making of Moreau de Saint-Méry's Intellectual World* (Chapel Hill: Omohundro Institute of Early American History and Culture/University of North Carolina Press, 2023), 30.

43. Quoted from Johnson, *Encyclopédie noire*, 3. About Moreau de Saint-Méry's mixed-race daughter, Aménaïde, see Johnson, *Encyclopédie noire*, 3, 25–30.

44. Moreau De Saint-Méry, *Description topographique, physique, civile, politique et historique de la partie française de l'isle Saint-Domingue*, 2 vols. (Philadelphia: Printed by the author, 1797–1798), 1:86.

45. Moreau De Saint-Méry, *Description topographique*, 1:71–99, esp. 71.

46. Yvan Debbasch, *Couleur et liberté: Le jeu du critère ethnique dans un ordre juridique esclavagiste Tome I : L'affranchi dans les possessions françaises de la Caraïbe (1635–1833)* (Paris : Dalloz, 1967), 61–66.

47. Marvin, "Bourbon Island Creoles," 5.

48. Marvin, "Bourbon Island Creoles," 72, 16, 121.

49. Marvin, "Bourbon Island Creoles," 56 (quotation).

50. Marvin, "Bourbon Island Creoles," 247; Peabody, *Madeleine's Children*, 8.

51. Claude Wanquet, *Histoire d'une révolution: la Réunion 1789–1803*, 3 vols. (Marseille: Jeanne Laffitte, 1980) 1:218, 3:375.

52. Marvin, "Bourbon Island Creoles," 150; Wanquet, *Histoire d'une révolution*, 1:218, 3:382.

53. "Arrêt de Réglement. Vu le réquisitoire du procureur général et ses conclusions des 5 et 16 Novembre 1778," Article X, in Étienne Delaleu, *Code Des Iles de France et de Bourbon*, 2nd ed. (Port-Louis: Tristan Mallac and Co., 1826), 13.

54. "Lettre du 15 fructidor an VII (1er septembre 1799)," cited in Wanquet, *Histoire d'une révolution*, 3:385.

55. Marvin, "Bourbon Island Creoles," 17, 123–130.

56. Marvin, "Bourbon Island Creoles," 136–137, 142 (quotation).

57. Dubois, *Avengers of the New World*, 80–81.

58. Marvin, "Bourbon Island Creoles," 149–151.

59. "28 Mars 1792–Décret relatif aux moyens d'apaiser les troubles des colonies," in *Collection Complète des Lois, Décrets, Ordonnances, Réglemens, et Avis du Conseil-d'État (De 1788 à*

1830 inclusivement), vol. 4, 2nd ed., ed. J. B. Duvergier, (Paris: A. Guyot and Scribe, 1834), 90–91, 90 (quotation).

60. Marvin, "Bourbon Island Creoles," 211–212; Florence Gauthier, "The Role of the Saint-Domingue Deputation in the Abolition of Slavery," in *The Abolitions of Slavery: From Léger Félicité Sonthonax to Victor Schoelcher, 1793, 1794, 1848*, ed. Marcel Dorigny (New York: Berghahn Books/Unesco Publishing, 2003), 167–179.

61. ADR L 307 "Pétition de la Colonie de Bourbon à l'assemblée nationale." See also Marvin, "Bourbon Island Creoles," 126 (quotations), 127–128; Noël, *Amours et familles interdites*, 573.

62. Marvin, "Bourbon Island Creoles," 149–151.

63. Marvin, "Bourbon Island Creoles," 237.

Acknowledgments

Because geographical, historical, and disciplinary boundaries are nothing more than shifting human inventions, I have made it a point to try to inhabit multiple spaces in my research. I feel tremendously lucky to have had the privilege, while researching and writing this book, of getting insights and feedback from an extraordinarily diverse range of scholars from many places and disciplines and across fields including French colonial history, Atlantic history, Indian Ocean history, Caribbean history, African history, French studies, Latin American studies, Black studies, Race and ethnic studies, and Indigenous studies.

I am very grateful to Richard Drayton and David Todd for "converting" me to the field of French colonial history during the year I spent at King's College London in 2009–2010. William O'Reilly helped facilitate this transition after my return to Cambridge University in 2010. I can't thank him enough for his support, recommendations, and mentorship. I am lucky to have benefited from the teaching and guidance of many other scholars in Cambridge and London, including Chris Bayly, Melissa Calaresu, Saul Dubow, Laura Gowing, Shruti Kapila, Mary Laven, Craig Muldrew, Mark Nicholls, Ulinka Rublack, Sujit Sivasundaram, Alexandra Walsham, and Peter Warner. They took the time to nurture what they saw in me all those years ago, and for this, I will always be grateful to them.

Some of my greatest debts of gratitude are to the anonymous reviewers of this book, to my dearest friend Nathan Marvin, and to François-Joseph Ruggiu and Sue Peabody. They have all read this entire book, and I am immensely grateful to them for their support, feedback, and recommendations throughout the years. My heartfelt thanks also go to Emma Rothschild and Brett Rushforth, who both read a first iteration of this manuscript several years ago and whose comments and reading recommendations have had a transformational impact on the manuscript.

I am also very grateful to my research assistant, Jérémy Boutier. In addition to having researched some of the materials discussed in this book, he has diligently double-checked most footnote references in this manuscript one by one, over the course of many months. Jérémy: *je te remercie infiniment d'avoir accompli ce travail titanesque; c'est un privilège de travailler avec toi.* I am also grateful to my wonderful Radcliffe Research Partners Karson Baldwin, Diarra Faye, and Madeleine Riskin-Kutz for their help tackling the secondary literature and researching some of the sources for this book. Here, I want to single out Madeleine Riskin-Kutz for conducting the last stages of the research for this book in the French archives. *Un grand merci à toi!*

There is another very important group of people who have generously commented on specific chapters or passages of this book or offered crucial support and reading recommendations. These include: Danna Agmon, Richard Allen, Saliha Belmessous, Philip Boucher, Kelly Brignac, Mackenzie Cooley, Myriam Cottias, Elizabeth Cross, Prosper Ève, Malick Ghachem, John Garrigus, Arad Gigi, Leonard Hodges, Jean-Pierre Le Glaunec, Julie Hardwick, Elizabeth Heijmans, Rachel Jean-Baptiste, Destin Jenkins, Rhys Jones, Michaela Kleber, Joseph La Hausse de la Louvière, Julie Marquet, Tessa Murphy, Santiago Muñoz-Arbeláez, Jennifer Palmer, Frédéric Régent, Daniel Robinson, Pernille Roge, Dominique Somda, Philip Stern, Rob Taber, Yevan Terrien, Barbara Traver, Richard Turits, Guido van Meersbergen, and Sophie White. I also wish to thank Jean-Michel André, René Estienne, Chantal Plévert, and the other members of the Association des Amis du Service Historique de la Défense in Lorient for their generous support, which has allowed me to design the map displayed in the Introduction of this book, based on their wonderful database "Mémoire des Hommes," section "Compagnie des Indes," subsection "Armements des navires."

I also extend my heartfelt thanks to Josh Piker, Julia Gaffield, and the staff and anonymous readers of the *William and Mary Quarterly* for their valuable feedback and support. Portions of Chapter 4 were originally published as "Beyond the Atlantic: Unifying Racial Policies across the Early French Empire," the *William and Mary Quarterly*, Vol. 68, No. 1 (January 2024): 3–36. This article was the recipient of the Douglass Adair Memorial Award (2024) and the Article Prize of the French Colonial Historical Society (2025).

Throughout the years, I have been lucky to interact with scholars at various institutions in France, the United Kingdom, Australia, and the United States. I am tremendously grateful to my colleagues at Newnham College in Cambridge, and especially to the members of the History Group, for their feedback and recommendations when I began to turn my graduate research into a book in 2016–2017. Special thanks to Aniket Kumar, Kate Fleet, Fiona Lejosne, Jenny Mander, Gabriela Ramos, and Alexandra Vukovich for their early comments.

When I moved to the United States, the Center for Comparative Studies in Race and Ethnicity (CCSRE) at Stanford welcomed me with open arms. Being there was the most eye-opening experience I have had in my entire life. This was a turning point in my research, and my project changed dramatically as I began to rewrite the book.

My warmest thanks to Jennifer DeVere Brody, Alaina Morgan, Paula Moya, and Jamele Watkins for their advice and continuous support. Thank you also to Marsha Challoner and Heidi M. López for making my experience at CCSRE so special and for their continued friendship.

During my time at Stanford, I have also had the privilege to receive feedback from a wide range of brilliant scholars from the Slavery Group, the Mellon Program in the Humanities, the Humanities Center, the History Department, and the Division of Literatures, Cultures, and Languages. These include Colleen Anderson, Jim Campbell, J. P. Daughton, Adrian Daub, Brooke Durham, Dan Edelstein, Paula Findlen, Héctor Hoyos, Nicole T. Hughes, Philippa Levine, Shawon Kinew, Elizabeth Marcus, Grant Parker, David Palumbo-Liu, Aileen Robinson, Luca Scholz, Londa Schiebinger, Miranda Spieler, Sixiang Wang, J'Nese Williams, Caroline Winterer, and Adrien Zakar.

My time at the Harvard Radcliffe Institute allowed me to receive additional feedback from another set of brilliant scholars as I was revising my manuscript for the second time. Special thanks to Vincent Brown, Ralph Eubanks, Amy Erdman Farrell, Amelia Glaser, Ariela Gross, Jessica Marie Johnson, Silyane Larcher, Mary Lewis, Robin Mitchell, and Scott Stevens for their thoughtful advice, support, and mentorship during that very productive year.

At Harvard, I also formed a close relationship with my superb editor, Emily Silk. I cannot thank her enough for her guidance, support, and recommendations throughout the years. Other sources of support during the production process have come from my writing coach, Amy Brown; my wonderful line editors Elizabeth Brodgen and Sam Stark; Alex and Malcolm Swanston, who both made the maps; and the entire team at Harvard University Press. I thank them for their time and patience.

I am also grateful for the continued support of my colleagues at Tulane, UT Austin, and Duke while writing this book. In particular, I would like to thank Laura Rosanne Adderley, Marc Bizer, Benjamin Brower, Indrani Chatterjee, Abena Dove Osseo-Asare, Fayçal Falaky, Jana Lipman, Elisabeth McMahon, Charles Mignot, Felicia McCarren, Steven Mintz, Jonathan Morton, Aaron O'Connell, Vernon Palmer, Randy Sparks, and Alexandra Wettlaufer. As I was completing my last revisions at Duke, I also received useful recommendations and support from Sarah Balakrishnan, Juliana Barr, Calvin Ryan Cheung-Miaw, Hannah Conway, Thavolia Glymph, Malachi Hacohen, Reeve Huston, Adrian Lentz-Smith, Cecilia Marquez, John Martin, Tamika Nunley, Jocelyn Olcott, Sumathi Ramaswamy, Thomas Robisheaux, and Peter Sigal.

In addition to my home institutions, I am also grateful to the many programs that have supported this book project throughout the years. These include the Radcliffe Institute at Harvard, the Andrew W. Mellon Foundation, the Arts and Humanities Research Council of the United Kingdom, the Kluge Center of the Library of Congress, the Center for History and Economics at Harvard and Cambridge, the Newton Trust, and the Humanities Research Center of the Australian National University.

This book has also benefited from intellectual exchanges with Arthur Asseraf, Guillaume Blanc, Trevor Burnard, Vincent Cousseau, Alexandre Dubé, Laurent Dubois, Flavio Eichmann, Elizabeth Ellis, Allan Greer, Gilles Havard, Yala Kidukidi, Emily Marker, Christopher Miller, Philip Morgan, Aissata Kane Lo, Naiima Khahaifa, Jessica Pierre-Louis, Dominique Rogers, Isabel Schnee, Jennifer Session, Yan Slobodkin, Noel Smyth, Pierre Singaravélou, and Jack Soll. My friend Cécile Feza Bushidi left us far too soon. She was a constant source of support ever since I met her in England, and she has been on my mind every day of the last few months as I was finishing this book.

Among those who have supported this project, some, like Cécile, have passed away. My dearest friend Mary White was the most gracious host, and she also knew New Orleans and the Louisiana archives better than anyone. She offered almost daily feedback on this project over the course of many months, and she also edited the first draft of this book. I loved her, and I am very sorry that she will not get the chance to hold this book in her hands; it would have meant a lot to her. Gwendolyn Hall, Pier Larson, and Laurie Wood were also very generous with their time. I am very grateful for their comments and reading recommendations. Their works have been an enormous source of inspiration, and I hope to have honored their memory throughout this book.

Last but not least, I would like to thank my family for their support. Special thanks to the entire Annerose family in Guadeloupe and the hexagon for their continued encouragement, to Anne Marsh for leaving her Texas homeland to become a permanent part of our family and allow me to finish this book, and to Joshua for being the perfect son. I am especially grateful to my parents, Pierre and Christiane Lamotte, who worked very hard so I could become the first member of my family to go to college.

My greatest debt of gratitude is to my husband, Daniel Ohayon, who has been very patient with me since I began to write this book. He read and reread it countless times and never stopped believing in me. I can say with confidence that this book would never have seen the light of day without him. Thank you, Daniel. You are my rock and the love of my life. This book is for you.

Index

Page numbers in *italics* refer to tables.